Raunds
The origin and growth of a midland village AD 450–1500

Excavations in north Raunds, Northamptonshire 1977–87

Frontispiece: The digging team at Furnells manor in 1981 mimic the actions of daily life in the ninth-century timber hall – sitting and standing around the central hearth, welcoming a visitor at the door and sleeping in the end chamber

Raunds

The origin and growth of a midland village AD 450–1500

Excavations in north Raunds, Northamptonshire 1977–87

RAUNDS AREA PROJECT

Michel Audouy
and Andy Chapman (editor)

with major contributions by

Paul Blinkhorn, Andrew Boddington, Graham Cadman, Gillian Campbell, Paul Courtney, Simon Davis, Nick Griffiths, Gwynne Oakley, Terry Pearson and Hugh Richmond

contributions by

Max Adams, Marion Archibald, Pat Chapman, J A Davis, Varian Denham, Martin Howe, Stephen Parry, Mark Robinson, Michael Shaw and Alan Vince

illustrated by

Leslie Collet and Alex Thompson, and including work by Paul Goff, Dorrie Orchard, Christopher Jones and Pat Walsh

Oxbow Books

Published by
Oxbow Books, Oxford, UK

© Oxbow Books, Michel Audouy and Andy Chapman 2009

ISBN 978 1 84217 337 4

A CIP record for this book is available from The British Library

This book is available direct from

Oxbow Books, Oxford, UK
(Phone: 01865–241249; Fax: 01865–794449)

and

The David Brown Book Company
PO Box 511, Oakville, CT 06779, USA
(Phone: 860–945–9329; Fax: 860–945–9468)

or from our website

www.oxbowbooks.com

Printed and bound in Great Britain by
Short Run Press Ltd, Exeter

Contents

Acknowledgements viii
Tables x
Illustrations xi
Preface by Andy Chapman xiv
Summary xv
Résumé xvi
Zusammenfassung xvii

PART 1

1 Introduction

Background 1
The excavations and the Raunds Area Project 1
Topography and geology 9
The medieval landscape 9
The structure of the report 12
The site archives 13

2 Historical Background

Domesday Raunds by Paul Courtney 14
North Raunds by Paul Courtney 14
The parish church of St Peter by Hugh Richmond 18
Abbreviations and references 21

3 A Panorama of Settlement Development

The pre-Saxon landscape 22
Summary of the Saxon and medieval chronology 24
Early–middle Saxon settlement and the middle Saxon farm (AD 450–850) 25
Late Saxon village formation (AD 850–1100) 28
The medieval manors and the village (AD 1100–1350/1400) 39
Late-medieval decline and relocation (AD 1350/1400–1500) 45
The early post-medieval village (AD 1500 onward) 50
From village to town 50

4 Archaeology and History

The virtues of large scale excavation 51
Archaeology and the physical evidence of historical change 51
Domesday book and the manorial status of Furnells and the Cottons by Paul Courtney 55
The rise and fall of the medieval village 57

PART 2

5 The Archaeological Evidence

Identification, retrieval and analysis 58
    Excavation strategy 58
    Post-excavation background 59
    Nature of the evidence and analytical strategy 59
    Relative chronology 59
    The radiocarbon dates 60
The pre-Saxon landscape 62
Furnells manor 62
    Early–middle Saxon settlement (AD 450–650) 63
    The Anglo-Scandinavian farm (AD 850–900/950) 66
    Plot formation and the late Saxon manor (AD 900/950–1100) 74
    The late Saxon church and churchyard (AD 950–1150) 84
    The aisled hall (AD 1100–1200) 89
    The medieval church (AD 1150–1350/1400) 93
    The western manor (AD 1200–1350/1400) 94
    The eastern manor (AD 1350/1400–1450) 100
    Demolition of the eastern manor (AD 1450–1500) 106
Langham Road 107
    Early Saxon settlement (AD 450–650) 107
    The middle Saxon farm (AD 650–850) 108
    The late Saxon boundaries and farm (AD 900/950–1200) 111
    The medieval tenement plots and field boundaries (AD 1200–1350/1400) 118
    Post-medieval activity 120
Burystead 121
    Early–middle Saxon settlement (AD 450–850) 122
    Plot boundaries and late Saxon/Saxo-Norman settlement (AD 900/950–1200) 125
    A manorial farm and tenement plots (AD 1200–1350/1400) 131
    Late medieval and post-medieval buildings (AD 1350/1400 onward) 134
Midland Road 137
    Late Saxon and medieval occupation 137
    The late medieval and post-medieval buildings (AD 1300–1600) 138
    Post-medieval tenements (AD 1600 onward) 138

Bibliography: Parts 1 & 2 143
Index: Parts 1 & 2 145

PART 3 (on CD inside back cover)

6 The Saxon and Medieval Pottery

Introduction by Varian Denham 151
The pottery from Furnells by Terry Pearson... 151
Furnells: a reappraisal of the ceramic dating by Michel Audouy and Paul Blinkhorn 170
The pottery from Langham Road and Burystead by Paul Blinkhorn... 173

7 The Saxon and Medieval Finds

Introduction... 195
Other finds from Furnells by Gwynne Oakley 195
Other finds from Langham Road and Burystead by Nick Griffiths.. 207

8 The Animal Bone

Introduction 214
Animal bone from Furnells by Alison Locker, Mark Robinson and Varian Denham 214
Animal bone from Langham Road and Burystead by Simon Davis 214

9 Plant and Invertebrate Remains by Gillian Campbell and Mark Robinson

Introduction 222
Evidence from Furnells.. 224
Charred plant remains from Langham Road 228
Plant remains from Burystead.. 230
Plant remains from the Midland Road frontage 240
Other sites in north Raunds 243
General discussion 244

Bibliography: Part 3 249

Acknowledgements

The excavations in north Raunds form part of the Raunds Area Project (RAP), which has been managed jointly by English Heritage and Northamptonshire County Council. The excavations and most of the post-excavation analysis took place between 10 and over 25 years ago. At that distance in time it is no longer possible to provide a full list of acknowledgements to the numerous individuals who have contributed to the many aspects of the project, and apologies are offered to anyone who has been omitted. For Northamptonshire Archaeology, the fieldwork was all conducted under the management of the county archaeologist, the late Alan Hannan, and Glenn Foard contributed much of the academic drive that led to the creation of the Raunds Area Project. For English Heritage, project management of the fieldwork was provided by John Hinchcliffe and in post-excavation by Varian Denham and Brian Kerr, while the final process of report editing has been supervised by Helen Keeley. The excavations fell under several Inspectors of Ancient Monuments; Glyn Coppack, Brian Davison, Paul Gosling, Tony Fleming and Mike Parker-Pearson.

Excavation at Furnells manor was directed by Andy Boddington from 1977 to 1980 and from 1980 to 1982 by Graham Cadman. Without doubt, it was the energy of Andy Boddington in those early years that carried the Furnells excavations so far beyond their initial objectives, and set the scene for all that has followed in Raunds. The site supervisors were Christine Addison, Andy Chapman, Ian Charles, Martin Cook, Peter Durnford, Mike Emery, Rod Fitzgerald, Christopher Jones, John Newman and Shahed Power. A full report on the late Saxon and medieval churches and churchyard at Furnells has already appeared in a separate volume (Boddington 1996).

The fields to the west of Furnells were subject to trial excavation undertaken by Shahed Power and Dave Windell, with this continuing into 1984 under the direction of Michel Audouy. An area of particular interest was enlarged to become the Langham Road excavation, which was directed by Michel Audouy in 1984, with Michael Webster as site supervisor. The excavation of Burystead and the Midland Road frontage was directed by Michel Audouy between 1985 and 1987, with Steve Webster as site supervisor throughout, assisted by Melanie Whewell and Jim Hunter. Running concurrently with these excavations, Steve Parry directed the Raunds Area Survey, while Dave Windell directed the excavation in the Nene valley of the deserted medieval hamlet of West Cotton, as well as providing overall management for the three fieldwork projects.

Not the least, mention must also be made of the diggers who worked on these sites, who are far too numerous to mention individually. Throughout the excavations, the core of the teams was made up of local people employed through the various Manpower Services Commission programmes then in operation, supplemented through the summer by volunteers paid a basic subsistence allowance.

The post-excavation analysis on the excavations at Furnells was carried out in the mid to late 1980s by a team led by Graham Cadman, and his draft report was edited by Max Adams. Following the decision to absorb the Furnells report within a single volume covering all the excavations in north Raunds, that single report was compiled by Michel Audouy in the early 1990s. Following the completion of the report in 1993 there was a long hiatus but, following the departure of Michel Audouy from archaeology and the receipt of comments from an external referee, work on basic editing and the incorporation of referee's comments was carried out by Pat Chapman under the direction and management of Andy Chapman at the end of the 1990s. Following a further hiatus, the final copy editing of the report, which has included some text revisions and a major reorganisation of the structure of the report, has been carried out by Andy Chapman over the first half of 2005, with editing and proof reading by Pat Chapman. The report was finalised for typesetting between November 2007 and February 2008.

Many people have been involved in the analysis of material from the north Raunds sites, and those who have produced specialist reports and smaller contributions are acknowledged directly in this volume. However, in reading this report it must be noted that the specialist contributions were all compiled prior to 1993, although Paul Blinkhorn updated the pottery report in the late 1990s, and they cannot reflect developments that have occurred in more recent years.

In the process of final editing, the interpretation of the chronology and development of the major structures has been reviewed and incorporates ideas that were developed in the late 1990s during the drafting of text for a proposed volume synthesising the results of the work on all aspects of the medieval archaeology of the Raunds Area. The draft for this volume was compiled under the direction of Michael Shaw. Michel Audouy and Andy Chapman contributed detailed reviews of the excavated evidence from north Raunds and the deserted hamlet of West Cotton, which was set within a broader context of settlement development provided through the systematic fieldwork and trial trench excavation of the Raunds Area Survey team, led by Steve Parry. The documentary context was provided by the research of Paul Courtney, with Professor Chris Dyer as project advisor.

Funding for post-excavation has been provided by English Heritage, and the publication of the report has been funded by English Heritage through the Aggregates Levy Sustainability Fund.

The line drawings that accompany the report are mainly the work of Leslie Collet and Alex Thompson (née Thorne), and the reconstruction drawings are by Alex Thompson. The report also incorporates line drawings originally prepared by Paul Goff, Dorrie Orchard and Christopher Jones. Final amendments and additions have been made by Pat Walsh and Andy Chapman.

Tables

PART 1
Table 2.1 The Burystead manorial buildings 17
Table 3.1 The chronological sequence at north Raunds ... 25

PART 2
Table 5.1 The radiocarbon determinations for early–middle Saxon settlement 60
Table 5.2 The radiocarbon determinations for Furnells church and churchyard 61

PART 3 (CD)
Table 6.1 The petrological fabric classes for early–middle Saxon pottery 152
Table 6.2 Quantification by class and geological source for early–middle Saxon pottery 152
Table 6.3 Quantification of the late Saxon and Saxo-Norman assemblage 158
Table 6.4 The medieval and post-medieval pottery types 164
Table 6.5 Quantification of pottery per major structural phase 164
Table 6.6 Local and regional pottery imports 169
Table 6.7 The revised ceramic chronology for Furnells 171
Table 6.8 Average sherd weight of early–middle Saxon pottery from Langham Road 176
Table 6.9 Average sherd weight of early–middle Saxon pottery from Burystead 176
Table 6.10 Average sherd weight for St Neots-type ware from all phased contexts 176
Table 6.11 Ipswich Ware body sherd types at Burystead 181
Table 6.12 The late Saxon Ceramic Phase Dating 182
Table 6.13 Pottery from late Saxon phases at Burystead 184
Table 6.14 Average sherd weight per ceramic phase at Burystead 184
Table 6.15 Average number of sherds per context at Burystead 185
Table 6.16 Pottery from late Saxon phases at Langham Road 185
Table 6.17 Average sherd weight per ceramic phase at Langham Road 185
Table 6.18 Average number of sherds per context at Langham Road 185
Table 6.19 The medieval Ceramic Phase Dating 189
Table 6.20 The later medieval pottery from Burystead, Midland Road 190
Table 6.21 The average sherd weight at Burystead, Midland Road 190
Table 6.22 Sherds per context at Burystead, Midland Road 190
Table 6.23 The later medieval pottery from Burystead 191
Table 6.24 The average sherd weight at Burystead 191
Table 6.25 Sherds per context at Burystead 191
Table 6.26 The later medieval pottery from Langham Road 192
Table 6.27 The average sherd weight at Langham Road.. 192
Table 6.28 Sherds per context at Langham Road 193
Table 7.1 Coins from Furnells 206
Table 7.2 Coins from Langham Road 212
Table 7.3 Coins and tokens from Burystead 212
Table 7.4 Coins and tokens from the Midland Road Frontage 213
Table 8.1 Summary of faunal remains from Burystead and Langham Road 220
Table 8.2 Minimum number of animals, represented by teeth, fore- and hind-limb bones 221
Table 8.3 Grouped dental wear stages for sheep molars (percentages), with comparative data 221
Table 9.1 Environmental samples from Furnells: summary of context information 224
Table 9.2 Charred plant remains from Furnells 225–6
Table 9.3 Mineralised seeds and insects from cess pits at Furnells 227
Table 9.4 Charred and mineralised remains from Langham Road: early–middle Saxon, late Saxon and medieval contexts 229
Table 9.5 Charred and mineralised remains from Langham Road: medieval contexts 231–2
Table 9.6 Charred and mineralised remains from Burystead: early–middle Saxon contexts 233–4
Table 9.7 Charred and mineralised remains from Burystead: late Saxon contexts 235–6
Table 9.8 Charred and mineralised remains from Burystead: twelfth-century quarry pits 237–8
Table 9.9 Charred and mineralised remains from Burystead: medieval features 239–40
Table 9.10 Charred remains from the Midland Road frontage 241–2
Table 9.11 Charred remains from late Saxon features at Gells Garage 243–4

Illustrations

PART 1

Fig 1.1	The location of Raunds, and the boundary of the Raunds Area Project	2
Fig 1.2	Raunds: the location of the major excavations and the vale hamlets	3
Fig 1.3	Transcription of the Raunds estate map of 1798	4
Fig 1.4	The excavations in north Raunds, 1977–87	5
Fig 1.5	Advertising poster for site open days at Furnells manor, 1979	6
Fig 1.6	Front cover of leaflet advertising the launch of the Raunds Area Project in 1985	6
Fig 1.7	Aerial view of north Raunds in 1979, looking north-west, showing the excavation of Furnells manor (centre top), with the empty paddocks of Burystead lying north of the church of St Peter (right)	7
Fig 1.8	Aerial view of north Raunds in 1986, looking north, with housing development beginning to appear at Furnells (top left) and Burystead (centre right)	7
Fig 1.9	Aerial view of Furnells towards the end of excavation, 1981, showing the houses on Rotton Row (bottom left), the excavated churchyard (overgrown and containing spoil dumps) and the late Saxon timber buildings (top, with the aisled hall partly under polythene sheeting)	8
Fig 1.10	Aerial view of Burystead in 1987, looking west, showing the medieval dovecote (centre), with housing encroaching from the north (right) and also across Furnells and Langham Road (top)	8
Fig 1.11	The surface drift geology and contours of north Raunds, as recorded on the excavated areas	10
Fig 1.12	North Raunds, as depicted on the estate map of 1798	11
Fig 2.1	Raunds, the church of St Peter	19
Fig 3.1	North Raunds, settlement development (AD 450–1500)	23
Fig 3.2	North Raunds, early–middle Saxon settlement (AD 450–850)	26
Fig 3.3	Langham Road, reconstruction of the middle Saxon farm	28
Fig 3.4	North Raunds, late Saxon settlement (AD 850–1100)	29
Fig 3.5	Furnells, the creation of the manor; a) the Anglo-Scandinavian farm (AD 850–900/950) and b) the late Saxon plots and long range (AD 900/950)	30
Fig 3.6	Furnells, ninth-century post-built halls (left foreground and background), and the wall trenches and post-pits of the late Saxon aisled hall (centre), looking north-east	33
Fig 3.7	Furnells, the wall trenches of the late Saxon domestic range (centre) and ancillary buildings (top right), looking south-east	33
Fig 3.8	Furnells, the development of the manor; a) the long range, church and churchyard (AD 950–1100), b) the aisled hall (AD 1100–1150/1200), c) the western manor house (1150/1200–1350/1400) and d) the eastern manor house (AD 1350/1400–1500)	35
Fig 3.9	Furnells, the late Saxon and medieval churches, looking south, with the stone coffin and excavated graves in the background	36
Fig 3.10	Furnells, reconstruction of the late Saxon long range and the church (AD 950–1100)	37
Fig 3.11	Langham Road, the wall trenches of the timber buildings of the late Saxon farm, looking east	38
Fig 3.12	North Raunds, Saxo-Norman settlement (AD 1100–1200)	39
Fig 3.13	Burystead, the late Saxon and medieval settlement (AD 900/950–1200)	40
Fig 3.14	North Raunds, the medieval manors and village (AD 1200–1350/1400)	42
Fig 3.15	Furnells, reconstruction of the western manor and the second church (AD 1200–1350)	43
Fig 3.16	Bone tailpiece from a three-stringed musical instrument, showing perforations to hold the strings (top), a slot and a notch to hold the retaining cord (bottom) and decorated with two stylised faces	43
Fig 3.17	Thirteenth-century pottery contemporary with the western manor, including a Lyveden/Stanion aquamanile in the form of a ram (centre) and Lyveden/Stanion jugs, including one with elaborate decoration, perhaps representing stylised human figures (centre right)	44
Fig 3.18	North Raunds, the late medieval manors (AD 1350/1400–1500)	45
Fig 3.19	Furnells, reconstruction of the eastern manor (AD 1400)	46
Fig 3.20	Furnells, the earthworks (based on Hall et al 1988, fig 2)	48
Fig 3.21	Burystead, the late medieval farm buildings (AD 1350/1400–1500)	49
Fig 4.1	Furnells and Langham Road, a metrical model of the plot layout	54
Fig 4.2	Late Saxon long ranges, comparative plans	55

PART 2

Fig 5.1	Furnells, early–middle Saxon settlement (AD 450–650)	63
Fig 5.2	Furnells, sunken-featured building (SP100)	64
Fig 5.3	Furnells, stone-lined pit and associated pits (SP16)	64
Fig 5.4	Furnells, timber building (SP59)	65
Fig 5.5	Furnells, posthole group (SP63)	65
Fig 5.6	Furnells, earth-cut oven (SP76)	66
Fig 5.7	Furnells, the Anglo-Scandinavian farm (AD 850–900/950)	67
Fig 5.8	Furnells, the northern hall (building B, SP91)	69
Fig 5.9	Furnells, the post-pits of the northern hall, building B, looking east	70
Fig 5.10	Furnells, the western hall (building D, SP94)	70
Fig 5.11	Furnells, the southern hall (building S, SP99)	71
Fig 5.12	Furnells, the post-pits of the southern hall, building S, looking south	72
Fig 5.13	Furnells, posthole structure C (SP98)	72
Fig 5.14	Furnells, the eastern timber hall (building A, SP70)	73
Fig 5.15	Furnells, the late Saxon buildings and boundaries (AD 900/950–1200), shown in relation to the preceding settlement	75
Fig 5.16	Furnells, the late Saxon enclosure and boundary ditch system in relation to the preceding enclosure	76
Fig 5.17	Furnells, the late Saxon settlement (AD 900/950)	77
Fig 5.18	Furnells, the long range and aisled hall	80
Fig 5.19	Furnells, the long range (SP138)	foldout 80–81
Fig 5.20	Furnells, interpretative plan of the hall of the long range, showing principal posts (P) and doorways (D)	81
Fig 5.21	Furnells, ancillary building R (SP103)	82
Fig 5.22	Furnells, ancillary building F (SP104)	83
Fig 5.23	Furnells, ancillary building F (SP104), looking east, and showing the southern entrance and recutting of the square enclosure (SP 109) (right)	83
Fig 5.24	Furnells, ancillary building G (SP105)	84
Fig 5.25	Furnells, ancillary building G, looking east, and enclosure ditch (foreground)	85
Fig 5.26	Furnells, ancillary building E (SP95)	85
Fig 5.27	Furnells, the late Saxon settlement with the addition of the church and churchyard (AD 950–1100)	86
Fig 5.28	Furnells, the late Saxon and medieval churches, and major burials	87
Fig 5.29	Furnells, building P (SP60)	89
Fig 5.30	Furnells, the twelfth-century settlement with the aisled hall (AD 1100–1200)	90
Fig 5.31	Furnells, the aisled hall	91
Fig 5.32	Furnells, interpretative plan of aisled hall, showing aisle posts (P), the bay structure and doorways (D)	92
Fig 5.33	Furnells, the wall trenches and arcade posts (left) of the aisled hall, looking north	92
Fig 5.34	Furnells, the southern range (SP137)	93
Fig 5.35	Furnells, the western manor and the medieval church (AD 1200–1350/1400)	95
Fig 5.36	Furnells, the western manor house	foldout 96–97
Fig 5.37	Furnells, the western manor house, looking north, showing the parlour (foreground) and hall (centre)	97
Fig 5.38	Furnells, the north-west range (SP89), with baking oven (south) and malting/drying oven (north)	99
Fig 5.39	Furnells, malting complex (SP85), with oven (west) and tank (east)	100
Fig 5.40	Furnells, the new manor house (AD 1350/1400–1500)	101
Fig 5.41	Furnells, the eastern manor house (SP7)	102–103
Fig 5.42	Furnells, the eastern manor house hall (left) and service rooms (right), looking south-west	103
Fig 5.43	Furnells, the manor house service rooms, with partially flagged floors, looking east	103
Fig 5.44	Furnells, the manor house dovecote with remnants of a western range behind, looking west	104
Fig 5.45	Furnells, the north range, kitchen with corner oven and hearth (west), brewhouse with rectangular drying oven (east) and circular vat stand (west)	105
Fig 5.46	Furnells, the north range, looking east, with drying oven (top), bakehouse (centre) and circular vat stand (foreground)	106
Fig 5.47	Langham Road, early–middle Saxon settlement (AD 450–850)	108
Fig 5.48	Langham Road, sunken-featured building (LRSP22)	109
Fig 5.49	Langham Road, the middle Saxon farm (AD 650–850)	110
Fig 5.50	Langham Road, the middle Saxon farm, building LRSP01 in foreground, looking south-west	111
Fig 5.51	Langham Road, middle Saxon farm, timber hall (LRSP01)	111
Fig 5.52	Langham Road, middle Saxon farm, timber hall (LRSP02)	112
Fig 5.53	Langham Road, middle Saxon farm, timber hall (LRSP04)	113
Fig 5.54	Langham Road, middle Saxon farm, timber building (LRSP06)	113
Fig 5.55	Langham Road, middle Saxon farm, posthole structure (LRSP03)	113
Fig 5.56	Langham Road, middle Saxon farm, posthole structure (LRSP08)	114
Fig 5.57	Langham Road, the late Saxon settlement (AD 900/950–1200)	114
Fig 5.58	Langham Road, the late Saxon farm	115
Fig 5.59	Langham Road, late Saxon farm, timber hall (LRSP14)	116
Fig 5.60	Langham Road, late Saxon farm, timber hall (LRSP15)	117
Fig 5.61	Langham Road, late Saxon farm, timber hall (LRSP16)	117
Fig 5.62	Langham Road, late Saxon farm, timber hall (LRSP17)	117
Fig 5.63	Langham Road, late Saxon farm, timber building (LRSP13)	118
Fig 5.64	Langham Road, late Saxon farm, timber building (LRSP09)	119
Fig 5.65	Langham Road, the medieval tenement plots (AD 1200–1350/1400)	119
Fig 5.66	Langham Road, medieval timber building

Fig 5.67	Burystead, the early–middle Saxon settlement (AD 450–850) ... 123 (LRSP10) ... 121		ware (35–48) ... 159
Fig 5.68	Burystead, early–middle Saxon timber building (BSP08) ... 124	Fig 6.5	Late Saxon pottery from Furnells: St Neots-type ware (49–52) and Stamford ware (53–55) ... 160
Fig 5.69	Burystead, early–middle Saxon timber building (BSP08), looking south ... 124	Fig 6.6	Late Saxon pottery from Furnells: Thetford ware (56–57), Quartz-tempered ware (58) and Saxo-Norman coarsewares (59–63) ... 162
Fig 5.70	Burystead, early–middle Saxon timber building (BSP09) ... 125	Fig 6.7	Saxo-Norman wares from Furnells (64–66) ... 163
Fig 5.71	Burystead, early–middle Saxon timber building (BSP09), looking south-west ... 126	Fig 6.8	Medieval pottery from Furnells: Lyveden/Stanion aquamanile (67) and large jug (69) ... 166
Fig 5.72	Burystead, early–middle Saxon timber building (BSP11) ... 127	Fig 6.9	Early–middle Saxon pottery from Langham Road and Burystead (1–8 decorated sherds, 9 shelly ware vessel) ... 177
Fig 5.73	Burystead, early–middle Saxon sunken-featured building (BSP51) ... 127	Fig 6.10	Early–middle Saxon pottery from Langham Road and Burystead (10–15) ... 178
Fig 5.74	Burystead, the late Saxon to Saxo-Norman settlement (AD 900/950–1200) ... 128	Fig 6.11	Middle Saxon pottery from Langham Road and Burystead (16–21 Ipswich ware, 22–27 Maxey ware) ... 180
Fig 5.75	Burystead, the late Saxon boundary ditches (AD 950–1200) ... 129	Fig 6.12	Late Saxon pottery from Langham Road and Burystead (28–32 St Neots-type ware, 33 Stamford ware) ... 183
Fig 5.76	Burystead, late Saxon to Saxo-Norman timber building (BSP19) ... 130	Fig 6.13	St Neots-type ware rim forms from Langham Road and Burystead ... 186
Fig 5.77	Burystead, late Saxon to Saxo-Norman timber building (BSP20) ... 130	Fig 6.14	Medieval pottery from Langham Road and Burystead (34–35 calcitic coarseware, 36 Lyveden A bowl and 37 Potterspury ware) ... 188
Fig 5.78	Burystead, the manorial farm and tenement plots (AD 1200–1350/1400) ... 132	Fig 7.1	Roman, early–middle Saxon to late Saxon finds from Furnells (1–25) ... 197
Fig 5.79	Burystead, medieval malt oven (BSP33) ... 133	Fig 7.2	Early–middle to late Saxon worked bone and antler from Furnells (1–12) ... 198
Fig 5.80	Burystead, the sunken, stone-lined chamber of the malt oven, looking west ... 133	Fig 7.3	Late Saxon horse furnishings from Furnells (1–8) ... 200
Fig 5.81	Burystead, medieval dovecote (BSP34) ... 134	Fig 7.4	Late Saxon knives and sickle from Furnells (1–4) ... 201
Fig 5.82	Burystead, the circular dovecote (BSP34), looking north ... 135	Fig 7.5	Late Saxon bone gaming pieces from Furnells (1–3) ... 201
Fig 5.83	Burystead, medieval building (BSP36) ... 136	Fig 7.6	Late Saxon padlocks from Furnells (1–3) ... 202
Fig 5.84	Burystead, late medieval and post-medieval buildings (AD 1350/1400 onward) ... 137	Fig 7.7	Medieval finds from Furnells (1–17) ... 203
Fig 5.85	Burystead, late medieval circular and square dovecotes (BSP35) ... 138	Fig 7.8	Late Saxon bone tailpiece and whistle from Furnells (1–2) ... 204
Fig 5.86	Burystead, the late medieval circular and square dovecotes, looking west ... 139	Fig 7.9	Medieval nine men's morris board from Furnells ... 204
Fig 5.87	Midland Road, late medieval buildings (AD 1300–1600) ... 139	Fig 7.10	Early–middle to late Saxon and medieval knives from Furnells (1–22) ... 205
Fig 5.88	Midland Road, late medieval building (SP06) ... 140	Fig 7.11	Early–middle to late Saxon finds from Langham Road and Burystead (1–9) ... 208
Fig 5.89	Midland Road, late medieval building (SP08) ... 140	Fig 7.12	Medieval finds from Langham Road and Burystead (11–26) ... 210
Fig 5.90	Midland Road, late medieval smithy (SP09) ... 140	Fig 7.13	Medieval finds from Langham Road and Burystead (27–29) ... 211
Fig 5.91	Midland Road, the smithy, showing the stone-lined drain (centre to top right) and the well (centre left), looking west ... 141	Fig 8.1	Tarsal bones and phalanges of sheep/goat and pig and a sheep/goat M^3 tooth with etched surfaces probably caused by partial digestion ... 216
Fig 5.92	Midland Road, post-medieval tenements (AD 1600 onward) ... 141	Fig 8.2	Internal and side view of two cattle incisors exhibiting a deep notch worn into the crown/root junction ... 219
Fig 5.93	Midland Road, post-medieval building (SP10) ... 142	Fig 9.1	Rachis fragments from tetraploid free-threshing wheat (left) and hexaploid free-threshing wheat (right). Scale 1mm divisions ... 223
Fig 5.94	Midland Road, post-medieval building (SP11) ... 142	Fig 9.2	Two views of a seed of cf. Melampryum arvense L. with central groove (left), with two other seeds to show variations in shape (right) ... 223

PART 3 (CD)

Fig 6.1	Early–middle Saxon pottery from Furnells (1–10 jars, 11–16 bowls) ... 154
Fig 6.2	Early–middle Saxon pottery from Furnells (17 bowl, 18 lamp, 19–23 biconical jars) ... 155
Fig 6.3	Early–middle Saxon pottery from Furnells (24–34 decorated sherds) ... 156
Fig 6.4	Late Saxon pottery from Furnells: St Neots-type

Preface

My first involvement with Raunds was on a July day in 1978 when I started work as a supervisor on the excavation at Furnells manor. I arrived, with my wife and six-month old daughter, in a Morris Minor Traveller with no working brakes, which we had bought with most of our savings, £120, only the week before – we needed the work and the money. We were joining Andy Boddington, the director, and fellow supervisor Graham Cadman; young archaeologists setting out on an adventure.

At the time, the scope of that adventure seemed ambitious enough: the total excavation of a recently discovered late Saxon church and churchyard, but this was to seem naively limited as events unfolded over the next few years. We had no idea at the time, while working on our initial six-month contracts to supervise the young and totally inexperienced diggers on the Youth Opportunities Programme (YOPs), that the excavations would eventually expand to several times their original extent to take in the whole manorial enclosure. We also had no idea that Furnells was to be only the prelude to the main performance, or that Raunds was destined to cast such a long shadow over our future careers and lives.

The mid 1980s saw the creation of the Raunds Area Project, as a joint initiative between Northamptonshire County Council and English Heritage. This new phase of fieldwork brought me, and my family, back to Raunds to work at the deserted hamlet of West Cotton for Dave Windell, in a team that was a bit older and wiser; benefiting from experience gained at Furnells and elsewhere. Michel Audouy took up the challenge of the work in Raunds, while Steve Parry led the Raunds Area Survey. The English Heritage teams were working just down the road at Roman Stanwick and the round barrows on Irthlingborough island. The scale of these projects made a significant local impact, and when West Cotton entered a team in the Raunds carnival weekend football tournament in the mid-1980s we discovered that, with up to 45 diggers, we were the second largest employer in Raunds.

For me, the day I arrived at Furnells is now quite literally half a lifetime ago, and our daughter is now older than I was then. Even after the passage of so many years, the ambition of that original project still sets it apart as an exceptional piece of work. It is to be regretted that for many reasons the report presented here does not do full justice to the original vision, too many years have passed and too many people have moved on for that to happen now. However, despite these reservations, the fieldwork carried out in north Raunds has provided us with an exceptionally clear view of the dynamic nature of the origin and growth of the village in medieval England, and a vision that belies the recurrent popular image of the village as one of the few static features in an ever changing world.

As editor of this volume, I am reaching the end of the road with feelings of qualified satisfaction that a duty has, at long last, been fulfilled, and a major piece of archaeological research made available. At the same time I am also aware of the failures, limitations and lost opportunities that lie along the long and tortuous road that has led to the production of this report.

Andy Chapman, Senior Archaeologist,
Northamptonshire Archaeology

October 2007

Summary

Over a period of ten years, a series of open area excavations at the northern end of the small town of Raunds, Northamptonshire, set on the valley slopes in a midland England river valley, examined the processes of village formation from the early Saxon period through to the desertion of the outlying manorial centres at the end of the medieval period. Behind continuity of place there is a complex pattern in which individual elements of settlement were frequently relocated in response to changing circumstances.

This was most clearly demonstrated at Furnells manor where there was a break between the early Saxon occupation, which may have been relocated to a nearby site in the middle Saxon period, and the establishment of a small enclosure and related timber buildings in the mid-ninth century. This initial higher-status focus, with Scandinavian associations, was absorbed into a formal plot system created by the mid-tenth century, probably following the English reconquest and the creation of the Danelaw. With the new plots came a new set of timber buildings, comprising a hall and domestic range with detached ancillary buildings, which can be seen as the residence of a minor thegn and having the organisation of a small manor house, with a distinct division into public and private space.

The subsequent development of this manor has been fully explored. A church and churchyard, eventually containing over 300 burials, was an early addition, and the church was later rebuilt on a larger scale. The hall had been rebuilt in stone by the beginning of the thirteenth century, but by the end of that century the church and churchyard were in disuse. Before the fifteenth century the manor house had been relocated onto the former church plot, but was itself abandoned after only some fifty years of use.

Meanwhile, on the opposite side of the valley, there was a parallel development of a manor and a church, which is still the parish church of Raunds, although only part of the manorial farm was available for excavation. From the fourteenth century the appearance of buildings fronting onto the main roads began the process that led to the emergence of the modern small town, with the deserted manorial plots left behind on the outskirts as pasture closes.

Résumé

Raunds est une petite ville des Midlands de l'Angleterre, située sur les flancs d'une petite vallée du comté du Northamptonshire. Pendant près d'une décennie, une série de fouilles programmées menée dans la partie nord de l'agglomération, a étudié le processus qui a conduit à la formation du Village, depuis la période du Haut Saxon (early Saxon), jusqu'à l'abandon des sites manoriaux à la fin du Moyen Age. Derrière cette continuité d'occupation, se cache une dynamique complexe au sein de laquelle les composantes individuelles de l'habitat furent fréquemment re-localisées, au gré des circonstances.

Ce mécanisme a été plus clairement démontré sur le site de Furnells. Habité depuis la période du Haut Saxon, l'endroit fut déserté au Saxon moyen (middle Saxon) lorsque le foyer d'occupation domestique fut déplacé, semble-t-il, de quelques centaines de mètres plus au sud. Les lieux demeurèrent inoccupés jusqu'à l'implantation, vers le milieu du neuvième siècle, d'un petit enclos auquel était associé un groupe de bâtiments. Ce fut le premier foyer d'occupation présentant les caractéristiques d'un rang social élevé. Dès le milieu du dixième siècle, ce complexe, aux affinités scandinaves évidentes, fut intégré à un système de parcelles agraires formellement établi, probablement à la suite de la re-conquête anglaise et de la création du territoire dit du "Danelaw". L'apparition de ce système parcellaire fut accompagnée de la construction d'un nouveau complexe de bâtiments, comprenant un hall doté d'ailes domestiques et de dépendances. L'ensemble peut être considéré comme étant la résidence d'un petit seigneur, ou thegn, comprenant un manoir de petite taille et exhibant une division distincte entre un espace public et un espace privé.

Les développements successifs de ce manoir ont été entièrement explorés. Assez rapidement, une église et un cimetière, qui contint jusqu'à 300 inhumations, lui furent ajoutés. Par la suite, une église de plus grande dimension remplaça la première. Le hall lui même fut reconstruit en maçonnerie sur le même emplacement au début du treizième siècle. Avant la fin de ce même siècle, l'église et le cimetière étaient tombés en désuétude. A l'orée du quinzième siècle, le corps de bâtiment du manoir avait déjà été déplacé sur le site de l'ancienne église. Lui même fut abandoné après seulement cinquante ans d'usage.

Dans un même temps, sur le versant opposé de la vallée, s'effectuait un développement parallèle sur le tènement dit de Burystead où se situaient un manoir et une église. Une partie seulement de la ferme manoriale a put être explorée alors que l'église est devenue et demeure toujours, sous une nouvelle forme, l'église paroissiale actuelle. A partir du quatorzième siècle, l'implantation systématique de bâtiments le long des routes principales marqua le début d'un processus d'où allait émerger la morphologie de la petite ville moderne, laissant les parcelles manoriales devenues des champs clos, en marge de l'agglomération.

Zusammenfassung

Während einer Zeitspanne von 10 Jahren studierten einige im Freien stattfindenden Ausgrabungsunternehmen am nördlichen Teil eines Dorfes namens Raunds, talaufwärts an den Talabhängen des Flusses in Northamptonshire in Mittel-England, wie Dorfsiedlungen sich ab Anfang der Zeit der Sachsen bis zu dem Verlassen der Gutshöfe am Ende des Mittelalters entwickelten. Obwohl sich Gruppen auf einem festen Ort aufhielten, gab es wegen den sich wandelnden Umständen der Siedler oft Umlagerungen der Siedlungsnutzstellen.

Am Gutshof Furnell kann man dieses sehr gut beobachten, denn dort gab es während der anfänglichen Sächsischen Besiedlung einen Zeitraum, in welchem während der mittel sächsischen Zeit die Einwohner des Hofes von einem Ort zu einem anderen Ort in der Nähe umzogen. Man findet hier auch eine kleine umzäunte gebaute Ansiedlung aus dem 9. Jahrhundert und dazugehörende Holzhäuser. Dieser anfängliche höhere Status von Skandinavischer Abstammung wurde Mitte des 10. Jahrhunderts in ein Großgrundstücksystem eingeteilt. Dies wahrscheinlich nach der Englischen Wiedereroberung und der Einführung der Danelaw, dem Dänischen Gesetzes. Mit den neuen Großgrundstücken entwickelte sich ein neuer Stil von Holzgebäuden, der aus einer Großhalle und Küchen mit getrennten Nebengebäuden bestand. Dadurch sieht man, dass dies der Wohnort eines Grossgrundbesitzers war, und eingerichtet war wie ein kleines Gutshaus, mit deutlicher Einteilung in öffentliche und private Räumlichkeiten.

Die darauffolgende Entwicklung eines solchen Gutshofes wurde ausführlich in allen Einzelheiten untersucht. Eine Kirche und ein Kirchfriedhof, mit nach und nach mehr als 300 Gräbern, wurde bald dazugebaut, und die Kirche wurde später in eine größere umgebaut. Das Kirchenschiff wurde Anfang des 13. Jahrhunderts aus Stein gebaut, aber am Ende desselben Jahrhunderts waren weder Kirche noch Kirchfriedhof in Gebrauch. Vor dem 15. Jahrhundert wurde der Gutshof auf das alte Kirchengrundstück umgesiedelt, aber dieser wurde auch nach einem Gebrauch von nur 50 Jahren verlassen.

In der Zwischenzeit gab es auf der anderen Seite des Tals eine parallele Ansiedlung bestehend aus einem Gutshof und einer Kirche, die noch heute die Gemeindekirche von Raunds ist, obwohl nur ein Teil des Gutshofes für die Ausgrabungsarbeiten frei war. Ab 14. Jahrhundert begannen die Gebäude die an den Hauptstrassen zum Vorschein kamen, sich eine Siedlung zu entwickeln, die allmählich das moderne Dorf wurde, welches mit den verlassenen Gutshofgrundstücken am Rand an die Weiden grenzt.

1 Introduction

Background

RAUNDS is a typical settlement of Midland England. It is one of many villages and small towns strung along the broad valley of the River Nene, which rises above Northampton and flows north-east across Northamptonshire and through Peterborough on its course towards the east coast at The Wash (Fig 1.1). At either side of the valley dissected plateaux form watersheds between the Nene and the neighbouring valleys of the Welland, to the north-west, and the Great Ouse, to the east. Raunds lies on the upper slopes of the valley side, straddling the confluence on a series of tributary streams that form the Raunds or Cotton Brook, which runs westward to the River Nene (Fig 1.2).

The place-name 'Rande' appears in the Domesday Book, with later variations such as Randes, Raund(e) and Rawns (Gover *et al* 1975). It probably derives from the Old English 'randum', meaning 'at the borders', or 'edges', which may refer to its topographical location on the western fringe of the former Saxon forest of Bromswold, or perhaps to a marginal territorial location. The origins of Raunds appear to lie in the coalescence of at least two discrete agglomerations of early settlement, one in north Raunds and another at Thorpe End, about 1km to the south (Parry 2006, 221–224). The dominance of these foci is still apparent in the 1798 Map of Enclosure, which shows an elongated village with a simple road system serving tenements and frontages which were only thinly occupied (Fig 1.3). The immediate surroundings comprised enclosed fields with most containing the ridge-and-furrow of previous cultivation.

Raunds was a village until well into the nineteenth century when the boot and shoe, and brick industries emerged as major components of the local economy, and it grew rapidly to small town status. The industrial and housing developments colonised the slopes of the valley to the south, leaving the derelict pasture closes on both stream banks in north Raunds undisturbed. Parts of the original core of the late Saxon and medieval settlement were thus fossilised in earthwork around the medieval parish church of St Mary, now St Peter's, which still overlooks Raunds from a vantage point high on the eastern stream bank.

Following the decline of the boot and shoe industries, a new role emerged in the 1970s with the growth of Raunds as a dormitory town. It was this new period of residential development, along with light industry and warehousing, which posed a threat to the closes at the northern end of Raunds and led to the series of excavations on both the western and eastern stream banks that have revealed so much of the story of the original development of the village.

The excavations and the Raunds Area Project

In 1976, in response to the threat of redevelopment, David Hall and members of the Northamptonshire Field Group recorded the earthworks and carried out a trial excavation in a paddock on the western stream bank at the site of medieval manor of Furnells (Fig 1.4: Hall *et al* 1988, fig 2 and plate b). The discovery of the remains of a medieval church and burials, including decorated late Saxon grave slabs prompted a response from the Northamptonshire County Council Archaeology Unit, and more extensive excavation began in the following year under the direction of Andy Boddington. The initial aim was the full excavation of the church and churchyard, but the project grew organically and eventually ran until 1982, under the direction of Graham Cadman, by which time much of the system of manorial closes had been excavated. Throughout this period contact with the local community was maintained both by the presence of local people within the excavation team and through regular site open days (Fig 1.5). To this day, there are still many local families with memories of those excavations. It may also be noted that throughout the excavation there was remarkably little vandalism, despite partially excavated burials often lying exposed over night.

The report on the excavation of the church and churchyard has already been published (Boddington 1996). While the chronology presented in that volume has now been revised, the broad presentation of the archaeology of the church and churchyard remains largely unchanged and will only be summarised briefly in this volume.

At the same time as the Furnells excavation, an assessment of the archaeological priorities for the county (Foard 1979) recognised that Furnells manor was not simply a valuable, isolated archaeological resource, but lay within a broader and largely intact historic landscape that was under threat from further development, including more housing and industry as well as road construction and mineral extraction. As a result, the Raunds Area Project was officially established in 1985, under the joint management

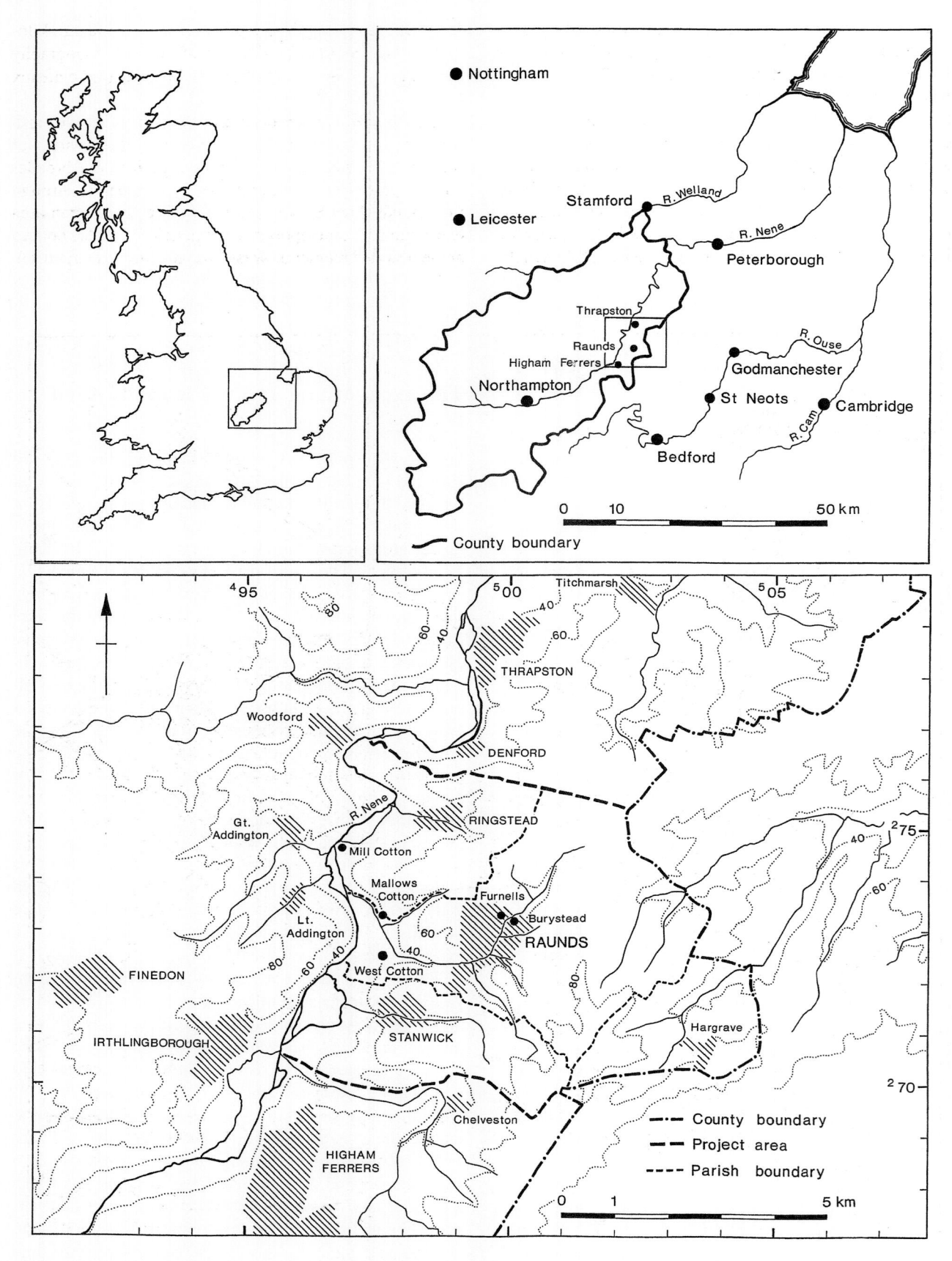

Fig 1.1: The location of Raunds, and the boundary of the Raunds Area Project © Crown copyright. All rights reserved. Northamptonshire County Council: Licence No. 100019331. Published 2007

of the Northamptonshire County Council Archaeology Unit and the Historic Buildings and Monuments Commission for England (English Heritage) (Fig 1.6). The aim of the project was the investigation of a range of elements of the historic landscape through the opportunistic rescue excavation of threatened sites, but with these set within a broader context through related programmes of field survey, documentary research and environmental analysis (Foard and Pearson 1985). The study area was bounded to the west by the River Nene and took in the parish of Raunds as well as the neighbouring parishes of Stanwick, Ringstead and Hargrave, a total area of forty square kilometres that included a full range of the local topography from the valley floor to the Boulder Clay covered plateaux (Fig 1.1).

This present report on archaeological work in north Raunds must therefore be viewed within the context of the Area Project. For the medieval period, the broader context of settlement development has been set through the Raunds Area Survey (Parry 2006) and the open area excavation of contemporary settlement in the valley bottom at the deserted hamlet of West Cotton (Chapman in press),

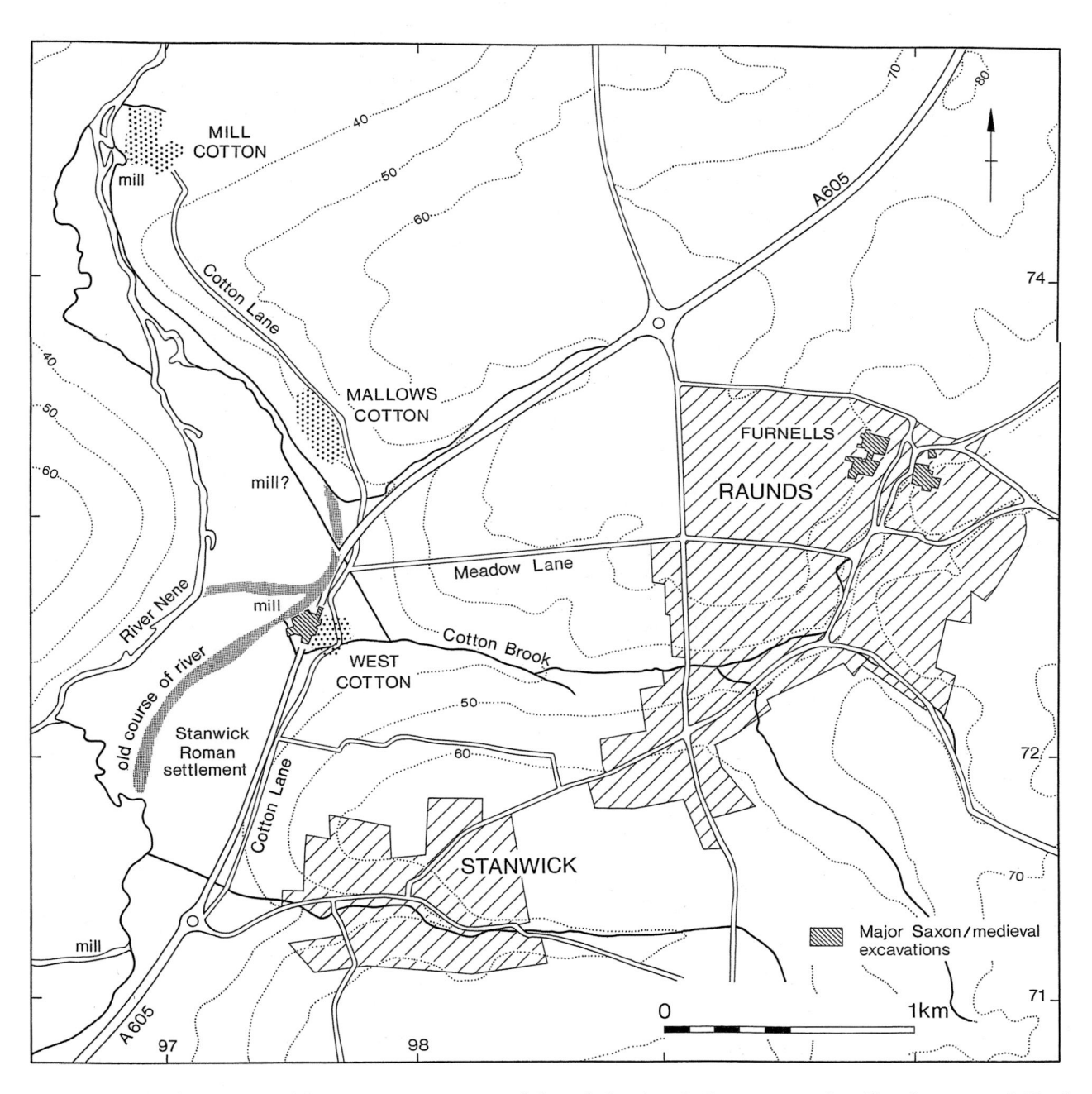

Fig 1.2: Raunds, the location of the major excavations and the vale hamlets © Crown copyright. All rights reserved. Northamptonshire County Council: Licence No. 100019331. Published 2007

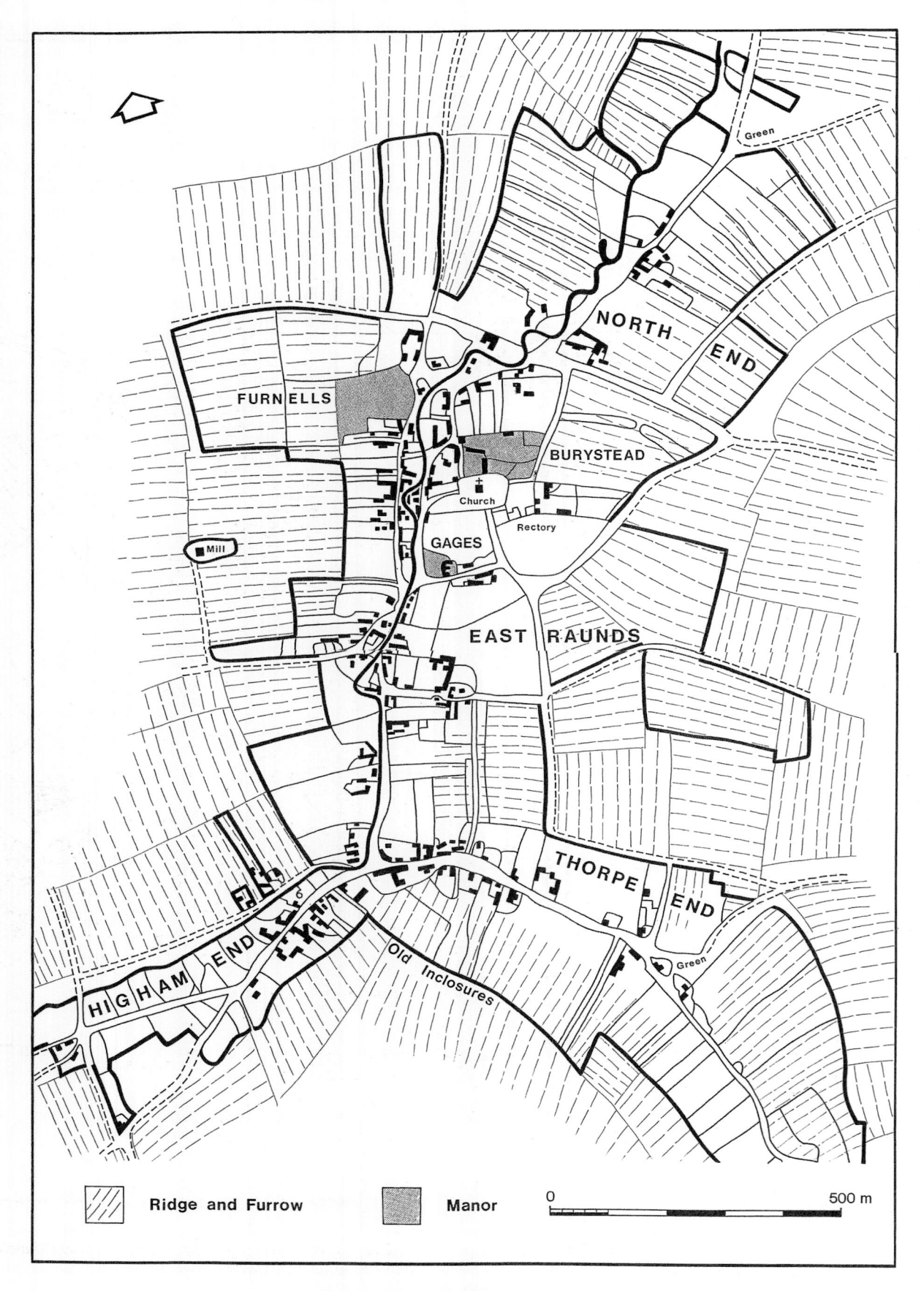

Fig 1.3: Transcription of the Raunds estate map of 1798

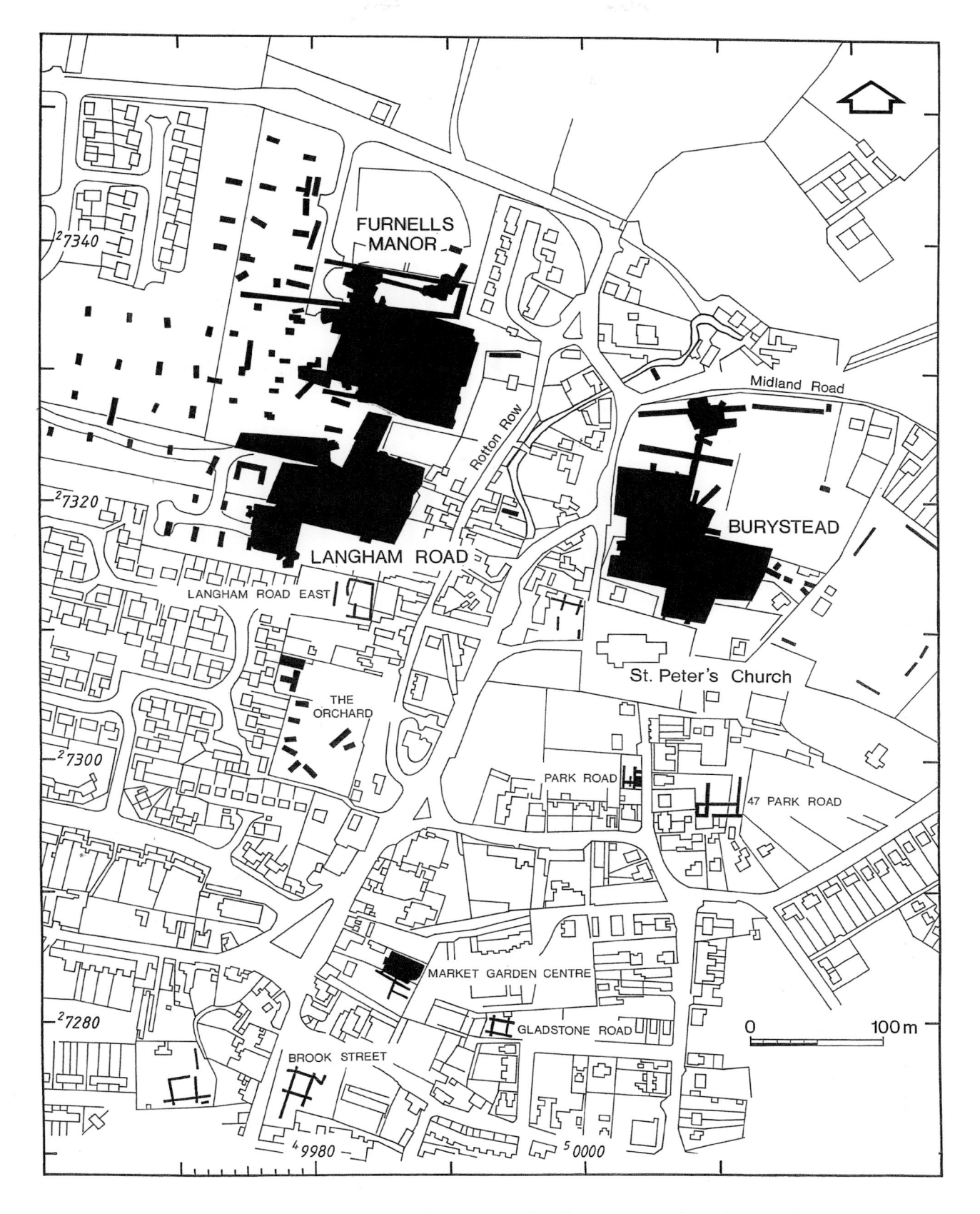

Fig 1.4: The excavations in north Raunds, 1977–87 © Crown copyright. All rights reserved. Northamptonshire County Council: Licence No. 100019331. Published 2007

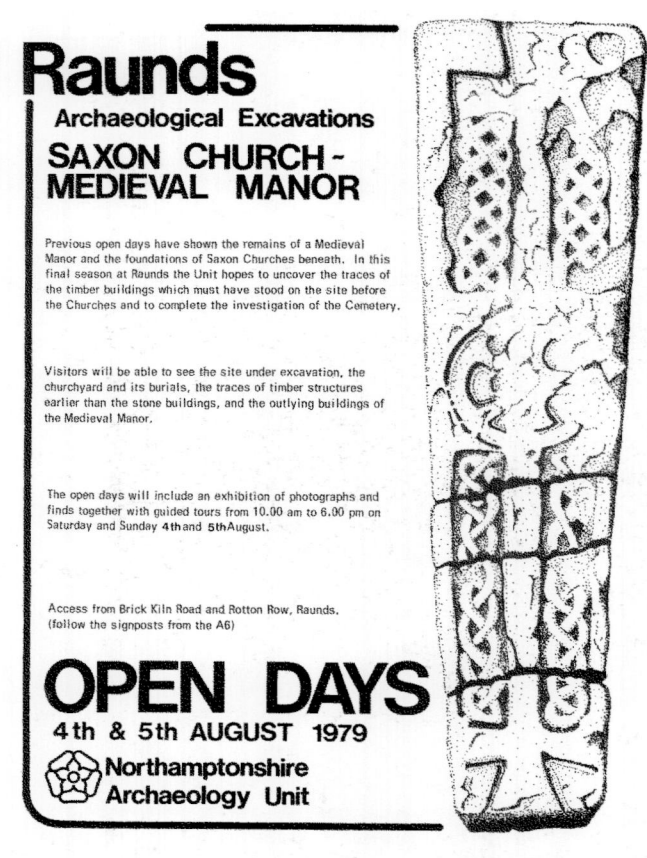

Fig 1.5: Advertising poster for site open days at Furnells manor, 1979

Fig 1.6: Front cover of leaflet advertising the launch of the Raunds Area Project in 1985

also conducted by the county archaeology unit. The earlier landscape history was studied at a similarly intensive level of fieldwork through the work of English Heritage, directed by Claire Halpin, and the county archaeology unit on the Neolithic and Bronze Age monument complex along the valley bottom (Harding and Healy 2007) and the work of English Heritage, under the direction of David Neal, on the Iron Age and Roman settlement at Stanwick, currently under post-excavation analysis and report preparation by Vicky Crosby (Crosby and Neal forthcoming). Through the late 1980s, local interest was still high, but the later excavations in north Raunds were never as visually attractive to the visitor, lacking the human element of the burials and buildings at Furnells. Furnells had also lain within an open landscape, while the later work often comprised a succession of smaller areas sometimes literally lying next to housing construction sites.

In north Raunds the pace of the archaeological investigation and its strategy were both initiated and governed by the rapid expansion of housing development (Figs 1.7 and 1.8). The excavations were therefore carried out in stages and involved a mix of techniques, ranging from extensive sampling by evaluation trenches to the area excavation of the available former foci of settlement. Following the excavation at Furnells from 1976 to 1982 (NGR: SP 999 733; Fig 1.9), two further major open area excavations were undertaken under the Raunds Area Project in the mid- to late-1980s (Fig 1.4). To the south of Furnells there was extensive excavation at Langham Road in 1984–5 (NGR: SP 998 732), and on the eastern stream a comparable area was examined between 1985 and 1987 at Burystead (NGR: TL 001 732; Fig 1.10), adjacent to the parish church, along with a small area to the north on the Midland Road frontage (NGR: TL 001 733, which explored parts of the late medieval to post-medieval tenements on the street frontage.

Other archaeological recording has been carried out elsewhere in north Raunds in the course of monitoring re-development, and small evaluation trenches have provided further valuable information concerning the extent of settlement activity at various periods. Although completion of fieldwork at Burystead in 1987 marked the end of

Fig 1.7: Aerial view of north Raunds in 1979, looking north-west, showing the excavation of Furnells manor (centre top), with the empty paddocks of Burystead lying north of the church of St Peter (right)

Fig 1.8: Aerial view of north Raunds in 1986, looking north, with housing development beginning to appear at Furnells (top left) and Burystead (centre right)

Fig 1.9: Aerial view of Furnells towards the end of excavation, 1981, showing the houses on Rotton Row (bottom left), the excavated churchyard (overgrown and containing spoil dumps) and the late Saxon timber buildings (top, with the aisled hall partly under polythene sheeting)

Fig 1.10: Aerial view of Burystead in 1987, looking west, showing the medieval dovecote (centre), with housing encroaching from the north (right) and also across Furnells and Langham Road (top)

large-scale excavations in north Raunds, the investigation of the origins of this Northamptonshire community still continues through occasional small scale excavations and watching briefs prompted by the monitoring of housing development (eg Morris 2002).

Topography and geology

The parish of Raunds extends up the valley slope from the river onto the plateau to embrace a full range of the geology and soils of the Jurassic belt. The valley bottom lies at around 35m OD while the modern town lies on the upper slopes of the valley close to the 60m (200ft) contour where it sprawls along both sides of the Raunds Brook at the confluence of several minor tributary streams (Fig 1.2). These streams run off the flanks of the adjacent plateau, which rises to a height of 75m OD between Raunds and Hargrave.

The Nene is a slow flowing river, where a complex of braided river channels has been reduced to no more than two major channels by a long-term process of channel siltation. This began as early as 5000BC (Harding and Healy 2007; Chapman 2004) and a major channel silted up as late as the twelfth century AD during the occupation of the adjacent medieval hamlet of West Cotton (Chapman in press). This final episode occurred during a period of intense alluviation, when the topography of the valley bottom was transformed by the burying of the glacial gravels beneath 1.0–2.0m of alluvial clayey silts. Along the margins of the floodplain there are exposures of Upper Lias clay, where spring lines emerge. On the valley slopes a range of Jurassic geologies of the Oolite series are exposed, including Northamptonshire Sands ironstone, Blisworth limestone and cornbrash, generally providing permeable geology and thus well-drained soils suitable for arable exploitation. On the upper slopes, Oxford Clay is exposed in places but the whole of the main plateau is capped by Boulder Clay, providing an impermeable geology and heavy intractable soils.

The north Raunds area straddles the upper slopes on either side of the northernmost tributary stream. The eastern side of the valley is dominated by Burystead and the parish church, where the erosive action of the stream has cut a steep scarp into the flanks of the hill. The western side of the valley, the site of Furnells and Langham Road, rises more gently towards a ridge that overlooks the River Nene.

The micro-geology of these sites is quite variable (Fig 1.11). At Furnells the manorial buildings and the church sat on the high point of a low ridge capped with clay. There is cornbrash limestone on the gentle northern slope, while to the south, between Furnells and Langham Road, a pronounced depression is filled with a red brown clayey loam, and this area was largely devoid of occupation. The Langham Road site straddled more even ground on similarly mixed exposures of cornbrash, clay and red loam. On the opposite side of the valley, the excavation site at Burystead straddled a slight promontory with the same mixed sequence, while at the Midland Road frontage, the lowest lying of the sites, there is only red loam.

The medieval landscape

Without pre-empting the discussion of the documentary evidence (Courtney below) or the description of the excavated evidence, to set the north Raunds excavations in context it is necessary to provide a brief summary of the broader pattern and hierarchy of medieval settlement.

The fieldwalking results of the Raunds Area Survey (Parry 2006) indicated that the pattern of early and middle Saxon settlement was one of small dispersed settlements, or farmsteads, scattered across the slopes of the valley side, with a tendency for the pairing of settlements on either side of the tributary streams. This pattern came to an abrupt end in the late Saxon period with the establishment of a more limited number of nucleated settlements and the setting out of the open field system.

Raunds was also always subordinate to Higham Ferrers, which lies to the immediate south, on the east bank of the Nene. Irthlingborough, on the west bank, had grown out of a seventh-century Mercian centre of Offa, perhaps originally founded within the Iron Age hillfort of Crowhill, which stood to the north of Irthlingborough, facing Stanwick. Higham may have succeeded Irthlingborough, but the early importance of Higham itself has recently been emphasised by the discovery of a middle Saxon estate centre lying to the north of medieval Higham and adjacent to Kings Meadow Lane, which probably fossilises a much earlier cross-valley route between Higham and Irthlingborough. A large enclosure and associated timber halls and barns are dated to the eighth century, and are interpreted as a purpose-built tribute centre for a royal estate (Hardy et al 2007). Higham was probably also the centre of an important late Saxon estate that had given its name to the hundred, and it had a market by the late eleventh century.

The importance of Higham was maintained throughout the medieval period when it acquired a castle and a college. Later medieval documents also indicate a major trading role, including the provision of malt to London, and it is likely that much of the agricultural surplus coming from Raunds would have passed through the market at Higham.

The historic form of Raunds is depicted on the estate map of 1798 (Fig 1.3). This shows Raunds to be a binary settlement, with distinct northern and southern ends, although with greater complexity within each end. To the south, distinct foci of settlement at Thorpe End and Higham End flank a tributary stream and the Raunds Brook. They are described in the survey volume (Parry 2006, 234–240), but are not considered further in this volume. At the North End, excavation and documentary evidence again show the presence of two distinct foci; on the west bank at Furnells

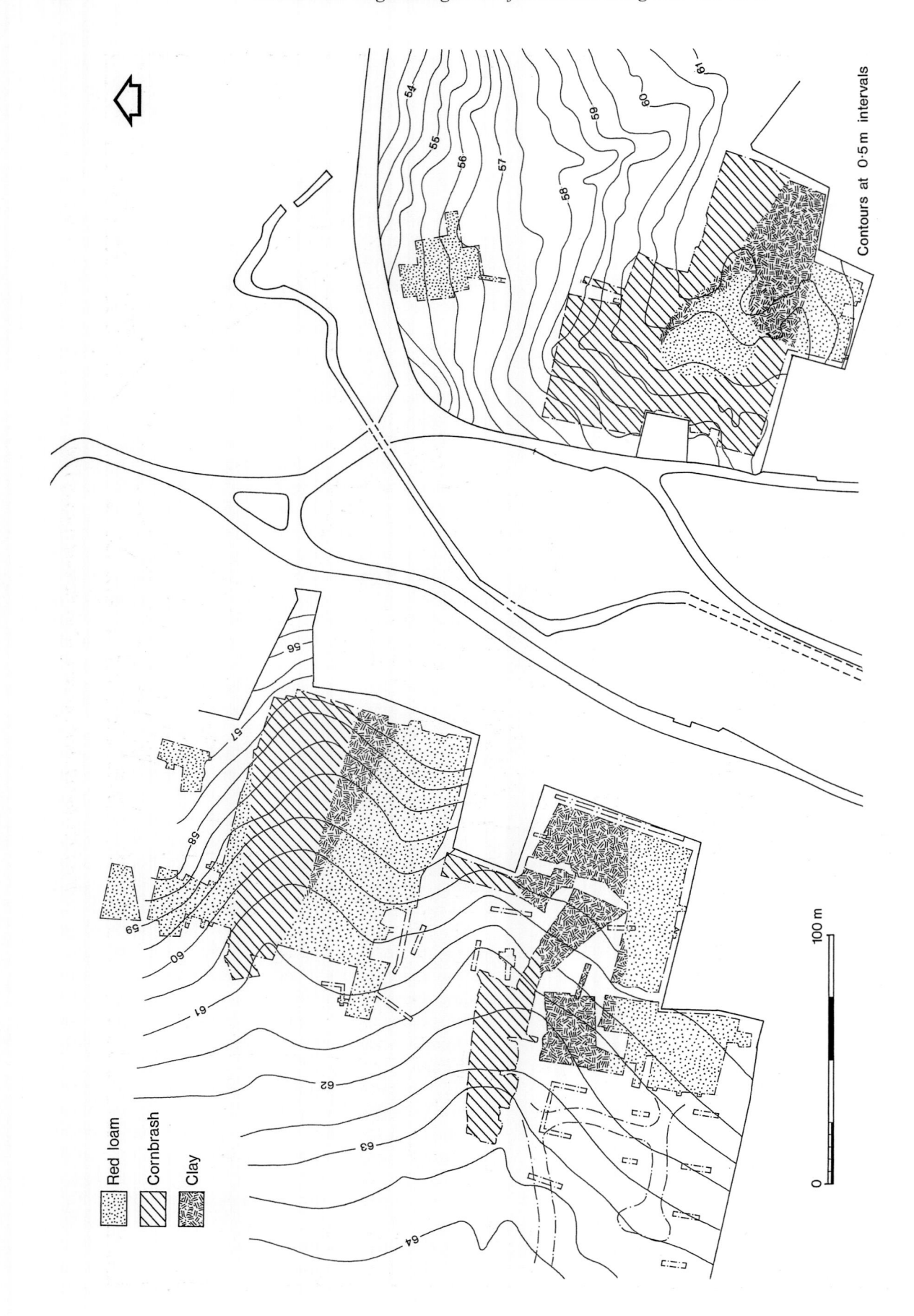

Fig 1.11: The surface drift geology and contours of north Raunds, as recorded on the excavated areas

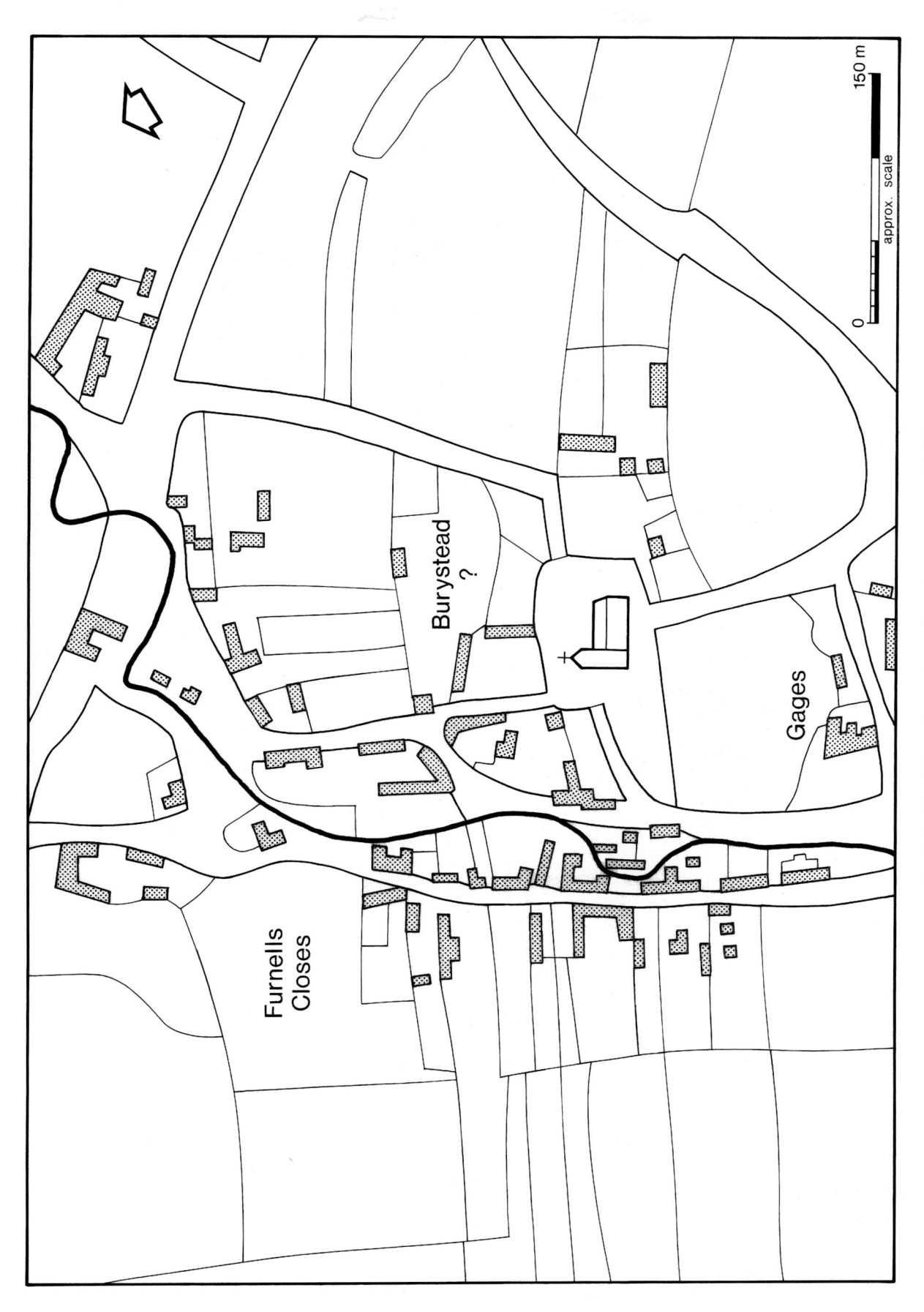

Fig 1.12: North Raunds, as depicted on the estate map of 1798

and on the east bank at Burystead (Fig 1.12). The intervening area, East Raunds, is related to later expansion linking the two ends, with Gages manor forming a late medieval and post-medieval focus. The presence of the original two ends is probably repeated in the medieval arrangement of the fields, where two independent three-field systems were in operation in the fourteenth century, and were recorded as North and Thorpe End fields in the sixteenth century (Hall 2006). Nucleated settlements formed from the late medieval fusion of a cluster of discrete original foci have been seen as a common phenomenon in the Nene valley close to the Bromswold, and elsewhere (Lewis et al 1997, 58).

The neighbouring settlements of Stanwick and Ringstead occupy similar locations on the upper slopes of the valley and, while both are smaller than Raunds, they would have followed broadly similar patterns of development through to the present day, as large villages around a manorial centre or centres and including a parish church. The minimal archaeological work conducted in these two villages is summarised in the Raunds Survey volume (Parry 2006, 160–167 and 221–214).

In addition to the surviving villages, there are the three deserted settlements of Mill Cotton, in Ringstead parish, and Mallows Cotton and West Cotton in Raunds (Fig 1.2). All three lay on the margin of the floodplain and were linked by the Cotton Lane, which would have provided direct access to Higham Ferrers to the south. This may have been a former minor Roman road that would have linked the Roman settlements at Ringstead, Mallows Cotton and Stanwick to a further settlement at Higham Ferrers.

The three valley bottom settlements formed significant elements of the landscape from the late Saxon period onward. By the end of the medieval period they had declined to become minor settlements dependent on the ever growing upland villages. A combination of archaeological and documentary evidence has shown that their final forms as peasant hamlets belies more illustrious origins as manorial centres in their own right. Mill Cotton in its heyday contained a grand moated manor house, the residence of the Chamberlyn family, major landowners in the district, as well as a watermill, which remained in use until the early 1900s, and a manorial chapel. The earthwork remains of this site were investigated under salvage conditions immediately prior to gravel extraction in the early 1970s (Parry 2006, 186–194), but little now remains of this village. At Mallows Cotton, the extensive village earthworks are well preserved and are scheduled as an Ancient Monument (Parry 2006, 177–185). Mallows Cotton also possessed a watermill and a manorial chapel.

At West Cotton, the smallest of the three deserted settlements, open area excavations in the 1980s, as part of the Raunds Area Project, uncovered half of the settlement. The results from this site, uncluttered by later activity, provide a model for the processes of village plot formation that were less perfectly seen and understood in north Raunds (Chapman in press). This small hamlet was also shown to have its origin in one, and perhaps two, late Saxon manors (one of which possessed a watermill) that lay at the lowest level of the manorial system. It also shows the processes of dynamic change that could occur within medieval settlements, with the loss of the watermill through alluviation in the twelfth century leading to the physical relocation of the manor house onto a neighbouring plot, and later to the sub-division and refurbishment of the manorial buildings to provide several peasant tenements.

The decline and eventual desertion of these marginal settlements was part of the same complex process that led to the abandonment of the manorial sites in north Raunds, as the landed gentry focused their estates on their principal manor houses, rather than maintaining a multiplicity of manorial centres, while the structure of the modern village emerged with the infilling of the frontages with rows of tenement plots.

The structure of the report
by Andy Chapman

This report is presented in three parts:

Part 1: Chapters 1 to 4 provide an introduction, the documentary evidence, a broad overview of the development of the sites in north Raunds and a discussion of the broader historical significance of the archaeological evidence. Part 1 can therefore be read as a self-contained summary and overview of the archaeology of north Raunds.

Part 2: Chapter 5 catalogues the major excavated structures and other significant feature groups, in particular providing illustrations and descriptions of the major buildings.

Part 3: Chapters 6 to 9 catalogue the material evidence of the pottery and other finds, as well as the animal bone and the environmental evidence.

Given the specialist nature of the chapters in Part 3, they will be available on a CD attached to the published volume and will also be available online through the Archaeological Data Service (ADS). It is also hoped that a limited number of these chapters will be produced in hard copy, although not formally bound as the main volume, so that they can be supplied to those who need this level of data.

In doing this the editor expects to have the wrath of many finds and environmental specialists descend upon him, but it is part of what many see as a necessary move away from the "traditional" paper archaeological report that contains all specialist contributions in full. The advent of the computer and their widespread availability, together with the capability to download data from the internet and to store it digitally, cannot be ignored. As unfortunate as many may find it, the day of the thick monograph that includes everything must be numbered when the more detailed and specific information can be quickly and cheaply disseminated in digital form to those who do need to consult it.

If it had been possible to foresee all these advances when the report was being put together in the early 1990s, the desirable aim would have been to integrate more of the specialist work into the panorama of settlement development, and to illustrate a wider selection of the material evidence within the main body of the text, but it has not been possible to do this within the scope of the final editing.

It is also intended that as a long-term resource, the full report will be made available online through ADS in a few years time, once sales of the paper copy have run their course.

The site archives

The archive of fieldwork records and the subsequent analysis of the evidence was organised in accordance with the principles of archaeological publication recommended by the Department of the Environment in 1975 (Frere 1975). During excavation a level II record was created by the allocation of stratigraphic context numbers to all discrete entities as the basis of a single context recording system (Boddington 1978). These were brought together in a numbered sequence of Stratigraphic Groups (prefix g) where they related to a single identifiable feature or event. Structural Phases (prefix SP) were created from groups displaying structural coherence, and these included buildings, posthole groups, and ditch systems. The Structural Phase (SP) references are used in this report. At Furnells, an additional alphabetical sequence was allocated to the major structures, eg Structure A (SP70). At Langham Road and Burystead the SP number codes were prefixed LRSP and BSP respectively. Small finds (prefix SF) have been catalogued according to structural phase and group.

Given the present lack of a county repository for archaeological archives in Northamptonshire, it is unlikely that either the finds or the paper records for the Raunds Area Project will become available for consultation or further research for some years. Some primary material and much of the secondary record is held in temporary store at the offices of Northamptonshire Archaeology, the contracting archaeology unit that took on the fieldwork role of the former Northamptonshire Archaeology Unit. The remainder is held in various temporary stores, with different aspects of the record held at different locations. These archives were under the supervision of the archaeological curatorial service of Northamptonshire County Council, formerly Northamptonshire Heritage. However, since 2006 this service has been reduced to little more than the maintenance of the county Sites and Monuments Record (SMR)/Historic Environment Record (HER), and the service is currently attached to the County Archive Service (Northamptonshire Record Office).

The future destiny of the records and finds from the work of all aspects of the Raunds Area Project is therefore unknown.

2 Historical Background

Domesday Raunds
by Paul Courtney

It has been postulated that Raunds, Ringstead and Hargrave once formed a discrete estate (Cadman and Foard 1984). The evidence of Domesday Book (DB), argues against such an interpretation. Domesday Book indicates that in the late eleventh century there were two chief holdings in Raunds. In 1066 Burgred, clearly a King's thegn, held a manor in Raunds which can be identified with Furnells (DB, I, f. 220c). The other chief holding in 1066 can be identified with the Burystead manor and was held by Gytha, wife of Ralph, earl of Hereford (DB, I, f.225d). Anne Williams (1989) has suggested that Ralph was for a time earl of Mercia and that he probably gained his Northamptonshire lands through his marriage to Gytha. She has also suggested that the spatial coincidence of Gytha's and Burgred's lands in the East Midlands suggest a familial connection. In 1086 William Peverel held Gytha's lands and Burgred had been replaced by Geoffrey de Mowbray, bishop of Coutances.

Domesday Book makes it quite clear that the Burystead estate in Raunds was not a 'manor' but a subordinate element of the soke of Higham. The usual curtness of circuit 4 of Domesday Book does not specify the status of Gytha's estate at Raunds, though mention is made of its 'appendages'. The presence of villeins and slaves suggests it was a 'berewick' (a detached portion of *inland* or demesne) with attached sokeland. The fact that it was not regarded as a manor does not mean that Burystead did not possess a hall (in legal terms a centre for the collection of renders and services), but it was clearly subordinate to the estate at Higham. It is perhaps conceivable that Gytha's share of Raunds was split off from a distinct Raunds estate and added on to the Higham estate at some point. However, given the presence of demesne it seems more likely that it would have been regarded as a distinct manor, with separate title by Domesday. Burgred's holding in Raunds was held by sake and soke; that is by charter (bookland). In contrast, his adjacent manor of Denford was held *libere* (freely), that is as allodial or familial land, held from an earlier date than the process of 'booking'. Domesday Book appears to show us an important comital manor based on Higham Ferrers in the process of fragmentation. Higham gave its name to the hundred and possessed a market in 1086. It would appear to have been the centre of an important late-Saxon estate, possibly with origins as a *villa regalis* or King's tun (see Courtney 2006a).

North Raunds
by Paul Courtney

The manorial landscape

The lands of Peverel and Coutances formed the two great fees that dominated medieval Raunds. The Peverel lands were held by the earl of Lancaster in the fourteenth century and later formed part of the duchy of Lancaster, held for most of its history by the crown. The Coutances lands came into the possession of the Clare family in the early twelfth century, and after their extinction in 1314 became part of the Gloucester fee held by the D'Audley and later the Stafford families.

The post-Norman manorial structure of Raunds had become highly complicated by the thirteenth century through the process of sub-infeudation, in which lands were granted away by the holders of its chief fees in return for hereditary knight service (see Courtney 2006a). However, three chief manors can be identified in Raunds: Furnells, Burystead and Gages. The first was the centre of the Coutances/Clare manor, the second was the heart of the Peverel/Lancaster estate, whilst Gages comprised lands in both fees. The manorial enclosures of all three lay in north Raunds (Fig 1.12). Indeed their significance is confirmed by the fact that they are the only manorial centres that can be located in the village.

Furnells manor

The manor of Furnells can be identified as the site of Burgred's manor in 1066 (Fig 1.12). Like most other late eleventh-century manors it was probably being farmed out for rent, and it appears to have been sub-infeudated by the thirteenth century. Thereafter it was held by a series of minor 'knightly' families who owed feudal dues to the Clares and their successors as feudal overlords. Manorial accounts were undoubtedly kept but were never incorporated into a major baronial archive and have been destroyed.

The manor appears to have been named after the Furneus or Furnellis family, who derived their name from a French place-name, probably Fourneux in Calvados (Reaney 1967, 60 and 1976, 128). The manor is first recorded in 1203–5 when Henry, son of Geoffrey, and Roger de Furneus disputed the rights to one knight's fee in Raunds and Ringstead (CRR, 3–5 John, 230 and 5–7 John, 72, 227–8, 230 and 291). Henry claimed that the manor was held by his grandfather, Hugh de St Lo who died seised of it in the reign of Henry I (1100–35). The dispute was apparently settled in the favour of the Furneus family as they continued to hold the fee. Roger de Furneus in 1284 is the last member of the family documented as holding the manor (FA, 4, 14). By 1314 he had been replaced as lord of Furnells by Eleanor de Trailly, but the manor was now assessed as only half a knight's fee instead of the whole knight's fee it had been in the thirteenth century (CIPM, c 5, 538). This either represents a reduction in the dues owed by the manor or just possibly that it was split into two moieties. If the latter, the non-Trailly moietie may have been incorporated into the second knight's fee held by John Champernowne in Barton, Raunds and Cranford, first recorded in 1314 (CCR, 1313–8, 138; CIPM, 5, 538). Unfortunately the Raunds component of the Champernowne estate cannot be defined on the ground nor can it be traced administratively after the mid-fifteenth century (CCR Hen IV, ii, 203–5; CIPM, 4, 59).

The Trailly family held over half-a-dozen manors, mostly in Bedfordshire (eg, CIPM, 10, 617 and 13, 210). In Northamptonshire they also held half a knight's fee from the Clare/Stafford family at Woodford across the River Nene from Ringstead and only 4 km from Furnells (VCH Northants 4, 258). Walter de Trailly held a fee in Raunds as early as 1276 but its nature is unclear (Rot Hund, 2, 10). An *inquisition post-mortem* (IPM) held at Northampton in 1289 notes that he held the advowson of Newton Bromswold (in Higham hundred), but states that he held no other fees in the county (CIPM, 2, 791). This statement, however, should be taken to mean merely that he held no fees in chief, that is, directly from the crown.

Eleanor de Trailly certainly held a half knight's fee in Raunds, as well as several Bedfordshire manors, from the Clare family in 1314 (CIPM, 5, 538). Unfortunately, there is no evidence as to whether the Trailly family continued to run Furnells manor directly or farmed it out. As late as 1403 an IPM of Edmund Stafford still records John de Trailly as holding the manor, though John died in 1400 (CIPM, 18, 100–2 and 838). John's heir was Reginald de Trailly, last of the male line, who died in 1402, leaving Margery de Huggerford as heir. However, as in previous Trailly's IPM no mention is made of those manors not held in chief (CIPM, 18, 643–5).

The later history of the Trailly manor is confused. Documents describing feudal relations in the later Middle Ages become scarcer and often contain antiquated information. There is also the possibility that they obscure the real pattern of sub-infeudation or sub-tenancy. The Greenes succeeded to the Trailly manor, including Furnells close, in the early fifteenth century. Up to 1399 their holding is described as 1/2 a fee in Middlecotes but in 1400 they are said to hold the manor of Cotes with lands in Raunds, Stanwick, Chelveston, Hargrave and other places for one knight's fee (CIPM, 18, 334; CPR 1399–1401, 551). The Greenes are also known to have had customary tenants in Raunds in 1389 (NRO SS 4243). At first sight, this seems to rule out both the Trailly manor, as Reynold de Trailly died in 1402, and the Clowne fee which is documented in 1403. It is conceivable, however, that Clowne or, more likely, the Traillys had already sold their manor to the Greenes but that this event is hidden by the conservative nature of the documents. The Greenes were a wealthy family with numerous manors in Northamptonshire as well as many other counties (see CIPM, 12, 355).

In the mid-fifteenth century the Staffords, earls of Wiltshire, succeeded the Greenes as lords of Furnells through marriage. However, the death of Edward Stafford in 1499 led to a long dispute over his inheritance, but eventually the estate was divided between John Mordaunt, Humphrey Brown and Sir Wistan Browne (VCH Northants 3, 328). In the later 1550s Sir Wistan's third of Furnells and Ringstead was acquired by lord Mordaunt (NRO SS 277, 3097, 3753). The Mordaunts, whose seat was at Drayton to the north of Raunds, became earls of Peterborough in 1628. The other third of Furnells was settled by Humphrey Browne in 1570 on his daughter Catherine and her husband, William Roper (NRO L(C) 2038).

The Duchy of Lancaster court rolls record various individuals who were ordered to clean the ditch below Furnells close or fined for allowing it to flood. These cases involved Henry Greene between 1452 and 1463, John Catlyn in 1448 and 1475 and Henry Catlyn between 1480 and 1484/5. In two cases the ditch is located more specifically at the south end of Furnells close (April 1483 and 1484/5). Henry Greene was, however, fined in October 1461 and May 1462 for allowing the ditches on both sides of the close to flood (NRO X705). The Catlyns were presumably farming the close from Henry Greene and subsequently the earl of Wiltshire. This evidence indicates that Furnells close had ditches, liable to flooding, at both its northern and southern ends. The two ditches presumably ran eastward down the valley into the brook.

In 1648 John Ekins transferred by deeds to Christopher Vivian and Thomas Ekins *'All that scite of the Manor of Furnells commonly called or knowne by the name of Furnells Close with a cottage therein standeinge'* (NRO S(G) 319). In 1708 Furnells close was mortgaged but the cottage is now described as having been formerly standing (NRO S(G) 330). A terrier of 1739 recorded *'three closes called Furnells Closes, in one of them stood the manor house or castle of Furnell's Mannor'* (NRO ML 124).

Gages manor

The seventeenth-century manor house still stands to the south of the parish church (Fig 1.12). In 1242–3 Henry de Raunds held 1/8 of a knight's fee in Raunds from the Ferrers family (later the duchy) and 1/4 of a fee from the Clares (BF, ii, 933 and 945). Herlewin de Raunds, presumably an ancestor, is documented in the county between 1176 and 1205 (PRS, 22 Hen II, 51 and CRR, 3, 307).

The de Raunds family continued to hold these fees into the fifteenth century. In the later fourteenth century, Sir

John Trailly, lord of Furnells, alienated Yelden (Bedfordshire), a Clare/Gloucester manor, to Edmund Hampden. The Traillys may have once had rights over the de Raunds family fee, as in 1428 Thomas de Raunds is recorded as holding 1/4 fee in Raunds of the lordship of Yelden (FA, 4, 45 and CIPM, 18, 100 and 644). After this date the 1/4 fee is no longer distinguished in the records. In the fifteenth century Thomas de Raunds' daughter married John Tawyer whose granddaughter married John Gage, who inherited the manor in 1474–5 (Visit Northants, 49–50 and 92; Bridges 1791, ii, 186). In 1582, taking advantage of its complicated origins, Robert Gage tried to argue that his manor did not lie between the limits of the duchy manorial court in Raunds. He was almost certainly unsuccessful as the duchy court rolls clearly show that part of his manor lay within duchy jurisdiction (PRO DL1/141/C9).

A duchy of Lancaster terrier of 1552–3 describes George Gage as holding four virgates from the duchy as a 1/4 knight's fee (NRO X706). In 1665 Gages manor was described as comprising three closes containing 32 acres, 120 acres of arable and ley, plus 12 acres of meadow. The manor site had barns, stables, a malt-house, dovecote and horse-powered malt mill. In addition there were recently purchased lands in Gages occupation as well as several hundred acres in the hands of tenants (NRO Clayton 152 and L(C) 1980). Gages new dwelling house is mentioned in 1614–5, implying that it had been newly re-built (PRO DL4/47/12).

Burystead manor

The Burystead (Middle English *'manor place'*) was the centre of the duchy of Lancaster manor in Raunds (Fig 1.12). It was the successor of the Domesday Book manor held by William Peverel. In the thirteenth century, during the hey-day of demesne farming, the manor was almost certainly worked by a steward for the direct profit of the lord, though no accounts survive for this period. The earliest bailiff's account for Raunds is for the accounting year Michaelmas 1313–14 (PRO DL29/1/3; translation in Kerr 1925, 80–6). This reveals that the manor, including 2991.5 acres of demesne arable, was farmed from April 20, 1314 by Thomas, earl of Lancaster to Sir Richard fitz Marmaduke for life. The farm was to reward fitz Marmaduke for his services as one of earl Thomas's indentured knightly retainers. Fitz Marmaduke was killed by a relative in 1318 and earl Thomas was executed for treason in 1322 (Kerr 1925, 81; Holmes l957, 137 and Maddicott 1970, 42 and 65).

Raunds was the first duchy manor to be farmed in Northamptonshire, though earl Thomas farmed out a number of manors in other counties to his retainers for life (Maddicott 1970, 42). The choice of Raunds presumably reflects that it was a peripheral component of the Higham estate. However, even at Higham Ferrers 50 acres of demesne were being let at will by 1348, reflecting the growing trend towards leasing (Somerville 1953, 95:fn.2).

The demesne at Rushden was also farmed out at some point between 1313–4 and 1355–6, presumably for commercial reasons (PRO DL29/1/3 and DL29/324/5292). Raunds continued to be farmed out for terms of life after the death of earl Thomas. A receiver's receipt of 1337 reveals that Joanna Waldesshef, whose family held a knight's fee in Stanwick and Ringstead, was farming the manor for life at five marks a year. She may have only been farming a portion, however, as similar receipts for the following year reveal that William de Hamptom and Richard de Coldale were both farming the *'manor of Raunds'* for life at only 20/- per annum (PRO DL28/32/14). An account roll shows that the demesne was again being run directly in 1355–6, but in 1363 the manor was farmed out for life to Henry Greene, lord of a manor in Middle Cotton (PRO DL29/324/5292; CPR 1361–4, 296). The lease appears to have been abandoned on his death, as the account roll of 1369–70 indicates that direct demesne farming had just been resumed and the previous year's harvest purchased from Greene's executor.

The resumption of direct management was probably a result of the inability to find lessees due to declining profitability. Notes were added to the Raunds accounts in 1372–3 and 1374–5 recording that the cost of cultivation exceeded the sale of grain by £11-11s-5d and £10-3s respectively. In 1380–1 and 1391–2 the portion of the demesne which was normally let at will was in hand because tenants could not be found. A valor of 1388 noted that the demesnes at Raunds and Higham were making a loss and recommended that they should both be farmed (Holmes 1957, 118). Higham was farmed for 10 years in 1389 and Raunds similarly in 1394 (PRO DL29/324/5314 and 5320). From this date onward Raunds was permanently farmed out to various individuals with leases of 7 to 21 years. The first farmer was William Marriot, vicar of Raunds, though, in contrast to the fourteenth century, most of his successors were peasant farmers from Raunds or neighbouring duchy villages. An exception was Sir Robert Tyrwhite of Kettleby (Lincolnshire), a duchy official, who held the lease from 1535–56. A more detailed study of the Burystead estate from the later thirteenth century onward has been published in the Raunds Survey volume (Courtney 2006b).

There is no evidence for lengthening of leases in the fifteenth century, or for very long leases of 40 years or more, as noted on some manors (Dyer 1968, 14). However, difficulties in finding lessees may have led to the rent declining from £10 in 1394 to a little over £6 by the mid-1430s. From 1566 the Burystead farm was held by members of the Ekins family, yeoman farmers of Stanwick. In 1602 it was leased to Thomas Ekins for three lives, still at an annual rent of only £6-9s-4d (PRO DL42/37A/f.62). Inflation must have made the farm increasingly attractive. In 1649 the freehold was purchased from the duchy by Dr Dolben with possession on termination of the last (Ekins) life, then aged 60 (PRO E317/44).

The Burystead manorial buildings

The fourteenth-century accounts record expenditure on repairs to manorial buildings at Burystead. A list of the buildings mentioned is given below, while the buildings in brackets are those which are likely to have existed but which are not recorded at this time.

Table 2.1: The Burystead manorial buildings

Domestic	Crop-related	Stock houses
steward chamber	barn	ox-house
brew-house	hay-house	dovecote
latrine	stable	pinfold
(hall*)	granary	(sheep-house)
(kitchen*)	kiln-house	—
(?bake-house)	—	—

* 15th-century reference

There would also have been a need for a building to store carts and other equipment. However, this may have lain beneath the hay-house (or hay-barn), as was common in the post-medieval period, rather than forming a separate building as at Cuxham (Harvey 1976, 727). The manorial court was surrounded by a stone wall with a chained gate. All of the buildings appear to have been thatched. The hay-house, the dovehouse (rebuilt in 1374–5), and the porch and buttressed barn were of stone, though the construction of the other out-buildings is uncertain. The barn would have been principally used to store cereals prior to processing and for winnowing. The latter process would have been carried out between the large opposing doors of the barns, which allowed the wind to blow away the chaff. Subsequently grain was stored in the granary and hay in the hay-house. In 1391–2 part of the exterior of the dovecote was also plastered, though this may imply no more than rough pointing. The dovehouse does not appear to have had an expensive potence, a swivelling ladder. A carpenter employed upon the hay-house in 1355–6 may have repaired the roof or flooring but a timber superstructure is possible.

The steward's chamber and granary are recorded (1355–6) as having been plastered and/or daubed *"ad p(l)iaust(r)and(um) et torchand(um)"*, which suggests infilling of stud walls. Certainly, repairs carried out in 1355–6 indicate that the *camera sen eschalli* or steward's chamber lay at first floor level and was of timber construction. Two posts beneath the *camera* were at fault and sills (horizontal timbers) either newly inserted, or more likely replaced, to carry them. In the same year the hurdled wall of an enclosure called the 'Intclos' was repaired. The accounts also note repairs to the pinfold, a gated and walled enclosure for keeping the straying stock of the tenants until a fine was paid. The kiln-house was newly built in 1555–6 and was probably responsible for much of the production of the exceptional sale of 126.5 quarters of malt in London that year.

Regular information on repairs no longer appear in the bailiff's accounts after the manor was leased out in 1395. The farmers were expected to maintain the buildings at their own cost as is made clear by the conditions of the leases given in memoranda at the end of the account rolls. Nevertheless both the bailiff's and receiver's accounts occasionally record sums spent by the duchy on repairs to manorial buildings at Raunds and elsewhere. The duchy also paid for repairs to the buildings of its urban and rural tenants, reflecting the weak position of landlords in the fifteenth century. These records are not always very specific but repairs 'within the manor' at Raunds probably refer to the Burystead enclosure. For instance, in 1454–5, £21-11s-8d was spent constructing a new building (*domus*) 'within the manor' (PRO DL29/327/5358). However, no doubt exists over the repairs carried out on the hall, dovecote and pinfold in 1444–5, and upon the gable above the kitchen in 1463–4. The princely sum of £43-17s-4d was also spent in 1444–5 on building a great barn. It is worth remembering that this sum was nearly seven years income from the Burystead lease (PRO DL29/341/554 and DL/328/5365).

The parochial landscape

The identification of Higham as the centre of a late Saxon estate suggests that its church was a primary minster. The advowsons of Higham, Raunds, Rushden and Irchester were all held by the Peverel fee in the twelfth century and all but St Katherine's, Irchester were dedicated to St Mary. A close connection between Raunds and Higham churches is indicated by a dispute over the advowson in 1237–8 between Williams de Ferrers, the prior of Lenton and the abbot of Thornton. It appears that Raunds and Higham shared a single priest (recently dead) and that King Richard (1189–99) had last presented (Bracton NB, 3, 1136: discussed in Franklin 1982, 32–5). It is possible that the priest was assisted by a hired chaplain, but the implication is that Raunds still formed part of the *parochia* or ecclesistical territory of Higham. Unfortunately there is no evidence to suggest the date at which St Peter's (formerly St Mary's), Raunds, acquired burial rights.

The layout of St Peter's church in Raunds suggests that it developed from a twelfth-century cruciform plan, typical of many minsters in Northamptonshire and elsewhere (VCH Northants 4, 34 and Richmond below). One must be wary, though, of interpreting status from architectural plan types (Franklin 1984). A case could be made for Raunds being a dependent church of the first rank. It might even have been of secondary minster status, which is still dependent upon Higham but originally served by its own community of priests. However, the cruciform plan may merely reflect that the Peverel family was willing to invest in an architecturally imposing church, whatever its status, in the twelfth century. St Peter's was certainly associated with a sizeable demesne manor (the Burystead), while Raunds parish was valued at 20 marks in 1256 and £40 in 1296, the same as Higham (Val Norwich, 273 and Tax Eccles, 40). Moreover the role of peasant communities in contributing to church building and repair should not be overlooked (Blair 1988, 8; Barlow 1963, 193 and Rosser 1988, 32).

If the above arguments are correct they provide a context which goes some way to explaining why the church of St Peter's became the sole parish church of Raunds in the twelfth century. The church at Furnells can be seen as a private church (*Eigenkirchen*) established by the lord on his bookland, as an expression of his manorial rights. The second law code of Edgar (960–2) indicates that a thegn with a church possessing a cemetery on his bookland was entitled to give it one third of its demesne tithe, the rest belonging to the minster (II Edgar 2: Councils, 97–8). It was also possible for an existing daughter church (*Feldcirce*) to be removed from the minster's *parochia* and become a private church when an estate was booked (ie created by charter) (Sawyer 1978, 248). Such a transition could have occurred at Furnells if the cemetery was pre-dated by a chapel, as has been suggested by the excavator (Boddington 1996, 14). The late Saxon period no doubt saw the foundation of many new churches within the *parochia* of Higham, both accompanying manorial fragmentation and to serve the scattered sokemen of what was to become the Peverel fee. We do not know to what extent this fragmentation proceeded with the permission of the minster. Elsewhere, minsters are known to have provided priests to new manorial churches in return for confirmation of their parochial rights to tithe and soul-scot (burial dues). However, the presence of a graveyard at Furnells would tend to suggest manorial encroachment upon minster rights through sufferance rather than cooperation (Blair 1988, 7–13).

In the course of the twelfth century, parochial rights became more defined and a general tidying up of the parochial landscape occurred. The Peverels may have exerted their right to a discrete Raunds parish through their possession of both the assumed primary minster at Higham and daughter of St Peter's, Raunds. The church at Furnells was presumably relegated to the status of a private chapel either without burial rights or with the mortuary payments going to St Peter's. Possibly the Clares, now lords of Furnells, received confirmation of the advowson of Ringstead (a chapelry of Denford) and Hargrave as part of a compromise with the Peverel fee (VCH Northants, 4, 44 and Monasticon, 6, 834).

The parish church of St Peter
by Hugh Richmond

There is no clear historical evidence for either of the churches in Raunds. There is no foundation date for St Peter's and the existence of the second church in Raunds on the Furnells manor is known entirely from excavation (Boddington 1996).

According to the Victoria County History (Northants 4, 44), St Peter's church was given to Lenton *c*1109 by William Peverel but it is not mentioned in any of the foundation charters to Lenton. It apparently appeared first in a charter which was seen by the antiquarian Thoroton but which has now disappeared. Thoroton transcribed the witness list only and included in it Robert Ferrers without the comital title, which suggests that William Peverel II may have granted Raunds to Lenton in 1121–38. On the other hand the VCH also claimed that Raunds was given to Thorton Abbey by William, earl of Aumale, at its foundation in 1139, a grant not mentioned in the surviving chronicle of the house. However, according to the same chronicle, Thorton did receive considerable augmentation of its endowment in the 1140s and by 1189 it included Raunds in a Royal *inspeximus*. The grant to Thorton may therefore indeed have taken place in 1139–57.

After William earl of Ferrers proved his claim to the church, the advowson remained with his successors, ultimately being in the hand of the dukes of Lancaster. In 1357 Raunds was appropriated to the Newark hospital in Leicester, a Duchy foundation, remaining a vicarage for the remainder of the medieval period. A will in 1547 shows that one aisle was dedicated to St Peter, according to Bridges (1791) the chapel at the end of the south aisle. In 1514 and 1517 bequests were made for the rebuilding of the steeple, though Serjeantson (1917) thought nothing of note was done. There was at least one guild in the church in the sixteenth century known sometimes as the Resurrection Guild and sometimes as the Sepulchre Guild, though these references might refer to two separate guilds.

The surviving fabric is mainly of thirteenth-century date with fourteenth- and fifteenth-century alterations, particularly refenestration. The surviving plan includes a nave aisled on both sides and a long chancel flanked on the south by a chapel of the same width as the aisle (Fig 2.1). A vestry, now demolished, stood on the north side of the chancel. At the west is a square tower and spire. The spire was carefully rebuilt after being struck by lightning in 1826. The church was restored *c*1873 by Scott.

The twelfth-century church

There is only one feature in the fabric datable to the twelfth century, the rear-arch of a round-headed window over the second bay from the west of the south arcade of the nave. The rectangular plinths, on which stand the double respond and the first pier to the west of the nave south arcade, have a width of 0.86m (2'10"), which is a com-

2. Historical Background

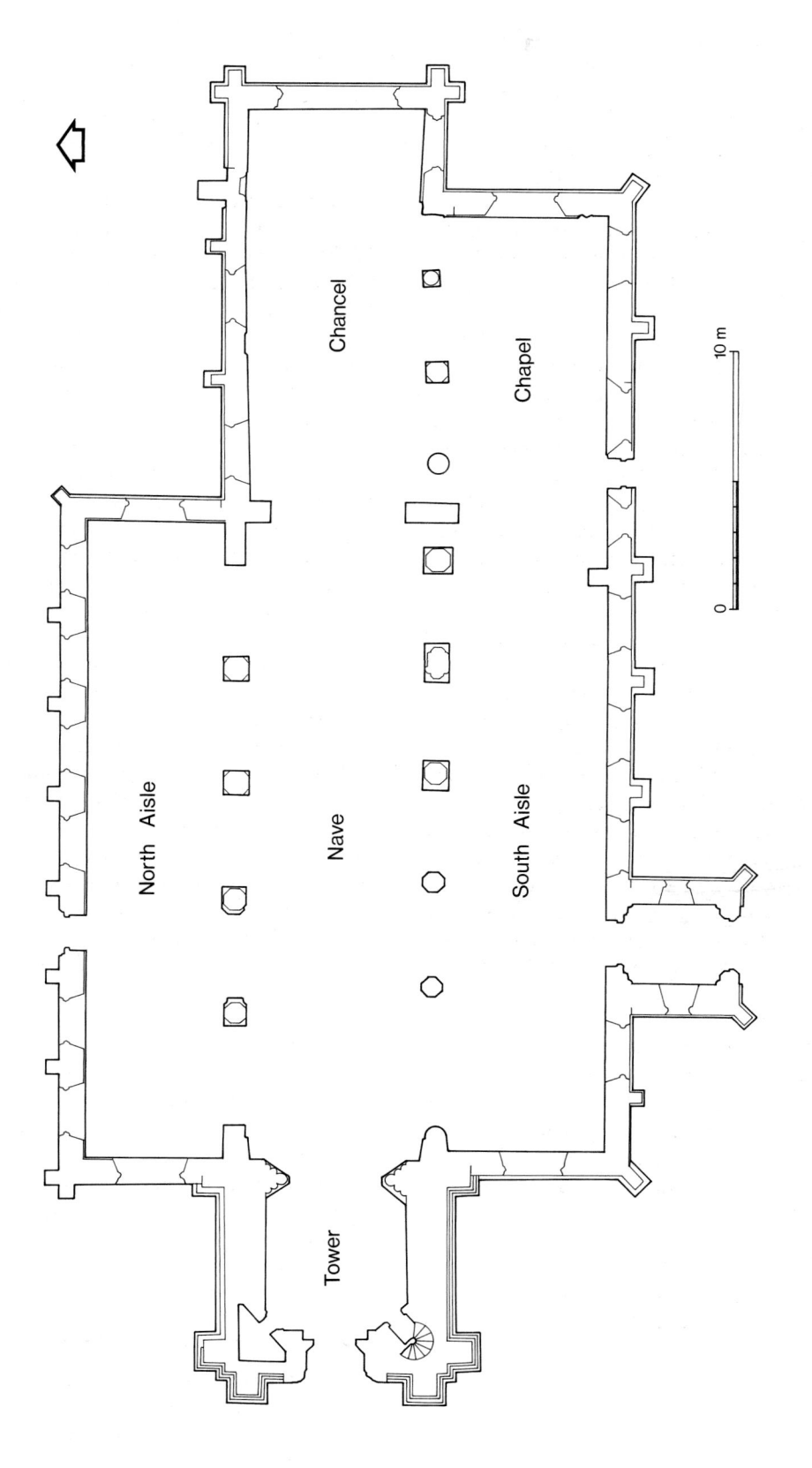

Fig 2.1: Raunds, the church of St Peter

mon twelfth-century wall thickness. Thus the plinths and the upper wall survive from the twelfth century, indicating that the twelfth-century church was first built with a nave which was subsequently aisled.

The symmetry of the west tower with the nave would indicate that the nave was of its present width before the tower was added in the thirteenth century. The west bay of the nave south arcade was presumably built wider than the next three uniform bays in order to join the early nave to the new tower. This would suggest that the Norman nave was shorter at the west than the present compartment.

There is no evidence for the twelfth-century chancel although its presence may be indicated by the misalignment in the south wall. Such misalignment is paralleled at Rothwell and Higham Ferrers.

The presence of a transverse chapel in the twelfth century is uncertain and depends on the interpretation of tenuous pieces of evidence. At the east, the shape of the penultimate pier from the west and the presence of part of an angle quoin in the fabric of the wall above may indicate the location of the angle of a transverse chapel. The plinth of the easternmost pier has a width of 1.09m that deviates from the standard 0.86m and therefore may survive from an earlier phase in the building's development. Indeed, the plinth may have supported the east respond of an archway from an unaisled nave into a south transverse chapel. The presence of such a compartment is suggested by the double respond at that point and the exposed footings below the present south wall.

The thirteenth-century church

The addition of a chapel to the south of the chancel may date to the early thirteenth century, if the south doorway is *in situ*. This is corroborated by a blocked window of thirteenth-century type in the south wall of the chancel chapel. The window also indicates that the compartment was built to its present width at that time. The fragment of a north jamb at the north end of the east wall may have belonged to the lancets of a former east window. The blocked window over the east pier of the arcade between chancel and chapel must survive from an earlier, unaisled phase of the chancel. The present arcade between chancel and chapel can be dated by the corbel on the east respond to $c1275$. The awkwardness of the bay spacing provides further evidence that the arcade is an insertion. It is possible that the arcade was originally of two bays, corresponding to the two complete central bays. The base of the central pier appears to date from the early thirteenth century and may survive *in situ* from the original arrangement. It therefore appears that in 1275, the arcade was enlarged to the whole length of the chapel but at the same time the original bay spacing was retained. A three-quarter bay replaced the east respond and a half bay the west respond. The construction of the great east window of the chancel may date from the period of the arcade rebuilding. The blocked window at the east end of the chancel north wall, which appears to be of thirteenth-century character, may belong with the east window and thus with a lengthening of the chancel. The vestry, which once stood to the north of the chancel, is dated by the doorway leading to it as fourteenth century but may have been of earlier origin.

The tower was constructed $c1225$ and it is likely that the formation and the spacing of the south arcade predate the tower. This is suggested by the wider west bay of the nave south arcade. The underlying reason for this arrangement must have been the need to connect the nave to the new tower that was, originally, constructed free standing. The south arcade of the nave, however, was constructed $c1300$ into its present form with the polygonal piers still probably following the earlier thirteenth-century spacing and scale. The double respond was retained although the capitals were remodelled. The archway into the transverse chapel which was probably incorporated into the south aisle at the same time, if not before, was removed and replaced by the present arcade of one and a half bays. The most probable explanation for this unusual arrangement is the desire on the one hand to maintain the scale of the nave arcade and on the other to mirror the earlier half arch at the west end of the chancel arcade. The south doorway indicates that the south aisle had reached its present width $c1225$. The footings visible at the east end of the south wall confirm that the aisle lined-up with the south wall of the transverse chapel. The internal jambs of some of the thirteenth-century windows survive. In the south porch, the angle shaft for a former vault, the outlines of which are preserved, shows that the south porch was originally of the same date as the south aisle.

In the mid-fourteenth century, the north arcade (except for the thirteenth-century west respond) was rebuilt to a uniform bay spacing and detailing and the north aisle refenestrated. The north wall was probably of thirteenth-century origin, since the north doorway, of $c1250$, appears to be *in situ* lining up with the south doorway. The moulding and ballflower in the chancel arch shows that the arch was also rebuilt in the mid-fourteenth century. It appears not to have been moved although the arrangement of the south side makes it look as if it is an insertion. The south aisle was also refenestrated in the mid- fourteenth century, to the same design as the east and west windows of the north aisle. In the later fifteenth century the nave and chancel walls were raised in height and a clerestory formed, extending the whole length of the nave. A vault was inserted in the tower, blocking the upper part of the tower arch and the lower part of the west window. The south porch was remodelled in two storeys. New windows were inserted in the chancel and chancel chapel.

Abbreviations and references

A wide range of documentary sources have been utilised. General published texts are listed in the bibliography, while the abbreviations used for specific documentary sources are listed below:

Bracton NB	Maitland, F W, (ed) 1887 *Bracton's Note Book*, 3 vols, London
Bridges, J, 1791	*The History and Antiquities of Northamptonshire*, Whalley, P, (ed)
CCR	*Calendar of Close Rolls*
CFR	*Calendar of Fine Rolls*
CIPM	*Calendar of Inquisitions Post Mortem*, Public Record Office
CIPM-Rec Comm	*Calendar of Inquisitions Post Mortem*, Record Commission Councils
	Whitelock, D, Brett, M, and Brooke, C N L, (eds) 1981 *Councils and Synods with other documents relating to the English Church I: AD 871–1204*, 2 vols, OUP
CPR	*Calendar of Patent Rolls*
CRR	*Calendar of Regis Rolls*
II Edgar	King Edgar's code at Andover (II and III Edgar, 959x963)
EHD I	Whitelock, D, (ed) 1955 *English Historical Documents: i, c AD500–1042*
EHD II	Douglas, D C, and Greenaway, G W, (eds) 1981, *English Historical Documents: ii, AD1042–1189*
FA	*Feudal Aids*
G E C	Gibbs, V, Doubleday, H A, and de Walden, H, (eds) 1910–36 *The complete Peerage by G E C*, 10 vols
Monasticon	Caley, J, Ellis, H, and Bandinell, B, (eds) 1817–30 *Monasticon Anglicanum*
NRO	*Northamptonshire Record Office*
PRO	*Public Record Office*
PRS	*Pipe Roll Society*
Rot. Hund.	*Rotuli Hundredorum temp. Hen. III and Edw. I*, Record Commission
Tax. Eccles	Astle, T, Ayscough, S, and Caley, J, (eds) 1802 *Taxatio Ecclesiastica Angliae et Walliae auctoritate P. Nicholai IV., circa AD 1291*, Rec Comm
Val. Norwich	Lunt, W E, (ed) 1926 *Valuation of Norwich*, Oxford
Visit. Northants	Metcalfe, W C, (ed) 1887 *The Visitations of Northamptonshire*, London
VCH Northants	1902 *The Victoria History of the County of Northampton*, **1**
VCH Northants	1930 *The Victoria History of the County of Northampton*, **3**
VCH Northants	1937 *The Victoria History of the County of Northampton*, **4**

3 A Panorama of Settlement Development

This chapter provides a broad, interpretative overview of the chronology and development of Saxon and medieval settlement across north Raunds, taking in the excavated sites of Furnells manor, Langham Road, Burystead and the Midland Road frontage (Fig 3.1). It draws on the detailed description of the excavated evidence and the analysis of all aspects of the material evidence including the pottery, other finds, the animal bone and the environmental evidence. This chapter also sets north Raunds within the broader pattern of contemporary settlement as understood from other aspects of the work of the Raunds Area Project, particularly the results of the Raunds Survey (Parry 2006) and the excavations at the nearby deserted hamlet of West Cotton (Chapman in press).

The pre-Saxon landscape

The work of the Raunds Area Project has identified a wide range of Neolithic and Bronze Age ritual monuments, predominantly strung along the floor of the Nene valley from West Cotton in the north and continuing well to the south of the Stanwick Roman settlement (Fig 1.2: Parry 2006, fig 4.2; Harding and Healy 2007; Chapman 2004). Early prehistoric settlement, however, remains poorly understood as it relies largely upon scatters of worked flint whose interpretation is debatable.

For the Iron Age, pottery does survive in the fields though its poor condition and limited dating potential precludes detailed interpretation. Nevertheless a pattern of gradual intensification of settlement and movement onto the Boulder Clay plateau to the east has been identified (Parry 2006, 60–65).

The pattern of Roman settlement and land-use was closely linked to the late Iron Age landscape, with apparent continuity at many settlements (Parry 2006, 72–84). The Roman settlement pattern displays a contrasting landscape of predominantly large settlements adjacent to the River Nene and small dispersed farms on the Boulder Clay plateau. This contrast is accentuated by the virtual absence of settlement on the upper slopes of the valley side, perhaps indicating that the slopes were controlled by and farmed from the settlements adjacent to the river. The excavations at Stanwick have provided a good indication of the form of one of these large riverine settlements (CAS undated; Parry 2006, 167–70). The site appears to have been continuously occupied from the Iron Age through to the fifth century AD. By the second century AD there was a series of farmsteads set within rectilinear enclosures. Three of the farmsteads became increasingly Romanised and one was converted in the late fourth century into a substantial winged corridor villa. A further small winged corridor villa was discovered in 1989–90 during excavations by the Oxford Archaeological Unit at Redlands Farm some 2km south-west of the Stanwick settlement (Keevill 1991). Other valley bottom Roman settlements east of the Mallows Cotton deserted medieval settlement and between Mill Cotton and Ringstead, have also been subject to limited excavation.

Within the survey area there appears to have been a high population, indicating an intensively exploited landscape, with an overall density of 1.0 site per km² during the early and middle Roman periods, and a slight decline to 0.75 sites per km² in the late Roman period (Parry 2006). Scatters of pottery carpet much of the intervening land, suggesting manuring and thus indicating that arable production formed a major component of a regime in which most of the land was farmed although, just as in the Middle Ages, this would not preclude periods of fallow or even temporary pasture allowing the maintenance of animal herds. A decline in the extent of the manure scatters suggests a decrease in grain production, starting in the late second and third centuries AD and accelerating in the later third and fourth centuries. The process appears to be closely linked with the fortunes of the nearby settlements which presumably provided the manure.

Gradual reorganisation and change in the second and third centuries AD led to a distinctly different pattern of settlement by the late Roman period. A decline in settlement numbers appears to have been largely confined to the Boulder Clay plateau, where ten farms were apparently abandoned. The overall changes indicate a concentration of settlement in selected locations which may reflect gradual nucleation or economic changes.

None of these activities had any direct effect on the study area in north Raunds, which remained essentially unsettled until the early Saxon period. The only material evidence comprises small quantities of worked flint, most notably two barbed and tanged arrowheads from the chancel of the first church at Furnells, most probably from a disturbed Bronze Age burial; a small quantity of Iron Age pottery from a small pit group at Langham Road, that attest to some limited occupation; and residual Roman pottery and coins, some of which may have arrived with cartloads

3. A Panorama of Settlement Development

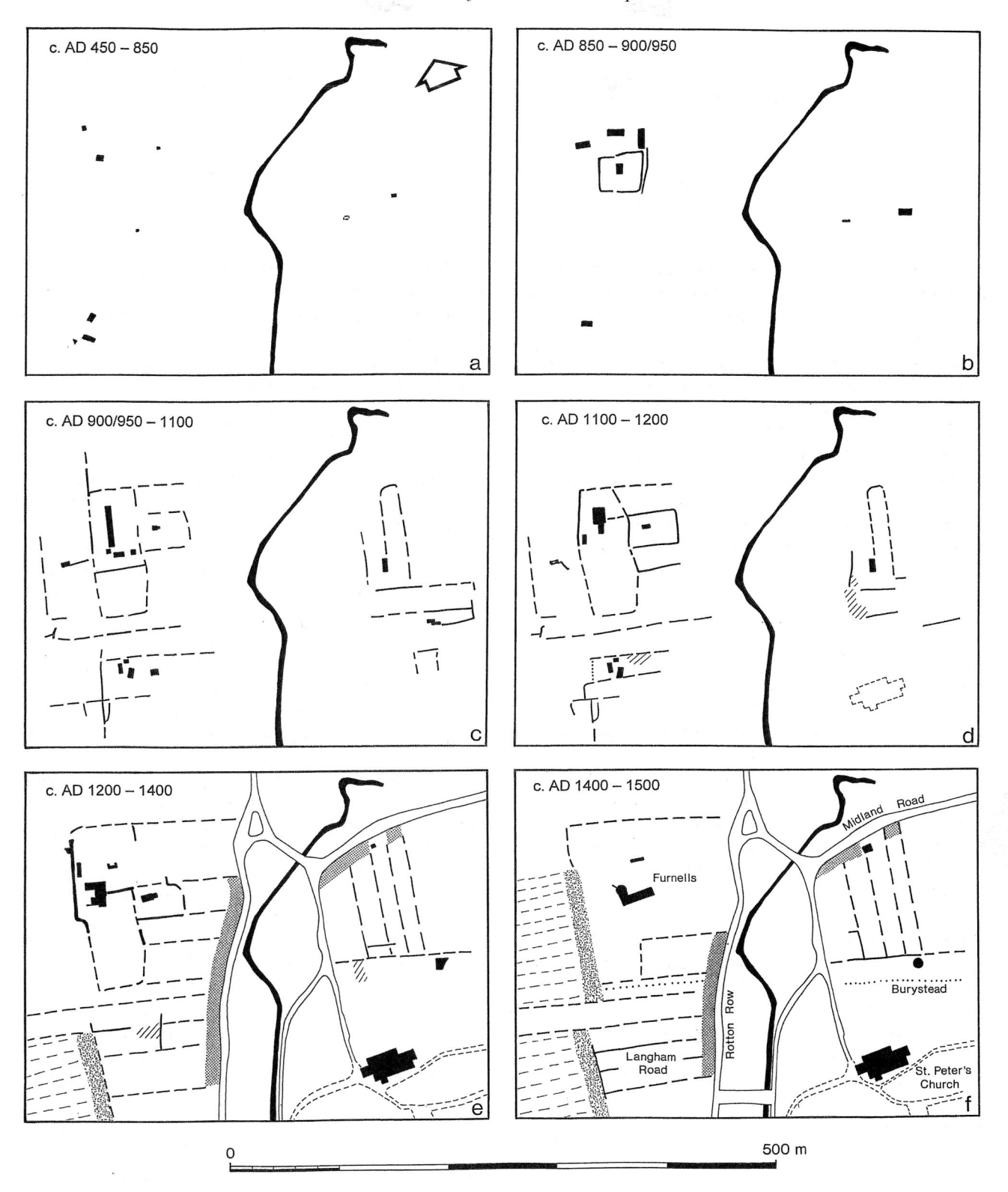

Fig 3.1: North Raunds, settlement development (AD 450–1500)

of stone robbed from the major Roman settlements in the valley.

Summary of the Saxon and medieval chronology

The archaeological evidence from the three excavated sites in north Raunds will be considered within four broad historical periods: the primary settlement of the early to middle Saxon period; the late Saxon formation of the manors and village, together with the post-Conquest modifications of that system; the high medieval manors and village tenement plots; and the late medieval decline of the manors and the growing dominance of tenements on the road frontages (Table 3.1 and Fig 3.1). Details of the archaeological evidence, particularly the descriptions of the many excavated structures and other features will be provided in Part 2: Chapter 5, while the material evidence is described and discussed in Part 3: Chapters 6–9.

All dates given within this report are based primarily on the Relative Seriated Phase Dating scheme, which derives from the analysis of the pottery from the north Raunds sites and was subsequently refined during the analysis of the material from West Cotton, Raunds (Chapter 6). The work of the respective pottery researchers at the Northampton Development Corporation working on the substantial assemblages from the excavations in Northampton through the 1970s and 1980s, Mike McCarthy, Mary Gryspeerdt and Varian Denham, had provided the solid chronological framework, which was later utilised by Terry Pearson and Paul Blinkhorn in the analysis of the Raunds assemblages. In addition, there is a small group of radiocarbon dates which assist in the dating of some specific early–middle Saxon features (Section 5.1, Table 5.1), and a group of radiocarbon dates from the early church and churchyard at Furnells that assist in dating the sequence of church development (Table 5.2).

However, there are many aspects of the chronology of the sites that are still imperfectly understood and imprecisely defined. It must therefore be recognised that all quoted dates inevitably have a *circa* attached to them, even when this has been omitted in the text.

It must also be noted that the chronology and the sequence of development presented here (Table 3.1) differs in some aspects from the published interim chronologies for the sequence at Furnells (eg Cadman *et al* 1983 and Foard 1985, fig 7), and in respect to the published report on the Furnells church and churchyard (Boddington 1996). It does differ less from the initial interpretations that emerged directly after the excavation (Cadman 1983).

A dating scheme for the church and churchyard at Furnells had been outlined in the early 1980s, both during and immediately after the excavation of the western part of the site, which included the contemporary manor houses. The chronology was therefore first established using the narrow base of the evidence and assemblages from the church and churchyard alone, which inevitably contained much residual material. Subsequently, the overall interpretation of the site, including the manor house sequence to the west, was constrained by the chronology previously established for the church and churchyard sequence.

In these interpretations, the presence of early Saxon wares was seen as a likely indicator of continuity of settlement through the early, middle and late Saxon periods. It was the recovery of quantities of middle Saxon Ipswich ware and Maxey-type ware at Langham Road and Burystead during the excavations of the mid 1980s that indicated the likelihood that Furnells, where these wares were absent, had not been intensively occupied through the middle Saxon period. This alone indicated that both the church and churchyard and some of the major timber buildings had been dated too early.

Further work in the early 1990s on the assemblages from other north Raunds sites and from West Cotton, and the establishment of the Relative Seriated Phase Dating scheme, further undermined the initial chronology for Furnells. Given these evident problems, the stratigraphy and chronology of key assemblages for Furnells were reappraised by Michel Audouy and Paul Blinkhorn (Chapter 6, Furnells: reappraisal of the ceramic dating of key structural phases). In addition, during the final editing of this volume, the radiocarbon dates from the first church and several closely related burials have also been reassessed, leading to slight revisions to the chronology of the development of the churches (Chapter 5, the radiocarbon dates).

In addition to the revised chronology, this volume contains two significant revisions to the proposed development sequence at Furnells. The interpretation of the development of the boundary ditch system was complicated by a lack of physical relationships and the inevitability that the pottery assemblages predominantly derived from the final phases of filling, with little material to provide secure dates for their origin. The approach adopted at the time saw the ditches as potentially forming a series of enclosures. The subsequent excavations at West Cotton illustrated more clearly that what was happening in the late Saxon formation of the settlements was the creation of a system of regular plots bounded by linear ditch systems. When this different basis for analysis was adopted, a new model emerged in which the small sub-square enclosure at Furnells was seen to be related to the earliest major timber buildings as the first phase of the late Saxon development; a return to the original post-excavation interpretation (Fig 3.1, b).

The second issue concerns the final fate of the medieval church at Furnells. The interpretation provided by Boddington (1996, 10–11 and fig 22) put together the insertion of a cross wall with rebuilding to the east to form a secular building, the church conversion phase, dated to within a century of the Norman Conquest. It was recognised at the time that the foundations of the inserted cross wall were of the same scale and form as the church building, and unlike any of the secular buildings at Furnells or other Raunds sites. It is now suggested that the inserted cross wall was

Table 3.1: The chronological sequence at north Raunds

Early–middle Saxon settlement	**AD 450–850**
Furnells: early Saxon settlement	AD 450–650
Langham Road: a middle Saxon farm	AD 650–850
Burystead, sparse early–middle Saxon settlement	AD 450–850
Late Saxon village formation	**AD 850–1100**
Furnells: an Anglo-Scandinavian farm	AD 850–900/950
Furnells: plot formation and the late Saxon manor	AD 900/950
Furnells: addition of church and churchyard	AD 950
Furnells: the late Saxon manor, church and churchyard	AD 950–1100
Langham Road: field boundaries and late Saxon farm	AD 900/950–1100
Burystead: plot boundaries and late Saxon settlement	AD 900/950–1100
The medieval manors and the village	**AD1100–1350/1400**
Furnells: the aisled hall	AD 1100–1200
Furnells: the medieval church	AD 1150–1200
Furnells: the western manor and medieval church	AD 1200–1350/1400
Langham Road: tenement plots and field boundaries	AD 1100–1350/1400
Burystead: plot boundaries and settlement	AD 1100–1200
Burystead: the manorial farm	AD 1200–1350/1400
The Midland Road frontage: medieval buildings	AD 1300–1350/1400
Late medieval decline	**AD 1350/1400–1500**
Furnells: The eastern manor	AD 1350/1400–1450
Furnells: the smithy	AD 1450–1500
Langham Road: tenement plots and field boundaries	AD 1350/1400–1500
Burystead: the manorial farm	AD 1350/1400–1500
Post-medieval relocation	
The Midland Road frontage: the smithy	16th century
The Midland Road frontage: domestic tenements	17th century onward

more likely to have been a further phase of church activity; probably the provision of a tower raised over the western end of the nave. This is an addition that can be accommodated within the revised and extended chronology for the church sequence (Table 3.1 and Fig 3.1).

Early–middle Saxon settlement and the middle Saxon farm (AD 450–850)

Within the Raunds area, the years between the decline of Roman Britain in the early fifth century to the emergence of the late Saxon state some four hundred years later is bedevilled by a lack of fine chronology. While the local pottery is well made and durable the date range for undecorated pieces spans both the early and middle Saxon periods (AD 450–850). Hence, while it provides a good impression of the overall settlement and land-use pattern for the early–middle Saxon period, it is essentially a near static representation of the more fluid reality. Any finer division relies upon the presence of pottery imported from outside the region, Maxey and Ipswich wares, which are usually dated AD 650–850.

The overall pattern of settlement and land-use is derived from the fieldwalking survey. The distribution of early–middle Saxon pottery is not even; there are extensive light scatters, areas with no sherds, but also distinct concentrations, some of which have been confirmed as settlement sites by limited excavation (Parry 2006, 91–97). The core areas of the pottery concentrations mostly range in size from 1 to 4ha and early–middle Saxon settlement may be suggested in some 22 locations which, if they were all contemporary, would provide a settlement density of 0.55 sites per km^2.

A major influence on settlement location appears to be proximity to streams or to the River Nene, with only three sites being over 300m distant. In at least six locations, including north Raunds and West Cotton, both sides of individual tributary valleys were occupied, sometimes with more than one discrete focus. Settlement appears to have retreated from the Boulder Clay watershed between the Nene and the upper reaches of the Great Ouse basin.

The early–middle Saxon pottery scatters also only rarely coincide with finds of Roman material, while there is little evidence of Saxon features on the excavated Roman sites, showing that there was no simple development from Roman villa to medieval manor.

Settlement along the Nene valley appears to be evenly distributed with sites generally 1–2km apart. Nine sites, including north Raunds, are set back from the river close to the junction of the permeable soils and the Boulder Clay plateau, thereby allowing the exploitation of a range of different soils; the remainder, including West Cotton, Mallows Cotton and Mill Cotton, occur close to the River Nene, perhaps located with the intention of utilising both the valley bottom as hay meadow and the light soils higher on the valley side.

The excavations in north Raunds and at West Cotton, together with small-scale investigating of sub-surface remains associated with pottery concentrations, have identified a range of features suggesting a pattern of open, unplanned settlement. While the overall areas covered appear extensive the density of buildings and other features is low.

In north Raunds settlement on both sides of the valley was spread over a total area of 16 hectares (Fig 3.2). No conclusive evidence of major boundaries was preserved and the edges of settlement were probably not formally demarcated.

Furnells: early Saxon settlement (AD 450–650)

At the excavated sites, disturbance from later activity had left the details of the early Saxon settlement unclear, but at all three sites it is likely that many of the scatter of undated postholes and small pits derived from small early Saxon post-built structures and related activity, even though full building plans rarely survived. At Furnells a substantial assemblage of early–middle Saxon pottery was recovered and the absence of middle Saxon imports suggests that this largely derives from the early Saxon period, although much of the pottery was residual in later features.

There was one classic sunken-featured building to the north-west (Fig 3.2). This produced a fairly typical range of domestic items including a pig-fibula pin, a heavy clay spindle whorl and a double-pointed bone weaving pick. A further sunken-featured building to the south, at the northern end of the Langham Road excavation, probably lay at the southern limit of this area of early Saxon settlement, which extended at least 100m north–south, covering 1ha or more. The southern sunken-featured building produced one of the few more closely datable finds, a sixth-century bronze girdle hanger. Between these two structures there was an extensive scatter of postholes, including several distinct concentrations, some associated with short lengths of linear slot, which may have been parts of small tim-

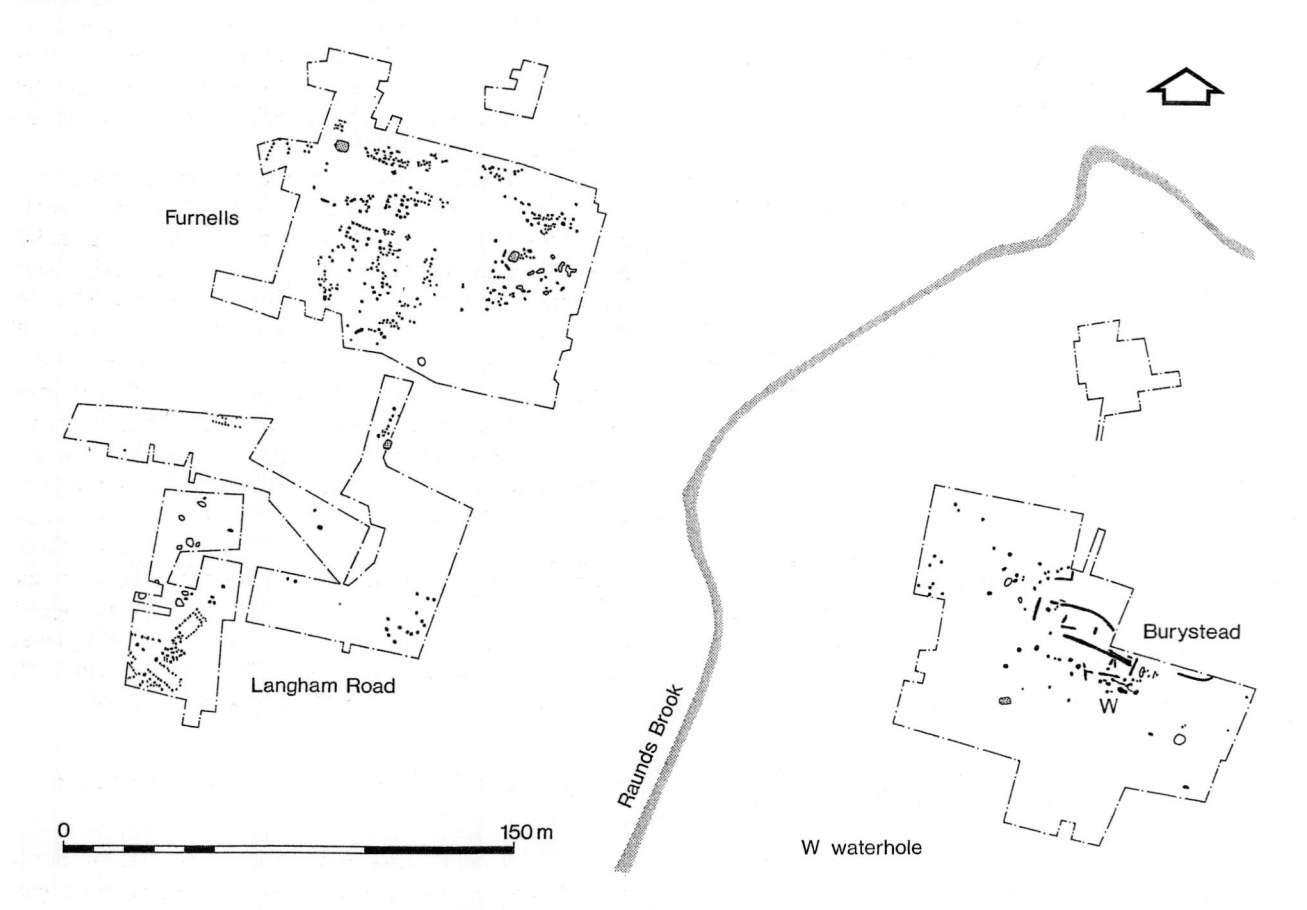

Fig 3.2: North Raunds, early–middle Saxon settlement (AD 450–850)

ber halls. These buildings were typically aligned either north–south or east–west, either along or across the general west–east slope, and were around 4.5m wide and less than 10m long.

Activity associated with the domestic occupation at Furnells included a square flat-bottomed pit to the east that was partly surfaced with stone, which included a square ironworking hearth bottom. In addition, a scatter of pits across this eastern area included clay-lined pits and pits containing dumped hearth debris. Charcoal from the final fill of one of these pits has given a radiocarbon date centred on the mid-sixth to the late seventh centuries (540–690 cal AD, 68% confidence, 1420±90 BP, Ha-5492) (Table 5.1). Irregular fragments of ironworking slag were also present in the fill of many of the graves around the late Saxon church. The evidence suggests that the eastern half of the Furnells site had been a centre for domestic industry, certainly including iron smithing, while the western half of the area held the main domestic buildings.

To the south-west, a small circular oven with a linear stokehole, containing charcoal and burnt clay, may have been a small drying and/or malting oven. Charcoal from the secondary fill of the oven has produced a radiocarbon date spanning a period from the mid-fifth to the mid-seventh centuries (440–660 Cal AD, 68% confidence, 1480±90 BP, Ha-4903). Towards the centre of the site a group of roughly parallel shallow gullies may have been a horticultural plot using spade cultivation.

The absence of middle Saxon imported pottery suggests that the settlement had been abandoned by around the middle of the seventh century; in broad agreement with the two radiocarbon dates. However, charcoal from a pit that produced a good assemblage of early–middle Saxon pottery has given a radiocarbon date centred on the middle Saxon period (690–890 Cal AD, 68% confidence, 1230±70 BP, Ha-5495), suggesting that there was at least some activity during these centuries. The pit was also cut by the western arm of the enclosure ditch for the Anglo-Scandinavian farm, indicating a date in the later ninth century for the reoccupation of the site.

Burystead: early–middle Saxon settlement (AD 450–850)

The clearest evidence for early Saxon settlement on the eastern stream bank came from a small excavation over 100m to the south of the Burystead excavations, and south of the parish church of St Peter, at Park Road. The truncated and disturbed remains of part of a cremation cemetery can perhaps be dated to the sixth century by the accompanying grave goods (Parry 2006, 225–229). Although its overall size is unknown, this cemetery presumably served at least part of the population of north Raunds in the early Saxon period.

A large quantity of early–middle Saxon pottery, including imported middle Saxon wares, was recovered during the Burystead excavations, possibly enough to suggest that it was more intensively occupied than the western stream bank during the middle Saxon period. Unfortunately, little pattern could be discerned in the features dated to this period, although both the features and the pottery distribution indicate that the centre of activity probably lay to north-east, in an area largely destroyed by post-medieval stone quarrying. To the south, a sunken-featured building, cut by a late Saxon plot boundary, may have been of early–middle Saxon date. A group of shallow ditches in the centre of the site may have formed parts of one or more enclosures. To the south of these there was a pit, partly lined with oak planking, which may have served as a waterhole or cistern. A radiocarbon date spanning the later seventh to mid-eighth centuries (670–760 Cal AD, 68% confidence, 1308±26 BP) was obtained from one of the planks and large sherds of Maxey-type ware were present in the fill.

Langham Road: a middle Saxon farm (AD 650–850)

While the Furnells area was largely deserted through the later seventh to mid-ninth centuries, a middle Saxon settlement focus lay immediately to the south, at the southern end of the Langham Road excavations (Fig 3.2). Here a group of posthole buildings may have formed a small farm (Fig 3.3), with the orderly arrangement suggesting a level of organisation and planning apparently absent in the earlier settlement. This may either have been a relocation of settlement from Furnells to a new site 100m to the south or a resettlement after a period of abandonment of the western stream bank.

The domestic quarters probably lay to the north in a post-built hall measuring 8.5m by 4.5m. A second similar building stood to the south, set at a right-angle. A circular timber structure between these halls was possibly a base for a stack or a granary, and a further timber hall lay to the south-west. A scatter of pottery, including sherds of Ipswich and Maxey-type wares, from some of the postholes and fanning out eastward suggests that related activities extended in that direction, perhaps across an open yard.

Given the presence of the imported pottery, the origin of the farm can have been no earlier than the mid to late-seventh century and it may have been in use as late as the mid-ninth century. However, although the posthole arrangements indicate that there was some replacement of posts, the simple single-phase plan form might suggest that this farm was not in use for as long as 200 years, leaving the question of continuity of settlement with both the preceding and following phases undetermined.

Early and middle Saxon settlement in north Raunds

The early–middle Saxon buildings recovered from north Raunds are unexceptional and may represent no more than one or two farmsteads shifting location over time, or a suc-

Fig 3.3: Langham Road, reconstruction of the middle Saxon farm

cession of unrelated, and short-lived farmsteads separated by periods of abandonment. The large quantity of pottery recovered does suggest that occupation at Furnells was not short-lived, although it contained only two sunken-featured buildings and perhaps some four or five small timber halls. It also appears to have had a small workshop area where iron smithing was practiced, although whether purely at a self-sufficient level or for trade cannot be determined.

In the middle Saxon period, the farm at the southern end of the Langham Road excavations does appear to have been sufficiently wealthy to acquire goods from some distance, while the recovery of a larger quantity of middle Saxon imported pottery from the Burystead area may suggest that there was a settlement of some importance on the eastern stream bank. However, through this period there is nothing to indicate that the settlement of north Raunds was more than relatively small-scale and only of local significance.

The agricultural base for these farms included the cultivation of free-threshing wheat and hulled six-row barley, with a higher proportion of barley present in the analysed samples than for subsequent periods. This may be a result of the role of barley being taken later by an increased use of rye and oats. It is also possible that the relative importance of barley in the early Saxon period and the lack of associated cereal processing debris may reflect a greater reliance on livestock as opposed to cereal growing.

Late Saxon village formation (AD 850–1100)

Following the dispersed pattern of the early–middle Saxon settlement, the late Saxon period saw the nucleation of settlement. This included the origin of the villages and the three vale hamlets, the Cottons, adjacent to the River Nene (Fig 1.2). The initial laying out of the open field system may have occurred at the same time as an integral part of a single and total reorganisation of the landscape, but this has proved more difficult to date with any precision.

The general process of settlement nucleation has been shown by the fieldwalking evidence (Parry 2006). Few early–middle Saxon pottery concentrations coincide with concentrations of late Saxon pottery, principally represented by St Neots-type ware which was apparently introduced into the area in small quantities from the late ninth century and in substantial amounts from the mid-tenth century. The absence of concentrations of late Saxon pottery in the area of the medieval open fields indicates that settlement had shifted to, and was confined within, the sites which developed into the medieval villages and hamlets (Fig 3.4). Indeed, the only concentrations which can be recognised lie within or on the periphery of these sites, indicating areas of shrunken settlement. Once established the general settlement pattern remained unchanged until a period of decline and contraction in the later Middle Ages when the hamlets and parts of the villages were deserted.

The major historical question in relation to the process of nucleation is whether it had its origin within the later ninth century, which would place it within the period of Danish control, or whether its origins lay in the tenth century following the English reconquest. To determine this we are largely dependent on the dating for the introduction of certain forms of St Neots-type ware, which were originally established for Northampton. The inevitable imprecision in this dating evidence poses many difficulties in attempting to set the appearance of this enclosed landscape within its historic context, but by comparing the morphology and chronologies of the two most complex development sequences, those at Furnells and the deserted hamlet of West Cotton, a probable consensus has emerged.

At Furnells the presence of an early St Neots-type ware form suggests a sequence of development commencing between the later ninth and earlier tenth centuries, and so probably within the period of Danish control. At West Cotton, however, the absence of early forms of St Neots-type ware suggests that the foundation of this settlement occurred slightly later, towards the middle of the tenth century, placing it within the decades following the reconquest in the early tenth-century.

This chronological difference is reflected in the differing settlement morphologies. At Furnells there was a transitional phase comprising a sequence of large post-built timber halls associated with a small ditched enclosure, the Anglo-Scandinavian farm (Fig 3.5a). By the mid-tenth century this had been absorbed into a regular plot system, which formed part of a major reorganisation of settlement in the wake of the reconquest (Fig 3.5b). It is this reorganisation, which included a distinctive new building complex with the walls founded in continuous slots, which is similar to the first hall complex at West Cotton, which also lay within a similar system of linear boundary ditches forming rectangular plots (Chapman in press).

It would only be at or immediately following this regulated process of nucleation that the surrounding landscape had been cleared of all dispersed settlement, thus enabling

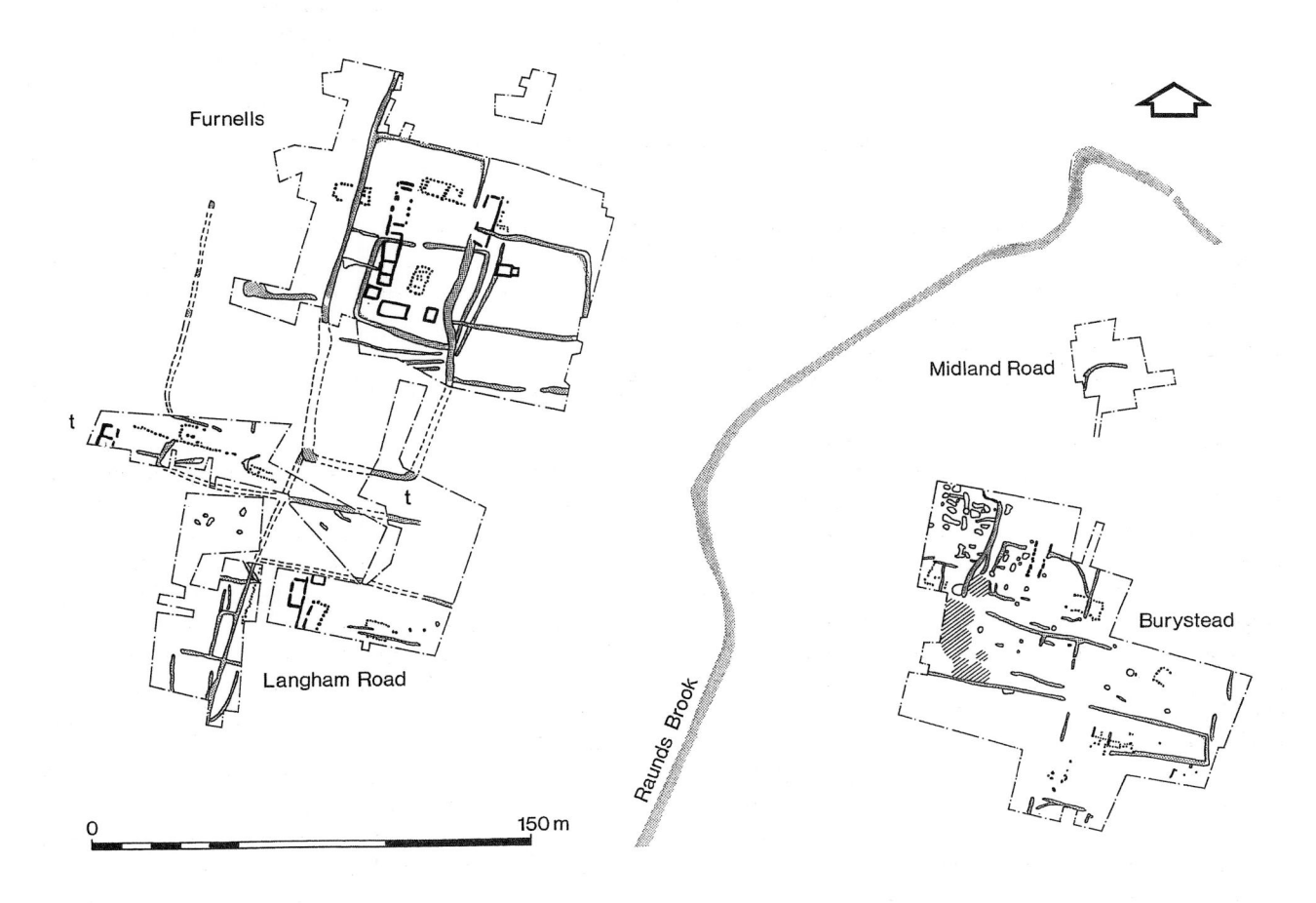

Fig 3.4: North Raunds, late Saxon settlement (AD 850–1100)

the full implementation of the open field system. However, the creation of the Anglo-Scandinavian farm might suggest that some initial process of nucleation had started in the later tenth century, under Danish control, even if its formalisation and regulation was a product of the decades following the reconquest.

Given the nature of the late Saxon reorganisation, the most readily apparent aspect of nucleation at the three excavated sites in north Raunds was the appearance of systems of linear boundary ditches that defined rectangular plots (Fig 3.4). In north Raunds this system had been much modified by later activity, but at West Cotton part of the original system survived as a row of rectangular plots, with later sub-divisions, which have been interpreted as being based on a primary unit of one-acre plots divided into half and quarter-acre units (Chapman in press). The north Raunds plots have not been analysed in as much detail but, once later modifications are allowed for, it is argued that they too were probably based on the same system of one-acre units (see Chapter 4 and Fig 4.1). There is a common appearance of plot widths of either 4 rods (c20m) or 8 rods (c40m), with one-acre plots typically measuring 40m (8 rods) wide by 100m (20 rods) long. In no instance can this system of metrification be applied with strict regularity over an extensive area, as local topography clearly prevented this from happening in the original setting out of the plots. Inevitably, many were created to conform to nominal acreages slightly less than the theoretical values.

One of the most prominent features of this new boundary system at both Furnells and Langham Road was a north–south linear ditch marking the western boundary of the settlement areas, and therefore forming a primary division between the settlement plots on the lower slopes adjacent to the stream and the field system on the slopes above. Once established, this boundary was maintained throughout the medieval period, although showing minor relocations as it was reformed over the centuries, and it still survived as a substantial earthwork in places when the excavations commenced in the 1970s.

This feature alone can be taken as epitomising the nature of the change that had occurred; with a dispersed landscape of individual settlements set within their own field systems giving way to a communal approach in which defined areas of settlement were set apart from the field system, with this physically marked on the ground by the ditch systems that were presumably dug by the populace in a grand episode of reorganisation. Despite the inevitable complaints of unfair land allocations that must have arisen, the system was sufficiently robust to serve for several hundred years, continuing to, and even beyond, the end of the feudal system.

Evidence from both Furnells and Langham Road may illustrate how existing settlements fared during this process

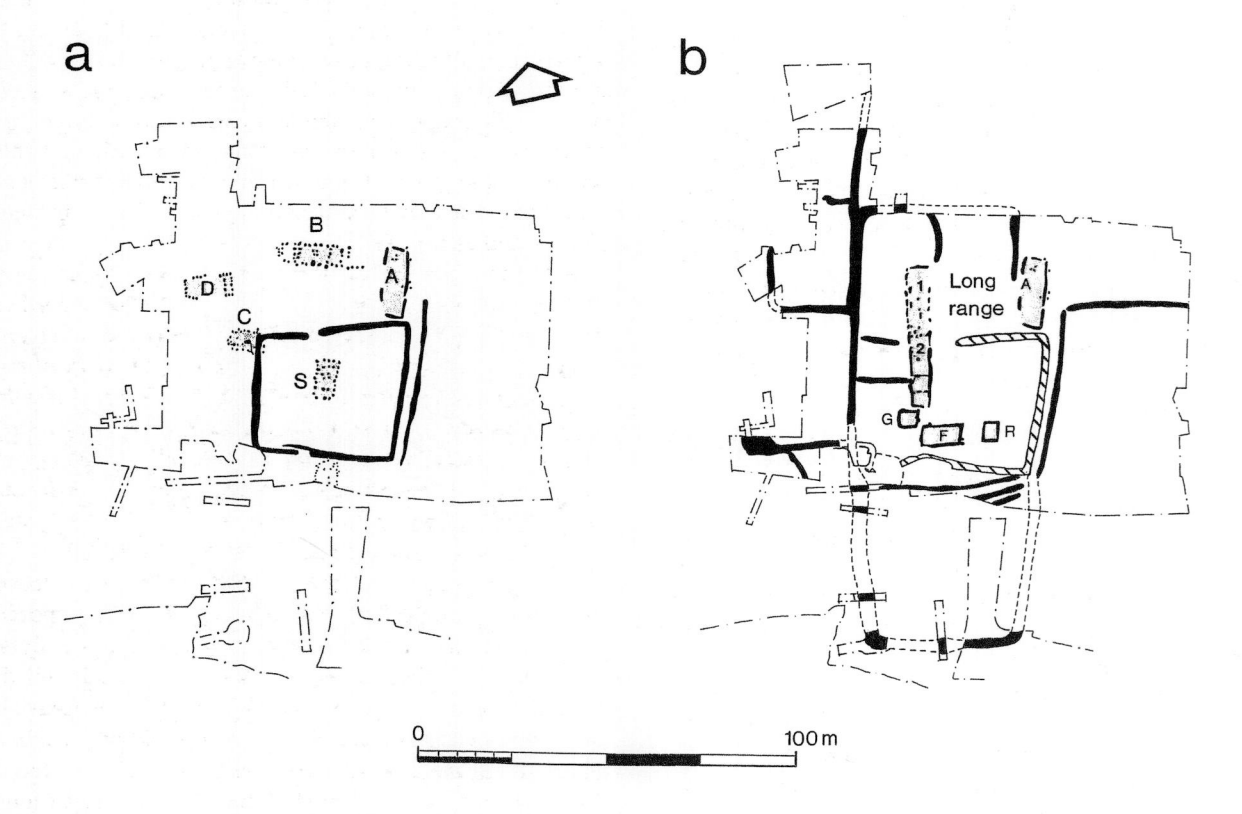

Fig 3.5: Furnells, the creation of the manor; a) the Anglo-Scandinavian farm (AD 850–900/950) and b) the late Saxon plots and long range (AD 900/950)

of reorganisation. At Furnells, the Anglo-Scandinavian farm survived the transition occupying the same plot, and its ditched enclosure was encompassed within the new boundary system. However, shortly afterwards a process of rebuilding began which saw the replacement of the individual post-built timber halls with a hall and domestic range built in a new construction method, utilising continuous foundation trenches for stave-built walls, along with smaller ancillary buildings. This may have accompanied a change of tenure, but it could also have been the adoption of newly prevailing building techniques reflecting a cultural change following in the wake of the reconquest.

In contrast, at Langham Road, the middle Saxon site was bisected by a late Saxon boundary ditch. This might only imply that the farm had been abandoned prior to the laying out of the boundary system, and was therefore not a physical impediment to it. However, a similar arrangement of buildings, mainly founded in construction slots, lay further to the east. They are dated to the late Saxon period, suggesting possible continuity of occupation but, if so, here the occupants were forced to rebuild on an adjacent area within the new plot system and east of the new boundary between the settlements and the field system.

Trial trenching carried out as part of the Raunds Area Survey to the south of the excavated sites has also shown that the ditched boundary systems were more widespread, and continued over a distance of 1km along the eastern flank of Raunds Brook, although the arrangements for individual plots could not be established (Parry 2006). They are mostly aligned upon the eighteenth-century road system implying that these principal routeways were in existence by the eleventh century and were presumably established as part of the process of reorganisation.

Within this larger area of formalised plots the actual intensity and character of settlement varied. The already important focus at Furnells was to continue to prosper, becoming the medieval manor with its church and churchyard. To the south, the Langham Road site appears to have comprised the back of a series of plots, probably peasant tenements or crofts, fronting onto a road to the east, Rotton Row, which runs along the western stream bank. A third level of society, landless peasants, may also be visible in this landscape. Between Furnells manor and the Langham Road tenements there may have been a trackway providing access to the open fields to the west. Within this 20m wide zone there were two small timber buildings that may have been peasant hovels built on the verges of the trackway.

To the east, at Burystead, plots running down to the Midland Road appear to have been comparable to the Langham Road plots, forming peasant crofts. The ditched plots on the higher ground to the south did not contain contemporary domestic buildings, which may have lain in an adjacent unexcavated plot. However, as these plots later formed part of the medieval manorial holding of Burystead, with the parish church to the immediate south, they may have pertained to a late Saxon holding of comparable status to that seen at Furnells.

Furnells: An Anglo-Scandinavian farm (AD 850–900/950)

The choice of location for this settlement was probably determined by the local topography. It lay on an east–west ridge of slightly higher ground that sloped gently to the east with a sharper fall beyond into the valley of the Raunds Brook. To the south the ground fell away gently before rising again to a further ridge on which the middle Saxon farm and later buildings at Langham Road were situated. Its establishment on the same location as the apparently un-associated early Saxon settlement is presumably one of coincidental use of a favourable location. Such a specific phase of new settlement can only be defined at Furnells. However, to the south at Langham Road, the presence of early St Neots-type ware may suggest that there was contemporary activity, perhaps a continuation of the middle Saxon farm.

The Anglo-Scandinavian farm comprised two principal elements: a major post-built timber hall to the north, building B, and a ditched enclosure containing a single post-built hall, S, to the south (Fig 3.5a). While the lack of stratigraphic connections and the problems of the pottery dating make it impossible to establish a definitive chronology for all of these separate aspects, there was a close physical relationship between the principal structures. The enclosure was slightly trapezoidal in plan, with a maximum width of 38m, and enclosed an area of 0.11ha. There were opposed northern and southern entrances, and the southern entrance had been elaborated at a later stage, perhaps including the provision of a timber gateway. The substantial post-built hall within the enclosure was aligned north–south, and was set immediately east of a direct line between the opposed entrances. If projected northward, this central axis aligns with the central doors of the northern hall, suggesting that it was a carefully planned arrangement of halls and enclosure.

A further, smaller timber hall, D, lay to the west, at a slightly oblique angle to the other structures, and a further structure, C, appeared to closely abut the north-western corner of the ditched enclosure. Between these northern buildings and the enclosure there was an open yard with the public access from the east, where it was to stay throughout the lifetime of the late Saxon and medieval manors. In fact, at the time of excavation in the 1970s the footpath access to Furnells Close from Rotton Row still lay on this same direct line over 1100 years later.

At a later stage, the eastern end of the area was closed by a substantial timber hall, building A, with opposed central doorways and walls founded in continuous slots, rather than principal posts in post-pits. The position of this building in the construction sequence is uncertain. It might have been a final addition to the Anglo-Scandinavian farm but, alternatively, it may have only been introduced slightly later, at the creation of the new late Saxon long range. Whatever the date of construction for this building, the way that it straddled the main access to the halls to the west, would suggest that its principal function was as a gatehouse controlling access to the hall beyond.

A second length of ditch ran closely parallel with the eastern arm of the enclosure, but this may also have been introduced as part of the formation of the late Saxon boundary system, see below. The palimpsest of pits and postholes lying to the east of the enclosure have been assigned to the early–middle Saxon period on the basis of the pottery from them, but it is possible that the group includes some features pertaining to this phase, which is otherwise devoid on any contemporary smaller features.

The provision of the hall to the north and a second hall within the enclosure to the south can be seen as defining two distinct aspects to the settlement; a private space within the enclosure and a public space, embodied in the provision of a substantial timber hall with direct access from the east. This arrangement indicates that this was not merely a domestic settlement and farm, but an establishment that also had a wider seigneurial function. We may therefore be seeing what could be called a proto-manor arrangement appearing in the later ninth century, within the period of Danish control. It is of significance that while the status of the Furnells site was apparently established under the Danes, this survived the reconquest and the reorganisation of the early to mid tenth century. The late Saxon reorganisation of settlement, whilst far-reaching and drastic, therefore utilised the existing role of the site and, in doing so, probably enhanced and formalised that role, and maintained a sense of continuity within a changing world, an approach that may have been central to maintaining social stability.

A Scandinavian influence at Furnells is evident in some of the recovered finds. Items of horse gear included a stirrup and pieces decorated with bosses (see Fig 7.3, 1–5). Whilst found in different contexts, they could have come from a single set or sets of a type described by Waterman (1959) when reporting a fine bridle from York and other pieces from London and Winchester. He noted similar boss-decorated harness sets in southern Norway. The restricted find spots in Britain could be interpreted as evidence of tenth to eleventh century Norse contacts. One of these pieces came from the enclosure ditch itself, although the other items were residual in later contexts within the same area.

Further evidence comes from two small hemispherical gaming pieces (see Fig 7.5, 1–2), which each have a rectangular hole in the flat base, one of which retains the remains of an iron peg. These are comparable to onion-shaped pieces from Goltho, Lincolnshire and appear to have Viking associations as naftafel pieces used on a portable pierced board, such as the one recovered from Ballinderry (MacGregor in Beresford 1987). One of the two pieces was from the enclosure ditch, while the other was from the eastern timber hall, building A.

The status of the occupants may also be indicated by the recovery of part of the skeleton of a buzzard (*Buteo buteo*), which might have been a captive bird. Local Scandinavian trade links are also indicated by an eleventh-century coin of Olaf Kyrre of Norway, found in the Langham Road excavations.

Furnells: Plot formation and the late Saxon manor (AD 900–950)

By the middle of the tenth century, the ditched enclosure at Furnells had been absorbed into a system of regular ditched plot boundaries that extended across both stream banks in north Raunds and beyond (Fig 3.4).

At Furnells, a major north–south ditch to the west of the existing enclosure was the boundary between the settlement plots and the field system on the higher ground to the west (Fig 3.5b). However, in its original form there were further ditches to the immediate west which may have bounded an infield system of small horticultural plots or stock paddocks lying between the settlement plots and the open fields higher on the western slopes. One of these adjacent infields contained a small pond, perhaps providing a water supply for stock.

The new ditch systems formed a single large plot that encompassed the existing post-built halls and the ditched enclosure, and all these elements were probably retained until after the new boundary system was established. As already discussed, the eastern timber hall, building A, at the north-eastern corner of the ditched enclosure, may have been either a final addition to the previous post-built complex or a new range contemporary with the introduction of the new boundaries and the new hall and domestic apartments. In particular, it may be noted that it would have stood directly opposite the new hall, where it clearly controlled all access into a northern courtyard, and may therefore be regarded as a formal gatehouse, a thegns gate. It is also noticeable how the northern post-built hall of the preceding phase lay on the northern side of the new courtyard, suggesting that there was a continuous process of building replacement, with the new hall constructed next to, rather than over, its predecessor, thus permitting continuity of occupation through the process of reorganisation and rebuilding.

The plot containing the new building range was 0.4ha (or approximately one acre) in area. The principal new building, the long range, was 37.4m long. The northern half comprised an open hall, heavily disturbed by the construction of its replacement, a broader aisled hall (Fig 3.6). The main walls were probably both founded in continuous wall trenches, and would have been stave built, as a façade of abutting posts, all load bearing. Various post-pits lay immediately inside the wall line but did not all form pairs. A pair on the eastern wall may have held the portal posts of an elaborate central doorway. An abutting range of smaller rooms, the domestic quarters, extended southward, and were also founded in continuous wall trenches. There were also three smaller detached ancillary buildings to the south, of similar build (Fig 3.7). The largest of these may have been a detached kitchen range, as suggested for

Fig 3.6: Furnells, ninth-century post-built halls (left foreground and background), and the wall trenches and post-pits of the late Saxon aisled hall (centre), looking north-east

Fig 3.7: Furnells, the wall trenches of the late Saxon domestic range (centre) and ancillary buildings (top right), looking south-east

a detached timber building adjacent to the contemporary long range complex at West Cotton, which had later been replaced by a stone kitchen range (Chapman in press).

At least the western half of the former ditched enclosure must have been backfilled to accommodate the new long range, but the ditches on the eastern side appeared to have been retained to form part of the eastern boundary of the new plot system. The retained part of the northern arm would have separated the hall end of the plot from the domestic ancillary buildings to the south, thus providing separate inner and outer courts, the private and public spaces, thus replicating in a new form the arrangement of the Anglo-Scandinavian farm. This indicates that the new arrangement had retained the larger seigneurial role of its predecessor, and may be characterised as the residence of a minor Saxon thegn.

The establishment of the long range complex at Furnells was the first of five major periods of building within the same plot system, indicating that it was with the establishment of the long range at around the middle of the tenth century that the formal manorial history of Furnells began, even if that had been foreshadowed by the high status Anglo-Scandinavian farm.

Furnells: The late Saxon manor and church (AD 950–1100)

The first major innovation, and a clear indicator of both the prosperity and the status of the long range complex, saw the foundation of a church and churchyard on a plot to the east of the long range (Figs 3.8a, 3.9 and 3.10). This was an addition appropriate to the residence of a minor thegn. Its construction may have followed quite rapidly, perhaps only some 10–20 years after the building of the long range, as radiocarbon dating indicates that the earliest burials date to the middle decades of the tenth century.

The church and churchyard formed the sole objective for the initial phase of excavation at Furnells in the late 1970s, and a full description has been reported separately (Boddington 1996).

That the foundation of the churchyard post-dates both the plot formation and the appearance of the long range complex is indicated by the reorganisation of the boundary system between the domestic plot and the new churchyard. In order to accommodate the addition of the churchyard within a nominal plot of around half an acre, a new eastern boundary for the domestic plot was formed some 10m to the west of the previous double-ditched boundary. To the south the new boundary ditch turned sharply back to the east to meet the earlier alignment. To provide some compensation for this loss of space within the domestic enclosure, the parallel length of the western boundary to the domestic plot was relocated westward, although only by some 4m (Fig 3.8b).

Why it was necessary to impinge upon the domestic plot in creating the churchyard, rather than setting it fully to the east, is uncertain, although the ground does fall away towards the Raunds Brook on this side, and the motivation may have been a desire to locate the entire churchyard in the prominent position provided by the ridge of higher ground.

The first church was small, only 8.0m long including the chancel, which was a slightly later addition to the original single-cell form (Boddington 1996, 16–22 and figs 10–19). The limestone foundations and a surviving wall course in rough-hewn limestone suggest that it was a stone construction to the full height of its walls, with a door towards the western end of the southern wall of the nave (see Fig 5.27). A pottery vessel buried beneath the floor is interpreted as a sacrarium or repository for sacred material, while a deep slot abutting the inner face of the west wall probably held timbers supporting a bellcote. The small chancel was added soon after the foundation of the church, and a stone base set against the east wall is interpreted as a clergy bench.

Burial within the churchyard appears to have commenced at or shortly after the building of the chancel, and the church lay central to a primary zone of graves laid out in well-ordered rows. At the eastern end of the primary zone, beyond the south-east corner of the church, a burial beneath a decorated grave cover is interpreted as a founder's grave. It may have lain within its own plot, and a stone foundation at the head end perhaps formed the base for a fine decorated cross, later broken up and reused.

Subsequent use of the cemetery included the clustering of stillborn and infant burials against the church walls, particularly around the chancel, and new outlying burial zones to the east and south-east were in less regular rows. A total of over 360 individuals were interred within the churchyard, indicating that it served as a communal burial ground, rather than merely as a manorial chapel with limited burial rights. The cemetery was in regular use for some 200 years, AD 950–1150, giving an average of just under two burials (1.8) per year. This is far more than would be appropriate for the occupants and direct dependants of the manor house, and it has been calculated that it might have served a population of about 40 people, half of whom were adults (Boddington 1996, 67).

A single in-situ stone coffin outside the door of the early church is of a form that appears after the Norman Conquest (Fig 3.9). Three adjacent graves had upright, rough hewn marker stones, suggesting that the stone coffin was the final addition to a group of high-status burials. There are fragments of worked stone that may come from broken-up stone coffins, and it has been suggested that four reburials of disarticulated bones in pits to the north of the church may have come from stone coffins removed at the building of the second church.

The building on the eastern side of the domestic enclosure, the possible gatehouse, must have fallen out of use at the creation of the churchyard, as it was cut by the ditch bounding the northern side of the cemetery. Thereafter, the access to the long range lay to the north of the cemetery

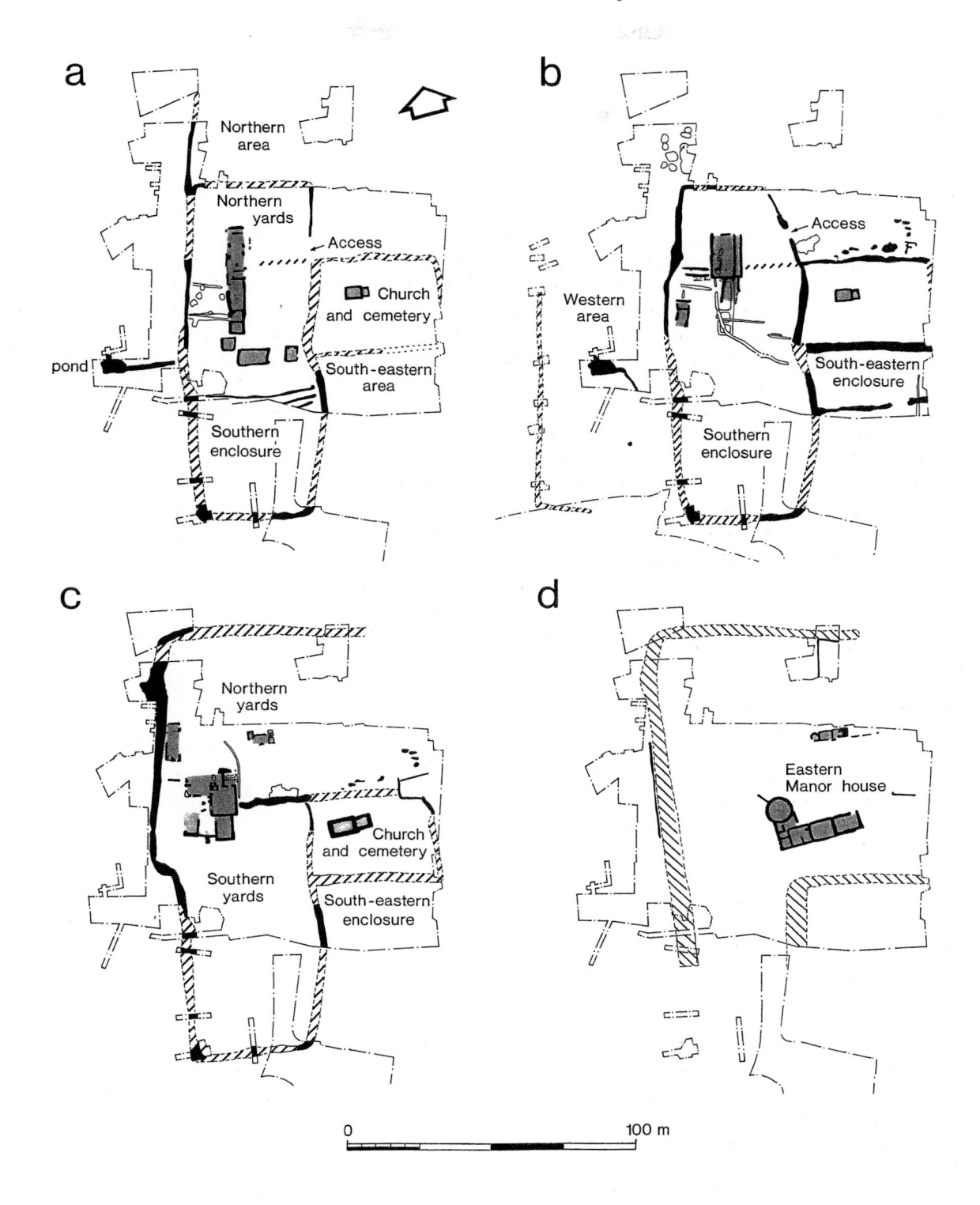

Fig 3.8: Furnells, the development of the manor; a) the long range, church and churchyard (AD 950–1100), b) the aisled hall (AD 1100–1150/1200), c) the western manor house (1150/1200–1350/1400) and d) the eastern manor house (AD 1350/1400–1500)

Fig 3.9: Furnells, the late Saxon and medieval churches, looking south, with the stone coffin and excavated graves in the background

through a simple opening in the ditch system (Fig 3.10).

It is probable that with the relocation of the eastern domestic plot boundary to accommodate the churchyard, a new northern boundary was also provided, to retain the division between the inner and outer courts. There was a major ditch system along this line, but it had been so thoroughly recut at later dates that any traces of earlier ditches had been removed.

The points of access to the churchyard itself were not established. The boundaries to the north, west and south contained no evident openings but as these ditches had all been recut, either simple openings had been lost within the palimpsest of cuts or bridging points had been provided across the open ditches. Access from the north and/or the west appear to be the most likely options. However, while the access to the domestic enclosure may originally have lain directly to the north of the churchyard boundary, through the eleventh and twelfth centuries a series of irregular shallow quarry pits were excavated into the cornbrash limestone to the immediate north of the churchyard boundary ditch, pushing the access to the domestic enclosure to the north of the quarry pits and restricting the places at which the churchyard could have been accessed from the north.

Other quarry pits lay to the north-west of the domestic enclosure, within the small enclosures of the postulated infield system. The brashy limestone from these pits may have been used for ancillary functions such as yard surfaces and hearths, but it is possible that some of the material may have been used as wall core in the construction of the second church or of the western manor in the later twelfth century. In addition, pits associated with a boundary ditch to the south of the churchyard would have produced quantities of sand and some gravel, perhaps used in the preparation of mortar for the earlier stone buildings on the site. The early quarries at both Furnells and Langham Road have been discussed previously (Cadman and Audouy 1990).

Langham Road: field boundaries and a late Saxon farm (AD 900/950–1100)

The stratification at Langham Road, Burystead and Midland Road was often insufficient to discriminate between events in the late Saxon period and the twelfth century. Hence many features on these sites are included on the general plans of both periods (Fig 3.4 and 3.12). Nevertheless, it is clear that, as at Furnells, systems of linear ditches forming rectangular plots had been created in the late Saxon

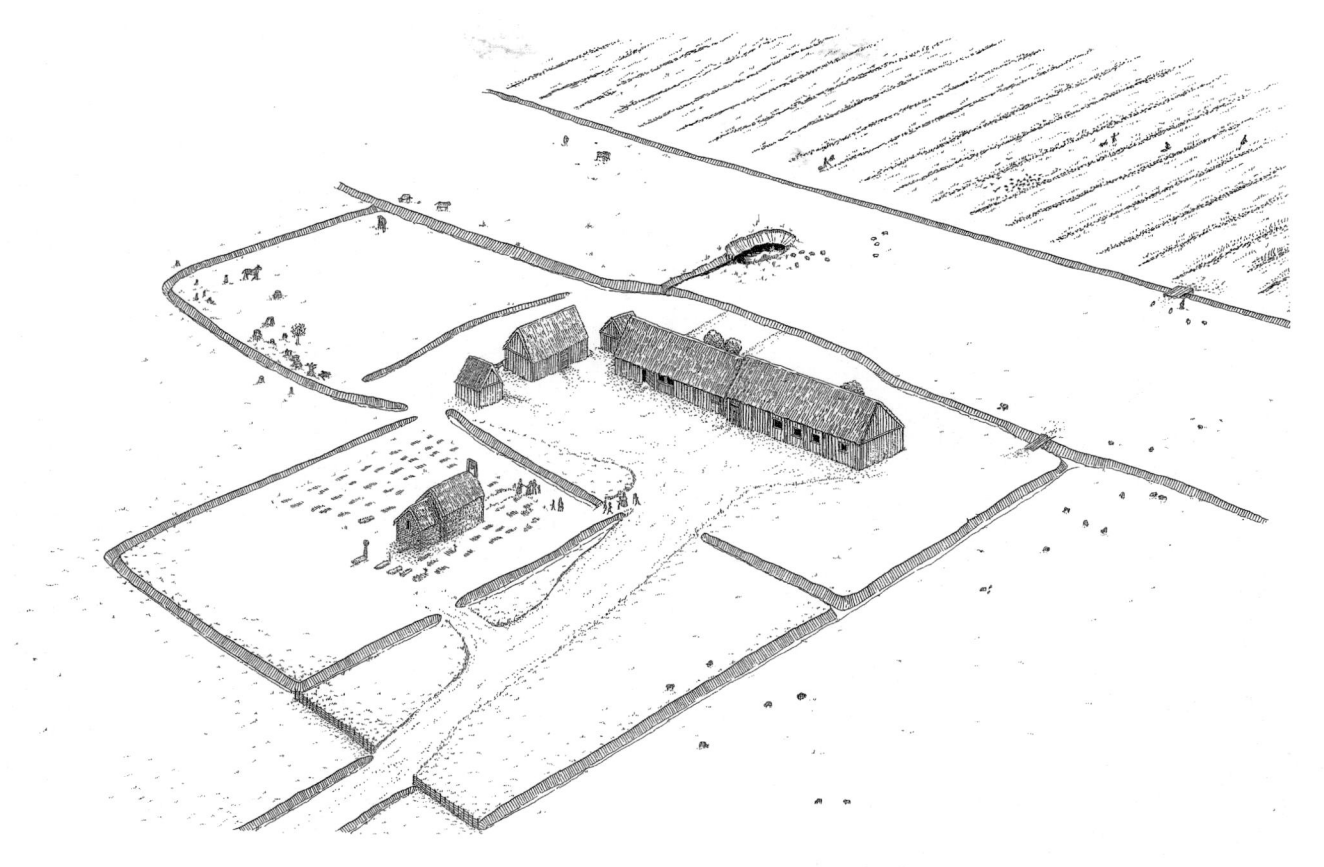

Fig 3.10: Furnells, reconstruction of the late Saxon long range and the church (AD 950–1100)

period and were then maintained and modified through the eleventh and twelfth centuries.

At Langham Road there were two groups of timber buildings broadly dated to these centuries. To the south-east there was a group of four closely associated buildings, with mixed slot and posthole constructions (Fig 3.11). These lay east of the main north–south boundary of the new plot system, and may have been a successor to the middle Saxon farm, which had lain to the west. A complex of minor ditches also lay to the west of the main north–south boundary suggesting, as seen at Furnells, that this area was probably an infield system perhaps used at least in part for stock control, with the open fields lying further to the west.

The new building complex lay within a plot that was probably 40m wide, while the western field boundary lay just over 100m west of Rotton Row. This suggests that the buildings formed a croft set within a toft one acre in extent. This is the first such toft to the south of the Furnells manorial plot, but there may have been further examples to the south.

At the very northern end of the Langham Road site there was a small posthole structure to the east and a slot construction to the west, which lay west of the boundary between the settlement and the fields, the only late Saxon buildings to do so (Fig 3.4). These may have been ancillary buildings to Furnells, but another possibility is that they lay within a 20m wide trackway, boundary by ditches, that separated Furnells manor from the tenement plots fronting onto Rotton Row (Fig 3.4, t). These buildings might mark the presence of a lower level of society, landless peasants building small houses of the verges of a trackway, which offered the only land available to them.

Burystead and Midland Road: plot boundaries and late Saxon settlement (AD 900/950–1100)

At Burystead, a well-ordered system of plots was created (Fig 3.4), which were to survive, with modifications, through to the post-medieval abandonment of the Burystead manor (Figs 3.12 and 3.14). In particular, the northernmost of the two east–west ditches was to remain unchanged to the post-medieval period. This was probably a major property division, forming the northern limit of the plots pertaining to the Burystead manor. The land to the north was divided by ditches aligned north–south into a series of tenement plots that extended to the Midland Road frontage. Here the basic pattern remained unchanged over the succeeding centuries, but the frequent realignments of the plot boundaries indicate that a more dynamic system of property tenure was in operation in this northern area.

Within the southern plots there was a single posthole

Fig 3.11: Langham Road, the wall trenches of the timber buildings of the late Saxon farm, looking east

and slot building and, to the west, an extensive group of quarry pits (Fig 3.13). Their presence here suggests that these were plots at the margins of the Burystead manorial holdings and, at this date, the most likely use of the quarried limestone was for the construction of a church, perhaps a late Saxon predecessor of the present parish church, which lies directly to the south. The location of the medieval manor house and its probable late Saxon predecessor has, unfortunately, not been located, but the only adjacent areas where it could have been situated are to either the east or south of the parish church.

Within the northern plots at Burystead there were at least three small posthole and slot buildings, and a scatter of irregular pits denote a range of associated domestic activities, including probably clay-pits. At this time the activity directly on the Midland Road frontage comprised only ditches and pits similar to elsewhere on the plots, showing that the domestic houses lay within their plots and not on the frontages.

The late Saxon economy

By the late Saxon/Saxo-Norman period the full range of cereal crops was being grown, both tetraploid and hexaploid varieties of free-threshing wheat, rye, six-row hulled barley and oats. Wheat was by far the most common crop at this period and, as has already been suggested, the apparent decrease in the importance of barley may be due to rye and oats being grown in its place. Remains of *Avena* sp. grain were recovered in similar numbers to barley which might suggest that they were grown in similar quantities, possibly as a mixture. Evidence from West Cotton (Campbell in press) indicates that oats and barley were grown as a dredge, though the comparatively large numbers of oat grains recovered from a ditch fill at Burystead suggest that it was also grown as an unmixed crop, possibly as fodder for draught animals.

There were few remains of rye, although their presence in a ditch fill at Burystead indicates that it was being deliberately cultivated, rather than occurring only as a volunteer in other cereal crops. Rye chaff far outnumbers

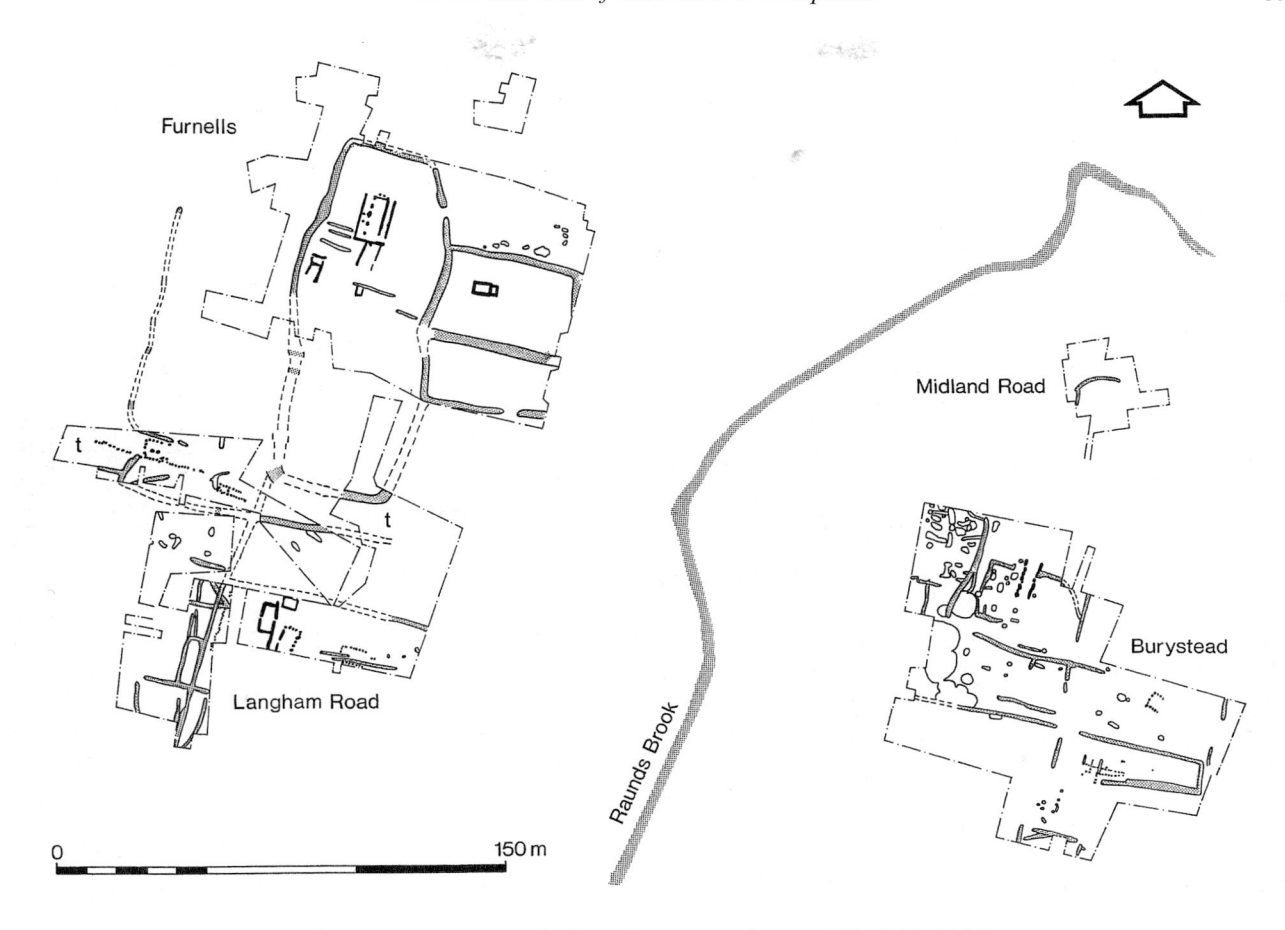

Fig 3.12: North Raunds, Saxo-Norman settlement (AD 1100–1200)

rye grain at the sites, a phenomenon also observed at West Cotton and at Stafford (L Moffett, pers comm), and it has been suggested that it is the result of the use of rye chaff as fuel or kindling in drying ovens. The samples from the late medieval bake/brewhouse at Furnells would support this interpretation for the use of both rye and rivet wheat chaff.

There is evidence for the cultivation of pea probably from the middle Saxon period onwards. The weed flora recovered from the late Saxon/Saxo-Norman samples is very similar to that found in the medieval assemblages with evidence for the cultivation of the same range of soil types and with a grassland element also present.

The medieval manors and the village (AD 1100–1350/1400)

This period covers an era of burgeoning economic and population growth and sees the full development of an intensively exploited landscape based on the open field system. The land was intensively farmed; arable had pushed to the margins of the townships by the late thirteenth century and probably long before. At West Cotton, ridge and furrow was sealed by alluvium on an area subsequently given over to meadow, suggesting that the arable here had been pushed to the furthest limit possible before the mid-twelfth century. The fieldwalking survey shows medieval pottery occurring in almost every furlong, suggesting intensive manuring to maintain soil fertility. Post-medieval documentation suggests that while the other villages in the Raunds study area, Stanwick and Hargrave, had a three-field system, Raunds, by far the largest of the settlements, had a double three-field system from at least the fourteenth century, which apparently relates to the two main settlement elements, the North End and Thorpe End.

By the time of Domesday Book the late Saxon estate centred upon Higham Ferrers was in a process of fragmentation, giving rise to a complex tenurial landscape. Two major holdings dominated the area. One fee belonged to the King's thegn Burgred at 1066 and had been granted to the Bishop of Coutances by 1086. This estate comprised lands and rents in Raunds, Ringstead, and the Cottons and included a manor in Raunds which can be identified with Furnells. It later belonged to the Clares (as part of the Honor of Gloucester) and the Staffords. Like most other eleventh-century manors it was probably being farmed out for rent. It appears to have been sub-infeudated by the thirteenth century. Thereafter it was held by a series of minor 'knightly' families who owed feudal dues to the Clares

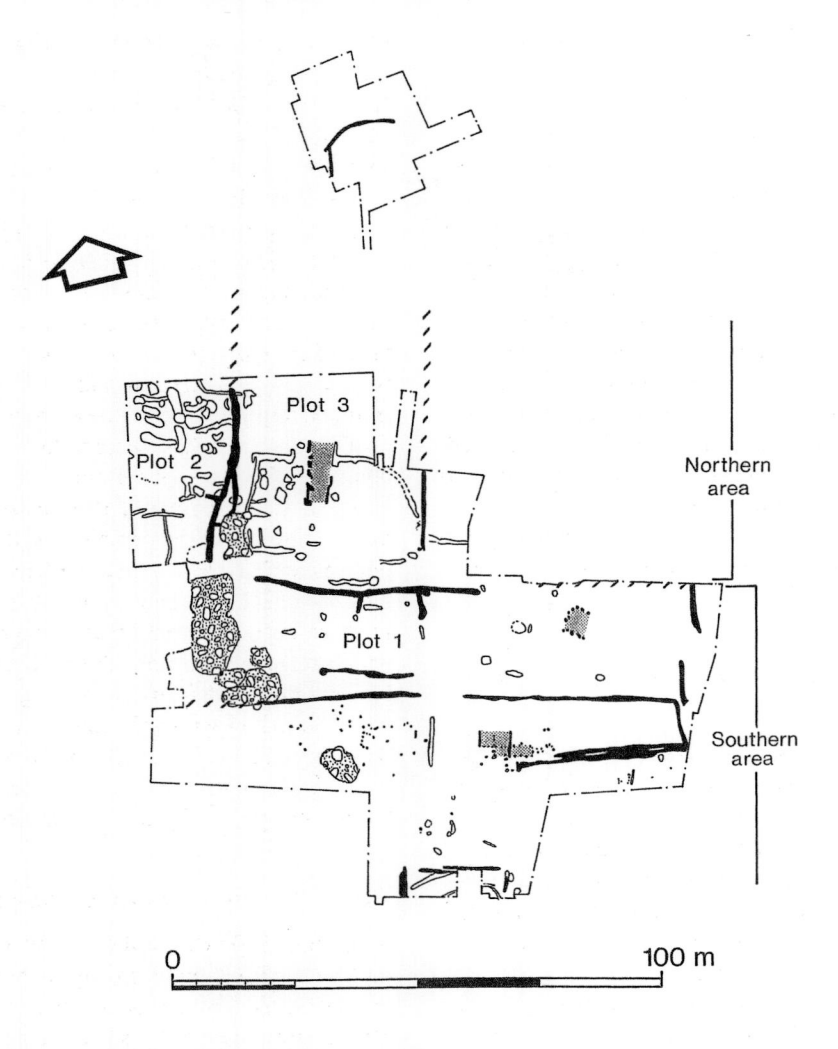

Fig 3.13: Burystead, the late Saxon and medieval settlement (AD 900/950–1200)

and their successors as overlords. No medieval manorial accounts survive and hence there is little information as to the form or layout of the manor. It continued to be known in the post-medieval period as the Gloucester fee. By the twelfth century the Clare/Gloucester fee had its chief court at Denford and the three main post-Conquest manors associated with the Cottons all owed suit to its court leet.

The other major fee belonged to the Countess Gytha in 1066 and was in the hands of William Peverel at Domesday. Subsequently it was held by the Ferrers family, the earls of Lancaster, and from 1351 formed part of the duchy of Lancaster. The manorial centre was at Higham Ferrers. Raunds Burystead, which possessed lands and tenants in Raunds, Ringstead, Hargrave and Stanwick, appears to have been a berewick (dependent demesne) in Domesday Book. In the thirteenth century, during the heyday of demesne farming, the manor was almost certainly worked by a steward for the direct profit of the lord though no accounts survive for this period. The fourteenth-century accounts record expenditure on repairs to manorial buildings.

Towards the end of the period overpopulation, crop failure and disease led to a period of decline although this is difficult to recognise in the archaeological record until the late medieval period.

Furnells: the aisled hall (AD 1100–1200)

At around 1100, the hall at the northern end of the long range was replaced by an imposing timber aisled hall (Fig 3.8b and 3.12). It was of the same length as its predecessor but with a marked increase in width (Fig 3.6). As with its predecessor, the complex palimpsest of features in this area has not aided the task of interpretation. The plan is certainly asymmetrical, with the paired wall trenches to the east slightly closer together than the aisle posts and the outer wall trench to the west. This might suggest that instead of an eastern aisle there was an attached pentice, forming a narrow fore building. The open hall would have been just over 4.0m wide, perhaps with the roof dropping lower at the rear over the single aisle, which added over 2.0m to the width of the hall. While the walls would again have been stave built, the aisle posts define this as a four-bay structure plus a half bay where it joined the rooms to the south.

The southern half of the range appears to have stood unaltered for some time, but it was later levelled and replaced by a much shorter timber range. New detached buildings probably included a kitchen range to the south-west. Other posthole and mixed posthole-and-slot buildings may have stood to the west and south of the long range and on the lower lying area to the south of the churchyard.

As indicated previously, there was probably always a ditch dividing the hall end and the domestic quarters, but this had been lost to later recutting along the same line. To the south, the boundaries between the domestic enclosure and the southern plot appear to have been backfilled, effectively enlarging the domestic enclosure, although no buildings were placed in this area.

While the domestic quarters were refurbished, the church and its attendant churchyard remained in use as before.

Furnells: the absence of a Norman manor house

While the late Saxon timber hall was rebuilt and enlarged as an aisled hall a few decades after the Norman Conquest, this rebuilding was only in timber, and it was to be around another 100 years before a stone hall was provided, at 1200. In contrast, at the hamlet of West Cotton, a site of lesser status, a Norman-style two-storey stone hall was built in the early 1100s, perhaps only a few decades after the rebuilding in timber at Furnells.

The absence of a Norman stone hall might suggest that in the early 1100s Furnells manor was such a minor holding that little attention or expense was devoted to it. Its fortunes perhaps only began to improve towards the middle of the twelfth century, when money was devoted first to the provision of a new church, to replace the out-dated and very small Saxon church, followed by the provision of a manor house in the newly emerging medieval style of parlour/solar, open hall, and service ranges.

It may therefore have been a period of neglect in the early 1100s that saw the site lose much of its earlier respect and status, and by the time the new church was built burial rights would appear to have been lost, presumably to the new and much grander church on the opposite side of the valley attached to the Burystead manor.

Furnells: the rebuilding of the church (AD 1150–1200)

Radiocarbon dating of burials that lay beneath the foundations of the second church, indicate that the demolition of the small late Saxon church and its replacement with a larger building could have occurred as early as AD 1150, suggesting that a new stone church was provided in advance of the building of a stone manor house. The enlarged second church comprised a stone-built nave and chancel. It was built on substantial pitched-stone foundations, but little survived about ground to indicate the position of doorways or internal features (Boddington 1996, 22–25 and figs 21–23). It was substantially larger than its predecessor but, at 15.2m for the nave and chancel, it was still small by the standards of its day. The southern wall lay over the southern wall of the earlier church, so that the higher-status burials to the south of the church were undisturbed by the rebuilding. A few burials, some of which may have been in stone coffins, probably to the west of the early church, had to be removed, but the bones were carefully collected and reburied in a series of pits immediately north of the new church.

The new church appears to have been only a manorial chapel, and there was certainly no general clearance and reuse of the churchyard. It is possible that some of the outlying zones of the cemetery to the east and south-east may have still been in use, perhaps including two small family plots, but there is no reliable dating for the burials in these outlying areas. It is also possible that the reuse of the stone coffin, with the breaking up of the original cover stone and its partial covering with a fragment from a broken-up cross shaft, may have been contemporary with the second church. Such a use would be consistent with its new status as a manorial chapel, with now only the immediate family being interred there.

Furnells: the western manor (AD 1200–1400)

At around 1200 the timber aisled hall was levelled and replaced on the same site by a new stone-built manor house, the western manor, and the ancillary buildings were also rebuilt in stone (Figs 3.14 and 3.15). They joined the church, which had been rebuilt some decades earlier.

To accommodate these new buildings within the manorial enclosure, the western boundary ditch was again relocated, moving it even further to the west. It may have been at this time that the infield enclosures, which appear to have lain between the domestic plots and the open field system, were abandoned, with the open fields then sharing a direct common boundary with the domestic plots.

Many of the minor ditches within the manorial enclosures appear to have fallen out of use at this time. This may have left the manor house set within a more expansive domestic enclosure, but it is also possible that some of the ditches may have been replaced by boundary walls for which no evidence had survived. The separation between the outer court, with its public access to the hall of the manor, and the private inner court, was certainly retained. It was at this time that the ditch was both widened and deepened, removing all traces of any earlier ditches.

The new manor house contained a square central hall, with an open hearth towards the southern end. To the north there were two service rooms with flagstone floors, and to the south there was a narrower parlour/solar wing. There were further poorly preserved buildings to the west, including a west wing that was probably a later addition.

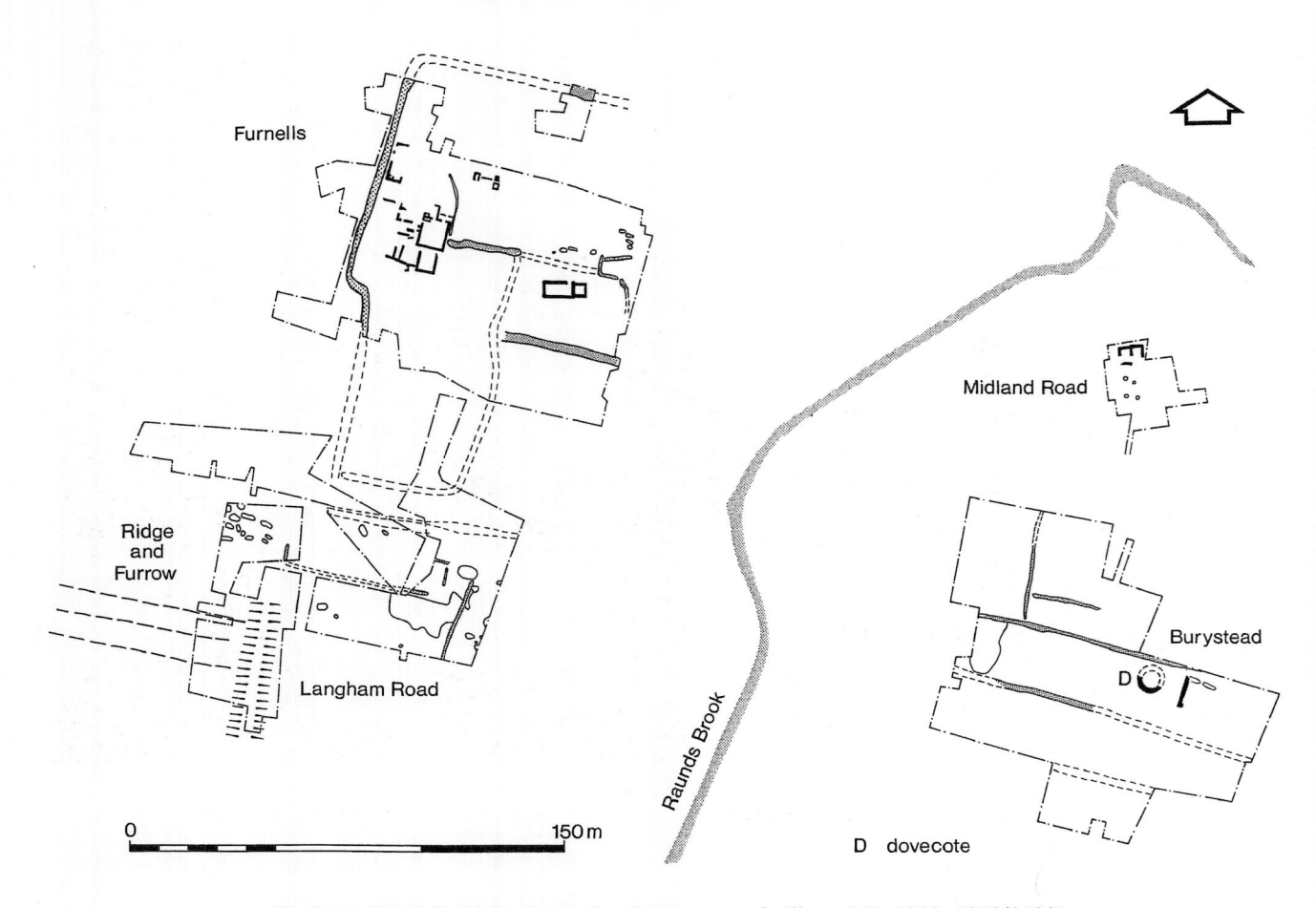

Fig 3.14: North Raunds, the medieval manors and village (AD 1200–1350/1400)

Adjacent to the parlour there was probably a small walled yard, which gave access to a latrine that emptied into a cess pit abutting the outer face of the yard wall. Beyond this stood a detached kitchen/bakehouse range containing a circular, corner baking oven. A similar juxtaposition of cess pit and kitchen/bakehouse range was seen in the contemporary manor house at West Cotton (Chapman in press).

Further buildings to the north-west and north-east of the manor house are probably slightly later additions, denoting continuing growth in the prosperity of the manor through the thirteenth century, when it was held by the Ferneus family. The kitchen/bakehouse range west of the manor house may have been replaced by a larger establishment to the north-west, which was a combined bakehouse/malting house with a circular baking oven in one corner and a sunken sub-rectangular malting/drying oven in the opposite corner.

To the north-east of the manor house there was a further malting complex, perhaps indicating the increasing importance of this saleable product, with the surplus probably going to market at nearby Higham. This expansion of malting facilities was also seen at West Cotton (Chapman in press). Any trace of a building enclosing the north-eastern malting oven had been lost. To its east there was a stone-lined tank and an adjacent area of limestone surface, perhaps respectively the steeping tank to promote sprouting, and the germinating floor to prepare the barley prior to drying in the oven to form the malt.

The new church would have served as the manorial chapel. It may have seen a final refurbishment in the thirteenth century. A wall was inserted across the nave and its construction exactly paralleled the construction of the other church walls, as a broad wall on pitched-stone foundations. This suggests that it belonged to the church sequence and not to a secular reuse, the church conversion phase, as postulated by the excavator (Boddington 1996, 10–11 and fig 22). It is suggested that this cross wall was inserted to support the provision of a tower raised over the western end of the nave.

The wealth and status of the western manor is evident in some of the recovered material possessions, particularly those from the spreads of demolition debris that overlay the levelled buildings. These include a silver gilt brooch with delicate filigree decoration and four settings for gems, and the bone tailpiece from a three-stringed musical instrument, decorated with two stylised faces with ring-and-dot eyes (Fig 3.16). In addition, some vessel glass, late thirteenth-

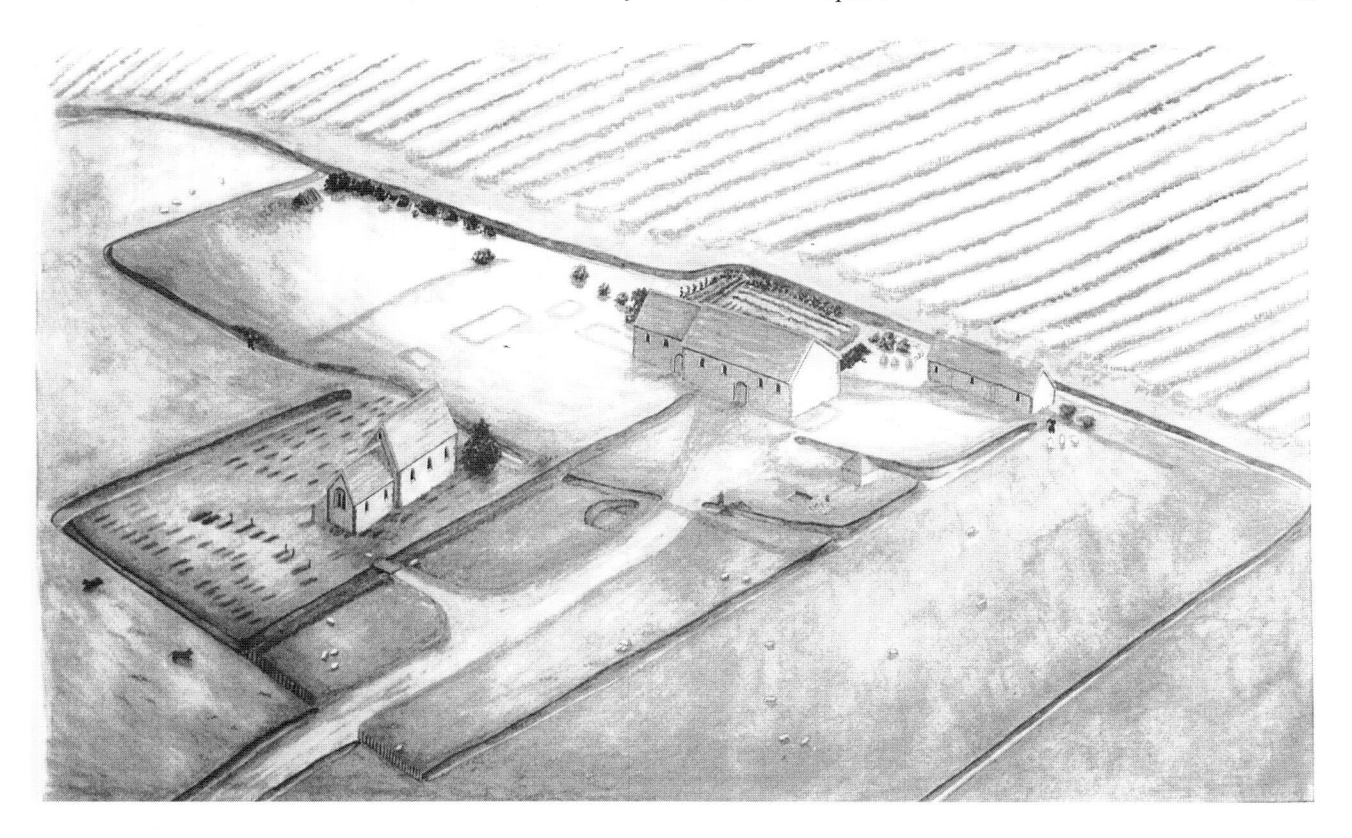

Fig 3.15: Furnells, reconstruction of the western manor and the second church (AD 1200–1350)

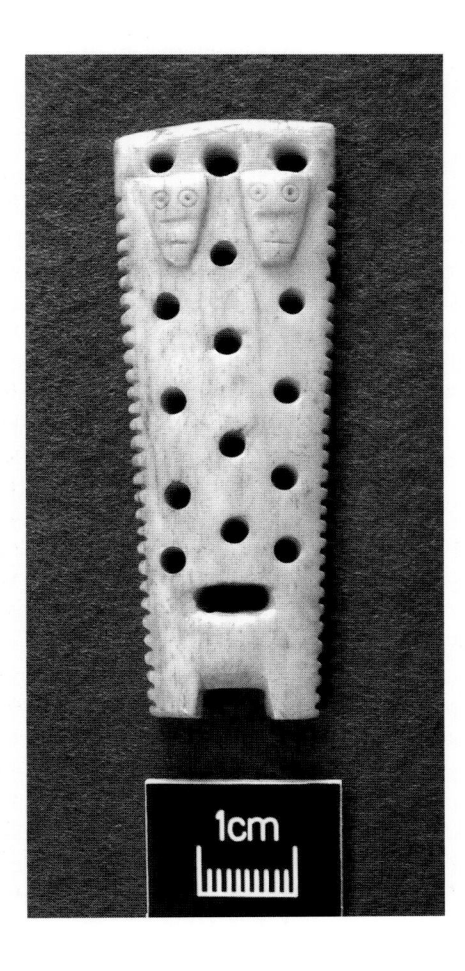

century coins of Edward I and an early fourteenth-century jetton also come from this period of greatest prosperity for Furnells manor. The range of pottery, besides the purely domestic wares, also includes a series of high-status vessels, possibly unique items commissioned by the owner of Furnells manor during the thirteenth century from the pottery industries at Stanion and Lyveden. The vessels include an aquamanile in the form of ram, a highly decorated jug with stylised human figures in white slip (Fig 3.17), and an extremely large jug with slip and trailed decoration (see Fig 6.8). More mundane activities are represented by the ubiquitous weaving tools and a glass linen-smoother.

Langham Road: tenement plots and field boundaries (AD 1100–1350/1400)

At Langham Road it proved impossible to distinguish twelfth-century occupation features from those for the late Saxon period (Figs 3.4 and 3.12). The system of plots continued largely unchanged and it was only at around the end of the twelfth century that the group of timber buildings were abandoned.

Fig 3.16: Bone tailpiece from a three-stringed musical instrument, showing perforations to hold the strings (top), a slot and a notch to hold the retaining cord (bottom) and decorated with two stylised faces

Fig 3.17: Thirteenth-century pottery contemporary with the western manor, including a Lyveden/Stanion aquamanile in the form of a ram (centre) and Lyveden/Stanion jugs, including one with elaborate decoration, perhaps representing stylised human figures (centre right)

From 1200 onward, no structures can be identified and it can be surmised that any buildings were located further to the east, as either part of a staged relocation towards the frontage or as a direct thirteenth-century formation of a frontage development along Rotton Row (Fig 3.14). As the frontage is still fully occupied it is unlikely that an opportunity will arise to examine this process further. As at Furnells to the north, the boundary system was simplified and eventually the most prominent feature was the low banked headland, rather the linear ditches alongside it, which marked the formal boundary between the open fields to the west and the domestic plots fronting onto Rotton Row to the east. The last generation of pits sealed by the headland contained pottery dated to the thirteenth–fourteenth centuries, showing that the final definition of the boundary of the field system was quite a late occurrence. To the north-west a cluster of pits may have been medieval clay pits excavated on the margins of the open field.

Within the plots there were irregular quarries through the brashy surface limestone and, in places, penetrating up to 2.0m into the better quality Blisworth limestone beneath. These presumably provided stone for new buildings. The soil and limestone rubble fills contained little domestic debris, perhaps suggesting that the quarries were deliberately infilled quite rapidly.

At the northern end of Langham Road, sometime after AD 1200 a timber building or a pen attached to a fence line was built within the trackway (Fig 3.12, t) that separated Furnells manor from the tenement plots to the south, perhaps as a continuation of the peasant occupation of this area. Confirmation that this area was a trackway is only available for the post-medieval period, when at least the eastern end had a metalled surface.

Burystead: plot boundaries and settlement (AD 1100–1200)

At Burystead the mixed finds assemblages has made it impossible to place any events specifically within the broad time bracket of the eleventh and twelfth centuries, so the small timber buildings may have been in use in either or both centuries (Fig 3.13), while the boundary systems appear to have continued on unchanged, apart from some sporadic re-digging of the ditches.

Burystead: the manorial farm (AD 1200–1350/1400)

It was only into the thirteenth century that the arrangement of the plots was formalised by the replacement of the major east–west boundary ditch by a substantial stone wall (Fig 3.14). In addition, a further wall ran northward towards the Midland Road frontage and this appears to correspond to a boundary shown on the enclosure plan of 1798 (Fig 1.3). These features, and the earliest phase of stone buildings in the southern plot, are assigned to this period on the basis of the latest date of the small quantities of pottery recovered from the fabric of the walls themselves, which suggests an origin in the fourteenth century.

The principal buildings in the southern plot, which is believed to have pertained to the Burystead manor, were a dovecote and a malting oven: two buildings that are mentioned specifically in the surviving accounts from the fourteenth century (see Chapter 2). The dovecote provides the first evidence that these were manorial plots, but these buildings were part of the manorial farm. The centre of the domestic activity in the medieval and later medieval periods must have been located elsewhere. This is also confirmed by the minimal quantities of medieval pottery from the excavated area. There were further scant remains of a group of stone buildings in the south-western part of the excavated area, which probably denote buildings shown on the Enclosure Map. Among them, a large perhaps originally circular area of pitched stones may represent the vestiges of a threshing floor, or even a horse-drawn mill, but otherwise the function of individual features remains indeterminate.

The manorial status of the southern plots may also be denoted by the presence of a small walled yard that lay beyond the excavation, but was terraced into the earlier medieval quarries that lay in the north-western corner of the manorial plots. This small enclosure has always been considered locally to be the village pound (Hall *et al* 1988). The possession of such a feature, used to keep stray animals pending retrieval by their owners after the payment of a fine, was a manorial prerogative and documentary evidence in north Raunds attests the presence of a pound at Burystead.

The Midland Road frontage: medieval buildings (AD 1300 onward)

The frontage of the Midland Road tenements does not appear to have been built on before the fourteenth century. Even then the buildings erected were small, and typically contained stone-lined drains, suggesting that they were ancillary buildings, perhaps cattle byres relocated to the frontage for ease of moving stock along the principal roads (Fig 3.14).

So, while this period does see the first appearance of a frontage, it was still perhaps not the sitting of main domestic buildings on the road frontage, which was to come slightly later.

Late-medieval decline and relocation (AD 1350/1400–1500)

During the fourteenth and fifteenth centuries there was a widespread shrinkage of settlement with desertion occurring both on the fringes and within the four villages, while the Cottons in the valley were largely abandoned (Fig 3.18). These changes can be identified within contemporary manorial accounts which note the desertion of individual properties, both as a direct result of, and following reorganisation after, the Black Death. The picture presented by the documentary evidence suggests gradual change and readjustment. The archaeological evidence is equivocal

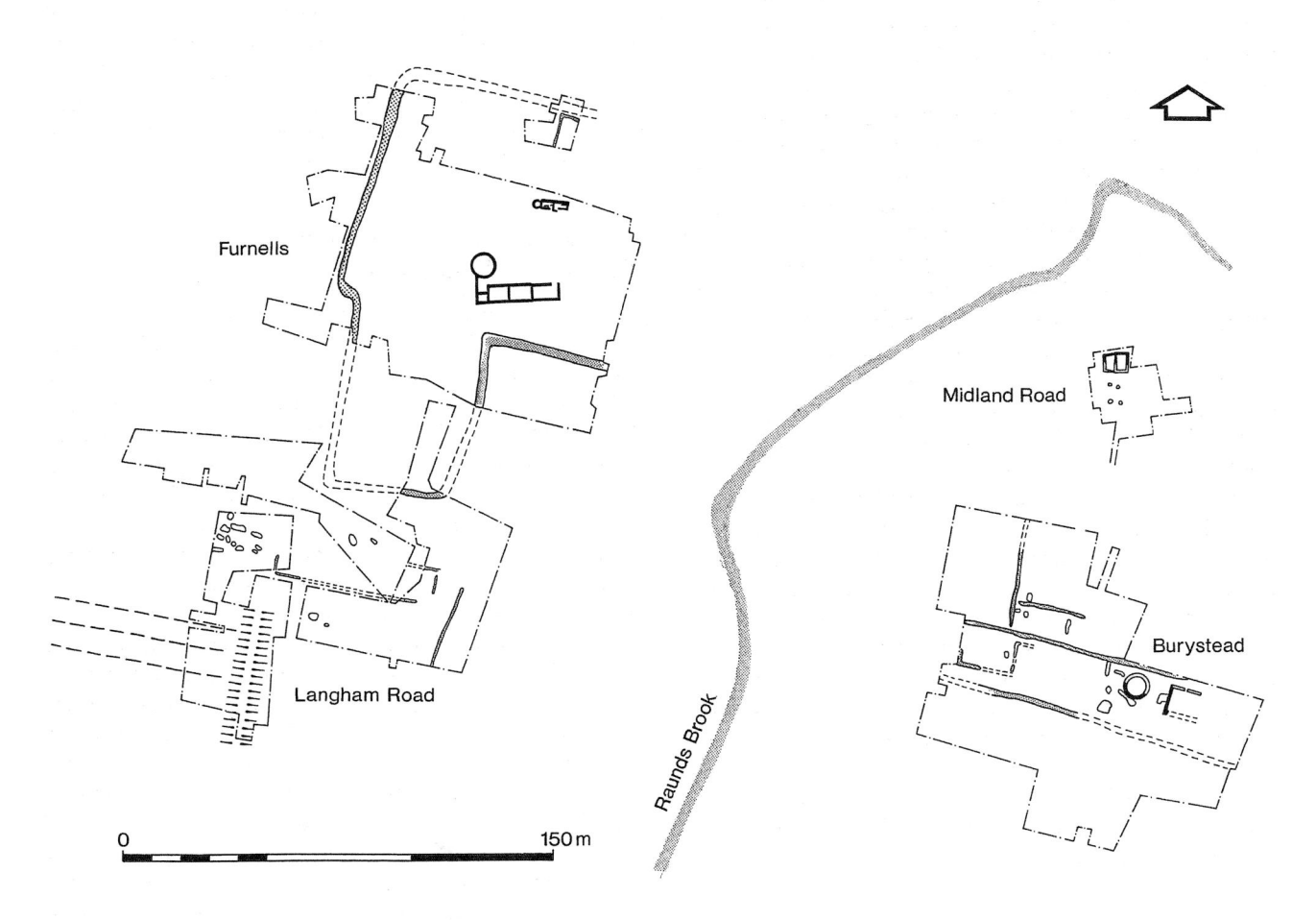

Fig 3.18: North Raunds, the late medieval manors (AD 1350/1400–1500)

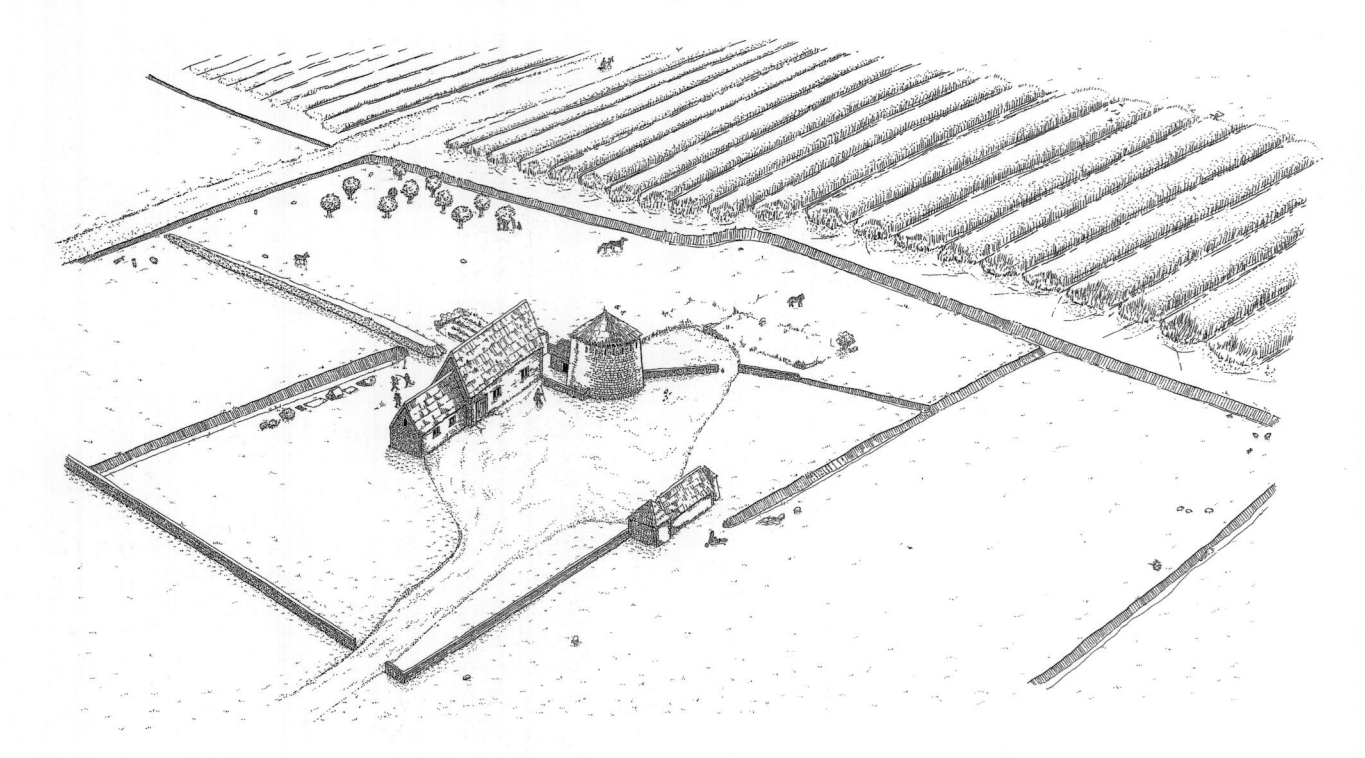

Fig 3.19: Furnells, reconstruction of the eastern manor (AD 1400)

and the dating of changes rests largely upon the introduction of late medieval reduced and oxidised wares for which the chronology is by no means securely established. A distinction between such events as the Great Famine of 1315–17, the Black Death of 1348–9 and subsequent calamities cannot therefore be easily made.

At Furnells the substance of the changing times may be embodied in the demolition of the old manor house and the building of a new manor house on the site of the redundant and levelled church (Figs 3.18 and 3.19). The new building probably coincided with a change in tenure, with the new manor no longer serving the seigneurial functions of its predecessors.

Contraction of settlement is perhaps shown by the decline in pottery collected from the hamlets and at the village edges. In some areas of medieval settlement there is almost a total absence of late medieval pottery, perhaps implying that after desertion these areas were maintained as pasture closes. The scale of changes within the villages is difficult to measure as it is uncertain how intensively these areas had been occupied previously. Nevertheless the eastern half of Thorpe End and much of North End in Raunds appears to have been abandoned prior to the widespread introduction of reduced ware in the fourteenth century.

The late medieval changes in the settlement pattern do not appear to have affected the manuring of the open fields. The density of sherds declines slightly, but the scatters continue up to the parish boundaries, suggesting that despite the population decline following the Black Death permanent pasture was still not widespread.

Furnells: the eastern manor (AD 1350/1400–1450)

In the later fourteenth century, Furnells manor was completely reorganised. The church, which may already have been redundant for some decades, was levelled, and a new manor house, the eastern manor, was constructed on the site of the church and its churchyard (Figs 3.18 and 3.19). The western manor was then levelled to the ground. This was the only physical relocation of the domestic quarters in over 500 years of settlement.

The new manor house comprised a central hall, with a parlour/solar to the east and a service wing to the west. The only features in the parlour end were the bases of narrow stone benches abutting the walls, while the hall contained the square stone base of a central open hearth.

The service wing contained a stone-lined trough, similar to features seen in the tenements at West Cotton (Chapman in press). Grey chemical staining and encrustation of the limestone suggests that they were used for some form of chemical processing, possibly the hand fulling of cloth to scour the natural greases and trampling to close the weave. The trough was later infilled and paved over. Immediately adjacent to the hall there was a stone plinth that probably supported a flight of timber stairs leading to an upper storey over the service wing. The westernmost service room contained two small openings into shallow garderobe pits set in the external wall face.

A free-standing dovecote lay to the north-west, but subsequently the open space between the dovecote and the manor house was walled-in to provide a small chamber with a flagstone floor, presumably used for storage, and a small walled yard metalled with limestone.

A detached kitchen range stood 30m north of the manor house. The eastern room contained a rectangular drying/malting oven and in the western room there was a rectangular fireplace against the side wall and a circular corner baking oven. A circular chamber at the west end of the building may have held the vat for the steeping of barley prior to sprouting and then drying to create the malt. Remnants of boundary walls suggest that there was a division between an eastern yard bounded by the manor house and the kitchen/bakehouse, and the area west of the dovecote, which the door of the dovecote door opened into (Figs 3.18 and 3.19). In addition, remnants of walls and a spread of stone rubble immediately west of the dovecote, which are visible on photographs but were not fully investigated, suggest the probable presence of a further stone building, which may have served an agricultural function as a barn and/or byre.

In the eastern manor, the arrangement of the buildings provided a distinction between the living quarters of the manor house, facing towards Rotton Row in the east, and the agricultural functions of the manor, as provided by the dovecote and a probable agricultural building, both facing the open fields to the west. By this date, the role of the manor house as a residence and the centre of a farm estate were probably its only functions. The hall no longer served seigneurial functions, and the reorganisation may have co-incided with a change of tenure, possibly the acquisition of Furnells by the Greene family, who owned many manors in both Northamptonshire and the surrounding counties.

The boundaries of the larger manorial enclosure appear to have remained largely unchanged. The main western ditch separating the manorial enclosure from the field system was retained, as was the ditch to the south of the manor house. The western edge of this same area was now marked by a low bank, which overlay part of the earlier ditch system.

Furnells: the smithy (AD 1450–1500)

The use of the new manor house at Furnells was short-lived, and before the end of the fifteenth century it had been abandoned, probably lying derelict and subject to intermittent scavenging of timber and stone. In the late fifteenth century the gutted remains of the hall were refurbished to accommodate the workshop of a smithy, with two small hearths or furnaces inserted into the western corners of the former hall. This use was probably short-lived. The hearths were sealed by a stone floor, perhaps related to a final use as an agricultural building, maybe a stock shed. By the end of the fifteenth century the ruins were levelled and manorial enclosure became a pasture close. The ghost of the final phase of manorial buildings survived in earthwork (Fig 3.20) until the housing development of the 1970s prompted its excavation in 1976.

Langham Road: tenement plots and field boundaries (AD 1350/1400–1500)

It proved impossible in most cases to distinguish late medieval from medieval features in these areas. At Langham Road the boundary system persisted but there continued to be little sign of occupation within the plots, which were presumably largely given over to horticulture or stock, with the open fields still to the west (Fig 3.18).

The plot boundaries still comprised a simple system of linear east–west ditches, which were retained into the post-medieval period until they were eventually replaced with stone boundary walls. More recent small-scale excavation in a plot to the south of the Langham Road site located an east–west boundary where successive late Saxon and medieval ditches were replaced by a stone wall in the sixteenth century (Morris 2002). This wall still stood until well into the twentieth century, and it was only finally levelled as the larger plots were broken up and sub-divided to allow infilling with modern housing.

Burystead; the manorial farm (AD 1350/1400–1500)

At Burystead the farm buildings, including the dovecote and malt house continued in use, set within a boundary system marked by stone walls (Fig 3.21). The dovecote was completely rebuilt twice. The first rebuilding was simply a new circular dovecote, but at a late date, probably no earlier than the end of the fourteenth century, it was demolished and replaced by a square dovecote, in the new fashion. Within the ruins of the second circular dovecote there was a deposit of eighteenth-century pottery and roof tile, possibly denoting the demolition date of the square dovecote.

Up to the time of excavation, a substantial stone wall still ran across the derelict closes, as the final reinstatement of the east–west boundary that had once marked the division between the plots pertaining to the Burystead manor and the tenement plots running down to the Midland Road.

The medieval and late medieval economy

There were very few soil samples from medieval features. However, wheat was still the most common cereal but there were also occasional finds of barley, rye and oat, although the two latter grains were less common than previously. Very few weed seeds were present but the proportion of leguminous weed seeds was generally higher than in earlier features. Otherwise, the weed flora was very similar to the late Saxon/Saxo-Norman assemblages with evidence for the cultivation of the same range of soil types and with a grassland element also present. There was very little chaff present in any of the samples.

There is evidence for the cultivation of pea probably from the middle Saxon period onwards and for horse/field bean (*Vicia faba* var. *minor*) from at least the twelfth century. In addition, seeds of cultivated common vetch

(*Vicia sativa* spp. *sativa*), which is grown for animal fodder, were identified in samples from twelfth-century deposits at Burystead. Particularly large numbers of legumes were recovered from post-medieval samples at the Midland Road frontage that may relate to the possible smithy. This may suggest a scenario where horses were fed, at least in part, on beans or vetch, whilst being shod or stabled in the smithy. A possible late medieval smithy at Furnells also produced a high percentage of large legume seeds.

There are occasional appearances of cultivated flax (*Linum usitatissimum*) in all periods and a single record of gold-of-pleasure (*Camelina sativa* cf. spp. *sativa*), which is grown for its oil, is also a typical weed of flax. The existence of five flax merchants in nearby Higham Ferrers in the medieval period attests to the importance of linen production in the area (Courtney pers comm). It has also been suggested that a stone-lined trough in the service wing of the eastern manor house may have been

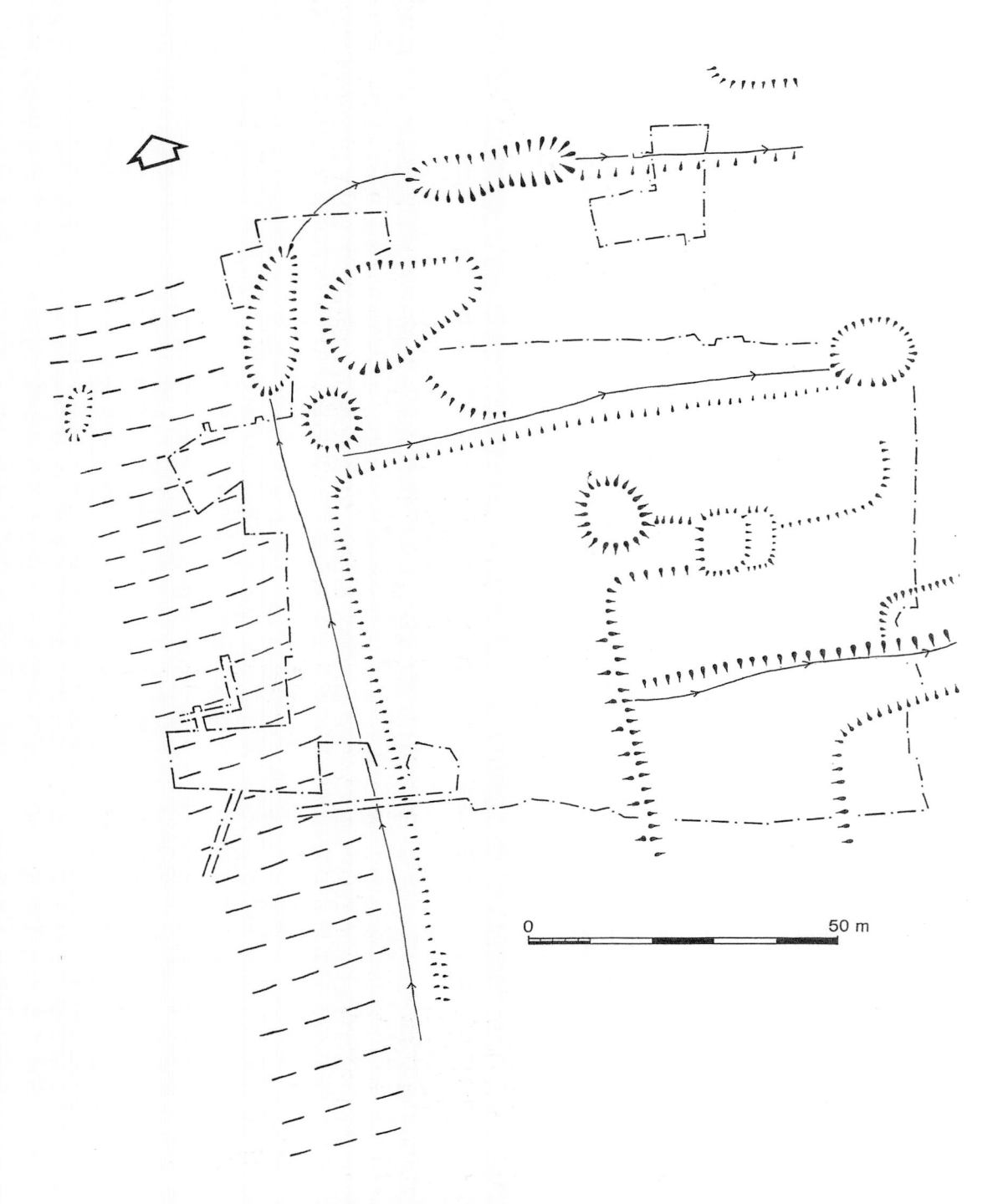

Fig 3.20: Furnells, the earthworks (based on Hall et al 1988, fig 2)

used for the fulling of cloth, perhaps also destined to go to market at Higham.

The recovery of large numbers of *Brassica* or *Sinapis* seeds in a medieval cess-pit at Furnells and black mustard (*Brassica nigra*) seeds in a late medieval oven at Burystead, suggest that this plant was being grown from the medieval period onwards either as a spice or for its oil. The presence of whole seeds mineralised in a cess-pit would suggest its use as a spice.

Bone preservation was generally poor, as there were few primary deposits and most bones had clearly been gnawed by dogs.

At Langham Road and Burystead the assemblages show only a slight increase in sheep, but not as marked as might be expected given the growth of the sheep trade in the medieval period. Age at death indicates animals were kept for wool and milk, and killed off for local consumption, but also with a steady kill-off of younger animals, more

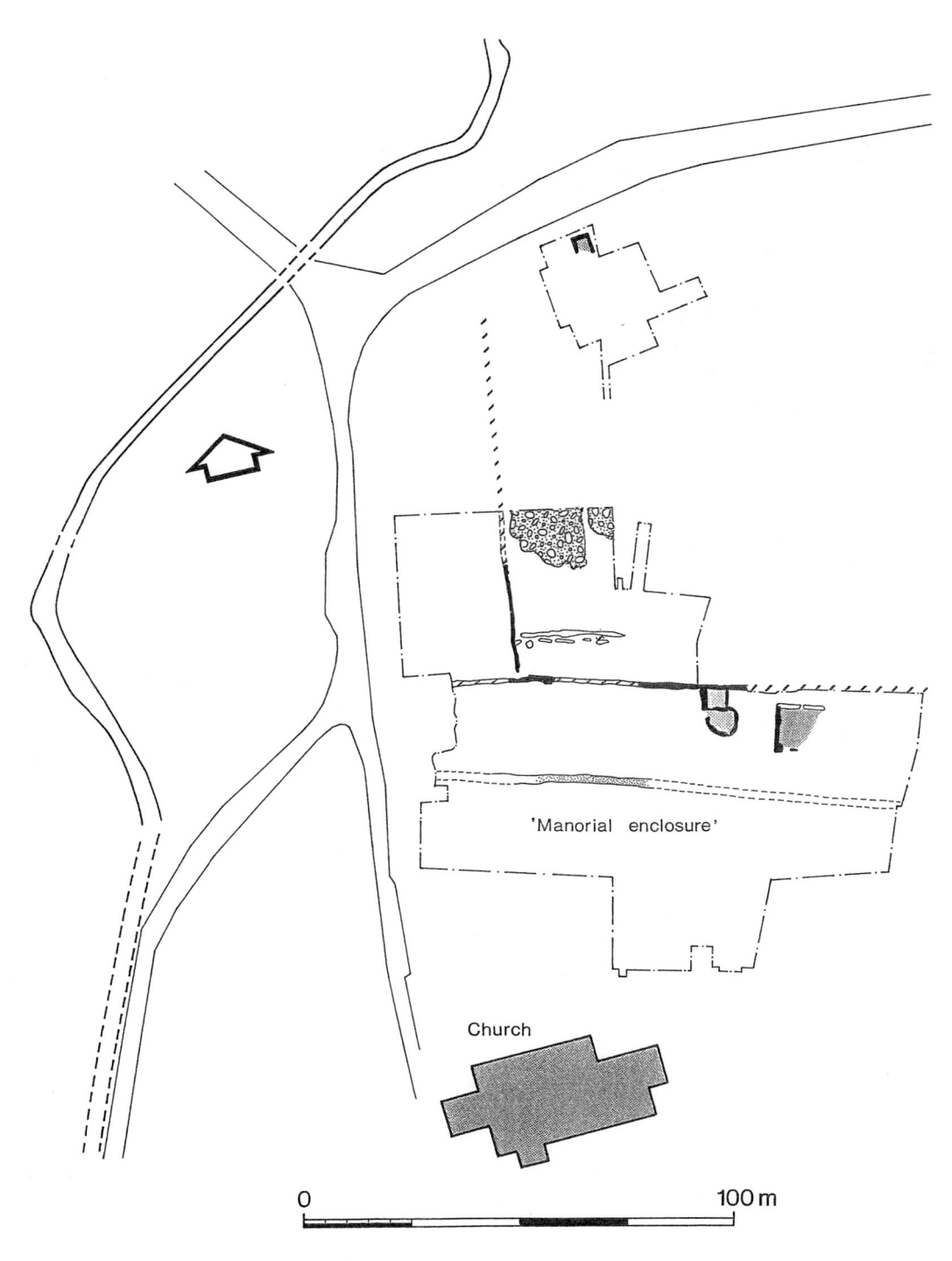

Fig 3.21: Burystead, the late medieval farm buildings (AD 1350/1400–1500)

so than from urban assemblages. One possibility is that mature animals were being sold into towns for the urban meat supply, with this causing a bias in their representation in the recovered assemblage.

At Burystead there was a high representation of horses, although much of this assemblage is of late medieval date or later. This includes a high proportion of old animals, perhaps suggesting that the Burystead closes were used for pasturing retired working animals. Two show skinning of horses and butchering for the consumption of horse meat, but whether fed to dogs or humans is unknown. An odd occurrence at Langham Road was the skull of a large dog or wolf from a medieval context, perhaps one of the last living wolves in England.

Birds are well represented in the assemblages. There is goose from the aisled hall at Furnells, and a goshawk from the eastern manor, while pigeon bones from the dovecote include a rock dove, *Columba livia*. Medieval pits at the Midland Road frontage included a common gull bone with knife marks suggesting consumption.

Fish were only rarely present. Thornback ray (*Raja clavata*) and cod (*Gadus Morhua*) were identified from medieval contexts and late medieval contexts at Midland Road contained herring and whiting.

The early post-medieval village (AD 1500 onward)

The later development of the village was beyond the remit of the Raunds Area Project, but the excavations on the Midland Road frontage provided an illustration of the relocation of domestic buildings from within their plots and onto the road frontages, which began in the 16th century.

Midland Road: the smithy (16th century)

Along Midland Road, the stone-founded medieval building was retained and phases of rebuilding can be discerned, ending with its eventual use, perhaps in the sixteenth century, as a smithy. This final phase is the first clear evidence of direct human usage of the buildings on the frontage. A determining factor in this case may have been the convenient location for a smith, whose activities would probably have included shoeing horses, showing an early appearance of the concept of consumer convenience.

Midland Road: the post-medieval tenements (17th century onward)

It was only into the seventeenth century that the smaller buildings were replaced by larger stone buildings that presumably mark the full development of domestic buildings along the Midland Road frontage. This frontage of small stone-footed cottages continued to be inhabited until the mid-twentieth century. Thus the tenements and rows outlived the manors, although their ancient layout continued to dominate the landscape around the parish church of St Peter at the core of the village.

From village to town

It is not within the scope of this study to trace the transformation of the post-medieval village into a Victorian small town with a local industry based primarily on the shoe factories and leather works, and with the consequent development of terraced housing for the workers and new shops to supply their needs.

At a superficial level it may be noted that much of the early stages of this process involved the development of vacant plots and paddocks, particularly around the southern margins of the village and along the main roads. The abandoned manorial plots of Furnells and Burystead, then pasture closes, were avoided, although both factory and housing development did occur further to the north along Midland Road.

As a result, by the later nineteenth century a village core of stone-built cottages and houses had become surrounded by the modern developments, often in brick rather than stone. The transformation of the core of the village to provide the facilities required for the ever growing small town was partly recorded photographically in the final decades of the nineteenth century and the opening decades of the twentieth. Reference may be made to the study of Hall *et al* (1988), which provides numerous before and after photographs recording this transformation in Raunds.

4 Archaeology and History

The virtues of large scale excavation

Large scale excavation is time-consuming, extremely expensive and, as the Raunds Area Project amply demonstrates, bringing the results to a published conclusion is a process that tends to leave many casualties in its wake; with the archaeology potentially one of those casualties.

However, the process also brings with it the benefits of scale and, as the Raunds Area Project also amply demonstrates, it is only as a result of the opportunity for cross-comparison between the three major excavations in north Raunds and a similar excavation at West Cotton in the valley, that individual events or building groups can be seen in a broader context as either typifying general and widespread changes of broad archaeological significance, or merely idiosyncrasies of the development of a single site with only a limited broader applicability. For early–middle Saxon settlement and the establishment of the open field system, the results of the Raunds Survey are also crucial.

Sites such as the deserted medieval hamlet of West Cotton, which previously were confidently regarded as secondary daughter settlements, can now be seen to have had a longer history and to have undergone a number of transformations in form and status, only the final stage of which can be read on the surface in the earthworks (Chapman in press). Similarly, in north Raunds, the North End of a bipartite medieval village, the manorial earthworks at Furnells were shown to conceal an unknown late Saxon church and churchyard while all surfaces traces of the earlier manorial buildings had been lost. The evidence illustrating the complex processes of reformation within the manorial plot in response to changing political and social circumstances were therefore only evident as a result of excavation. Conversely, at Burystead, the other manorial centre in north Raunds, the manor house confidently predicted from the documentary evidence was found, on excavation, to be absent. The plots had only been utilised for stone quarrying and, at a later date, contained the buildings of the demesne farm. The location of the manor house remains unknown, although clearly it is likely to have stood in another nearby plot close to the parish church.

So, despite the many advances in non-destructive fieldwork techniques and the potential of documentary analysis, it is clear that at present these can only tell part of the story, and large scale excavation is clearly a major tool in unravelling the complex physical truths of the processes involved in the evolution of manor and village.

The excavations in north Raunds have provided much new data for the entire period from the early Saxon settlement through to the desertion of manorial centres in the late medieval period, but most importantly they have addressed the issue of the nature and date of the reorganisation of settlement in the late Saxon period, and the relationship of these processes to the crucial historical episodes of the Danish occupation and the early tenth-century reconquest by the kings of Wessex, and thereafter the formation of the English village landscape.

The Raunds Area Project therefore demonstrates the benefits of using a wide-ranging, multi-disciplinary approach to the study of the history of a landscape. It is easy with hindsight to identify errors of judgement and areas where further work would have been beneficial, or even where detailed work was perhaps unnecessary. Nevertheless, the positive benefits of the study of the landscape as a totality have been amply demonstrated and will hopefully lead to further, similar studies elsewhere.

Archaeology and the physical evidence of historical change

The settlement of north Raunds emerged against a background of matter of great moment, which included the Danish presence during the ninth century, the return of the Danelaw to English lordship in the early tenth century, and the internecine warfare and eventual conquest of England which took place during the eleventh century.

The interaction between these events and a small settlement of the Midlands is of course impossible to establish event by event. However, from the archaeological record we can draw a number of broad inferences although, despite the scale of the works, there is still so much that is uncertain, particularly the lack of precise dating, that others may wish to interpret this evidence differently.

Once the evidence for a widespread reorganisation of settlement had emerged from the excavations, two major related issues were whether this reorganisation could be ascribed to the period of the Danelaw or to the reconquest, and the nature of the relationship between the establishment of the formalised settlement plots and the establishment of the open field system.

Neither question can be said to have been answered definitively at any single site, largely due to the problems of dating, but when the work at all three north Raunds sites as well as at West Cotton is taken into account, the similarities and contrasts in both physical development and the associated material remains has enabled the construction of a robust chronological model. The differences between this model and the provisional chronological sequences for Furnells, provides an illustration of the benefits that have accrued through the scale of the work at so many separate locations.

Early–middle Saxon dispersed settlement

The model for the early–middle Saxon dispersed settlement pattern, and its demise, has come from the work of the Raunds Survey (Parry 2006). Within north Raunds there was evidently an early Saxon settlement at Furnells comprising an untidy arrangement of buildings, and something similar was present on the opposite stream bank at Burystead. This provides a further example of early settlements on either side of water courses, as seen within the broader picture provided by the survey.

The settlement at Furnells was either abandoned by the late seventh century or had been relocated south to Langham Road, where a cluster of small timber houses formed a small but well arranged farm dated to the middle Saxon by the presence of imported Maxey ware and Ipswich ware, which was absent at Furnells. At Burystead occupation continued through the middle Saxon period, as indicated by the pottery and a radiocarbon date from a timber-lined water pit, but again there was too much disturbance for any form to the settlement to be defined.

The Danish settlement

The first evidence for the presence of settlement with an enhanced status, and perhaps providing a central and dominant role within the broader community, comes with the re-establishment of occupation at Furnells in the mid-ninth century. The so-called Anglo-Scandinavian farm has not only a more formal structure, but one that appears to make a clear distinction between public and private spaces; with a timber hall to the north at the end of the main access route from the east, while a similar hall set within a ditched enclosure to the south provided a private space, and one from which all ancillary buildings appear to have been excluded. This does suggest the appearance of a central authority and perhaps one to which other nearby settlements owed dues in cash, kind and service, recognised and paid through attendance at the hall.

The establishment before the end of the ninth century of what may, rather clumsily, be called a proto-manor must therefore date to the period of the Danish settlement of eastern England. From the evidence it is not possible to directly link these events in north Raunds to the larger landscape, but it is possible that the appearance of a central place in north Raunds was not unrelated to the progressive abandonment of dispersed settlement and the beginnings of the process of nucleation within a more limited number of locations, the villages and perhaps some of the vale hamlets, although not at West Cotton, and clustering around higher-status foci.

The reconquest

It appears to be only following the reconquest by the kings of Wessex in the early tenth century and the establishment of the Danelaw, which effectively occupied the area east of Roman Watling Street, the present A5, that a further major step in the process of nucleation was taken; the controlled reorganisation of the very structure of the emerging nucleated settlements.

The evidence at Furnells shows that this did not happen in isolation as an imperious replanning showing no respect for existing conventions and practices. The high-status residence at Furnells was retained and incorporated into the new arrangement, inaugurating a period of long-term stability in the settlement pattern. From this point onwards, the manorial status of Furnells can not only be recognised but, most importantly, can be characterised. Indeed, far from overthrowing the existing systems, the reorganisation may have overlain it and, in so doing, strengthened the growth of what was to become the manorial system following the Norman Conquest of the eleventh century.

The late Saxon village

The basis of the late Saxon reorganisation was the establishment of a co-ordinated and consistent land allocation to all members of society. The digging of ditches to mark these plots would have been a huge undertaking entailing a major expenditure of manpower. However, the ultimate success of this process can be measured by the survival of so many elements of the system through the succeeding centuries. In fact, it would not be an overstatement to say that it was the physical act of marking these plots on the ground, and the consequent allocation of the defined land parcels, that was the primary act of transforming a vague process of nucleation around high status foci to a concrete realisation of a structured and hierarchical village society, with its manor house, church, tenements and watermills, creating a sustainable and near self-sufficient community. There can be few conscious acts of social re-planning that have stood the test of time so well.

The evidence from north Raunds therefore addresses a number of questions raised in the study of medieval settlement in Central England. In a recent assessment (Lewis *et al* 2001), lacking any quantity of excavated evidence, it was suggested that that the weight of probability would favour a gradual and piecemeal development of nucleated settlement, rather than a single cataclysmic transformation, with many settlements perhaps only becoming ordered and nucleated as late as the twelfth century (*ibid*, 182–183). The evidence from north Raunds, if more widely applicable, would suggest that this is an unnecessarily conservative view, with the process of formal plot formation that lies at the heart of creating the ordered settlement across north

Raunds, quite clearly originating in the decades before the mid-tenth century and apparently as a single act.

The suggestion is that while there may have been distinct stages of development, the late Saxon introduction of regular plots formalising a process of nucleation around a high status foci that had begun in the late ninth century, was a sudden and dramatic event, which may not be unique to the Raunds area. Perhaps the secret lay in good management of the process to dispel or defuse the potential for such an event to be as cataclysmic for the society as it evidently was for the physical landscape.

The metrication of the village planning by Andy Chapman

The physical reality of the planning comprised the definition of blocks of rectangular ditched plots. The analysis of the settlement plan at West Cotton, which was generally less disturbed than the north Raunds sites, has shown that these were typically based on nominal one-acre plots, with sub-divisions into half and quarter-acres (Chapman in press). At West Cotton and less certainly at Furnells, Langham Road and Burystead the basic metrication for these plots has been established as a one-acre plot that was 20 rods (100m) long by 8 rods (40m) wide, with the half-acre plots usually simply half that length, 10 rods (50m), with these split lengthwise to form quarter-acre plots, 10 rods (50m) long by 4 rods (20m) wide.

A model for the plot formation at Furnells and Langham Road has been constructed (Fig 4.1). Its metrication is based on the standardised rod of 16.5 feet (5.03m), as defined in later medieval documents (Zupko 1968, 144–5). It may also be noted that the settlement plot acres were half the length and twice the width of the statutory acre applicable to land allocation in the fields, as also defined in later medieval documents (Zupko 1968, 3–4). On the ground it is easiest to define extant plot widths, and at West Cotton, Furnells and Langham Road (Fig 4.1), and Burystead there are clear examples of widths of 40m (8 rods) and 20m (4 rods). Lengths are more difficult to determine with any precision as the plot ends lay at the common boundaries, such as the roads, which have been liable to realignment and drift. However, at all the sites it is possible to infer the probable former existence of plot lengths of 20 rods (100m). In addition, the complexities of landscape topography obviously rarely permitted the simple provision of accurate rectangular plots of the correct acreage, and in many instances what was actually provided were clearly nominal plots, typically slightly on the small size.

The extent of the late Saxon land allocation within Raunds has been shown by the three main excavations and by trial excavations by the Survey team, with late Saxon boundary ditches located for a total distance of around 1km. The method of setting out the plots may be indicated on the west bank at north Raunds, where there is a dislocation in the western boundary system between the manorial plots of Furnells and the tenement plots to the south at Langham Road. This suggests that we are not looking at a single co-ordinated setting out over the entire extent of the village which, as noted above, would be impossible anyway given topographical constraints. The process was most probably one of setting out successive blocks of several acres of plots at a time. The setting out of the manorial plot at Furnells was therefore probably separate from but closely related to, the setting out of tenement plots to the south at Langham Road.

The open fields

A significant dislocation between the boundary systems at Furnells and Langham Road occurred in the main western boundary, a ditch system that at Furnells still formed a prominent earthwork up to the time of the excavations. This boundary was evidently the division between the closes and tenements of Furnells manor and Langahm Road, and the open field system on the higher ground to the west.

While there was a dislocation in the late Saxon setting out of this boundary, it only amounted to a few metres, indicating that the blocks of settlement plots at Furnells and Langham Road were being set out with respect to a common recognised boundary between the settlement and the fields. While it cannot be demonstrated, it seems likely that the two processes of settlement and field system reorganisation may well have been introduced as a single package. However, as we have seen with the settlement reorganisation, this does not preclude the possibility that this was the formalisation of processes that had already begun under the Danes in the ninth century.

Pre-conquest manors

The tenth-century reorganisation was also marked by the establishment of a new building complex at Furnells. As already indicated, the new plot system had respected the presence of the Anglo-Scandinavian farm, and was created around it. Similarly, the new buildings stood slightly apart from the two main existing post-built halls, so we can imagine these still occupied while the new buildings were going up next door.

At the heart of the new complex at Furnells was a remarkable structure, the long range. This timber building complex, characterised by the foundations being set in continuous wall trenches, comprised an open hall to the north, with an attached series of rooms *en suite*, presumed to be the private quarters, to the south. This form of structure was, however, far from unique to Furnells. At West Cotton, there was a hall of closely comparable size, although the attached domestic quarters were less extensive (Fig 4.2). The hall at West Cotton was later widened slightly, when it was converted to an aisled hall, while a similar conversion of the hall at Furnells was on a much grander scale, and increased the width of the hall significantly. However, the initial similarities are so close that they appear to have issued from the same standard design model.

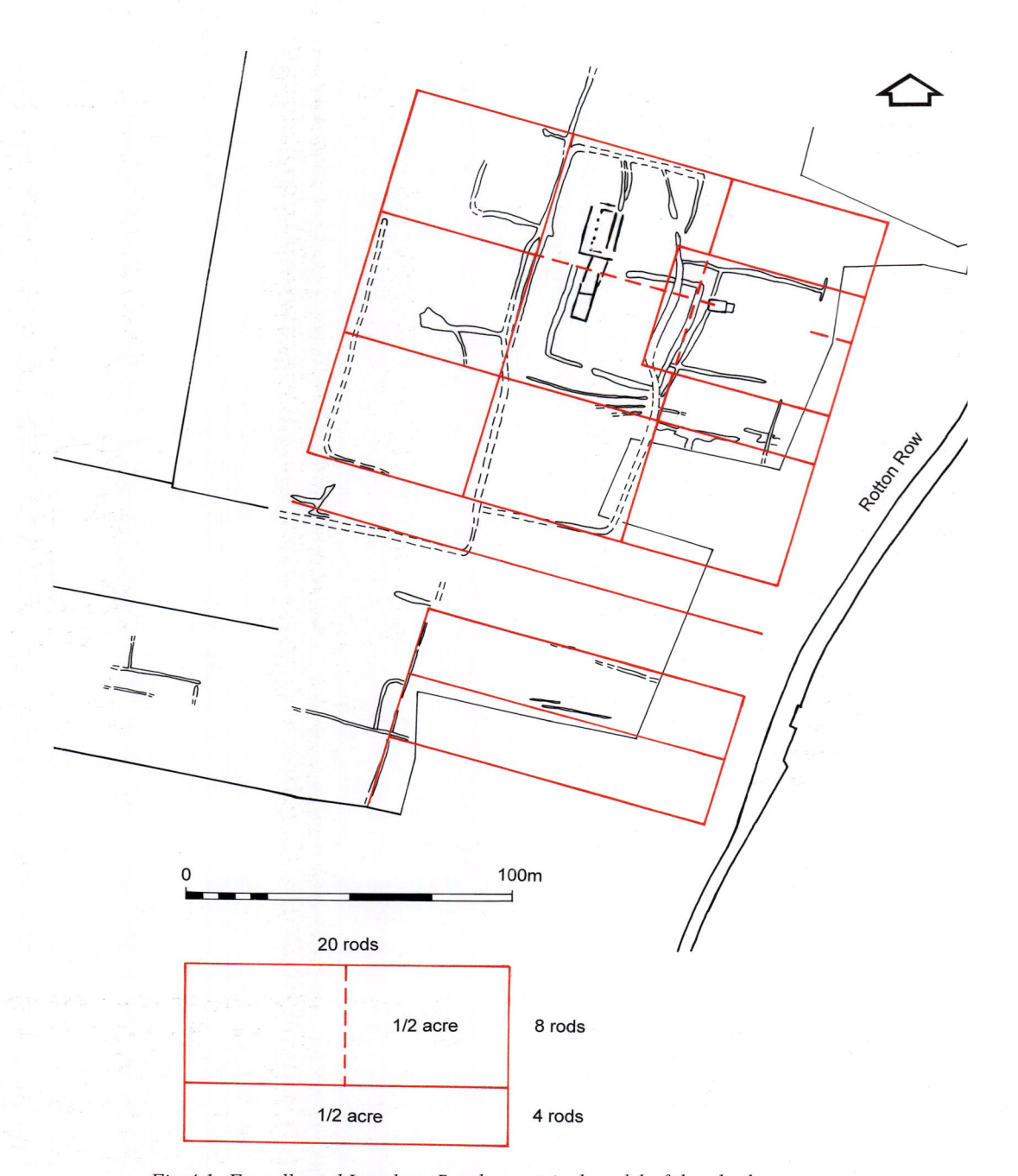

Fig 4.1: Furnells and Langham Road, a metrical model of the plot layout

Such standardisation was more widespread, as the characteristics of the late Saxon settlements and buildings at Raunds can be identified over a much larger territory. In particular, contemporary and almost identical structures are known in Lincolnshire at Goltho (Beresford 1987) and a further example, from beyond the Danelaw, comes from Faccombe Netherton in Hampshire (Fairbrother 1990) (Fig 4.2). Another example, also from Hampshire at Brighton Hill South, apparently only appeared in the mid-eleventh century (Fasham and Keevill 1995, 77–146). Not only were there close similarities of size and layout but, in the case of Furnells, Goltho and Faccombe Netherton, there was also a common development of a larger aisled hall in the eleventh or twelfth centuries. A tentative conclusion would be that these long ranges represent an Anglo-Saxon, possibly Wessex tradition, which was implanted following the reconquest of the Danish occupied lands in the early tenth century.

It is not only the long ranges themselves that are so similar. At all of these sites the arrangement of the accom-

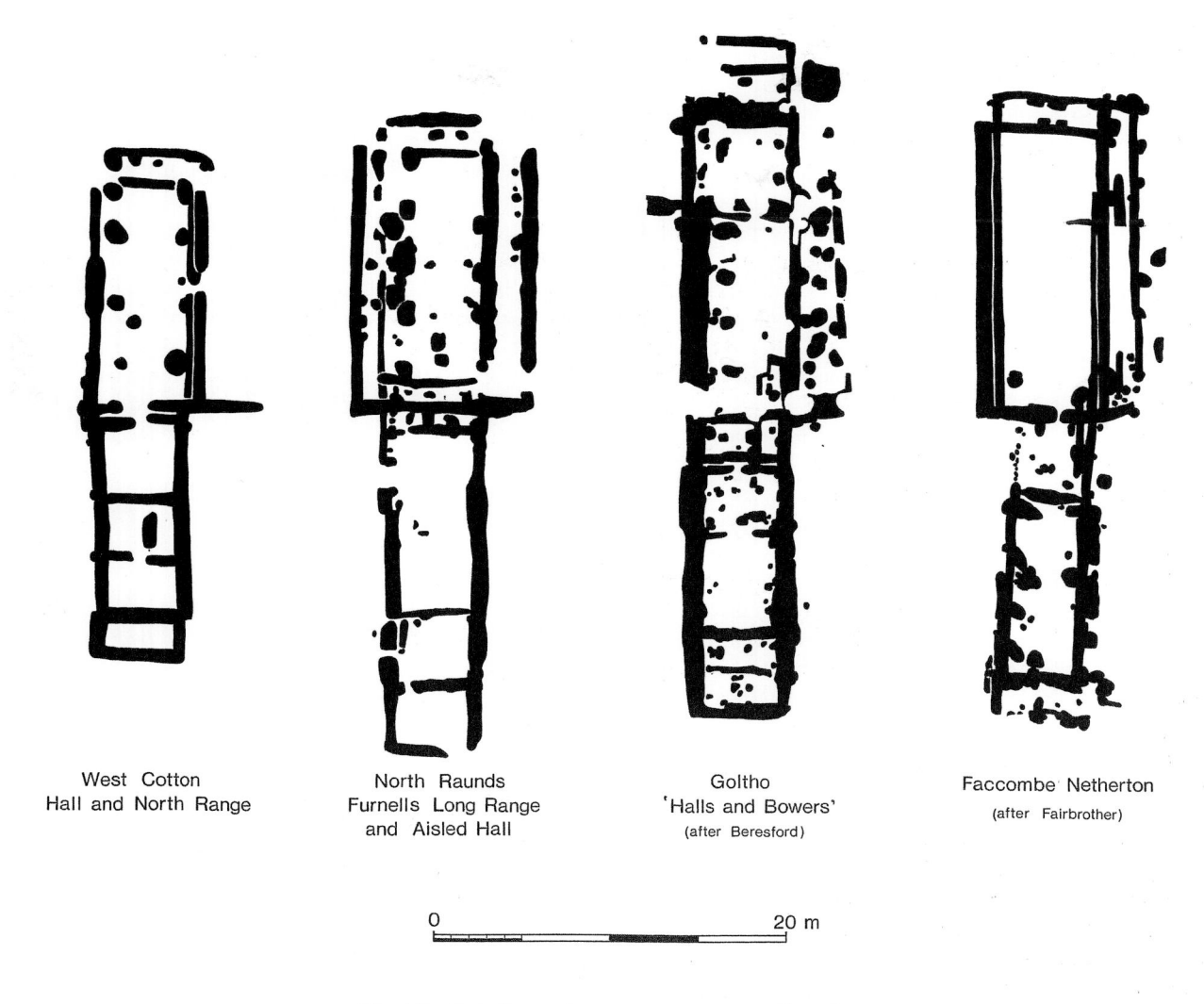

Fig 4.2: Late Saxon long ranges, comparative plans

panying buildings also followed the same pattern. The hall end of the long range was approached directly by the principal access to the site, thus forming the public space, while there was typically a physical boundary, usually a ditch system, blocking access to the adjacent private space of the attached apartments, which faced onto an enclosed courtyard surrounded by the ancillary buildings, including a detached kitchen range.

The archaeological traits of these building complexes, as well as the presence by the end of the tenth century of a church at Furnells and a watermill at West Cotton, are attributes which would be expected of a medieval manor. The inevitable conclusion is that their early occurrence bears witness to what is in effect a pre-Conquest manorial system, with the hall acting as a local administrative centre. In addition, by the end of the tenth century the status of Furnells was further reinforced by the provision of a small church set within a churchyard. This included a founder's grave marked by an interlace grave slab, probably with a similarly decorated free-standing cross shaft at its head.

Domesday Book and the manorial status of Furnells and the Cottons
by Paul Courtney

Domesday Book (I,220) makes it quite plain that Burgred held his manor in Raunds by sake and soke, which is an indication of bookright. The centre of this manor was probably Furnells and its demesne was described as follows: 2 demesne ploughs, 4 slaves, 4 villeins, and 6 bordars with 2 (tenant) ploughs, a mill worth 34s 8d and 100 eels and 20 acres of meadow. A subordinate entry also lists that 3 sokemen in Raunds held 2 hides, Robert 1 hide, Geoffrey 1 hide and Algar 1.5 virgates. In demesne they held 6.5 ploughs, and had 7 villeins, 4 bordars and 2 slaves with 2 (tenant ploughs), and a mill worth 12d. Domesday Book cannot be regarded, however, as giving a full list of the inhabitants of Raunds. Certainly later medieval records suggest that Ringstead, which was not mentioned in Domesday Book, was dominated by free tenants, who may have been the descendants of eleventh-century sokemen.

It is possible that Ringstead was included under Denford in Domesday Book, of which it was later a chapelry, but it is just as likely that its inhabitants are only recorded as part of the overall manorial value of Burgred's manor in Raunds, a not uncommon feature of Domesday Book sokemen (see Walmersley 1968 and Roffe 1990, 332–3).

The holdings of Burgred's three sokemen and three named men cannot be identified on the ground, though they probably included Mill Cotton, Mallows Cotton and West Cotton. The 12d mill certainly seems likely to have been the one excavated at West Cotton. The three Cottons are first recorded in the Northamptonshire survey of the twelfth century (VCH Northants 1, 377) and can be traced as knight's fees of the Clare/Gloucester fee from the thirteenth century onwards. The Cottons were, however, clearly not regarded by Domesday Book as manors and must have been subordinate to Burgred's presumed hall at Furnells.

There is no agreed definition of the term manor (Latin *manerium*) among modern historians nor was there in the medieval past. Indeed, a case can be made that the term manorialism, like that other imprecise concept, feudalism, should be abandoned by modern historians (Brown 1974, 1088). The origins of the English manor, economically defined as a lord's estate with a demesne (home farm) and dependent tenants owing rents and services, are now seen to lie well within the Anglo-Saxon period (Aston 1958). A great variety in both size and organisation of manors already existed by the time of Domesday Book. Indeed there were manors which had no demesne and no unfree tenants. By the fourteenth century the term *manerium* was also slowly assuming a legal meaning, not fully formalised until the seventeenth century, regarding a lord's juridical rights, especially his right to hold manorial courts. Such a legal definition, however, is not applicable to earlier centuries (Holdsworth 1922, 181).

The word *manerium* was introduced to England by the Normans and is a latinisation of the old french *manoir*, a dwelling, a word derived from the latin word *manere*, to remain (OED *sub* manor). Stenton (1971, 480) saw the latin *manerium* as an equivalent to the old english *heafod botl*, a chief dwelling, a term he argues was being used by the end of the tenth century to cover not only the house of a lord but the adjacent lands which contributed to its maintenance. In Domesday Book the term *manerium* was used to define the centre of an estate. However, many subordinate units which were not regarded by Domesday Book as manors (eg the Peverel holding in Raunds) possessed demesnes, subordinate peasantry and presumably halls at which dues and services were rendered. Some scholars, following Maitland (1897) rather than Round (1900) have seen the Domesday Book manor and not the vill as a geld collection centre (eg Palmer 1987). The complex relationship between manor and vill (the latter being clearly the unit of geld assessment) in northern England, however, suggests that this is unlikely (Roffe 1981). Furthermore the implied alienation of royal rights would be totally out of character with the policy of the Wessex dynasty in this period (D R Roffe pers comm). Modern working definitions of the term manor include a "centre for payment of dues in cash, kind and service" (Chibnall 1986, 136) and "equivalent to the rights that a lord had in land and men round his residence" (Miller 1966).

The question of whether West Cotton should be regarded as a manor is to some extent merely a matter of semantics. It does, however, lead us onto the rather more interesting, if equally thorny, question of its social and tenurial status prior to 1066. As we have seen, Domesday Book sheds no light on the tenurial status of the Cottons beyond the fact that they were clearly not regarded as manors. They may have been held in 1066 as sokeland (land held freely by a sokeman who owed soke dues to a lord), as loanland (leased, often for three lives), or as an appurtenance to an office (similar to dregnage and thegnage tenure in the north).

Domesday Book suggests there was an overlap in economic status between the lesser thegns and the wealthier freemen. Thegns, for instance, are recorded at Eaton, Carlton and Headon in Nottinghamshire with holdings worth a few shillings (DB, I, fos 284–5; Stenton 1910, 22 and 63); while a *liber homo* at Bungay in Suffolk held 5 carucates with 22 villeins, 22 bordars and 3 serfs (DB, II, f.330; VCH Suffolk I, 372–3). Abels (1988, 144) has argued that some sokemen and *liberi homines* attended the King's army alongside thegns either to discharge their own tenurial obligations or those of their landlord. There was, however, a sharp distinction in social standing as is shown by the six-fold difference in Mercia between the wergeld (blood-price) of a thegn and an ordinary freeman (EHD I, 443). An early eleventh-century source indicates that if a *ceorl* (freeman) prospered so as to possess "fully five hides of his own, a bell and a *burgh*-gate, a seat and special office in the King's hall, then was he henceforth entitled to the rights of a thegn". One manuscript also adds a church and a kitchen to the list (EHD I, 432; Lieberman 1903, 456).

The later manorial history and archaeology of Furnells strongly suggest that it can be identified with the hall of Burgred's manor in 1066. This manor was held by bookright and had probably been granted off from the Higham estate. Most likely it was being farmed for an annual rent in the eleventh century. West Cotton was clearly not regarded by Domesday Book as a manor and must have been subordinate to Burgred's hall. The tenure and social status (whether median thegn or sokeman/freeman) of the holder of West Cotton are far from clear. One must distinguish between the hall as an architectural type, as revealed by excavation, and the hall as a legal concept as revealed by the documents. However, it is possible that West Cotton had its own unfree tenants who rendered rent and labour services at its hall. Indeed in economic rather than tenurial terms it may have differed little in its operation to Furnells. In regard to the material culture of the two sites, it is not impossible that the residents of the Cottons could have been of higher status and wealth than the farmer who actually lived at Furnells.

The rise and fall of the medieval village

The archaeological evidence from north Raunds for the processes of village formation through the ninth and tenth centuries has provided new evidence of national importance in understanding the nature and origin of those processes. In contrast, the evidence for the later development of the village, from the Norman Conquest onward, is adding important information, but in relation to processes that are already far better understood both archaeologically and through the historical record. The latter centuries are therefore only briefly set within their historic context.

Medieval village development

There were no immediate consequences of the Norman Conquest that are evident in the archaeological record. Indeed, at Langham Road and Burystead most of the features can only be broadly dated to the tenth–eleventh centuries, showing a pattern of continuity in which the established boundary systems were maintained by periodic cleaning and recutting. At Langham Road, the small middle Saxon farm, perhaps levelled at the creation of the boundary system as it lay on the margin of the newly established open field, was replaced by a similar arrangement of timber halls, providing a contrast to the establishment at Furnells. The farm placed to the rear of its plot, was in use until the end of the twelfth century, when it was perhaps relocated eastward onto the eastern half of the plot as a first stage in the move towards the development of the road frontage.

At Furnells, the twelfth century saw the refurbishment of the hall, with its rebuilding as wider aisled hall. The small late Saxon church and churchyard continued in use, although at some stage the focus of the late Saxon founder's grave, with its interlace decorated grave slab, was replaced by a new focus of high class burials. These included a number of stone coffins outside the door of the church. However, through the earlier twelfth century the site may been in a period of decline as it never acquired a stone Norman hall, even though its lesser neighbour at West Cotton did.

It was in the thirteenth century that Furnells manor reached the apogee of its development, when in the hands of the Furneus family. A new church had been provided after the middle of the twelfth century, and at around the end of the century the timber buildings were cleared to make way for a stone-built manor house. While the hall stood throughout, the detached ancillary buildings underwent a number of modifications, suggesting that the manor was at the centre of a buoyant and developing economy, with the processing of malt as a cash crop for the markets at Higham the most readily identifiable aspect. The chapel was later also enhanced by the raising of a tower over the nave, even though it was then only a manorial chapel, with burial rights transferred to the much grander church that had arisen on the other side of the valley attached to the Burystead manor. At Burystead, the plots to the north of the new church, previously utilised as stone quarries, acquired buildings of the manorial demesne farm, including a dovecote and malt house. This expansion at Burystead indicates that this too was a manor at the centre of a buoyant and developing agricultural economy.

Late medieval decline

The travails of the fourteenth century, culminating in the Black Death of 1348–50, led to many changes in society, and the decline of the manorial system was a consequence of these changes. At Furnells this saw a radical reorganisation of the manorial enclosure. Both the western manor house and the church were levelled, and a new house was built over the remains of the church, thus moving the manor house towards the frontage and away from the rear of the plot where the major domestic buildings had stood for the previous 400 years. This may have occurred following the purchase of the manor by the Greene family, marking the economic rise of a farming family effectively supplanting the manorial system both as one of the major movers in the running of the agricultural regime, along with other similar families, and then occupying and rebuilding the very manor houses themselves. In this we see the beginnings of the post-medieval squirarchy, which adopted the manners and something of the status of their former overlords.

By the sixteenth century the physical reformation of the medieval village was also well advanced. The new manor house at Furnells was abandoned and, after a period of semi-dereliction and casual reuse, it was demolished. At the same time, the use of a building on the road frontage at Midland Road as a smithy marked the first step towards bringing the domestic residences of the rich and poor off their plots and onto the road frontages, where the story moves beyond the evidence acquired through the excavations of the Raunds Area Project in north Raunds.

5 The Archaeological Evidence

Identification, retrieval and analysis

The archaeology of north Raunds is a resource that may contribute to a variety of research areas. The extent to which the information may be significant is, however, dependent upon its potential for generating sound inferences, offering a high level of interpretation.

An assessment of the detail of the archaeological evidence from north Raunds indicates several negative characteristics, reflecting impacts which undoubtedly must affect its ultimate level of interpretation. These include the tendency of activities to erode rather than accumulate deposits, the dryness of the site which has affected the preservation of organic remains, and a high level of cultural disturbance characterised by the general lack of primary stratified deposits and a fragmentary and mixed finds assemblage. Archaeological excavation and the techniques of its recording and subsequent analysis also have had an influence on the final level of interpretation. However, the preservation of the three sites is at least average, if not somewhat above average, for such settlement areas left abandoned on the margins of living villages. In particular, the common availability of stone and its use in major domestic buildings from the late twelfth century onward has provided more complete and interpretable building plans than would be available from areas where timber buildings were the norm.

Also counterbalancing the negative effects, there is the exceptional scale and scope of the work involved both in north Raunds and with the closely comparable material from nearby West Cotton (Chapman in press). The recovery of numerous near contemporary building plans at separate sites and the examination of the associated features and boundary systems has enabled general patterns of planning, organisation and building practices to be distinguished from individual idiosyncrasies, and this more than compensates for any small-scale problems deriving from any inadequacies of excavation, analysis, interpretation or a lack of sufficient reliable dating evidence.

What has emerged is a comprehensive model for the origins and development of the north Raunds area, whilst accepting that some individual elements of this model cannot be fully validated by the detailed site record and are dependant on analogy with similar and better quality and/or better-dated evidence from other parts of the overall project.

Excavation strategy

The main sites were investigated by open area excavation, although in all cases the total areas exposed were achieved in a series of smaller stages, so that a full view was only available towards the end of the process. The topsoil and subsoil was always removed by mechanical excavator fitted with a toothless bucket. The sites had not been ploughed since their abandonment and were all pasture closes under grass. Inevitably, some quantity of unstratified cultural material will have been lost at this stage.

The archaeological surfaces exposed by machine stripping were cleaned by hand and all stratified deposits and associated cut features were excavated fully, apart from parts of major ditch systems and some of the quarried areas, which were selectively sampled. Smaller machine-dug trenches and observations of general development construction trenches were also employed at the periphery of the main open areas, to determine the general extent and nature of former activity.

The ease of recognising features varied greatly with the type of subsoil and weather conditions. The clay subsoil caused problems as frequently it was either too wet or too dry for effective excavation, and some features are likely to have been missed. The Cornbrash caused no more than minor difficulties, as only smaller postholes with fills consisting of limestone fragments were hard to identify.

Artefacts, including animal bones, were collected by hand. The faunal assemblage from north Raunds is characterised by a poor state of preservation and a high ratio of teeth to bone, and the bulk of the material was inevitably derived from secondly deposits, such as the boundary ditches, where recutting and cleaning inevitably led to much mixing of soils, as indicated by the high percentages of residual pottery.

A comprehensive environmental sampling policy was applied at Langham Road and Burystead in the later 1980s but not at Furnells in the late 1970s to early 1980s, where a limited wet-sieving programme retrieved smaller mammal and bird bones from selected features, such as hearths, pits and occupation surfaces. As the sites did not include any deposits which had remained permanently waterlogged, classes of material usually associated with such deposits (insects, pollen, waterlogged plant remains) were not available for study and the archaeobotanical record was limited to material that had been preserved through charring or, in a few cases, had become mineralised through contact with cess.

In spite of their common conceptual framework, each excavation was funded and undertaken independently as a localised reaction to a specific development in Raunds. This inevitably restricted the choice of location and the timing of the archaeological investigation, but provided opportunities of scale only rarely available.

Post-excavation background

The post-excavation programme of each site and the concomitant compilation of a research archive was the responsibility of the individual site directors. The series of post-excavation programmes commenced with that of Furnells. As with the site recording policies, this work set an analytical framework which was to become common to all subsequent excavations in north Raunds, thereby creating a series of compatible research archives which have enabled the results to be integrated into this report.

Throughout the programme of analysis, the identification and initial interpretation of the main structural elements of each site was therefore carried out by the individual responsible for the excavation. In the case of Furnells, an overall chronology was established shortly after the end of the excavations (Cadman *et al* 1983). The model was refined during subsequent analysis and culminated in the production of a first draft report in 1989. In the course of the integration of all the north Raunds sites into a single report, the stratigraphic and ceramic evidence from Furnells was reappraised. This resulted in a revised phasing and chronology, which forms the basis for the present report. The further reconsideration of the north Raunds evidence while drafting texts for the proposed medieval synthesis volume in the 1990s has also been incorporated.

Nature of the evidence and analytical strategy

Generally, significant vertical stratification was only encountered directly over and adjacent to former medieval stone buildings. The depth of accumulation was generally shallow, 500mm, with the exception of the late medieval, eastern manor and underlying churches at Furnell, where it attained 1.0m in places.

Elsewhere, stratification consisted of one to two horizons of agricultural subsoil that sealed truncated cut archaeological features. This soil cover was generally 300–500mm thick with the exception of a surviving headland from the former open field cultivation at Langham Road where an accumulation of up to 1m was recorded at the south-western end of the site. The headland was made up of two broad horizons of soils and sealed middle Saxon remains.

On the eastern stream bank, the covering of soil was on average some 300mm deep, but increasing in places to 500–600mm in the south-western corner of the Midland Road site and the extreme southern part of the Burystead site. The underlying archaeological remains consisted mainly of patchy layers of rubble and features cut into the natural geology.

The cumulative effect of periodic building repair, replacement or their systematic robbing, together with the routine maintenance of ditches, the quarrying of stone, agricultural practices and other such activities, resulted in the loss of primary deposits, such as floors and the ground surface of the early settlement, and the displacement of any cultural material within these deposits.

Poor survival of undisturbed archaeological soils at each site implies that any structural activity that did not penetrate the subsoil will have left little direct evidence.

The range of manufacturing techniques which were probably practised in the area is only indirectly reflected by the building techniques, the presence of slag from smelting or smithing, spindle-whorls and loomweights for spinning and weaving, bone needles for sewing and a range of other tools found in mixed deposits.

Relative chronology

At site level, individual phasing was achieved on stratigraphical grounds wherever possible. At Furnells two good relative sequences could be established, one for the late Saxon and medieval halls and the other for the churches and the late medieval manor. Likewise, at the Midland Road frontage, a relative sequence linked several phases of late medieval to early post-medieval buildings. Elsewhere, however, stratification was poor and inter-relationships between features were scarce. In consequence, only the broadest chronological approach is possible, though within each major period the significant phases of the better-stratified part of any site can be discussed. Generally, however, the phasing of a large number of features which stood in stratigraphical isolation has been based entirely on the characteristics of the pottery assemblage they contained. The dating of stratigraphically isolated buildings is especially difficult since in most instances the fill of the component postholes or slots cannot be related directly to either construction or demolition. Even in the case of the better-stratified series of buildings at Furnells the degree of contamination, both residual and intrusive, has hampered precise dating. On all sites, and particularly at Langham Road and Burystead, a large number of isolated features did not contain ceramics, and many of these did not conform to a particular pattern, so that they cannot be associated with any specific use or period of activity.

The only absolute dating from north Raunds is provided by 13 radiocarbon results taken on samples of charcoal and bone from Furnells and a single charcoal sample from Burystead (see below). Their value is limited in that none is representative of a context which formed part of a good relative sequence. Most came from isolated pits or postholes and others derive from the skeletal remains from selected graves in the churchyard.

Similarly, such coins as were found occurred outside the main relative sequences and therefore are of little help in the calendar dating of phases.

The radiocarbon dates

Nine samples of human bone from burials at Furnells were submitted for radiocarbon dating as part of the programme of analysis of the church and churchyard sequence (Boddington 1996, 72). A further four samples from Furnells were submitted to the Harwell Laboratory as part of the broader analysis of the site, and a single sample from Burystead was submitted to the Queen's University Laboratory, Belfast.

Early–middle Saxon chronology

Two of the samples from Furnells are from pre-graveyard contexts: comprising charcoal from a hearth, SP1, and charcoal from the final fill of a pit, SP18. The first of these has given an unacceptably early date in the late Iron Age to early Roman, while the second date spans the mid-sixth to late seventh centuries. Charcoal from a pit oven, SP76, has a similar date spanning the mid-fifth to late seventh centuries. These confirm the broad presence of early Saxon settlement at Furnells, with a possible abandonment, or at least a decline, in the mid-seventh century.

The sample from Burystead was part of the wood lining of a well or water hole, the backfill of which contained middle Saxon Maxey-type ware. The radiocarbon date spans the later-seventh to mid-eighth centuries, coinciding with the first century of the 200 hundred year currency of Maxey ware.

The fourth date from Furnells came from charcoal from a pit within a pit group, SP122, which was cut by the western arm of the enclosure of the Anglo-Scandinavian farm (SP109). The date spans at least the late seventh to mid-eighth centuries, and suggests that despite the absence of imported middle Saxon pottery there was still some activity on the site in the middle Saxon period.

This small group of radiocarbon dates provide some support for the proposed chronologies based on the pottery dating, but are too few in number and typically have standard deviations that are too large to permit any finer chronological distinctions.

The construction of the churches at Furnells manor
by Andy Chapman

With the widespread agreement that there were fundamental problems with the dating of the sequence at Furnells manor, as expressed in Cadman *et al* 1983 and Boddington 1996, Audouy and Blinkhorn reappraised the ceramic chronology in 1990–91 by looking at key stratigraphic groups and the associated pottery assemblages (this volume, Chapter 6; Table 6.7).

This analysis was central to the revision of the chronological sequence at Furnells, but it is now suggested by the editor that as the known problem was that key aspects of the site had been dated too early, the tendency of the reappraisal was to seek the latest possible date for these key events. In so doing, the chronology was swung in the opposite direction, with a tendency to be too late rather than too early. The only relevant data directly available for further analysis are the group of nine radiocarbon dates from the early church and burials in the vicinity of the church (Boddington 1996, 72 and table 24 & fig 70).

Table 5.1: The radiocarbon determinations for early–middle Saxon settlement

Lab. number	Context	Sample type	Conventional date BP	Calibrated date Cal AD 68% confidence 95% confidence
Har-5492	Furnells: hearth SP1, pre-churchyard	Wood charcoal	2000±120	Cal BC 170–130 Cal BC 360–250
Har-4903	Furnells: pit oven SP76 Early–middle Saxon pit	Wood charcoal	1480±90	440–650 390–690
Har-5493	Furnells: hollow SP18 pre-churchyard	Wood charcoal	1420±90	540–690 420–780
UB-3420	Burystead: BSP1, Middle Saxon water hole	Waterlogged wood	1308±26	670–760 660–770
Har-5495	Furnells: SP122 Early–middle Saxon pit	Wood charcoal	1230±70	690–880 660–960

Radiocarbon dating laboratories: Har-Harwell and UB-The Queen's University of Belfast
Radiocarbon calibration program: CALIB 5.0 (2005), M Stuiver and P J Reimer
Calibration data set: IntCal O4

5. The Archaeological Evidence

Table 5.2: The radiocarbon determinations for Furnells church and churchyard

Lab. number	Context	Sample type	Conventional date BP	Calibrated date Cal AD 68% confidence 95% confidence
Har-5013	Burial 5266, Under wall of chancel of second church	Human bone	1320±70	640–780 600–880
Har-5014	Burial 5223, East of second church Cut by burial 5222	Human bone	1110±90	780–1020 680–1150
Har-5020	Burial 5298, Under western wall of second church	Human bone	1100±80	820–1030 700–1160
Har-5016	Burial 5254, Under wall of chancel of second church	Wood charcoal	1080±70	880–1030 770–1160
Har-5015	First church, chancel	Wood charcoal	1040±70	890–1120 810–1170
Har-5012	Burial 5286, South of church East of stone coffin	Human bone	1000±70	970–1160 890–1190
Har-5010	Burial 5222, East of second church Cuts burial 5223	Human bone	970±70	1010–1160 890–1220
Har-5011	Burial 5299, Under western wall of second church	Human bone	960±60	1020–1160 980–1220
Har-5019	Burial 5178, North of stone coffin	Human bone	930±70	1020–1170 980–1260

Radiocarbon dating laboratory: Harwell
Radiocarbon calibration program: OxCal v3.10 Bronk Ramsey(2005)

Atmospheric data from Reimer et al (2004);OxCal v3.10 Bronk Ramsey (2005); cub r:5 sd:12 prob usp[chron]

Har-5013 (5266) 1320±70BP
Har-5014 (5223) 1110±90BP
Har-5020 (5298) 1100±80BP
Har-5016 (5254) 1080±70BP
Har-5015 (church) 1040±70BP
Har-5012 (5286) 1000±70BP
Har-5010 (5222) 970±70BP
Har-5011 (5299) 960±60BP
Har-5019 (5178) 930±70BP

CalBC/CalAD   500CalAD   1000CalAD   1500CalAD

Calibrated date

These radiocarbon dates have been recalibrated and plotted (Table 5.2) in order to examine two keys points in the chronology: the construction of the first church and the commencement of burial within the churchyard, and the date of construction of the second church.

The date from Burial 5266 is unacceptably early for the use of the churchyard and is not considered further. The burials were all interments lying close to the early church and four (5266, 5298, 5254 and 5299) lay beneath the foundations of the second church and evidently pre-dated its construction (Boddington 1996, fig 25). Burial 5178 lay adjacent to and pre-dated the stone coffin. Burial 5222 lay immediately east of the chancel of the second church on an extreme alignment, and was therefore considered to be potentially one of the few burials post-dating the construction of the second church.

The dates for Burials 5223, 5298 and 5254 all indicate that the cemetery was in active use by the middle decades of the 10th century. This is consistent with the ceramic dating, which provides a date between AD 900 and 950 for the establishment for the late Saxon plot system and long range. The analysis of plot layout has indicated that the church and cemetery was not part of the original arrangement and was a later addition, but the radiocarbon dating would suggest that the interval between these two events may have been short, perhaps only some 10–20 years, and far too short to be recognised within the ceramic assemblage. As a result, the introduction of the church is now dated to the middle decades of the tenth century, rather than the late tenth century date resulting from the reappraisal of the pottery (see Table 6.7).

The radiocarbon dating of the burials also indicates that use of this central part of the churchyard continued at least into the early decades of the twelfth century, and perhaps to around AD 1150. It is uncertain if burial in the churchyard had largely ceased some time prior to the building of the second church or more closely coincided with that event, but a date range of 1150–1200 for the construction of the second church seems more likely than that a period of more than 50 years elapsed between the cessation of burial and the construction of the second church no earlier than AD 1200.

An earlier date would also be consistent with the balance of the pottery evidence, as the late date of 1200 is dependant on three sherds of pottery from the fill of a single grave, Burial 5298. This burial has also given a radiocarbon date of 700–1160 Cal AD (98% confidence, 1100±80BP, Har-5020) indicating that this individual had most probably been interred well before 1150. The pottery can therefore be regarded as intrusive and not indicative of the date of burial.

The pre-Saxon landscape

Although the sites that comprise the settlement area of north Raunds show little indication of earlier activity, the landscape of the Raunds Area Project has revealed a far broader picture along the Nene valley. This area was a centre of human activity from the ceremonial monuments of the Neolithic and Bronze Age at West Cotton and Irthlingborough (Harding and Healy in press), through to the Iron Age and Roman settlement excavated at Stanwick (Crosby and Neal forthcoming) and revealed elsewhere in both excavation and by the work of the Raunds Survey (Parry 2006). The area occupied by the village of Raunds was perhaps peripheral until the arrival of the Saxons.

Three trial trenches, part of an extensive evaluation in 1982, excavated around 150m to the west of the main site at Furnells revealed traces of shallow linear features and depressions. An associated single sherd of pottery and a few struck flint flakes suggest a Bronze Age date. In addition, two late Neolithic/early Bronze Age flint barbed and tanged arrowheads were found in the chancel of the late Saxon church (Boddington 1996, 21, 93, fig 20). A small quantity of other struck and worked flints were also recovered as residual finds.

The earliest direct evidence of human activity is provided by a small but widely distributed collection of Iron Age pottery, which at Langham Road was associated with a few features including a small hearth, up to 800mm wide, which was lined with a single layer of limestone and round pebbles.

The Roman period is likewise represented by a small quantity of contemporary ceramics and a few coins. These finds are unlikely to denote direct activity and were most probably brought to north Raunds in the Saxon and medieval periods, either as curios, for use in jewellery, medicine or pigment, or recovered during episodes of stone robbing. One Roman coin pierced for suspension was found at Burystead and a sherd of Samian ware from Furnells had been finely grated. The absence of associated features indicates that the area was not settled in the Roman period.

Furnells manor

In 1976, David Hall and the Northamptonshire Field Group excavated trial trenches on earthworks within a pasture close west of Rotton Row (Fig 1.4). Finding a medieval manor house was not unexpected, but the presence of several graves, including two late Saxon decorated grave slabs and a stone coffin, was a surprise. They indicated that a late Saxon and Norman church and churchyard lay beneath the late medieval manor house.

Open area excavations began the following year with the objective of fully excavating both the church and its cemetery. The initial area took in only the eastern manor house and the underlying churches, but in the summer of 1977 this was extended to the full limits of the cemetery by the simple process of working outwards with the machine stripping until no further burials were encountered. Thereafter, there were additional extensions in succeeding years. Initially these were primarily to allow for the exploration of the boundary ditch system. When this work resulted in the discovery of outlying buildings of various dates, there were further extensions which eventually took in the ancillary buildings to the north and the western manor complex to the west. These extensions ran up to, and in places beyond, the boundary ditch between the manorial plots and the open fields to the west. At its final limits the site extended up to 120m east–west by 95m north–south, taking in a total area of 0.86ha.

The excavations at Furnells came to an end in 1982. The southern site boundary had been the limit of the development area, which lay within the manorial plot system. The northernmost end of the Langham Road excavations of the later 1980s took in the southernmost part of the plots pertaining to Furnells manor, and reference should be made to the relevant parts of the Langham Road section of the chapter for descriptions of features in this southern area. In the following account of the development of the Furnells manor site, the church and cemetery are only briefly summarised as these have been previously published (Boddington 1996), although the chronology is revised and the final phase of use reinterpreted.

Furnells manor: Early–middle Saxon settlement (AD 450–650)

The early settlement comprised a profusion of small features such as postholes, pits and hollows, which were distributed across the site without any apparent boundaries (Fig 5.1). The majority of these cut the natural subsoil,

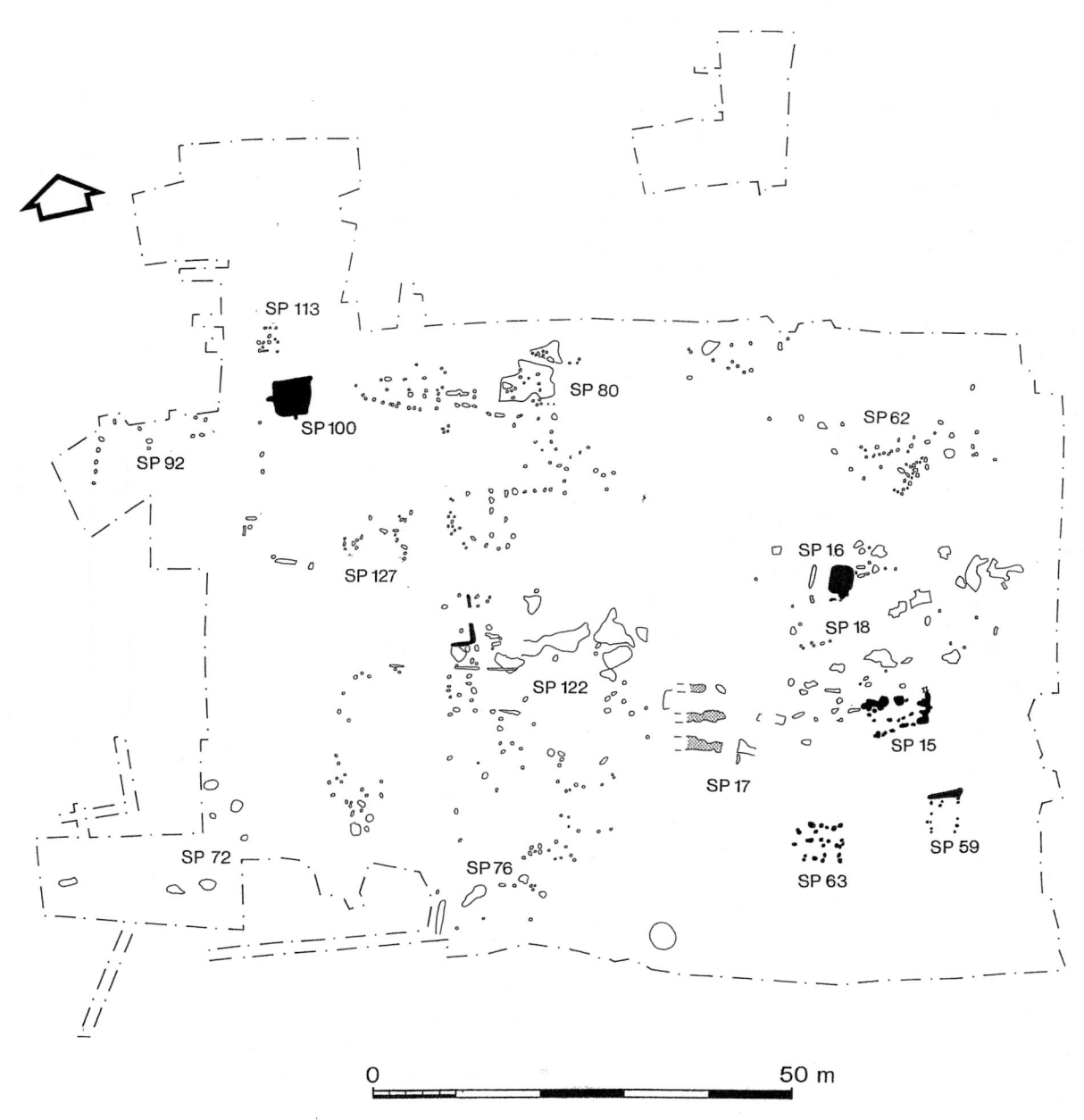

Fig 5.1: Furnells, early–middle Saxon settlement (AD 450–650)

although there was a small area of stratified deposits to the east, beneath the late Saxon church. Some of these features can be securely dated by the pottery assemblages, but much of the early–middle Saxon pottery was recovered as residual material in later contexts. In addition, many of the smaller earth-cut features are undated. At least some of those depicted probably belonged to later periods of occupation.

The minimal stratification, combined with the difficulty of dating the early–middle Saxon pottery, makes it impossible to advance a secure chronology and sequence of development within the period. Accordingly, the evidence is considered only as a palimpsest of features and the information is organized on the basis of physical characteristics and spatial distribution. However, the absence of any imported middle Saxon pottery suggests that the main phase of early Saxon occupation had come to an end by the middle or late-seventh century, and two radiocarbon dates confirm this date range. However, a further radiocarbon date suggests that there was at least some sporadic activity on the site during the eighth and ninth centuries.

The settlement probably comprised a loose grouping of several small post-built halls, although no complete building plans were recovered. There was a sunken-featured building to the north-west (Fig 5.1, SP100), while a further sunken-featured building at the northern end of the Langham Road excavations probably also belonged with these buildings (see Fig 5.47, LRSP22). Around and between these features there were numerous pits, hollows and scattered postholes but it is possible in only a few instances to relate the evidence to a specific activity; such as small-scale cultivation in the central area and a drying or malting oven to the south (SP76). The presence of much ferrous slag and a hearth bottom also indicates that iron smithing was carried out on the eastern part of the site.

Despite the unprepossessing appearance of the settlement evidence, the recovery of over 11000 sherds of early–middle Saxon pottery shows that it was certainly a domestic settlement of considerable scale and duration.

Sunken-featured building (SP100)

This structure lay in the north-western corner of the site (Fig 5.1). It was 4.7m long by 4.1m wide and 0.30m deep, but the eastern end and part of the northern side had been truncated by later features (Fig 5.2). It was cut into limestone but its base showed no signs of wear, perhaps indicating that it had been covered by a suspended floor. Postholes lay at the midpoint of the eastern and western ends. They were 0.45m and 0.30m deep and contained stone packing. There was also a shallow linear gully along the western end of the structure, and an elongated posthole lay at right angles. A further posthole lay beyond the southern edge of the feature.

The primary fill, which comprised a brown, humic clay containing limestone fragments, charcoal flecks and pebbles, contained 25 sherds of early–middle Saxon pottery; a pin worked from a pig fibula [small find (SF)1003]; fragments of a spindle-whorl [SF 1001] and a Roman Denarius.

Stone-lined pit (SP16)

This feature lay to the east, beneath the first church (Fig 5.1). The square pit, measuring 3.0m by 2.8m, was 0.25m deep and the flat base had been lined with unworn, roughly laid limestone (Fig 5.3). The fill contained 44 sherds of

Fig 5.2: Furnells, sunken-featured building (SP100)

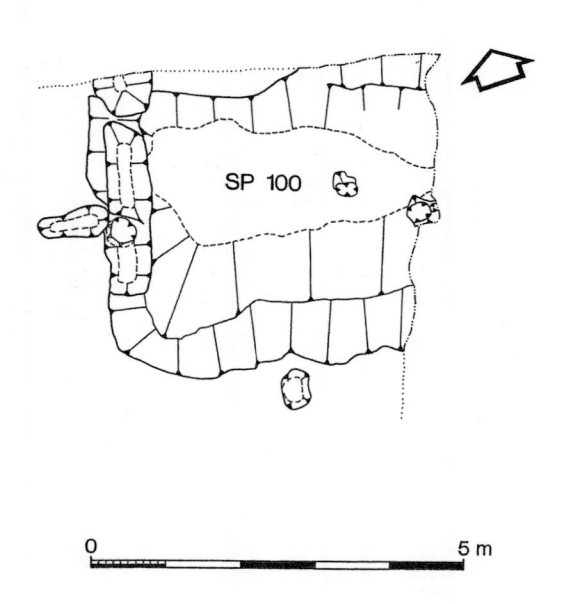

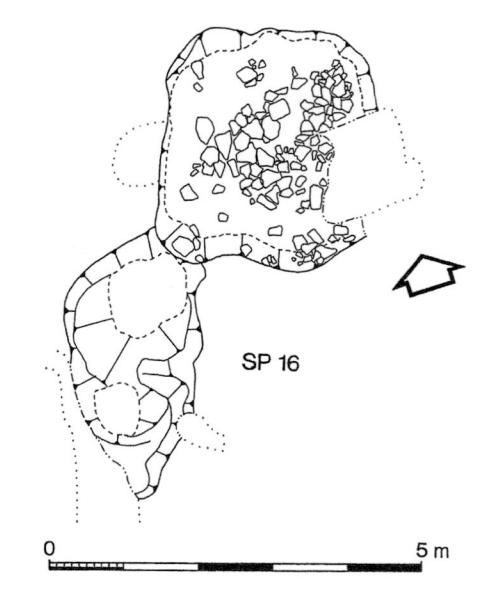

Fig 5.3: Furnells, stone-lined pit and associated pits (SP 16)

early–middle Saxon pottery; while three sherds of late Saxon pottery probably represent contamination of the upper fills. The stone lining included a hearth bottom, measuring approximately 200mm square, indicating that iron smithing was being carried out nearby. The absence of postholes either within or around the feature casts doubt on its initial interpretation as a sunken-featured building. It appears to have been associated with an adjacent pit group, which lay immediately to the south-west. The pits fills contained 86 sherds of early–middle Saxon pottery and a single intrusive sherd of St Neots-type ware.

Posthole structure (SP15)

To the south-east of the stone-lined pit (Fig 5.1), a group of 23 postholes in an area of *c*20 sq m may have represented some form of sub-rectangular structure. The group had been heavily disturbed by graves in the overlying cemetery. The fill of the postholes yielded five sherds of early Saxon pottery.

Posthole and slot structure (SP59)

This structure lay in the south-east corner of the site and comprised post-built long walls with a slot forming the northern end wall (Fig 5.4). No trace of a southern wall was recovered. It was 4.5m long by 3.0m wide. The slot fills produced six sherds of early Saxon pottery and two of St Neots-type ware.

Posthole Structure (SP63)

Also to the south-east, this structure comprised a cluster of postholes set within a roughly rectangular area measuring 6.0m by 4.5m (Fig 5.5). The individual wall-lines cannot be clearly distinguished and the assumed interior also contained a rough east–west line of postholes. The postholes produced 14 sherds of early Saxon pottery and a single sherd of St Neots-type ware.

Posthole structure (SP92)

A cluster of postholes to the north-west (Fig 5.1) could have been the remains of a poorly defined structure, measuring 7.30m by 6m. Seven sherds of early Saxon pottery were retrieved from posthole fills.

Linear gullies (SP17)

Near the centre of the site there were three irregular but parallel linear gullies (Fig 5.1). They had been truncated to the east and west by later features. They had a maximum surviving length of 4.0m, and ranged from 0.80m–1.3m wide and 0.25–0.50m deep. They were flat based and steep-sided and are interpreted as spade-cut furrows associated with small-scale cultivation. Eleven sherds of early Saxon pottery were retrieved from the fills.

Feature group (SP18)

A scatter of postholes, gullies and irregular pits and hollows lay across an extensive area on the eastern part of the site (Fig 5.1). Some of these contained dumped burnt debris and small amounts of iron working slag, and slag was also recovered from the overlying graves. This, together with the hearth bottom from the nearby stone-lined pit (SP16), indicates that this eastern area was a centre for iron smithing in the early Saxon period. Charcoal from one pit has given a radiocarbon date of 540–690 Cal AD (68% confidence, 1420±90 BP, Har-5493).

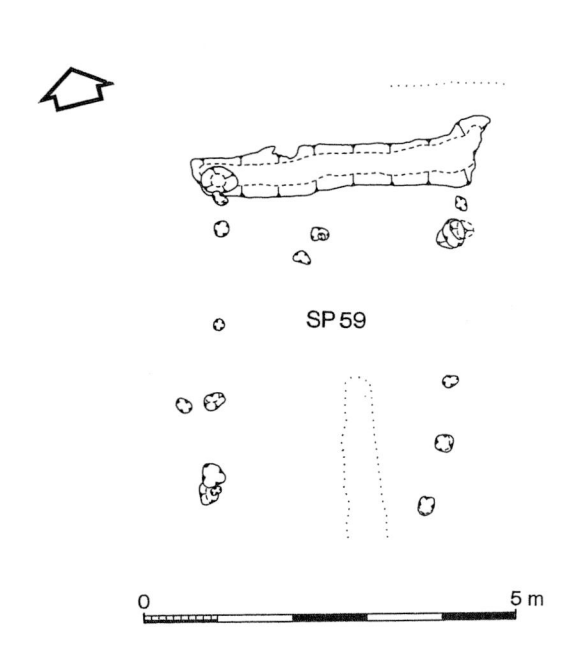

Fig 5.4: Furnells, timber building (SP59)

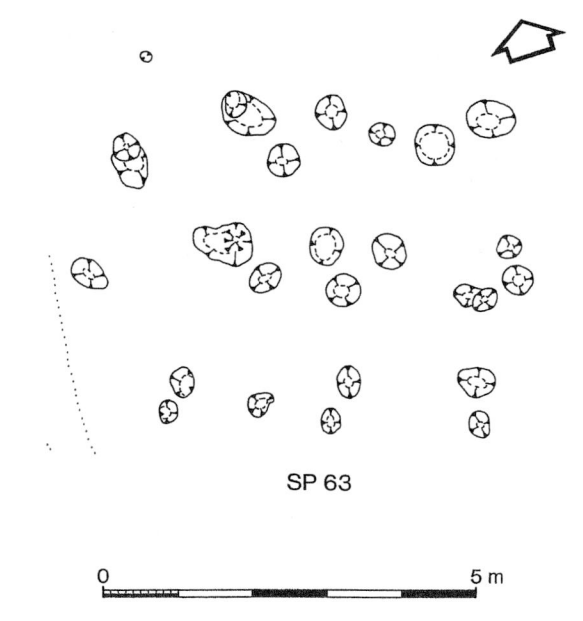

Fig 5.5: Furnells, posthole group (SP63)

Pit group (SP72)

A sparse scatter of pits lay close to the south-western limit of excavation (Fig 5.1). Many of these features are likely to have originated in the early Saxon period although the dating, based on a few sherds of pottery, is tentative.

Posthole scatter (SP62)

A scatter of 62 features in the north-eastern corner of the site, comprised mostly postholes cut into the natural limestone, although no individual structures are identifiable (Fig 5.1). Forty-three sherds of early Saxon pottery were retrieved, however, 29 sherds of later pottery suggest that at least some of these features belonged with the late Saxon and medieval occupation.

Oven/corn dryer (SP76)

A group of pits, postholes, gullies and slots close to the southern edge of the site (Fig 5.1), included an earth-cut oven or corn dryer. This comprised a shallow circular pit, 1.20m in diameter and up to 0.40m deep, with a linear flue to the south-west, 2.25m long by 0.80m wide and 0.20m deep (Fig 5.6). A layer of silt was overlain by a deposit of charcoal and burnt clay, with the latter probably derived from a collapsed superstructure. Charcoal from the secondary fill produced a radiocarbon date of 440–650 Cal AD (68% confidence, 1480±90 BP, Har-4903).

Posthole and pit groups (SP80 and SP113)

These groups lay close to the northern and north-western limits of excavation and comprised two small clusters of postholes and shallow pits (Fig 5.1), which produced a small assemblage of early–middle Saxon pottery.

Feature group (SP127)

This group includes 300 features from the western area of the site, comprising postholes and some pits and stakeholes (Fig 5.1).

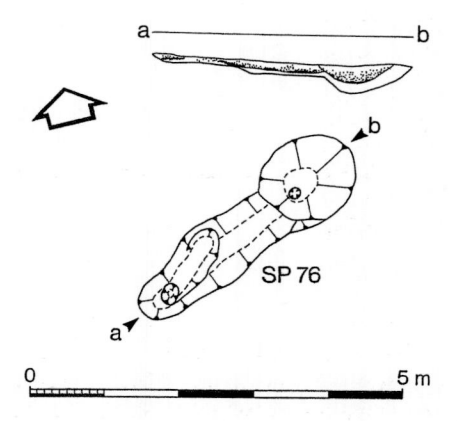

Fig 5.6: Furnells, earth-cut oven (SP76)

Feature group (SP122)

This group of postholes and pits occupied much of the central area of the site (Fig 5.1). Two of the pits contained most of the several hundred sherds of early–middle Saxon pottery from this area. The larger of these two pits was 2.0m long by 1.2m and 0.36m deep. Charcoal fragments from the smaller pit have given a date range of 690–880 Cal AD (68% confidence, 1230±70 BP, Har-5495), a date indicating that there was some activity on the site between the eighth and ninth centuries, despite the absence of contemporary imported middle Saxon pottery.

On the northern margin of this group a gully forming a reverse L-shape, measuring 6.0 by 2.9m, may be the remnants of a small timber structure.

Furnells manor: The Anglo-Scandinavian farm (AD 850–900/950)

This is the most problematic period at Furnells. Immediately following excavation the provisional interpretation was that a sub-square ditched enclosure and major post-built halls pre-dated the appearance of the network of boundary ditches, although the enclosure and halls were then ascribed a middle Saxon date. During post-excavation the model for this phase of settlement was revised, setting the post-built halls within an outer enclosure formed from various elements of the larger-scale ditch network (see Cadman 1983, fig 3; Foard 1985, fig 7 or Current Archaeology 106, 325–327).

As already discussed, it was the recovery of quantities of imported middle Saxon pottery at the nearby Langham Road and Burystead excavations that raised questions concerning both the dating of the sequence at Furnells and the assumption of continuity of settlement. Taking into account the review of the pottery dating and the nature of the evidence derived from the other nearby sites and at West Cotton, the revised sequence of development is one that has returned to something closer to the excavator's original thinking. The dating is based on the absence of imported middle Saxon pottery and the presence of some early forms of St Neots-type ware. The characterisation of this settlement as an Anglo-Scandinavian farm follows from the dating of this activity to the period of Danish control of the region, and to the presence of various finds, including an assemblage of horse harness fittings (see Fig 7.3) and some gaming pieces (see Fig 7.5), which exhibit Scandinavian influence.

The basic arrangement of the settlement comprised a major timber hall (B, SP91) to the north, with a second slightly smaller hall to the south (S, SP99) standing within a square ditched enclosure (SP 109) (Fig 5.7). This arrangement can be seen to encompass the two elements of public and private space. A smaller timber hall (D, SP94) formed an ancillary building to the west. A further minor timber building (C, SP98) either abutted or was cut by the corner of the ditched enclosure.

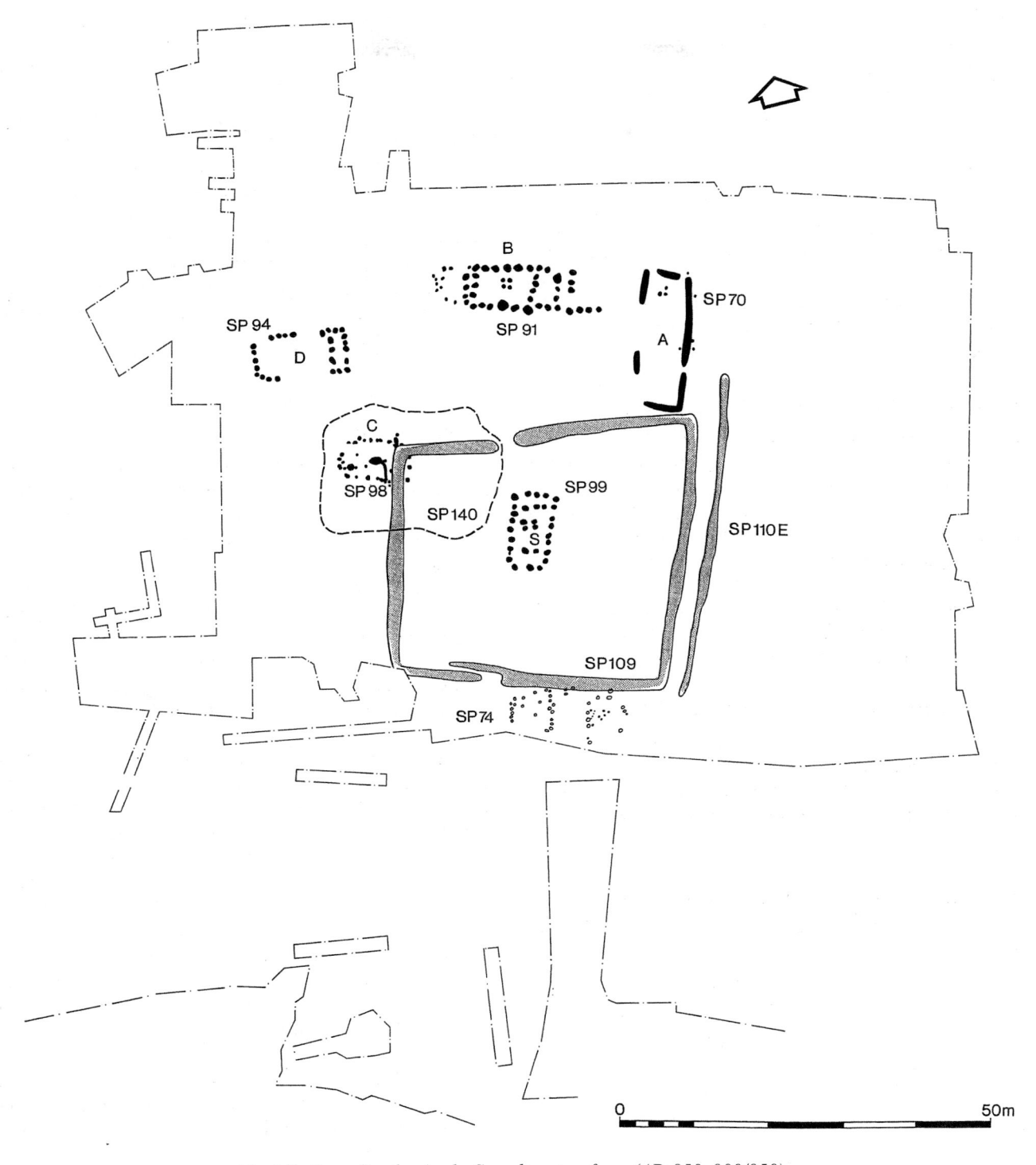

Fig 5.7: Furnells, the Anglo-Scandinavian farm (AD 850–900/950)

A further major timber hall (A, SP70), lying to the east, was of a different build as it was founded in construction trenches. It was certainly of a later date, and may have been either a late addition to the Anglo-Scandinavian farm or was constructed as part of the late Saxon manor complex. There is insufficient dating evidence to determine which.

The apparent absence of smaller features, such as post-holes and pits, within this period is a result of the lack of dating evidence. A proportion of those appearing on the early–middle Saxon plan (Fig 5.1) probably belonged to this period.

The enclosure (SP109 and SP111)

The ditched enclosure was roughly square in plan, measuring up to 35m north–south by 38m east–west, enclosing an area of c0.11ha (Fig 5.7). There were opposed entrances to the north and south. These lay to the west of centre and in line with the doorway of the northern hall (SP 91). Both were initially simple openings, 2.1m and 2.4m wide.

The enclosure ditch, at up to 2.20m wide by 0.80m deep, was wider and deeper than most of the ditches of the succeeding boundary network. A distinct slot, possibly caused by cleaning, was present on the western arm, but similar evidence did not survive elsewhere.

Of the 1141 sherds of pottery that were recovered from the ditch fills, 583 were from early–middle Saxon wares and 408 of St Neots-type ware. The large quantity of late Saxon pottery reflects the retention of the parts of the ditch system into the initial late Saxon plot layout. Smaller quantities of medieval pottery are considered to be contamination from later activity, probably largely from the fills of the subsidence hollow above the ditch silting.

The southern arm of the enclosure was recut. This included the provision of a length of U-profiled slot set inside the original entrance opening (Fig 5.7 and see Fig 5.23). It is suggested that this may have been related to the provision of a timber gateway to control access through this entrance. The date of this refurbishment is uncertain, and it may have occurred in the late Saxon period, with the southern arm of the enclosure incorporated into the late Saxon plot boundaries.

A detached length of ditch running parallel with the eastern arm of the enclosure is also difficult to date (Fig 5.7, SP110E). It may have been introduced at or soon after the construction of the enclosure, but recutting of the northern end most probably occurred at the formation of the late Saxon plot system, suggesting that it was either incorporated into the later boundary system or was part of the later ditch system.

The northern hall (Building B, SP91)

This substantial timber hall stood to the north on an area of limestone bedrock (Fig 5.7). The building was 12.5m long by 5.5m wide, with the long walls defined by eight opposed pairs of post-pits, indicating that it was of a frame construction (Figs 5.8 and 5.9). Many of the post-pits had either evident recuts, or were oval in plan, suggesting the later replacement of many of the timbers. In some cases, post packing was relatively undisturbed and preserved the distorted outline of circular posts that had been between 200–300mm in diameter. The central pairs of post-pits were larger, marking opposed central doorways. Small external postholes at the doorways could indicate the provision of either porches or perhaps steps providing access to a raised timber floor.

The long walls were 10m long but the end walls lay a further 1.0m beyond this, and comprised three smaller post-pits lying fully within the width of the building, so that the corners of the building were not square. This suggests the provision of a hipped roof rather than a plain gable end. The overall length to width ratio for the building was 2.3:1, but taking only the long walls into consideration and excluding the extended end walls, the ratio would be closer to 2:1.

The central room occupied six of the nine bays and was 7.7m long. Four small postholes in the centre of the room, but just west of a direct line between the doorways, formed a rectangle measuring 1.4m by 1.0m. This may denote the location of a central hearth, perhaps set within a timber hearth box. To the east, a line of internal postholes set between the penultimate pair of wall posts formed an end chamber just over 2.0m wide. To the west a line of three postholes between the terminal post-pits formed an end chamber just over 1.0m wide, presumably used for storage.

Further postholes continued the line of the southern wall to both the west and east, and groups of postholes 3.0m to the west of the building and 2.0m to the east may indicate the provision of lean-to extensions. The arrangement of this building, with its hipped roof and lean-to extensions, would appear to have achieved the maximum floor space for the minimum supporting wall structure. The building and the extensions would have formed a timber façade at least 20m long, which would have formed the northern side of the public open space between the hall and the enclosure.

The majority of the pottery recovered from the post-pits, over 200 sherds, was of early–middle Saxon date. These were mostly small and fragmentary and can be considered residual. There were also 21 sherds from a single early–middle Saxon pot, a debased biconical urn, incorporated in the packing of the eastern post-pit of the southern doorway. Twenty-two sherds of late Saxon pottery from the backfill of some postholes indicate the date of demolition.

Two pins fashioned from pig fibula from one of the postholes are either residual from the previous occupation or continue a tradition of such implements into the late Saxon period.

The western timber hall (Building D, SP94)

This post-built hall was 12.0m long by 5.5m wide (Fig 5.10), with a length to width ratio close to 2:1. The long walls were formed of closely-spaced paired post-pits. There may have been eleven in each wall, but the central part, probably including the doorways, had been lost to a later ditch. The eastern end of the building was square, with a line of seven similarly-sized post-pits forming the gable end. The western end wall comprised five post-pits not spanning the width of the building and lying 1.0m beyond the long walls. This again suggests the provision of a hipped roof. In some post-pits limestone post-packing had preserved the outline of posts approximately 200mm in diameter.

5. The Archaeological Evidence

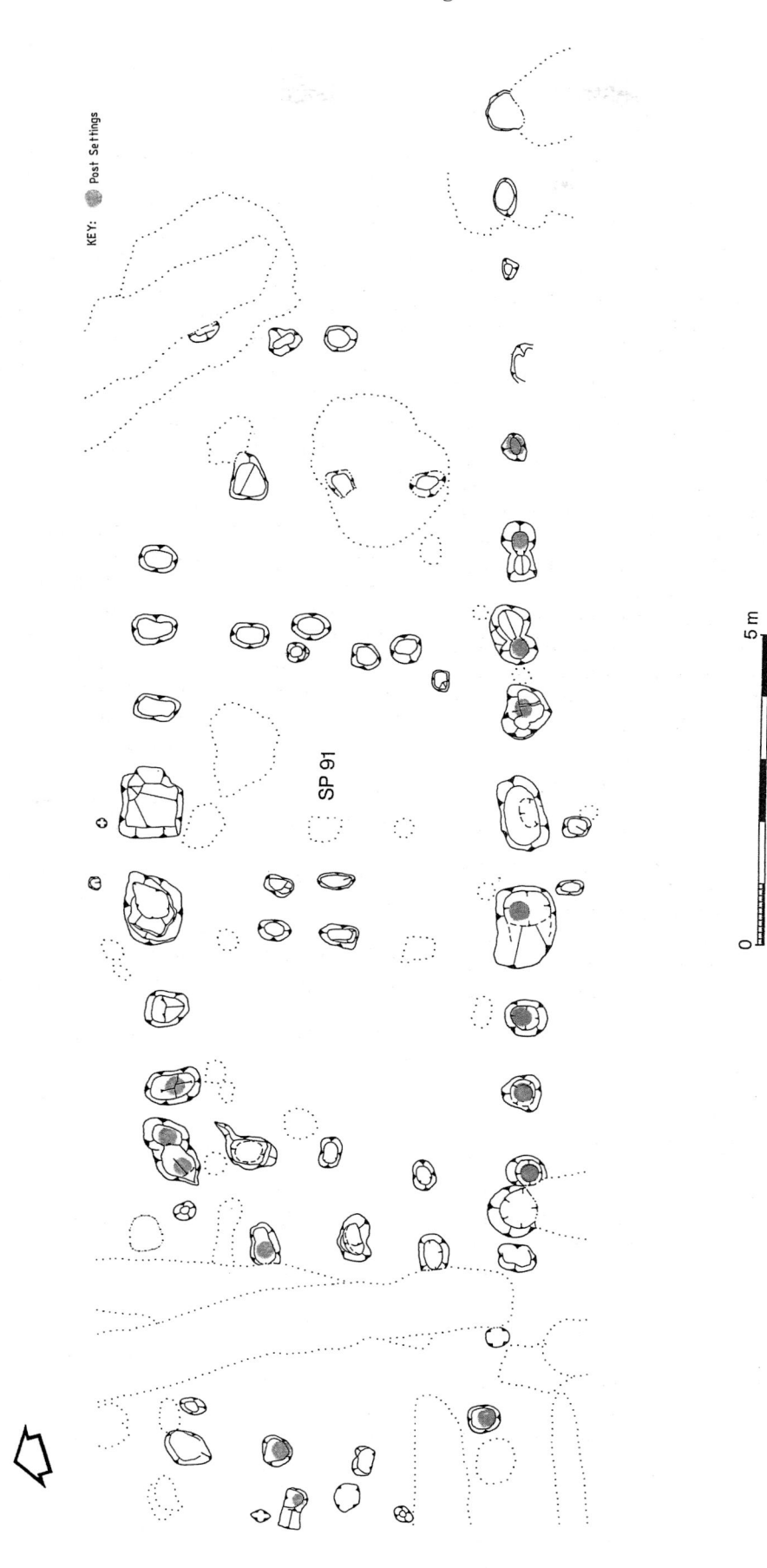

KEY: ● Post Settings

SP 91

Fig 5.8: Furnells, the northern hall (building B, SP91)

Fig 5.9: Furnells, the post-pits of the northern hall, building B, looking east

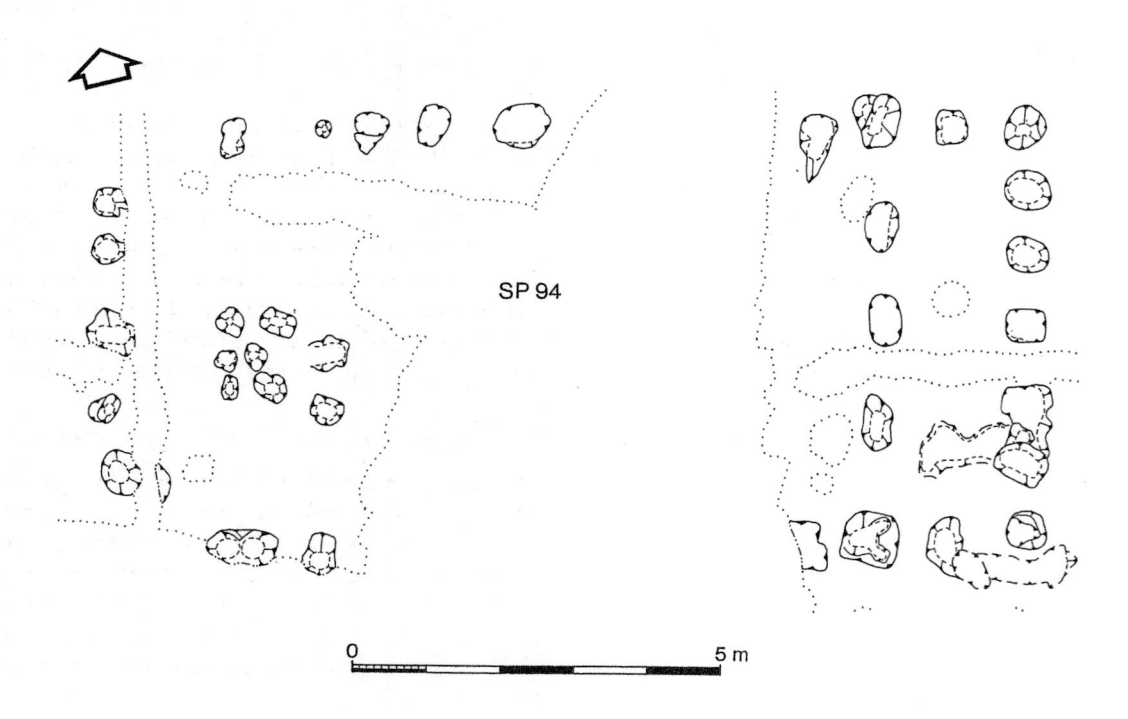

Fig 5.10: Furnells, the western hall (building D, SP94)

An internal line of three post-pits formed an eastern end chamber, 1.7m wide. To the west there was a cluster of small postholes of unknown function.

Eighty-four sherds of early–middle Saxon pottery were recovered from the fills of the postholes, along with four sherds of later Saxon pottery that relate to demolition. Other finds include fragments of burnt clay and slag.

The southern timber hall (Building S, SP99)

The timber hall within the ditched enclosure (Figs 5.11 and 5.12) was 9.7m long by 5.2m wide, with a length to width ratio close to 2:1. The long walls were formed from eight opposed pairs of post-pits, although the two northernmost pairs were smaller. There was no clear distinction in the post-pits to indicate which had held door posts, but opposed central doorways seems the most likely option. The long walls were 8.5m long with the end walls just under 1.0m beyond this, and comprising three post-pits set within the width of the building, which yet again suggests the provision of a hipped roof. Two internal posts to the south and three to the north indicate the provision of end chambers up to 2.0m wide. The line of the northern partition wall runs at quite an angle to the end walls, so that the chamber was significantly narrower to the east.

Within the central room, four postholes and an associated patch of loamy silt containing charcoal and burnt clay may indicate the site of a former hearth, perhaps comprising a timber hearth box.

Fifteen small and abraded sherds of early–middle Saxon pottery probably represent secondary deposition. No later pottery was recovered.

Posthole structure (C, SP98)

This rectilinear arrangement of postholes may have been a pen or a byre rather than a domestic building. It abutted the north-western corner of the ditched enclosure, but this relationship is problematic as the excavator included a few postholes lying within the enclosure as potentially part of the structure, which would imply that it pre-dated the enclosure (Fig 5.13).

The structure was 7.0m long by 5.0m wide, measured to the edge of the enclosure ditch. The postholes on the long sides appeared to have been paired, while at the western end there was a profusion of postholes. A short length of the gully at the north-eastern corner may have been part of an original eastern wall, set along the upper edge of the adjacent ditch and later lost to erosion of the ditch edge.

The presence of an internal pit and gully suggest that the structure was perhaps a pen or byre. The oval pit had a post or stake-hole at each end, and a shallow gully ran southwards, just passing through the line of the southern wall.

It is unclear whether the 144 sherds of early–middle Saxon pottery from the postholes had been used for packing or were incorporated during demolition. Their presence is not surprising, however, as the structure lay in an area of 'grey earth' (SP140, see below), a preserved soil horizon which contained a dense scatter of early–middle Saxon pottery. In addition, there were 14 sherds of St Neots-type ware together with a fragment of a connecting plate from a single-sided comb of probable late Saxon date.

The eastern timber hall (Building A, SP70)

The eastern timber hall is distinct from the buildings already described in that rather than being post-built, it was of post-in-trench construction, with this probably indicating that it was stave-built, with the walls comprising continuous lines of abutting timbers of similar proportions and load-bearing capacity. It was constructed mainly on limestone bedrock but its southern end was founded on Blisworth clay.

This building was 19.0m long by up to 6.0m wide, a length to width ratio of 3:1, with the long walls slightly bowed (Fig 5.14). Little remained of the western wall trench, but the eastern wall was better preserved and allow-

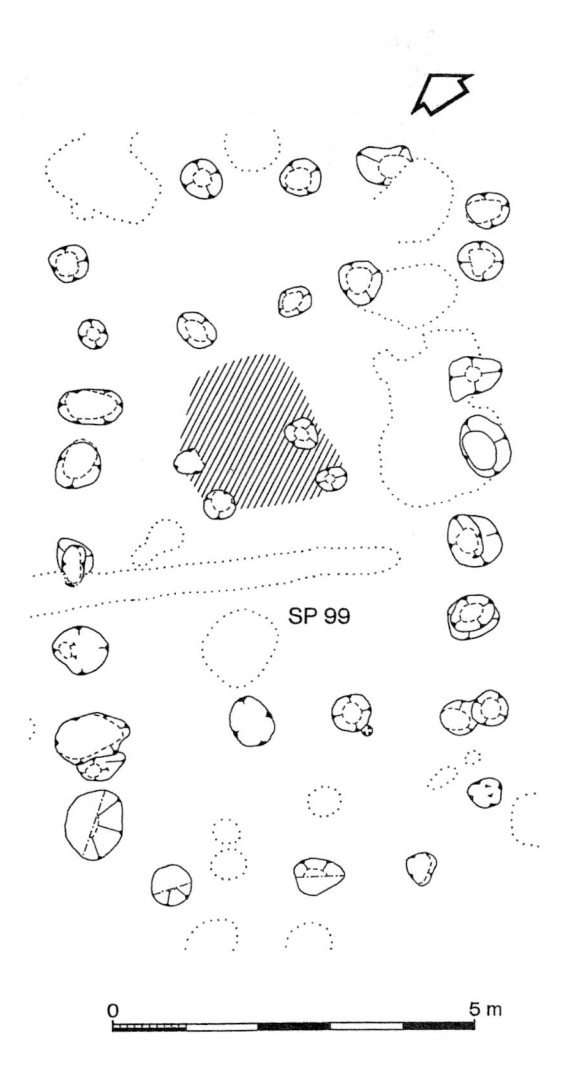

Fig 5.11: Furnells, the southern hall (building S, SP99)

Fig 5.12: Furnells, the southern hall, looking south

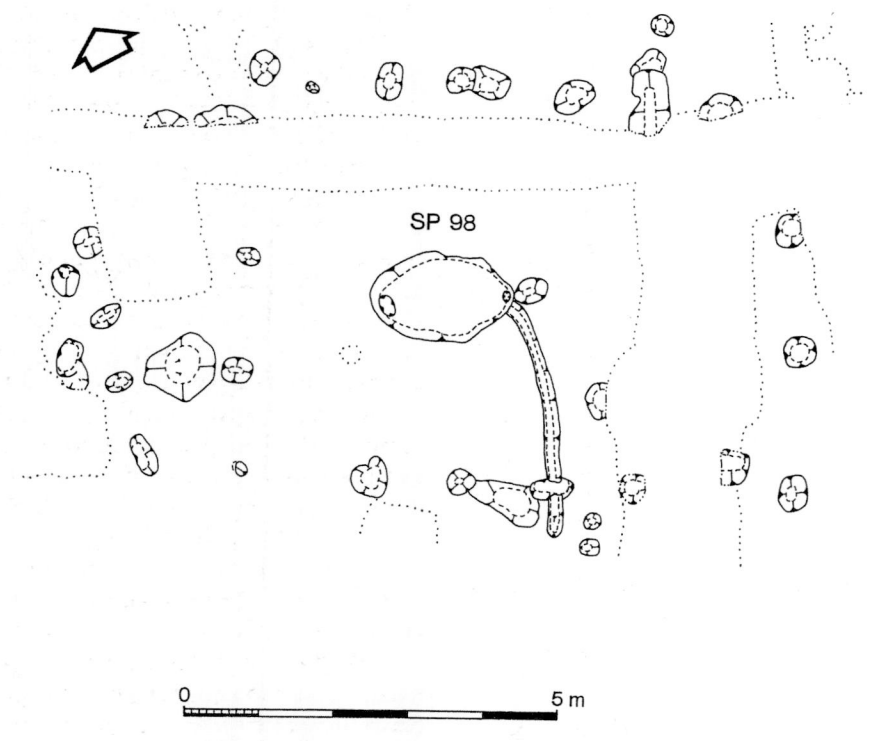

Fig 5.13: Furnells, posthole structure C (SP98)

5. The Archaeological Evidence

ed the form of the building to be partly reconstructed. The presence of a central doorway was indicated by a length of slot, 4.0m long by 0.60m–0.80m wide and 0.40m deep, slightly deeper than the rest of the wall trench. Some timber impressions were preserved at the northern end of the central slot, and these suggest that more substantial, or at least taller, uprights, perhaps forming an impressive door surround, had flanked a central doorway at least 1.0m wide.

To the south of the doorway there appeared to be a single length of wall trench, 7.5m long running to the southern end of the building. In contrast, the wall to the north of the doorway comprised two distinct sections; a 4.5m length to the north of the doorway and a separate 3.0m length that was offset slightly to the west. There appeared to be a similar offset on the western wall trench, which was not as well preserved. This may suggest that there was a northern chamber, 3.0m long, which was slightly narrower than the rest of the building. There may have been either an accompanying difference in the respective roof lines or perhaps the provision of a hipped roof over the northern chamber. Parts of the wall trenches for the southern and northern end walls were recovered, and these were closely comparable to the long walls.

The position of timbers was indicated by shallow depressions in the base of the wall trenches together with occasional discrete clusters of limestone fragments; the remnants of disturbed packing. The spacing of individual posts ranged between 240–440mm centre-to-centre and the majority were 200mm in diameter. The uneven survival of post-settings and the absence of post-pipes suggest that when the building was demolished the posts had been extracted and not left to decay *in situ*.

There were a number of small postholes just beyond the northern wall and immediately adjacent to the east wall, which may have been related to the construction of the building. There were also a few internal postholes that were possibly contemporary with the building.

Forty-five small and abraded sherds of early–middle Saxon pottery together with three sherds of St Neots-type ware were recovered from the fills of the wall trenches. In addition, 13 sherds of Saxo-Norman and three sherds of medieval pottery were also recovered but all but one of these sherds came from the southern wall trench, which had been disturbed by both later ditches and graves.

The date of construction of this building has not been firmly established. The construction technique indicates that it was of a later date than the post-built halls of the Anglo-Scandinavian farm. It is possible that it was added to this building complex, lying immediately north of the corner of the ditched enclosure. It would have acted as a gatehouse, controlling access to both the northern hall and the enclosure. It was certainly in use contemporary with the long range of the late Saxon manor and may have been built as part of this complex. It would have controlled access to the main domestic buildings, in this case the new long range, and it can perhaps be regarded

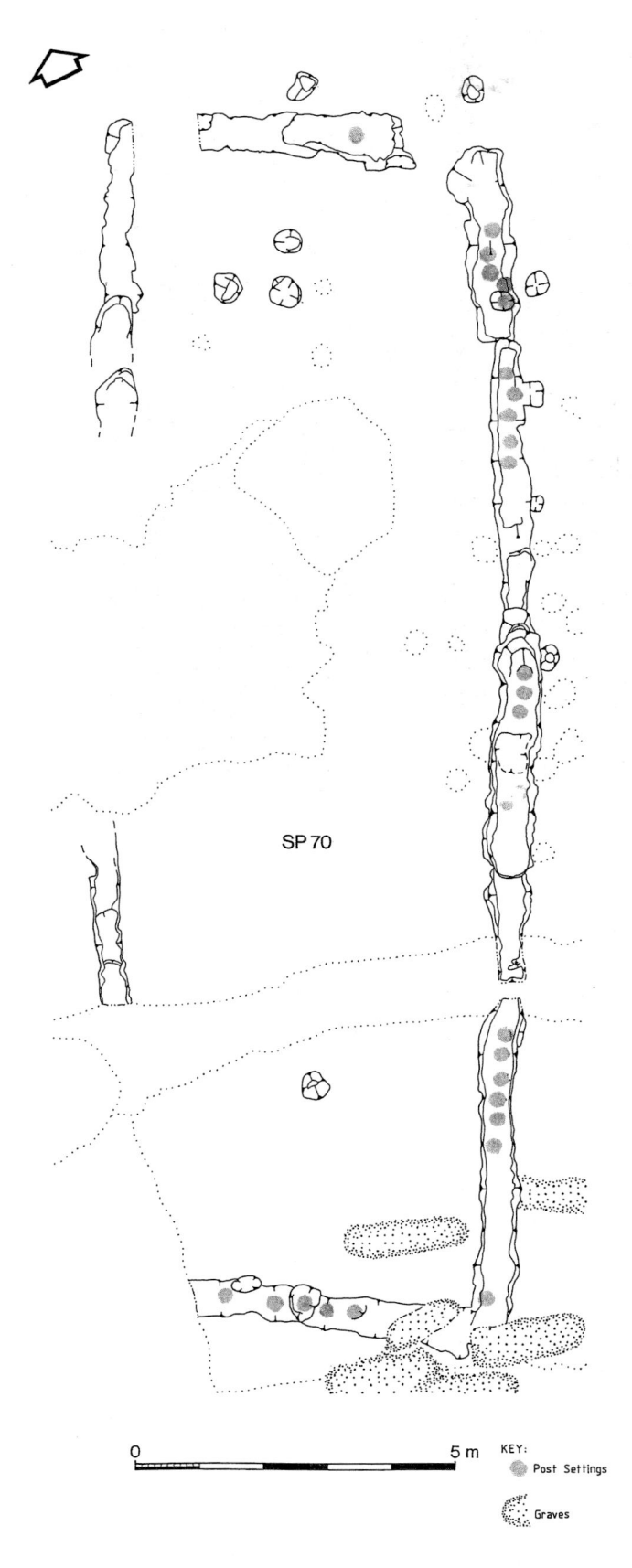

Fig 5.14: Furnells, the eastern timber hall (building A, SP70)

as an example of a thegns gate, a feature referred to in contemporary documents. It is certain that it only had a short period of use, as it had been levelled by the mid-tenth century, when the boundaries of the newly created churchyard, and subsequently several graves, cut across it, see below.

Posthole structures (Building K, SP74)

A minor building complex to the south might also be contemporary with the Anglo-Scandinavian farm (Fig 5.7, SP74). Two posthole groups might denote light timber buildings or pens lying immediately outside the southern entrance to the enclosure. These had been assigned to the late Saxon period, see below, although as they fell out of use before the digging of the ditches bounding the southern side of the late Saxon domestic enclosure an earlier origin is possible.

The western structure was 6m wide and in excess of 7m long, with the long walls defined by two lines of closely-spaced postholes. To the east there was a similar, but less orderly, group of postholes forming a structure perhaps 5m wide and in excess of 6m long.

The "grey earth" (SP140)

Across a roughly rectangular area, measuring 25m east–west by 17m north–south, on the western part of the site, there was a remnant soil horizon referred to during excavation as the "grey earth", due to its distinctive appearance as a layer of dark grey, humic clayey loam. It appears to have been preserved in the area beneath the southern, domestic wing of the late Saxon long range, and extended to both the west and east of this.

It was suggested by the excavator that it was perhaps an early–middle Saxon midden, with this accounting for the quantities of early–middle Saxon pottery recovered from it. Alternatively, it may just represent an isolated area in which a general soil horizon had been preserved due to the presence of a series of later overlying buildings and surfaces.

The soil horizon had a maximum thickness of 500mm. Although it may have been a preserved early–middle Saxon soil, it had clearly undergone much reworking during the subsequent occupation, with a consequent mixing of late Saxon pottery and finds with the earlier material. It appears to have been sealed by surfaces dating to the 13th century, contemporary with the medieval western manor house.

Furnells manor: Plot formation and the late Saxon manor (AD 900/950–1100)

In the decades prior to the mid-tenth century there was a major reorganisation of the site. A system of linear ditches were introduced to demarcate the outer boundaries of the settlement and to define its internal spatial organisation (Figs 5.15 and 5.16). In particular, a major ditch to the west defined the boundary between the settlement and the field system.

This new arrangement showed a close respect for the existing enclosure and buildings, and the southern and eastern arms of the enclosure appear to have been incorporated into the new boundary system. The new domestic area therefore occupied the same space as its predecessor, probably indicating direct continuity of settlement. Indeed, the new buildings did not impinge on any of the major existing buildings, so it can be envisaged that life continued in the old post-built timber ranges while the new hall and apartments were under construction. At the centre of the new arrangement was the long range, with a hall to the north and domestic apartments to the south, with detached ancillary buildings to the south (Fig 5.17). This arrangement, especially with the later addition of a church, shows that we are looking at the holding of a minor late Saxon thegn, effectively a small late Saxon manor.

The layout of the ditch system shows that the church and churchyard were not part of the original plan. However, by the mid-tenth century the eastern boundary of the domestic plot had been relocated westward to make space for the incorporation of the church plot adjacent to the domestic centre (see Fig 5.27). The principal access to the domestic buildings lay to the north of the churchyard, leading directly to the hall of the long range, but the possible gatehouse must have been removed when the churchyard was established. Some minor buildings, ditches and quarry pits lay to the south-east, to the south of the churchyard, and appear to be part of an associated area of lower status occupation. A complex of ditches to the south-west of the main building complex, which also included a pond, suggests a busy area with access between the ancillary buildings and the fields to the west, probably reflecting the agricultural basis to the economy of the late Saxon manor.

The boundary ditch system and associated features

The individual ditches varied considerably. None was wider than 1.5m and their depths did not exceed 0.7m and was often much less. Many contained a shallow slot at the base, possibly the result of cleaning, and many had been recut on a number of occasions.

The general absence of refuse from the fills might also be a result of such regular maintenance and recutting, although rubbish may simply not have been systematically deposited in the ditches. The pottery from the ditch fills ranged in date from early–middle Saxon to medieval, including quantities of late Saxon pottery, particularly St Neots-type ware. Given the extent of cleaning and recutting, the assemblages are well mixed and only provide secure dates for their final filling, which for the minor ditch systems was typically in the twelfth century, prior to the introduction of the stone-built western manor house. In addition, the typical homogeneous clay fills of the ditches made it difficult to define separate fills. The consequent recovery

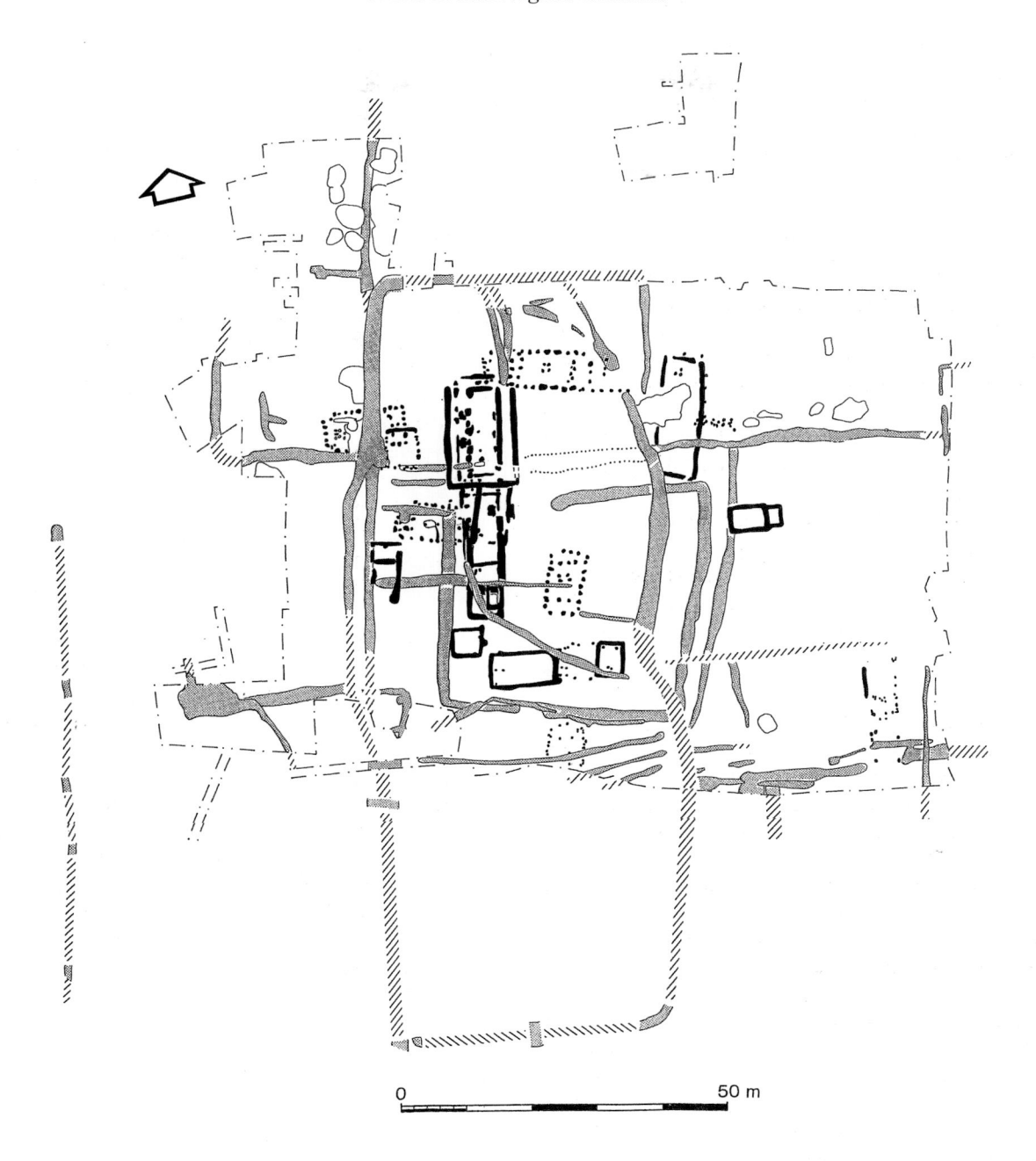

Fig 5.15: Furnells, the late Saxon buildings and boundaries (AD 900/950–1200), shown in relation to the preceding settlement

of pottery under single context numbers spanning the entire fill sequence for many of the excavated ditch sections, has made it impossible to provide any more precise analysis of the ditch chronologies.

At Langham Road and Burystead (see below) it is suggested that the boundary systems defined plots broadly conforming to standard widths and areas based on multiples of the 16.5 foot rod (5.03m), and typically involving the use of one-acre plots that were either 8 rods (40m) wide by 20 rods (100m) long or 10 rods wide by 16 rods long, and sub-divisions of these into half and quarter-acre plots (Zupko 1968).

That metrical control was also practiced in the setting out of the boundaries at Furnells is indicated by the less complex parts of the system. An outlying ditch (SP114) lay 50m to the west of the main western boundary (SP110W) (Fig 5.16), suggesting the use of a 10-rod measurement. The domestic area was more complex in form, but it may be suggested that the domestic core occupied a one-acre plot, 10 rods (50m) wide by 16 rods (80m) long, as indicated on the model layout (Fig 4.1). It may also be noted that the similar long range at West Cotton has also been shown to have lain within a one-acre plot (Chapman in press). There may have been a similar one-acre plot to

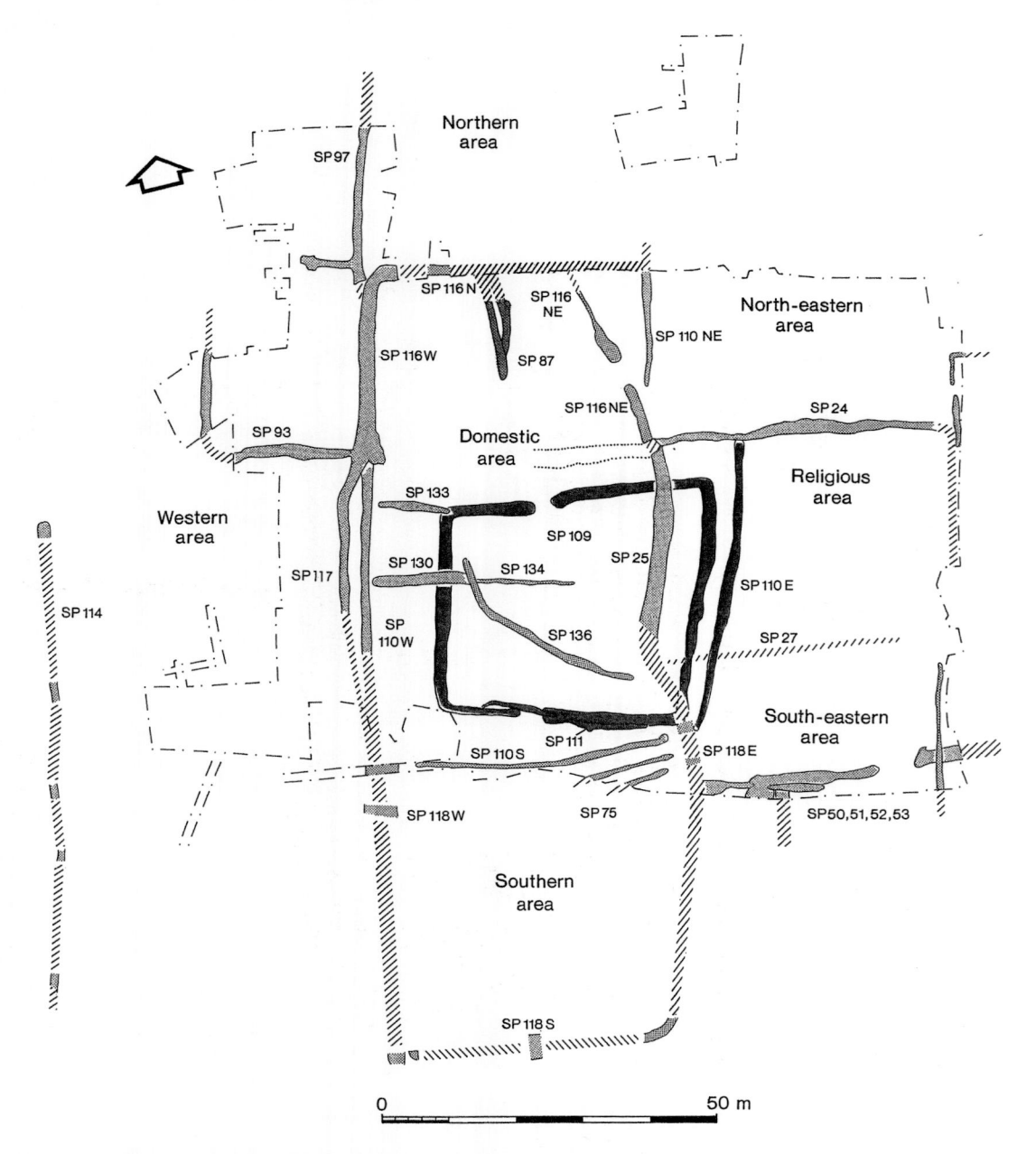

Fig 5.16: Furnells, the late Saxon enclosure and boundary ditch system in relation to the preceding enclosure

the east, covering the access and much of the church and cemetery area. The present rear property boundary along Rotton Row is slightly short of this, as the model would suggest a boundary line 10m further to the east. The block of land south of the domestic core, the southern enclosures, would have added a further one-acre plot to the manorial holding.

There is also some evidence to suggest that while there may have been a single process of reorganisation involving the setting out of ditched plots across the whole of north Raunds, the practical means of achieving this was by the laying out of individual blocks of directly associated plots. This conclusion is drawn from the break in the main western boundary, possibly where a trackway separated the manorial plots at Furnells and the lower-status tenement plots at Langham Road, and the alignment of the respective western boundaries were also offset by some 5m (Fig 4.1). It is therefore suggested that the plots pertaining to Furnells were laid out as a single group, while Langham Road was established independently on an adjacent block of land, but utilising the same principles of plot dimensions and overall sizes.

5. The Archaeological Evidence

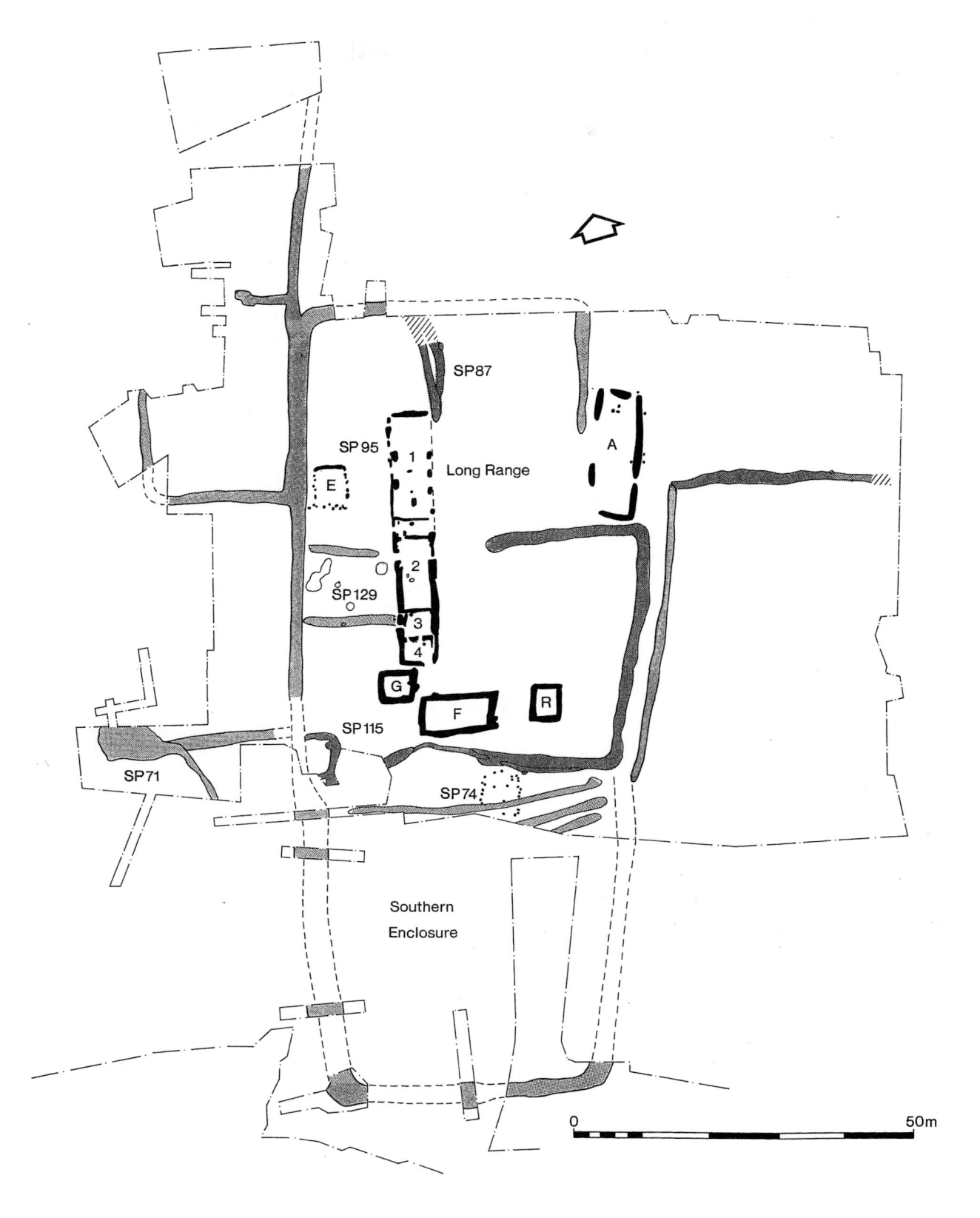

Fig 5.17: Furnells, the late Saxon settlement (AD 900/950)

The western boundary

Although much altered over the centuries, there was probably a single continuous, or near continuous, ditch defining the western boundary from the origin of the system, with this essentially defining the boundary between settlement and the field system (Fig 5.16).

Two lengths of ditch survived relatively unaltered from the original system. The ditch flanking the domestic area (SP110W) was typically 1.1m wide and 0.35m deep. Of 125 pottery sherds recovered, 98 were early–middle Saxon wares, 26 were of St Neots-type ware, and there was a single medieval sherd, probably intrusive. This confirms that the original ditch flanking the domestic area had fallen out of use at an early date, probably by the end of the tenth century (see below).

The continuation of this ditch further to the north (SP97), was evidently maintained for longer as it was up to 0.8m deep with a basal slot, perhaps due to cleaning. This length of ditch produced a total of 319 sherds, including 298 small and eroded early–middle Saxon sherds, derived from a concentration of early activity in this area. Later pottery was also present and included eight sherds of St Neots-type ware and eight sherds of twelfth-century coarse ware, indicating that this northern ditch length had been abandoned by the end of the twelfth century.

The major change to the western boundary was the relocation of a length adjacent to the domestic area 3m westward (SP117), probably in order to provide additional space within the domestic plot to compensate for the loss of area that resulted from the introduction of the churchyard.

The length of the western ditch flanking the northern end of the domestic enclosure was also recut at this time. The new ditch (SP116W) was 1.9m wide and up to 0.95m deep, with a U-shaped profile. Up to three recuts were identified although most of its course had been disturbed by later activity. At its northern end this ditch turned eastward to form a northern boundary (SP116N). Unfortunately, this boundary lay largely just beyond the excavated area and was not investigated further.

Of 577 pottery sherds from the various fills of the later ditches, 137 were of early–middle Saxon date, 311 late Saxon, and 133 Saxo-Norman, indicating that this ditch system was in use through the twelfth century but not beyond.

The western area

While in the later medieval settlement the main western ditch system marked a simple division between the settlement plots and the open fields, the situation was more complex in the late Saxon period. At this time there were further ditch systems and other features to the west of this boundary. A similar arrangement occurred at Langham Road in the late Saxon period (see below), and it would appear that in both instances there were enclosed functional areas that formed intermediate zones between the settlement and the open fields.

At Furnells the actual boundary of the field system may have been marked by a ditch (Fig 5.16, SP114) 50m to the west of the main boundary. It was located intermittently in a series of trial trenches. There was a butt end to the north. To the south, within the Langham Road excavation (Fig 5.57, LRSP32), it turned eastward onto the same alignment as the southern end of the Furnells settlement plots.

The pond (SP71)

The pond was oval, measuring 10m by 8m, and up to 0.8m deep (Fig 5.17). It had been dug into the natural clay that lay beneath the red loam subsoil. The deepest part was at the south-eastern corner, where the sides appeared to have been shaped, possibly to accommodate a lost timber revetment and perhaps a sluice to regulate the flow of water. From here a ditch ran eastwards for 16m, presumably linking to the main western boundary. This was later replaced by a narrower and shallower gully that ran south-eastward on a new alignment.

The loam and clay silts filling the pond contained almost exclusively early–middle Saxon pottery, while the fills of the secondary gully contained an assemblage that included both early–middle Saxon pottery and St Neots-type wares.

Ditched enclosures and quarries

To the north of the pond, lengths of gully formed a small enclosure, 30m long by 22m wide, abutting the western boundary ditch (Fig 5.16, SP93).

Within this enclosure there were two irregular shallow quarry pits (see Fig 5.27, SP102), set close beside the boundary ditch. To the immediate north of the enclosure there was a larger group of quarry pits (SP96) that lay on both sides of the western boundary ditch. As with the other quarries, these may have been used to supply cornbrash limestone used in the construction of the first church, see below.

The southern boundary of the domestic area

All of the late Saxon buildings lay north of the southern arm of the existing enclosure, suggesting that this ditch was retained to form the southern boundary of the new domestic area. It may have been at this time that the southern arm of the enclosure ditch was recut with the entrance possibly furnished with a timber gateway. At the south-western corner of the domestic enclosure the ditch recut continued westward towards a further complex of gullies and pits (Fig 5.17, SP115). This area was apparently related to access between the southern end of the domestic area and the pond and fields to the west. A coin of Edgar (AD 959–975) came from these features, together with sherds of St Neots-type wares.

To the south of the enclosure there were a further three ditches that all appear to be part of a new multiple southern boundary to the domestic area. The disposition of these ditches appears to permit access into the domestic area from the west, while the convergence of the ditches to the east appears to block access from this direction. These ditches may either be original or a later addition following the removal of the two minor timber structures (SP74), which belonged either to the Anglo-Scandinavian farm or the early use of the late Saxon manor.

The northernmost of the three ditches (Fig 5.16, SP110S) was up to 0.7m wide and 0.3m deep. Only 10 pottery sherds were recovered from its fill; six were early–middle Saxon and four late Saxon. Only the eastern ends of the other two ditch systems (SP75) were excavated, and of the 37 sherds of pottery from these, 17 are of early–middle Saxon type, with the remainder late Saxon.

The eastern boundary of the domestic area

The original eastern boundary was probably formed by the retained eastern arm of the existing enclosure and the ditch running parallel to it (Fig 5.16, SP110E). The recut northern end of this ditch terminated immediately adjacent to the east–west boundary ditch flanking the access to the late Saxon hall (SP24). There was no eastern boundary further to the north, as the access to the hall was controlled by a major building range (Fig 5.17, building A), which formed a gatehouse, the thegn's gate, either retained from the previous arrangement or contemporary with the new long range. To the north of this building there was a further eastern boundary ditch (Fig 5.16, SP110NE), but this was offset to the west of the building.

The eastern boundary line was also continued southward by the addition of a new ditch (SP118E), although the full complexity of the ditch systems in this area was not fully resolved in excavation.

With the introduction of the church and churchyard in the mid-tenth century, the original eastern boundary ditches were infilled and the boundary was relocated 10m to the west (Fig 5.16, SP25). To the south this new ditch dog-legged eastward to join the more southerly ditch (SP118E) that had not been realigned.

The gatehouse to the north (Building A) must have been demolished at this time, as the ditch (SP24) that flanked the approach to the hall and formed the northern boundary of the churchyard, was extended westward cutting across the southern end of the building. The longevity of this ditch system, which was retained until the building of the eastern manor house in the fourteenth century, was illustrated by the long sequence of recutting.

With the demolition of the gatehouse, the entrance the domestic area became a simple opening in the ditch system. At some stage, a new ditch (Fig 5.16, SP116 NE) was set at an oblique angle across this area. It had a simple, 4.0m wide, opening providing access to the domestic enclosure. This entrance lay to the north of its predecessor, perhaps as a result of the appearance of shallow stone quarry pits to the east (Fig 5.27, SP73 and SP61) adjacent to the northern churchyard boundary ditch. These quarries may have provided limestone for the construction of the first church. The ditches at this entrance produced some medieval pottery, indicating that this new eastern boundary was to remain in use until after the construction of the western manor house at the beginning of the thirteenth century.

The north-eastern area

Access from the east, from a precursor of Rotton Row along the western side of the Raunds Brook, would have been across this area, but no metalling or other indications of former trackways survived.

It may be noted that at the time of the excavation access to the pasture closes from Rotton Row was still along this same line, which lay beyond the northernmost of the houses fronting onto Rotton Row. This suggests that the location of this access had been fossilised in the street pattern along Rotton Row for over a thousand years, and survived even once the manor it had served was long gone.

The buildings of the late Saxon manor (AD 900/950–1100)

The domestic area contained a major timber building complex, the long range, which comprised two adjoining structures, an open hall to the north and a suite of attached chambers to the south (Fig 5.17, and Figs 3.6 and 3.7). To the south there were also three free-standing ancillary ranges, the largest of which may have been a detached kitchen range, and a further minor building may have stood to the west of the long range. The possible gatehouse to the east (building A), which was contemporary with at least the early use of the long range, has already been described. In all cases all that survived were the construction trenches, and there were no floors or other occupation deposits associated with these buildings.

The buildings surrounded a central yard that extended 50m north–south. However, it is suspected that there would have been a division between the public space facing the hall to the north, and the private or domestic space to the south. This division may have been provided initially by the retention of part of the northern arm of the existing enclosure. The southern yard would have measured 20m north–south by 27m wide. With the later introduction of the churchyard boundaries, the width was reduced to 20m, but the length of the domestic yard was probably increased to 26m by the provision of a new boundary slightly further to the north. Any direct evidence for this new northern ditch had been removed by a later ditch along the same line (Fig 5.27, dotted outline). This surviving ditch was contemporary with the western manor house, but is assumed to have replaced earlier ditches on the same line.

No yard surfaces had survived either to the north or within the enclosed yard to the south.

The long range (SP138)

The long range, which straddled Cornbrash to the north and Blisworth clay to the south, had a total length of 38.5m, including both the hall to the north and the abutting domestic apartments to the south (Figs 5.18 and 5.19). The plan form is closely paralleled by the contemporary long range at nearby West Cotton and also by broadly contemporary hall ranges at a number of sites including Goltho, Lincolnshire and Faccombe Netherton, Hampshire (Chapter 4 and Fig 4.2).

The hall

The hall was 19.0m long and 6.5m wide, with a length to width ratio of 3:1 (Figs 5.19 and 5.20). The damage caused by later rebuilding as an aisled hall and by the construction of the stone-built western manor, and the uncertain phasing of some of the palimpsest of cut features in this area, has made it difficult to fully interpret the plan form and the internal arrangement of the hall. Indeed, even the basic plan form was not established in excavation and was only defined during the post-excavation programme. The excavation of a near contemporary hall range at West Cotton in the late 1980s has been a major influence on the final interpretation, as presented below.

The preferred interpretation is that the hall end of the range comprised two separate but conjoined elements, the hall and a slightly wider northern chamber (Fig 5.20). Towards the southern end of the hall, an internal partition formed an ante-chamber between the hall and the apartments to the south. Internally, the northern chamber was 6.5m long by c6.0m wide, while the central open hall was 9.0m long by c5.5m wide, with a 2.5m long ante-chamber to the south.

No eastern wall trench survived, but it is most likely that it was closely similar to the western wall trench and had been removed by the more substantial and deeper wall trench of the later aisled hall, which had directly and perhaps deliberately, utilised the line of the earlier wall.

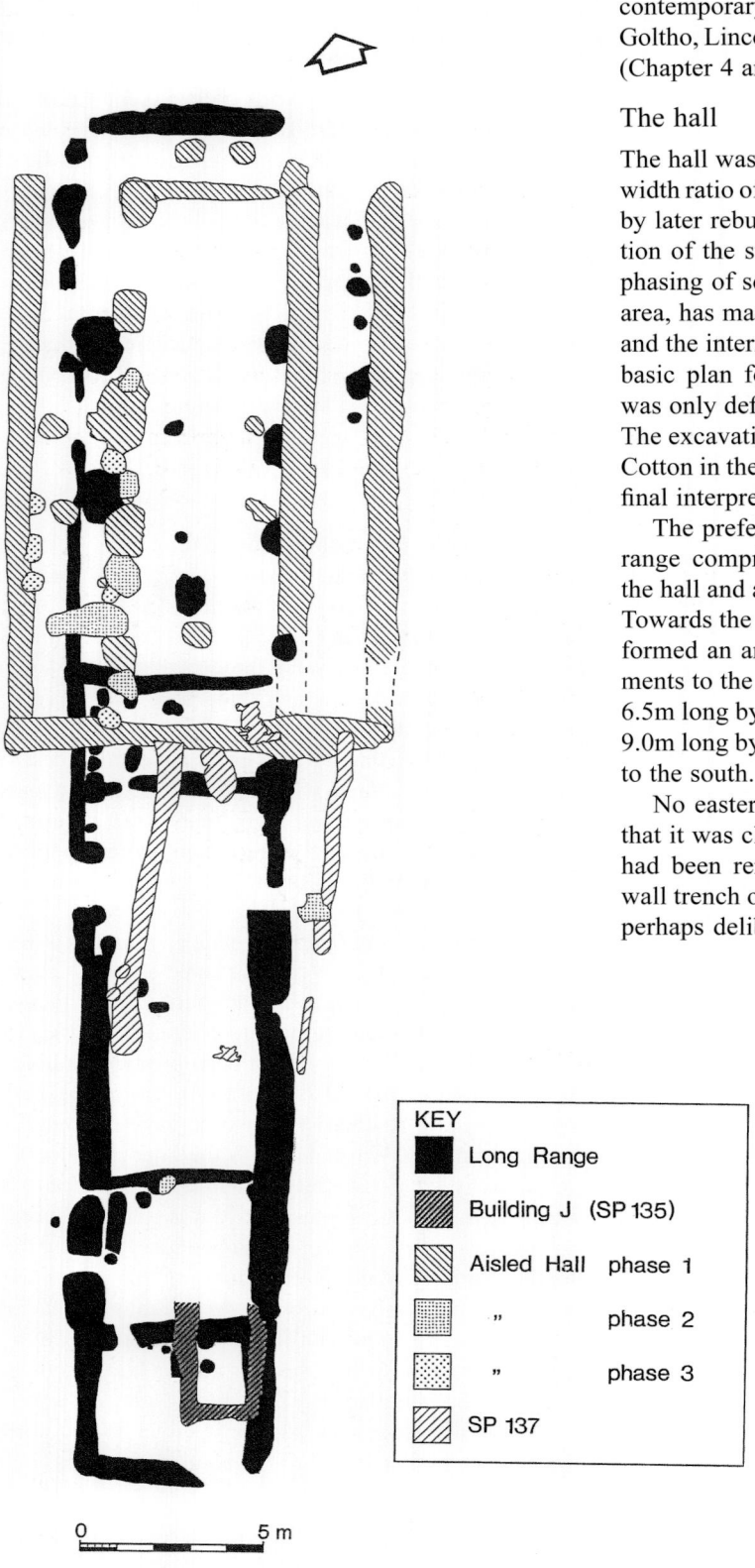

Fig 5.18: Furnells, the long range and aisled hall

At the centre of the eastern wall, on its inner edge, there was a pair of substantial post-pits, set 1.5m apart, which may have held the portal posts of the main door surround, which would have had an opening perhaps 2.0m wide (Fig 5.20, D1).

The western wall was founded in a narrow construction trench, 0.40–0.50m wide, which had been heavily truncated by later activity, so that no more than the bottom 200mm survived. To the north, a 1.0m wide break probably formed a doorway opening, set slightly north of centre (Fig 5.20, D2). To the north of this doorway the wall trench terminated at a transverse post or plank setting adjacent to a larger post-pit (P4). To the north of this the western wall was marked by disturbed remnants of a wall trench that lay slightly west of the remainder of the western wall, indicating that the northern end of the building was a little wider, and possibly forming a northern chamber of separate build. The positioning of paired post-pits (P3 and P4) at the junction of the hall and this postulated northern chamber support this interpretation. The only other paired post-pits (P1 and P2) lay at the southern end of the hall, suggesting that the two sets of paired post-pits held timber frames forming the gable ends of the hall. The northern chamber was therefore an abutting extension to the hall.

A difficulty with this interpretation is the absence of an evident partition wall between the hall and the northern chamber. However, this area had been disturbed by a stone-lined drain within the later manor house, which may have removed all traces of a shallow wall trench or postholes supporting a partition wall.

While it is suggested that the hall comprised two structural elements, hall and northern chamber, the placing of the main doorway in the centre of the whole building implies that it was conceived as a single entity. The doorway placing can therefore be seen as an architectural device to impress visitors. Viewed from the outside the central doorway would suggest that the hall ran the full length of the range, and only on entering would the hall be seen to be smaller on the inside than it appeared on the outside.

At the northern end of the building there was a detached length of wall trench. It stopped slightly short of the main walls, and there was an evident post-setting only in the western end of the trench. This might suggest that the end of the northern chamber had a hipped, rather than a gabled, roof. A pair of rectangular cuts in the base of this wall trench may suggest the provision of a 1.0m wide doorway (D3), just west of centre. A transverse wall trench 2.0m south of the northern wall (Fig 5.19) is of uncertain phasing, but is most likely to have held the northern wall of the later aisled hall (see Fig 5.30).

At the southern end of the hall, the wall trench ran between two post-pits (P1 and P2) presumed to have held a timber-framed gable end. The wall trench terminated short of the western wall, where there may have been a doorway (D4).

A transverse wall trench 3.0m north of the southern wall may also belong with this building (Figs 5.19 and 5.20). It contained remnants of stone-packed elongated postholes, perhaps denoting plank-settings. It would have held an internal partition forming a southern chamber, 2.5m long, perhaps serving as an ante-chamber, controlling movement between the public hall and the private apartments to the south.

There was little surviving detail associated with the wall trenches to define the nature of the timber construction. At nearby West Cotton, a well-preserved length of wall trench contained uniform closely-spaced depressions in the base that suggested the presence of stave-built walls, comprising closely-set timbers of similar size that shared the roof load, rather than this being carried by a limited number of principal posts with infilling between. It is likely that the hall at Furnells was of a similar construction, although the gable ends of the hall had separate timber frames that were set inside the stave-built walls.

The interpretation presented accounts for the majority, but not all, of the excavated features. A single large post-pit (P5) just inside the western wall trench and opposite the main doorway has no obvious structural role, while a post-pit (P6) towards the southern end of the postulated eastern wall is similarly unexplained.

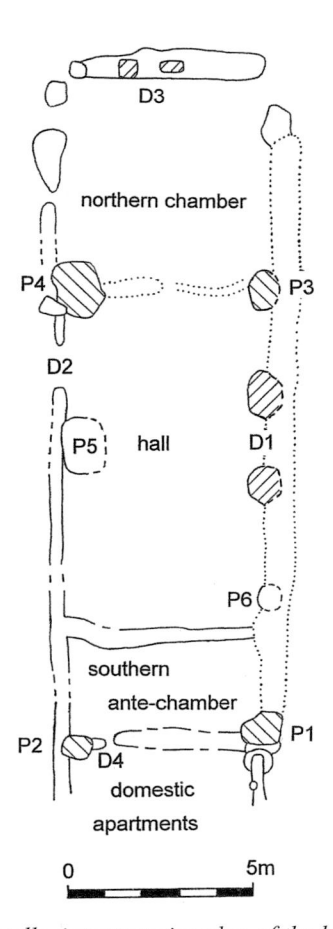

Fig 5.20: Furnells, interpretative plan of the hall of the long range, showing principal posts (P) and doorways (D)

The domestic chambers

The domestic range was 18.5m long by 4.8m wide, slightly narrower than the hall (Fig 5.19). The southernmost chamber, room 4, which was 3.4m long, had been excavated as a separate structure prior to the identification of the rest of the range, but the building does appear to have been of a single build. The length to width ratio was nearly 4:1.

The western and eastern walls were founded in wall trenches that contained some surviving dispersed post-settings in the bases, and some deeper post-pits may have held timber door surrounds. The southern end wall was continuous with the side walls, as were the divisions between rooms 3 and 4. The absence of principal posts indicates that this range was entirely a post-in-trench construction, probably stave built.

Rooms 2 and 3 originally appear to have formed a single room, three-bays, 14m long, unless evidence of lightly built partition walls had been lost. There was probably a near central doorway in the eastern wall, where there was a break in the wall trench and post-pits that may have held a door surround. Post-pits within the western wall trench suggest the provision of two doorways, towards the northern and southern ends of the wall. An extensive area of scorched natural, contaminated by charcoal, at the southern end of the room, may have derived from a hearth or a brazier stand, and traces of a possible clay floor survived close by. This burnt area was cut by a shallow gully that was probably a later partition wall, shortening room 2 to 10m long and creating a new square chamber (room 3), 4m long. An internal slot adjacent to the western wall indicates the provision of some substantial internal timber fixture or fitting.

Building R (SP103)

The three buildings to the south of the long range (Fig 5.17) shared a common construction technique of continuous wall trenches, and the fills all produced similar pottery assemblages.

Building R was a small rectangular building, 4.5m long by 3.6m wide (Fig 5.21). There was a single continuous wall trench of uniform depth, although a slightly deeper slot in the south-east corner might have held a sill beneath a 1.0m wide corner doorway. No impressions of posts were recovered from the base of the wall trench. A pair of postholes inside the northern wall may have held structural timbers or some substantial internal fitting running the length of the northern wall, and set at the opposite end of the building from the doorway.

One of the internal postholes contained 24 sherds of early–middle Saxon pottery. Two sherds of early–middle Saxon pottery were recovered from the wall trench fills, along with a single sherd of a St Neots-type ware.

Building F (SP104)

This was a large rectangular building, 9.4m long by 4.8m wide (Figs 5.22 and 5.23). The continuous wall trench generally had a uniform depth of 300mm, although at the south-western corner it was wider and shallower, at 150mm deep. The paired postholes in the northern wall, set 1.0m apart, might indicate the presence of a central doorway, while similar post-settings in the southern wall trench might define the eastern side of an opposed doorway. Further post-settings were preserved in the base of the western wall trench, including a central pair of elongated slots that may have held paired planks. The function of these is unknown, although they might have flanked a further doorway or supported some specific structural feature related to the function of the room.

At the south-eastern corner there was an additional length of slot running eastward, and there may have been a similar feature at the disturbed north-eastern corner. There was a similar feature on building G (SP105), see below, and similarly extended corners have been seen on the late Saxon timber buildings at West Cotton (Chapman in press). They are presumed to have held some form of buttressing or raking posts.

Pottery was scarce; 27 sherds of early–middle Saxon and seven of St Neots-type ware were recovered.

While the function of this building is unknown, a timber building at West Cotton with a similar relationship to the long range, was replaced in the twelfth century by a stone-built kitchen range. It is suggested, therefore, that this timber building may also have functioned as a detached kitchen range.

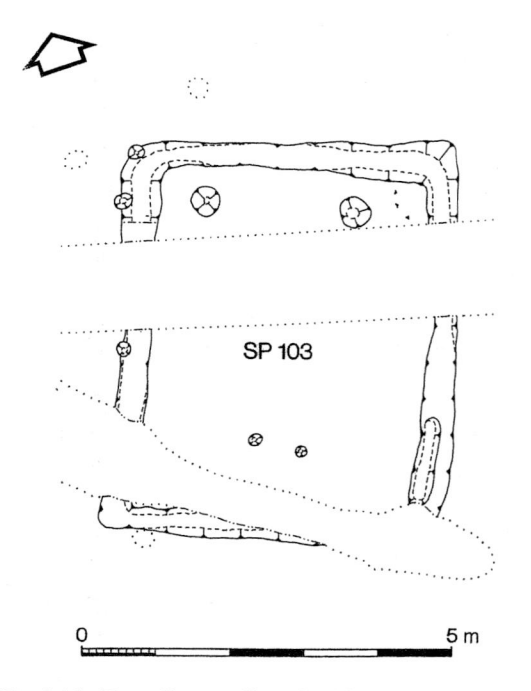

Fig 5.21: Furnells, ancillary building R (SP103)

5. The Archaeological Evidence

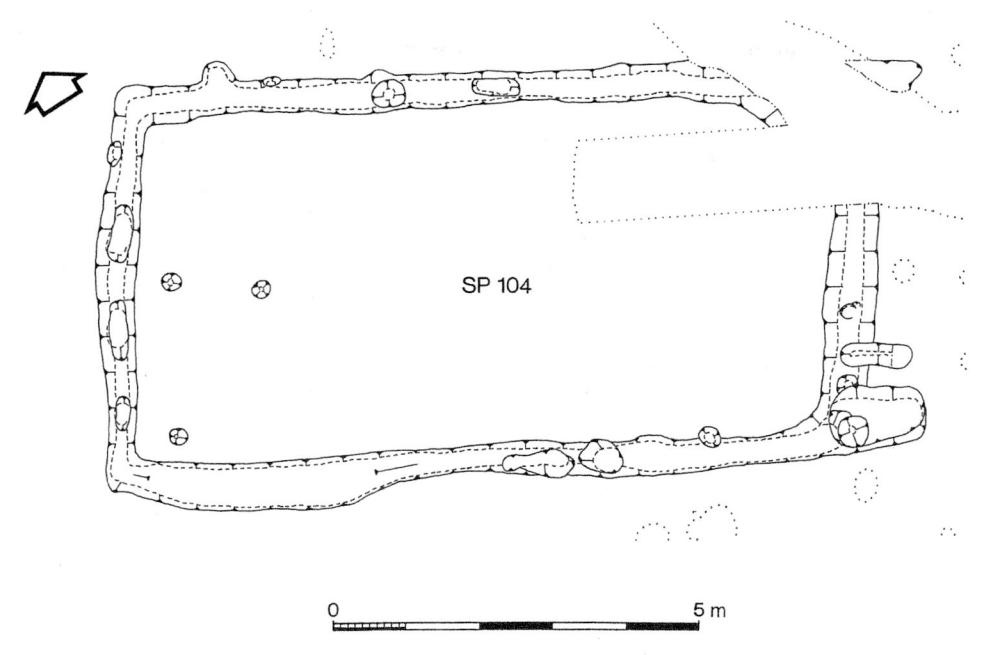

Fig 5.22: Furnells, ancillary building F (SP104)

Fig 5.23: Furnells, ancillary building F (SP104), looking east, and showing the southern entrance and recutting of the square enclosure (SP 109) (right)

Building G (SP105)

This was a near square building, measuring 3.9m by 4.3m (Figs 5.24 and 5.25). A deep, narrow slot in the base of the southern wall trench may indicate where deeper post-settings supported door surrounds. There were two impressions of posts in the base of the eastern wall trench, and an adjacent shallow circular hollow cut the outer edge of the wall trench.

Six early–middle Saxon and eight St Neots-type sherds were recovered from the fills of the wall trenches and the pit.

Features north of the long range

Two phases of ditch ran northward from the north-east corner of the long range (Fig 5.17, SP87). They would have blocked access around the northern end of the building and probably also functioned as drains, and would have emptied into the northern boundary ditch. Prolonged collection of water in the gullies was denoted by the accumulation of silt within them and the formation of iron panning and water abrasion of the edges and surfaces of the associated pottery. The gully was later deliberately back-filled and it contained a large quantity of dumped debris. This probably occurred in the early twelfth century, as the debris included 177 sherds of early-middle Saxon pottery, 223 sherds of late Saxon pottery and only eight sherds of Saxo-Norman pottery, suggesting that it had been infilled at the building of the aisled hall.

Remnant layers of compacted soils to the north of the hall (not illustrated), may have been parts of yard surfaces adjacent to the building.

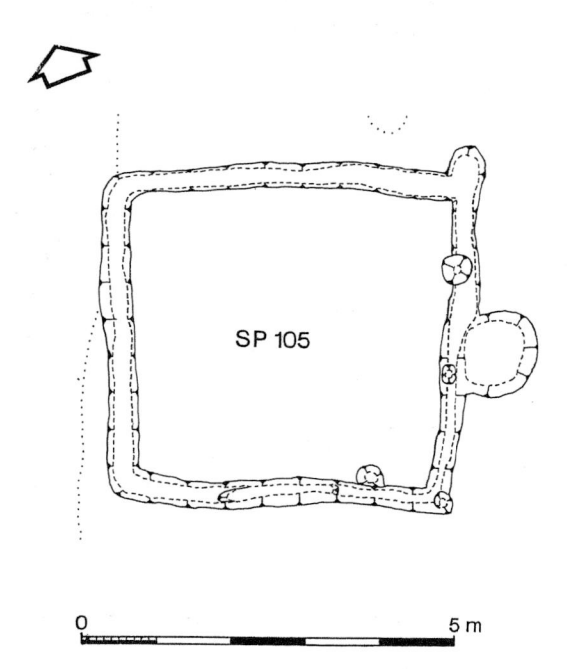

Fig 5.24: Furnells, ancillary building G (SP105)

Features west of the long range

There were two short lengths of ditch (Fig 5.16, SP130 and SP133) lying 10m apart, which ran westward from the long range (Fig 5.17). They also may have served as both boundaries and/or drains. Between them there was a group of pits (Fig 5.17, SP129), which are broadly dated to the lifetime of the long range and aisled hall. One of these contained cess deposits, and may have served as a garderobe to domestic apartments of the long range.

Building E (SP95)

Whilst the main group of ancillary buildings lay to the south of the hall, a single slot and posthole structure, 6.0m long by 5m wide, lay to the west, adjacent to the western boundary ditch (Fig 5.17). It is broadly dated as contemporary with the long range and aisled hall.

The north wall was defined by a shallow trench with a single elongated plank or posthole at the north-west corner (Fig 5.26). The other sides were formed by postholes, though it is possible that the truncated southern wall may originally have been like its northern counterpart.

Twenty-four sherds of early Saxon pottery were recovered, mostly from the northern gully, together with 13 sherds of late Saxon and Saxo-Norman pottery.

Furnells manor: The late Saxon church and churchyard (AD 950–1150)

The sequence and chronology of the church and churchyard, which were constructed to the east of the domestic area, relies upon a range of evidence.

The pottery assemblage from a length of ditch beneath the church provides a *terminus post quem* for its construction of AD 900. However, the infilling of these ditches and the relocation of the boundary line further to the west has already been cited as clear evidence that the church and churchyard were a later addition to the late Saxon manorial holding, necessarily placing them no earlier than the mid-tenth century (Fig 5.27).

The pottery from the grave fills is composed of residual early–middle Saxon wares, several hundred sherds of late Saxon wares and less than a score of Saxo-Norman and medieval pieces. All of the ceramic types that were present at the adjacent domestic site were represented in the later Saxon assemblage from the churchyard. By contrast, the domestic area produced a large quantity of Saxo-Norman pottery, indicating that the religious area was effectively sealed from the secular activity at some time prior to the introduction of these wares. In particular, this must have occurred before the eleventh century when pottery of Cotswold Oolitic type was especially prevalent in the adjacent domestic area.

The radiocarbon dating of burials considered to be among the earliest generation of inhumations within the graveyard suggests that the first interments occurred at around the mid-tenth century (as already discussed, and

Fig 5.25: Furnells, ancillary building G, looking east, and enclosure ditch (foreground)

see Boddington 1996, 72). This suggests that the addition of the church and churchyard occurred in the mid-tenth century, perhaps within a couple of decades of the establishment of the late Saxon manor.

The late Saxon church (SP3 & SP4)

The soil layers beneath the first church (SP3) were considered by the excavators to have resulted from the levelling of the area preparatory to building construction. The first church was very small, comprising a single cell measuring 4.5m by 3.1m (Fig 5.28 and Fig 3.9). The walls were of rough-hewn limestone bonded with mortar and resting on two layers of clay-bonded limestone foundations. The presence of decayed mortar in later contexts suggests that the walls were plastered, probably both internally and externally, while the recovered fragments from architectural pieces indicate the provision of decorative door and window surrounds.

There was a door towards the western end of the southern wall, and an elongated stone-lined pit abutting the inner face of the western wall may have held the uprights supporting a timber bellcote. To the east, a complete pottery vessel placed in a shallow pit and sealed beneath a floor of small irregular pieces of limestone, may have

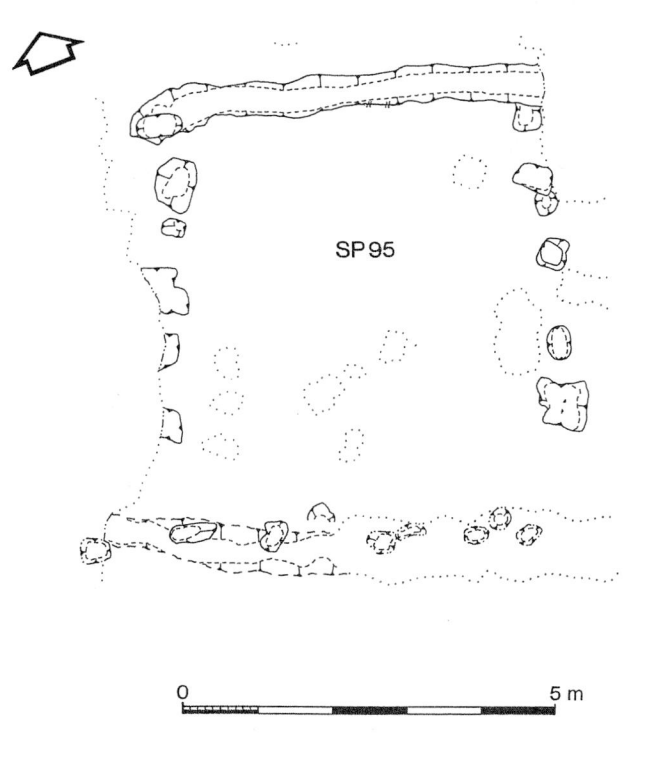

Fig 5.26: Furnells, ancillary building E (SP95)

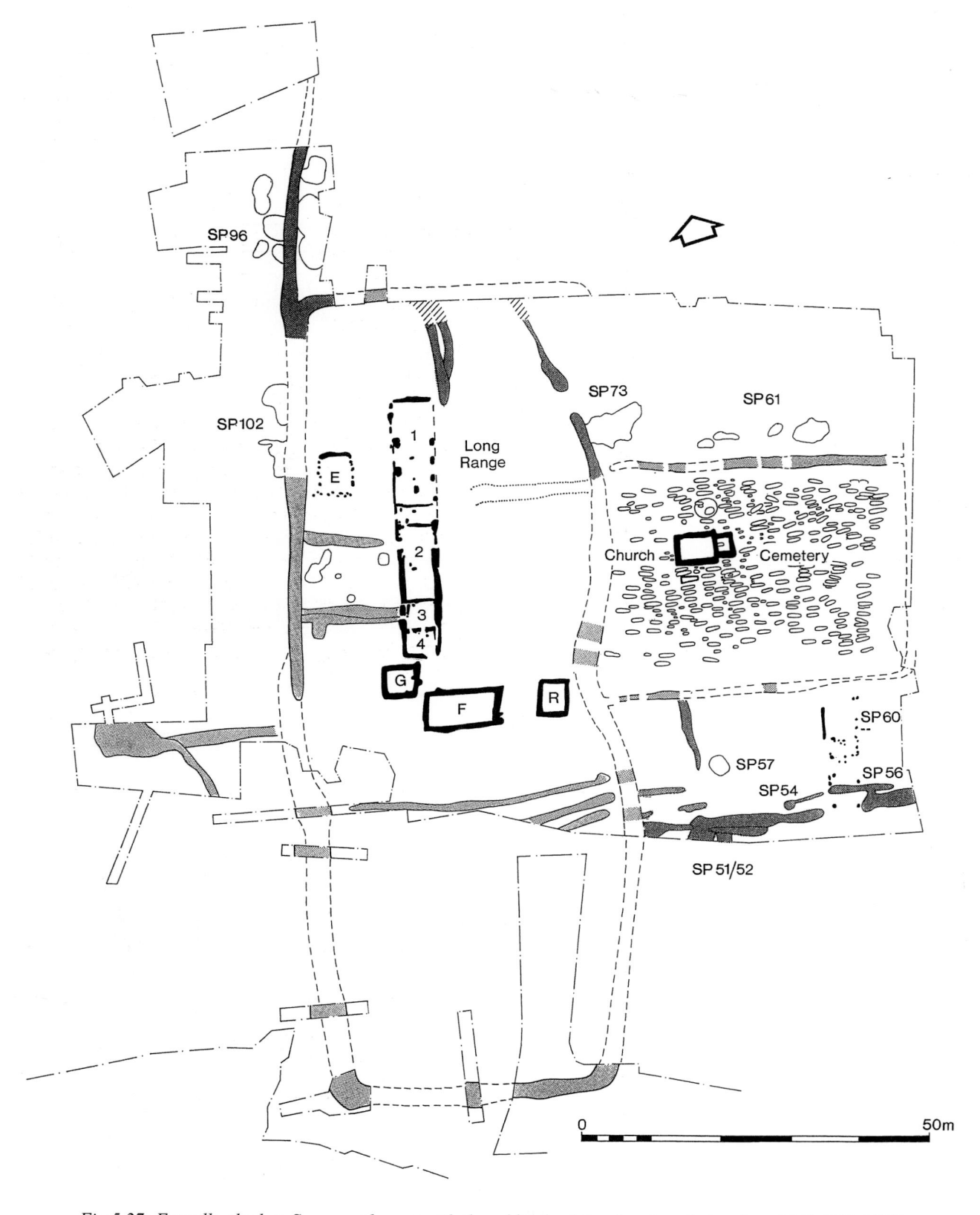

Fig 5.27: Furnells, the late Saxon settlement with the addition of the church and churchyard (AD 950–1100)

been placed here during the consecration of the church. It was perhaps used a *sacrarium* and later as a *piscina*, situated to the immediate west of the altar, which would have stood at the end of the nave. These features provide rare evidence for late Saxon liturgical practice (see Parsons in Boddington 1996, 58–66).

A small chancel (SP4), measuring 2.65 by 3.1m, was constructed slightly later, but built in the same fashion as the nave. The chancel contained a stone-foundation against the eastern wall, which has been interpreted as the base of a clergy bench. Behind it, remnants of original wall plaster survived. As all the adjacent burials respect the chancel, it would appear that burial only commenced following its construction.

The construction of the church is the earliest recognised use of building stone on the site, and provides a context for the appearance of several extensive but shallow stones quarries around the margins of the late Saxon ditched plots to the north (Fig 5.27, SP61 and SP73), south (SP51 and 52) and also to the west (SP102) and north-west (SP96).

The churchyard boundaries

The northern and western boundaries of the churchyard have already been discussed in relation to both the access to the domestic area and the relocation of the original eastern boundary of the domestic enclosure. The western boundary ditch (SP25), was 1.5m–2.5m wide and 0.8m deep, but was later recut (SP26) to 1.20m–2.0m wide and up to 0.5m deep.

The eastern boundary

Immediately adjacent to the eastern limit of excavation a single trial trench located a clay-filled ditch, cutting tenacious clay natural, which may have been an eastern boundary to the churchyard. There were certainly no burials within several metres of this ditch, indicating that the churchyard.

The southern boundary (SP27)

The original southern boundary of the churchyard was probably the earliest of a sequence of ditches, the latest of which was contemporary with the late medieval eastern manor. This ditch system ran along the top of a slope, with the area to the south lying at a lower level than the churchyard.

The churchyard (SP20)

The religious and demographic aspects of the cemetery have been discussed at length elsewhere (Boddington 1996, 67). The *in situ* or disturbed remains of 363 individuals were recovered; with an estimated total population of some 380–390. A full range of the populace is represented from neonates to elderly individuals, with a demographic profile that would be expected for such a rural community. There was a high level of infant mortality. For adult males there was a fairly even death rate, while for females there was a peak death rate for ages in the 20s, no doubt resulting directly or indirectly from childbirth, and a steady death rate thereafter.

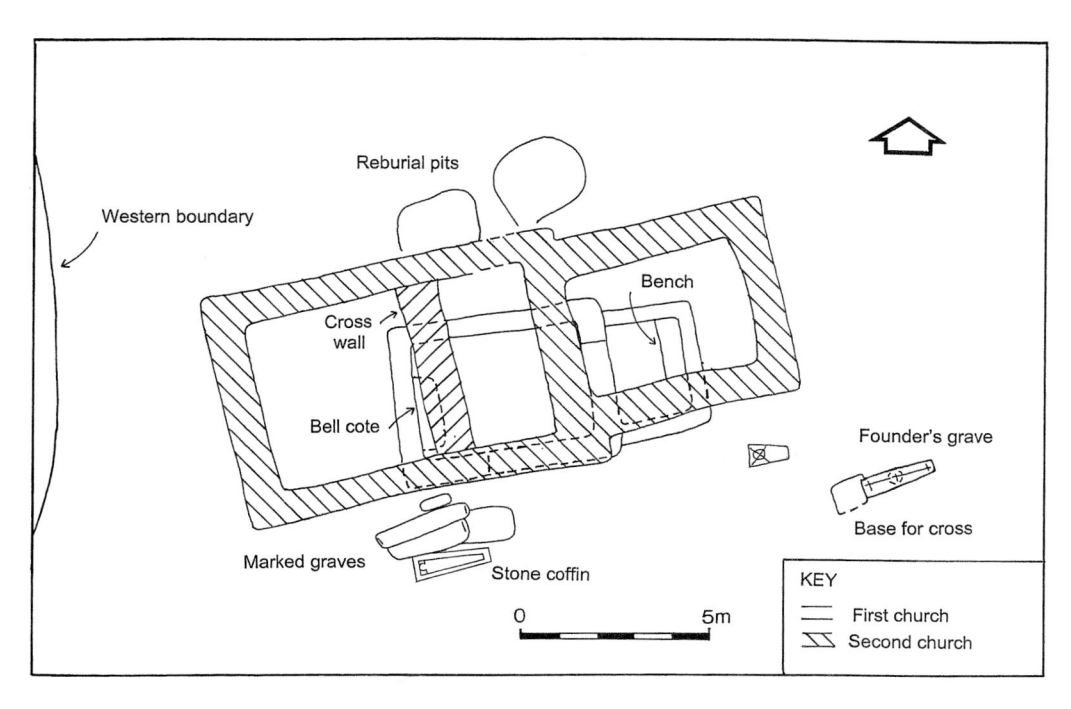

Fig 5.28: Furnells, the late Saxon and medieval churches, and major burials

An area to the south-east of the church has been interpreted as a founder's plot (Fig 5.28). The grave of a man, aged 35–45 years, was marked by a fine grave slab in Barnack stone, decorated with interlace (Boddington 1996, figs 94–96). A stone footing at the head end may have been the base for a free-standing cross, and parts of a broken up cross, decorated with interface, had been used as an improvised cover for the stone coffin. To the north-west of the founder's grave, an infant burial was marked by a smaller grave slab decorated with a simple encircled St Andrew's cross (Boddington 1996, figs 97–99).

Around the first church the cemetery developed in an orderly manner. There were seven rows of burials across the southern part of the cemetery, and the rows to the east continued northward past the end of the church. There were also three shorter rows to the north of the church. This scheme was subject to later infilling, but disturbance of earlier graves was relatively uncommon, and when it did occur the disturbed bones had invariably been carefully collected and redeposited within the new grave. There were later extensions of less well-ordered row systems to the east and south-east, as well as the insertion of individual burials within available gaps within the cemetery area, and the insertion of infant and child burials close to the walls of the church, particularly around the chancel.

Whilst shrouded burials in earth-cut graves appear to have been the norm, the disposition of some burials indicates the use of wooden coffins, and a high proportion of the graves exhibit the use of placed stones around the head and under, around and over other parts of the body as well.

A second group of high-status burials lay to the immediate south-west of the church, next to the doorway. The earlier phases included burials in wooden coffins and burials with end marker stones and, finally, the provision of a stone coffin with a head recess, characteristic of a post-conquest date in the later eleventh or twelfth centuries (Boddington 1996, figs 88 and 89). These individuals may be the successive occupiers of the late Saxon and medieval manor houses to the west. However, the recovery of fragments from perhaps another four stone coffins from the foundations of the second church indicates that further high-class burials had been disturbed at the later rebuilding, see below. These may also have lain around the south-western corner of the original church, where there are evident gaps in the row structure.

It has been argued that the majority of the excavated burials were contemporary with the first church, with this partly indicated by the evident absence of a second overall phase of use, which would have resulted in overlapping row systems and much intercutting of graves and disturbance of burials.

The south-eastern area

The system of boundary ditches enclosed a small area, measuring 20m north-south by at least 35m east-west, on the lower lying ground to the south of the churchyard, which was a focus for activity only in the tenth and eleventh centuries (Fig 5.27).

The southern boundary of this area was a particularly complex system of interconnecting pits and ditches (SP51/52 and SP56). These were up to 1.5m deep and may well have been quarries used for the extraction of fine sand and gravel, perhaps supplying the raw material for the mortar used in the construction of the first church.

The pits appear to have been backfilled quite rapidly, and the quantities of domestic waste incorporated into the fills must have either come from the long range complex or other nearby buildings. The dumped waste included ash, charcoal, smithing slag, limestone, pottery and animal bone. The pottery was dominated by St Neots-type ware storage jars, together with sherds of Stamford ware, while the assemblage of artefacts included fragments of horse harness fittings with Scandinavian connotations. The deposits of charcoal also included charred seeds from free-threshing hexaploid and tetraploid wheat, together with the remains of unidentified herbage and a few large legumes.

Subsequently, the boundary line was probably reinstated by the digging of shallower ditches, and a few sherds of pottery dated to the thirteenth century, from the lower fills of two pits, illustrate the longevity of this boundary system.

Building P (SP60)

This small timber building was 8.0m long by 4.7m wide (Fig 5.29). A room to the north was defined by parallel wall trenches, while a short, narrower southern chamber, only 2.5m long by 4.0m wide, was defined by postholes.

Further to the south there were traces of a possible surface, where scorching could indicate the position of a hearth. This might suggest that the building had been longer, or that an external surface lay between the building and part of the boundary ditch system (SP56). The small assemblage of 33 sherds included 13 of early–middle Saxon date and 13 of St Neots-type wares. This area lies beyond the domestic enclosure, and it might be part of an associated lower-status domestic area serving the thegn occupying the long range, with the debris from the nearby ditches reflecting involvement with the daily round of crop processing and light industry.

The southern areas

The partial definition of boundary ditches extending southward from the domestic enclosure, largely located within the Langham Road excavation site, appears to define a southern enclosure (Fig 5.27). In the limited part of the interior investigated there were no contemporary features.

Furnells manor: The aisled hall (AD 1100–1200)

At around the beginning of the twelfth century the original hall was levelled and replaced by a broader aisled hall (Fig 5.30). The domestic range to the south was probably retained for a while, but this too was subsequently levelled and replaced by a much shorter range. In addition, there was a separate building to the south-west, perhaps a kitchen range.

The pottery assemblage associated with the aisled hall and the underlying hall of the long range provides a *terminus post quem* for construction of AD 1100, and the more than 1200 sherds of pottery recovered from the aisled hall and associated deposits suggest that occupation continued through the twelfth century.

The aisled hall (SP142)

The aisled hall was 16.0m long by 10.5m wide (Figs 5.31–5.33). As already discussed in relation to the hall of the original long range, there are problems in attempting to unravel and interpret the palimpsest of wall trenches and post-pits in this area (Fig 5.18). The preferred interpretation is that the building comprised a hall, incorporating a western aisle supported by a row of aisle posts, while running the full length of the eastern side there was a narrow fore-building, or pentice, of separate build, as part of a formal façade to the public face of the building. The hall was 16.0m long by 8.0m wide, a length to width ratio of 2:1. Internally, the hall was 6.5m wide, comprising a central space 4.2m wide and a western aisle 2.3m wide (Figs 5.31 and 5.32). There may have been a continuous roof slope to the west, although the angle may have been less steep over the aisle to increase internal head room, while the fore-building would have had a separate roof, perhaps abutting the hall below full wall height, so that the hall could have been be lit from openings high in its eastern wall.

The two long walls of the hall and the wall supporting the fore-building were founded in continuous wall trenches, 0.90m wide by 0.50m deep. Only the southern end of the two eastern wall trenches had been lost to later disturbance. In the base of the wall trenches there were some evident changes in depth, and fragments of limestone packing and impressions of posts, but too few to provide a clear indication of the overall arrangement of the timbers, although the posts appear to have been typically 200–250mm in diameter. Given the absence of any paired post-pits, it is suggested that the long walls were stave built.

Along the two eastern wall trenches there were various changes in depth and some deeper hollows indicating post positions, and the main eastern doorway (Fig 5.32, D1) may have opened into the southern of the two central bays, facing an open hearth, although the evidence was not conclusive.

The arcade forming the western aisle comprised a line of four post-pits (P2–P5), up to 0.68m deep, which may

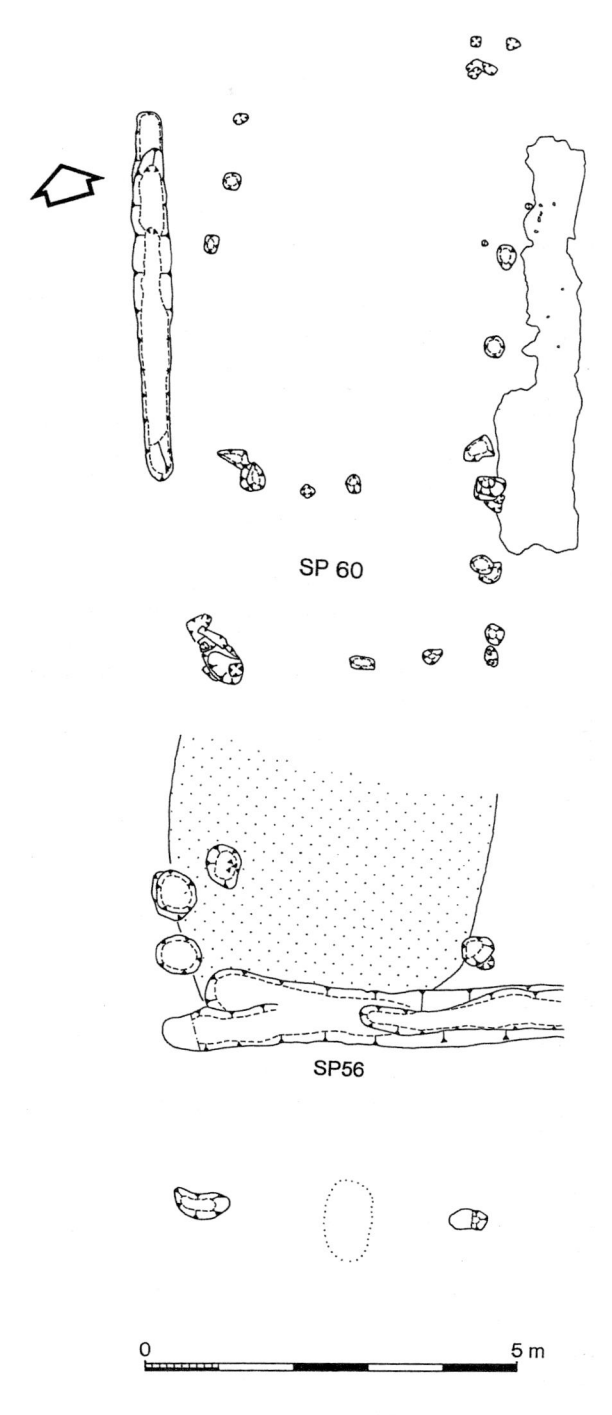

Fig 5.29: Furnells, building P (SP60)

have held uprights up to 500mm in diameter. These were regularly spaced at 3.2m centre-to-centre. This spacing was maintained to a post set in the northern wall trench (P1), but the spacing to the southern wall was only 1.9m. The interior therefore comprised five bays, with four consistently 3.2m long while there was a narrower bay, 2/3 of this length, at the southern end of the building (Fig 5.32). This may have been related to the need to butt the new hall

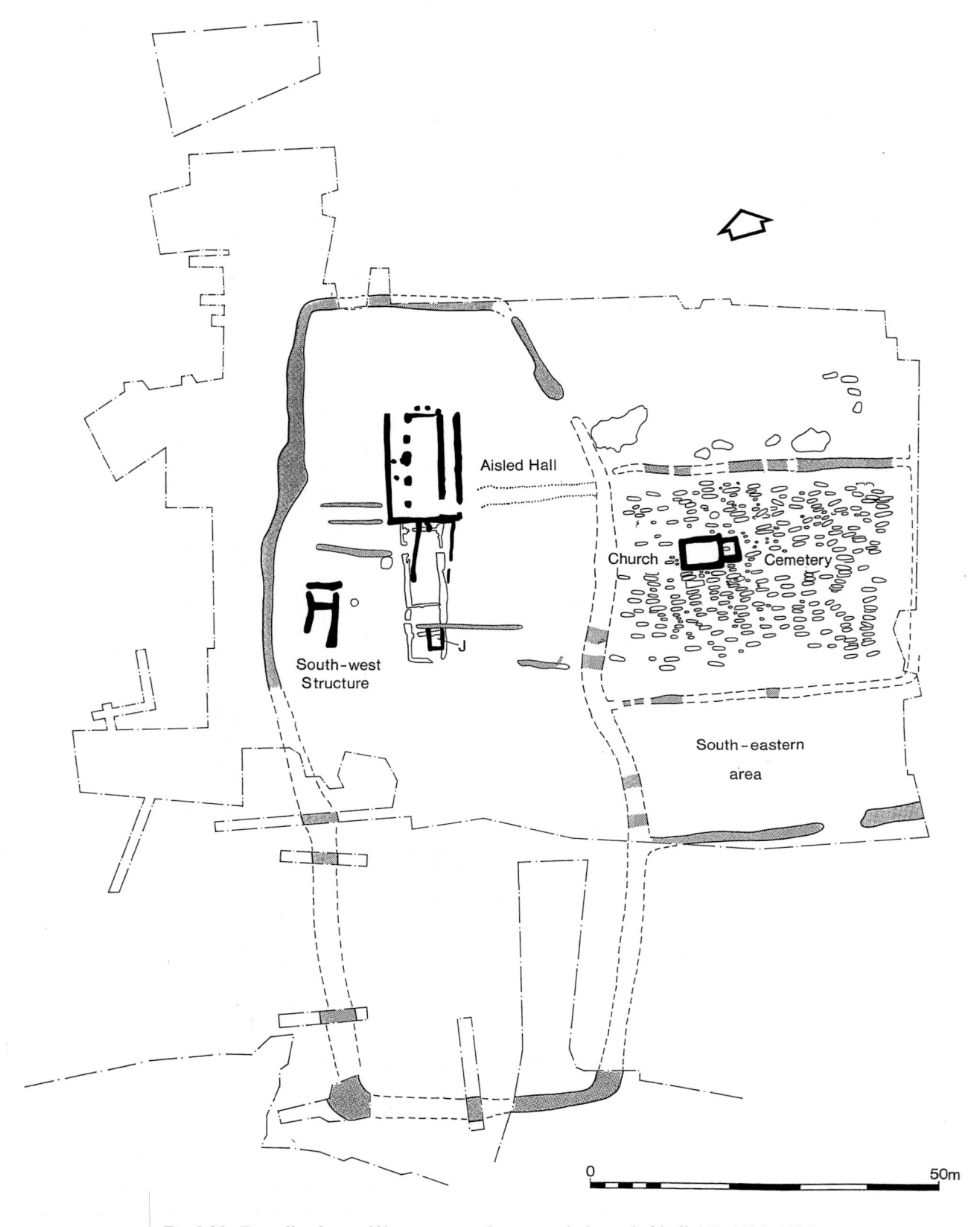

Fig 5.30: Furnells, the twelfth-century settlement with the aisled hall (AD 1100–1200)

Fig 5.31: Furnells, the aisled hall

against the retained gable end of the domestic apartments of the original long range, perhaps with a hipped roof over the partial bay rather than a plain gable end.

The northernmost aisle post (P2) stood alone, but south of this there where numerous additional post-pits of various sizes set between the original aisle posts, making interpretation problematic (Fig 5.32). If these also held aisle posts they would imply that there was at least three separate phases in which aisle posts in the southern half of the building were relocated, with resultant changes to the width and the number of bays, from five to six to four, which would seem to require concurrent rebuilding

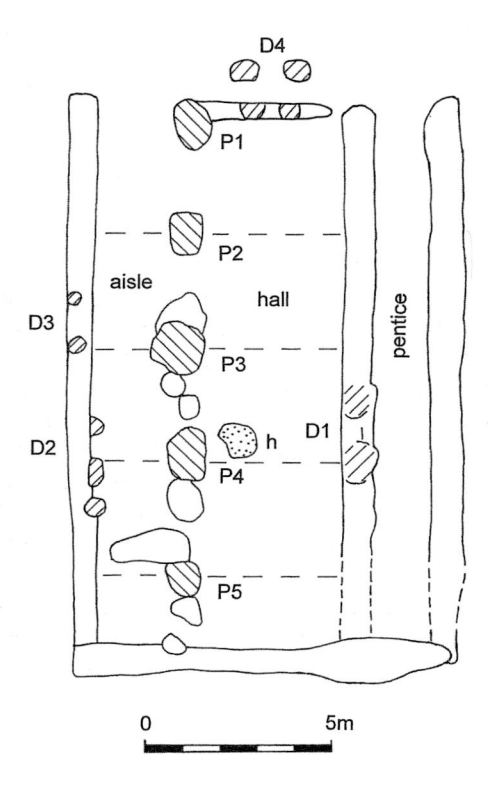

Fig 5.32: Furnells, interpretative plan of aisled hall, showing aisle posts (P), the bay structure and doorways (D)

of much of the roof. A possible model for this sequence was developed in post-excavation (see Fig 5.18, aisled hall, phases 1–3).

Given the structural implications of the multi-phase model, a simpler interpretation is now preferred. It is suggested that the bay structure remained constant while the intermediate post-pits related to the provision of partition walls forming individual chambers within the western aisle. Towards the southern end of the western wall, postholes along the inner edge of the wall trench may suggest the provision of a western doorway (D2), with an associated rough surface of limestone and clay. Deeper post-settings within the wall trench to the north might suggest that there was a more central western door (D3). The blocking of the openings in the western arcade may therefore have been to screen a rear door from the open hall, while a small chamber, 2.5m long by 2.0m wide, may have been formed at the southern end of the aisle.

The northern wall trench extended only across the hall, and contained two stone-packed postholes, 1.0m apart. These were matched by a pair of slightly larger postholes to the north, perhaps marking the provision of an end door with a porch (D4). The southern wall comprised a continuous wall trench running the full width of the building with no indication of a doorway setting.

Within the southern half of the open hall there was the sunken base, roughly 1.0m square, for a hearth (h), com-

Fig 5.33: Furnells, the wall trenches and arcade posts (left) of the aisled hall, looking north

prising small pieces of limestone set vertically into a bed of compact clay. The surface was thoroughly burnt and charcoal filled the intervening spaces. In addition, there were patchy areas of eroded limestone flooring within the western aisle and western part of the hall.

The southern range (SP137)

At some stage the old domestic range was levelled and replaced by a new, shorter range, which was 9.0m long by 4.8m wide (Fig 5.34). This abutted the south wall of the aisled hall, although it was not quite square-on to the hall. The long walls were founded in narrow, steep-sided trenches, and concentrations of limestone fragments are interpreted as post-packing.

There appears to have been a single chamber, and across the centre of the room there were deposits of limestone fragments that had been laid to fill a subsidence hollow over an underlying ditch. Above this, patches of clay and sandy mortar attest to the former existence of a more extensive floor.

The related pottery assemblage comprised more than 150 sherds of tenth to eleventh-century wares, while 85 sherds of residual early–middle Saxon material was also present.

Ditches west of the aisled hall (SP141)

At the south-western corner of the aisled hall there were two roughly parallel gullies, 2.5m apart, which ran westward towards the western boundary ditches (Fig 5.30). Parallel with the southern ditch, there was a line of postholes, which may have formed a boundary fence. A group of pits to the south of this (SP129) included a cess pit in use contemporary with either the long range or the aisled hall.

The south-western structure (SP128)

To the south-west of the aisled hall there were the disturbed remains of what may have been the first stone-built domestic range on the site (Fig 5.30). Two parallel robber trenches were associated with traces of rubble and mortar floors and truncated limestone walls that survived up to three courses, 260mm, high. It measured at least 6.0m long by 4.5m wide, and may have been longer than this. It was partly buried by a medieval kitchen range (SP125), suggesting that it may have been a detached, stone-walled kitchen range added to the aisled hall complex.

Fifteen sherds of early–middle Saxon pottery were recovered, together with 12 sherds of tenth to eleventh-century wares, a single sherd of Stamford ware and eight sherds of twelfth-century pottery.

Building J (SP135) and ditch systems south the aisled hall

To the south of the aisled hall a narrow ditch, running west–east cut across the line of the former late Saxon domestic range. A very small structure denoted by a continuous wall trench around three sides, abutted the southern side of the boundary ditch. It measured only 3.7m long by 2.5m wide, and is of unknown function (Figs 5.18).

Furnells manor: The medieval church (AD 1150–1350/1400)

The rebuilding of the church

The rebuilding of the church took place during the second half of the twelfth century, perhaps as early as 1150, well before the construction of the western manor house.

The construction date for the second church had always been problematic given the lack of associated and well stratified pottery assemblages. The radiocarbon dates for three burials that pre-dated its construction indicate that they had been interred by the middle of the twelfth century, if not well before (Chapter 5: The chronology; Table 5.2, Burials 5266, 5298 and 5254). A further burial (5299) pre-dating the second church was interred sometime between the late tenth and early thirteenth centuries (980–1220 Cal AD, 95% confidence, 960±60 BP, Har-5011).

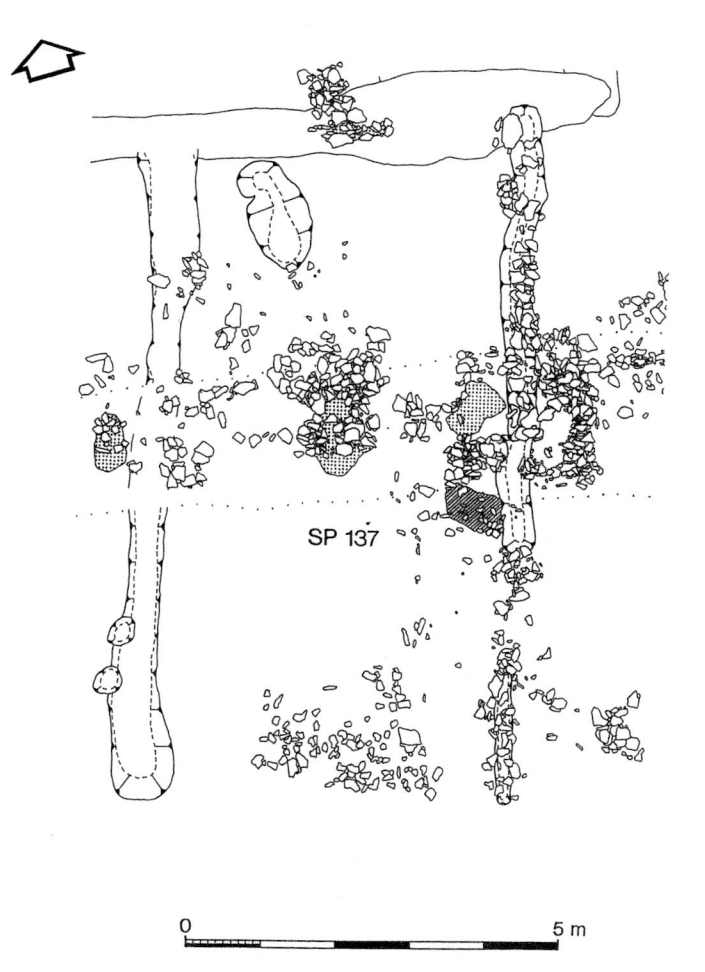

Fig 5.34: Furnells, the southern range (SP137)

A mid-twelfth century date is also consistent with the overall balance of the pottery evidence. The date of 1200 proposed in the review of the pottery (Chapter 6; Table 6.7) was dependant on three sherds from the fill of a single grave, Burial 5298. However, this burial has also given a radiocarbon date of 700–1160 Cal AD (98% confidence, 1100±80BP, Har-5020) indicating that this individual had most probably been interred well before 1150; so the pottery can be regarded as intrusive within this grave.

The nave of the new church was 7.55m long by 4.58m wide, and the chancel was 4.68m long by 3.48m wide (Figs 5.28, 5.35 and 3.9). The walls stood on broad foundations, 1.00m wide, while the depth was varied depending on the stability of the underlying ground, being shallowest where the new walls stood over the levelled walls of the first church. For the nave the foundations typically comprised two courses of pitched limestone, with three courses for the chancel.

The southern side of the new church coincided with the southern wall of the earlier church, so there was no disturbance of existing burials in this area. However, to the west and north earlier burials were disturbed and some, either intact or partially disturbed, survived beneath the walls of the new church. Four individuals were deposited as bundles of disarticulated bones in charnel pits to the north of the new church. The presence of even the smaller bones, and the recovery elsewhere of fragments of broken up stone coffins from the foundations of the new church, suggests that these individuals had probably been carefully removed from stone coffins, displaced as a result of the rebuilding, which had most probably stood close to the one surviving stone coffin.

Whether use of the churchyard for burial continued is uncertain. The lack of intercutting graves across the full extent of the cemetery does indicate that despite the building of the new church, there was no general churchyard clearance to enable a fresh churchyard to be laid out. However, it is possible that some of the use of the outlying burial zones to the east and south-east was contemporary with the second church. It is evident that use of the cemetery came to an end, even if coincidently, when most of the available churchyard area had been occupied. It is possible that the second church, either from its origin or at least soon after, was purely a manorial chapel, with burial rites held by the present parish church standing on the facing hillside to the south-east at Burystead.

It does appear that there was a late reuse of the stone coffin, with the original cover perhaps broken when the new interment was made. The lower part of the broken cover was re-used, while the head end of the coffin was covered with a fragment from a broken up late Saxon graveyard cross, decorated with interlace. The cross fragment had been trimmed and thinned to fit over the head end of the coffin.

The final use of the church

As previously outlined (Chapter 3), in addition to a new chronology a new interpretation is offered for the final episode in the use of the second church. The original interpretation was that there was an episode of rebuilding related to the conversion of the building from religious to secular use (Boddington 1996, 10–11 and fig 22). This "church conversion phase" put together the insertion of a cross wall in the nave with rebuilding to the east to form a simple rectangular building containing two rooms. It was argued that it had been constructed at around the middle of the twelfth century, within a century of the Norman Conquest, although the present review of the dating evidence has indicated that the building of the second church itself occurred no earlier than the mid-twelfth century.

The reinterpretation is based on the constructional form of the inserted cross wall. This was, at 1.1m wide, actually slightly wider than the existing church walls, and it was similarly founded on two courses of pitched limestone. This is unlike any of the other secular buildings at either Furnells or other Raunds sites. At both the southern and northern ends of this cross wall the foundations had been cut into the existing wall foundations by up to 0.4m, implying that the facings of the existing walls had been cut back so that cross wall could be securely bonded to them. However, to the north some larger wall stones were interpreted by the excavator as quoins and facing stones (Boddington 1996, fig 22), to imply that the standing cross wall had been cut fully through the existing church wall. This indicated that the structure had undergone major rebuilding of its basic fabric; the church conversion. It is now suggested that this observation was in error, and that the overall character of the inserted cross wall is consistent with it relating to a further phase of church activity. In this location, the cross wall created a near square chamber at the western end of the nave, with internal dimensions of 4.1m by 4.7m (Fig 5.28). This suggests that a tower was raised over the western end of the nave; an addition that can now be comfortably accommodated within the revised and extended chronology for the church sequence (Table 3.1).

The final date of disuse has not been established. Clearly the church was levelled before the construction of the eastern manor house in the late fourteenth century, but this may have followed a period of disuse, and perhaps at least partial demolition, that occurred somewhat earlier, perhaps in the early fourteenth century.

Furnells manor: The western manor (AD 1200–1350/1400)

At around the end of the twelfth century, the aisled hall complex was levelled and replaced by a stone-built, medieval manor house comprising a central hall with service rooms to the north and a domestic chamber to the south. Further rooms and yards, poorly preserved, lay to the

5. The Archaeological Evidence

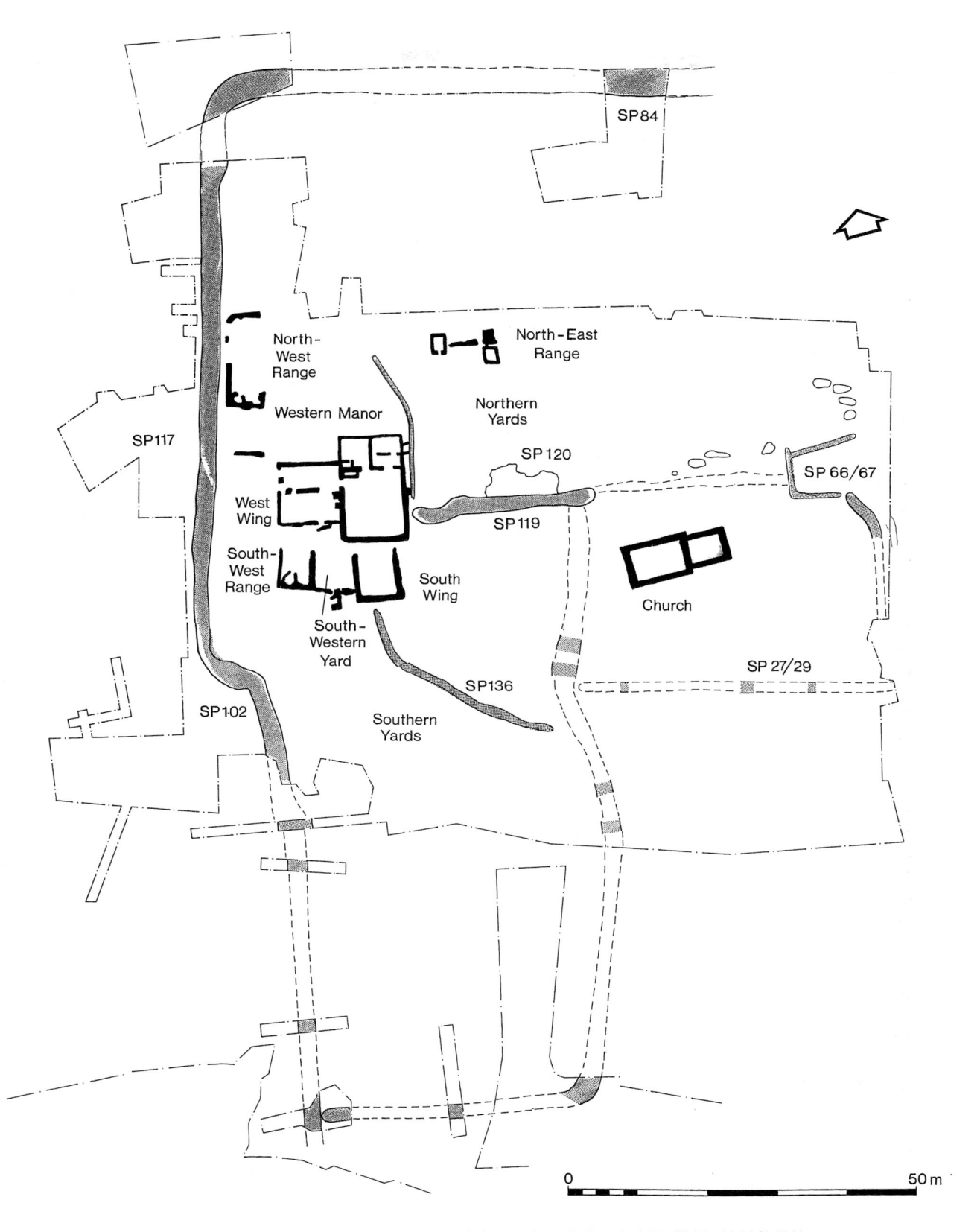

Fig 5.35: Furnells, the western manor and the medieval church (AD 1200–1350/1400)

west. To the north, perhaps as later additions, there was a kitchen/bakehouse and a malting complex. With the rebuilding of the manor, in addition to the rebuilding of the church some decades earlier, Furnells manor reached its zenith as a small medieval manor house (Fig 5.35).

A small quantity of medieval pottery from the underlying aisled hall provides a *terminus post quem* of AD 1200 for the erection of the building. Pottery from the fabric of the walls, floor levels and hearth spans the period AD 1200–1450. The majority of the associated finds and pottery came from the demolition levels. Quantities of residual pottery and finds within the demolition deposits indicate that there was much disturbance of earlier deposits during the process of demolishing and levelling this building.

Boundary ditches

Ditches continued to mark the boundaries throughout the medieval period. Several had been re-cut and there was some indication of the former presence of banks from which material had eroded and slipped into the open features. Different elements probably fell into disuse at different times, but most had become redundant by the fifteenth century.

The system was dominated by the western boundary (Fig 5.35). The length adjacent to the new manor house (SP117) was relocated a further 6.5–10m to the west of its former line, providing additional space for the new buildings. To the north, it joined an equally prominent northern boundary ditch (SP84). Both were still prominent earthworks when the excavations began.

The east–west boundary (SP119) between the corner of the churchyard and the manor house was recut making it broader and deeper, probably removing all traces of earlier ditches on this line. A large pottery assemblage came from the western end of the ditch, probably dumped there closely before or during the demolition of the manor house. The northern boundary of the churchyard was not certainly recut, but the existing ditches would still have formed a visible boundary. At the eastern end of the approach to the manor, there was a rectilinear arrangement of steep-sided slots (SP66/67). These may have been some form of timber structure, perhaps even a gateway controlling access to the manor.

The southern churchyard boundary was relocated slightly to the north (SP27), and disturbed a few graves. It appears to have also served as a quarry, with the local Blisworth limestone being dug out of its sides. The quarried stone may have been used in the construction of the second church (Boddington 1996, 14). Afterwards, the boundary was retained by digging a smaller ditch (SP29), which was cut into the backfill of the quarry. No pottery was recovered from quarry ditch SP27 but of the total of 77 sherds from SP29, 20 are early–middle Saxon, 46 late Saxon, four are Saxo-Norman, and seven are medieval. Following its abandonment, the large quarry ditch remained clearly visible as an earthwork. A further small quarry pit (SP120), lying to the east of the manor house, also dates to this period.

The southern area, which had probably been established in the preceding period, may have been retained in much the same form, with the western boundary still on its previous line (SP102) and linked to the new ditch at a dog-legged turn.

The western manor house (SP123)

The demolition of this building had been so thorough that associated floor levels only patchily survived, while the walls had been near totally robbed to leave only shallow robber trenches (Figs 5.36 and 5.37). The few surviving sections of walls stood to a maximum height of four courses, 270mm, and were constructed of a 7:1 ratio of local Blisworth and cornbrash limestone, with larger hewn blocks facing a rubble core. The walls were 630–680mm wide and no distinct foundation course was recognised. The western and eastern walls of the hall were supported by buttresses. The western buttress was the best preserved, measuring 0.9m by 0.8m, and was constructed as an integral part of the overall fabric. There was apparently no systematic use of quoins, but too little survived to be certain of this. Stones were set in a matrix of silty clay, although traces of fine sand may indicate the original presence of mortar bonding. A small quantity of residual pottery was retrieved from within the wall fabric, but there is no evidence of its extensive use as clinking.

The hall

The hall was 9.0m long by 7.5m wide (Fig 5.36). There was a doorway at the northern end of the west wall, where two underlying post-settings, 0.95m apart, indicated the provision of a timber door jamb. The presence of an opposed doorway in the eastern wall was indicated by external metalled surfaces defining the approach to it. The two doorways would have formed a cross-passage at the northern, upper end of the hall. The adjacent, northern wall was quite well preserved and contained two doorways, 1.0m and 1.4m wide, that gave access to the service rooms. Iron door-fittings were retrieved from deposits of fire debris close to these entrances.

A central hearth, 2.0m square, lay towards the southern end of the hall. The hearth base was constructed of pitched stone, up to two courses deep, set within a shallow hollow, but any former kerb stones had been removed. Spreads of charcoal and burnt clay extended to the east and north.

A stone base in the north-west corner of the hall, adjacent to the doorway, 1.9m long by 1.0m wide, survived up to two courses high and was formed of a rubble core edged with larger stones. It had probably supported wooden stairs leading to an upper storey over the service rooms to the north. Two postholes beneath the western end may have held upright timbers that supported the superstructure.

From the eastern end of the stone base a shallow slot ran southward for 5.0m, stopping 3.0m from the southern wall. It may indicate either the presence of an internal

Fig 5.37: Furnells, the western manor house, looking north, showing the parlour (foreground) and hall (centre)

screen set 1.5m from the western wall, or a support for a first-floor gallery also accessed from the timber stairs.

Despite extensive robbing, it was suggested by the excavator that the scattered larger limestone slabs across the interior were derived from a floor of rough hewn stone flags, but there was insufficient surviving to be certain of this.

The service rooms

The outer walls of the northern service rooms had been fully robbed. Along part of the northern wall a concentration of densely packed, pitched stone fragments, 4.15m long by 1.2m wide, were set in a trench 400mm deep, which may have consolidated an area of softer ground. Too few lengths of standing wall survived to determine the structural relationship between the hall and the service wing. However, the dividing wall between them was of the same width and build as the hall walls, and the lack of evidence for the outer walls of the service wing suggests that they were perhaps more shallowly founded. It is therefore suggested that the hall was of a single build with both the service wing and the southern wing abutted to it.

The presence of two service rooms was indicated by the pair of doorways and by the survival of a central partition wall, 0.4m wide, which stood up to three courses high. In both rooms there were remains of floors of roughly squared flagstones, which were up to 400mm long, and both floors were 300mm below the level of the hall floor.

The western service room was slightly the larger, at 3.8m wide by 4.25m long. The flooring survived adjacent to the partition wall, and in the south-western corner of the room there was a shallow, stone-lined pit, 1.1m long by 0.9m wide and 0.24m deep. A further shallow pit (SP88) to the north may also have been contemporary.

The eastern service room was 3.2m wide. It contained two stone-lined drains that ran eastward, crossing the line of eastern wall. Both probably connected with an external drain, see below, although one of the junctions had been lost. The eastern ends of both gullies were covered by flagstones, but the western ends were open. The fills of these drains yielded quantities of carbonised pulses (Table 9.2, samples 252 and 253).

Stone-lined drain (SP88)

A stone-lined and capped drain, 0.18m wide and 0.25m deep, ran parallel with the eastern wall of the hall and service wing, and drains from the eastern service room emptied into it (Fig 5.36). The drain continued to the north-west for about 10m before petering out. No pottery earlier than the twelfth century was recovered from the fill, and much was of the thirteenth century.

The south wing or parlour (SP123)

A single rectangular room, measuring 7.90m by 4.45m, lay to the south of the hall (Fig 5.36). The shallow robber-trenches contained orange sandy mortar and fragments of limestone, and they ended 1.6m short of the southern wall of the hall, suggesting the presence of opposed doorways. There was no evidence for direct access from the hall. No traces of flooring survived.

A curving ditch (SP136) that ran towards the south-east from the southern wall of the parloer, may have served as a drain (Fig 5.29).

A west wing (SP126)

The presence of a west wing was suggested by fragmentary traces of walls and surfaces to the west of the hall (Fig 5.36). The buttress on the western wall of the hall, which was encompassed within this wing, suggests that the wing was a later addition. The fragments of walls, faced with limestone blocks and surviving no more than two courses high, indicate that it was probably near square, measuring 7.5m north–south by 7.8m east–west. Remnants of an east-west wall suggest that it was divided into two elongated chambers. The northern chamber would have been 3.0m wide with direct access to the western hall door. The chamber to the south was 4.0m wide. Across the eastern half of this room a limestone and mortar floor surrounded a small hearth, less than 1m wide, which comprised a vertically pitched limestone kerb, with surviving deposits of clay, charcoal and silt.

The south-west range (SP125)

A detached kitchen/bakehouse range stood to the west of the south wing, or parlour (Fig 5.35). On the basis of the pottery recovered from the walls, it was probably built at around 1200, probably at the same time as the manor house. It may have replaced an earlier stone kitchen range (SP128) associated with the later use of the aisled hall. Only the walls forming the south-eastern corner had survived, and were up to five courses high. The floor space was 3.75m wide and, while the length is unknown, it must have been in excess of 5.0m and no more than 8.0m long.

In the south-western corner there was a circular oven, 1.40m in diameter. The base of the oven lay 150mm below the floor surface and the two surviving courses of limestone lining were intensely scorched. Scorching was also evident across the oven floor and within the sunken stokehole, and the floor was overlain by lenses of charcoal within a sandy silt matrix. To the east there were probable remnants of a flagstone floor, but no open hearth had survived.

Destruction debris and pottery overlying the levelled range indicates that it was abandoned during the second half of the thirteenth century, while the adjacent manor house was still in use, suggesting that it had been replaced by the larger kitchen and bakehouse (SP89) to the north-west of the manor house.

The south-western yard

Between the south wing of the hall and the south-west range there was a small yard, up to 5.5m wide, probably surfaced with limestone, and closed on the southern side by a wall running between the two buildings (Fig 5.36).

Abutting the southern side of this wall there was a garderobe or latrine pit, 2.0m long by 1.6m wide and up to 0.5m deep, lined with coursed limestone to the north and south, and limestone slabs to the east. It may have been for the private use of the residents of the parlour, and was presumably emptied on a regular basis, as no cess-like deposits survived and the stone rich fills were probably entirely derived from the levelling of the superstructure. Twenty-two sherds from a glazed jug of Stanion ware were recovered from the fill.

The north-west range (SP89)

This bakehouse/brewhouse was 13m long by 3.8m wide, although much had been lost to a modern sewer that cut across it (Fig 5.38). The ground laid walls of unmortared rough-hewn limestone were 0.60–0.70m wide, and survived to a maximum height of five courses. Some wall stones were scorched, indicating their reuse from an earlier structure, perhaps an earlier kitchen range.

In the south-west corner there was a circular baking oven, 1.39m in diameter, with a sunken floor and a heavily scorched stone lining. In the north-east corner there was a sub-rectangular malting or drying oven. The chamber was 1.5m long by 0.9m wide, and was more deeply sunken than the baking oven, with a longer stone-lined flue. Burning was confined to the oval hearth stone set at the mouth of the flue opening, indicating its use as a low temperature drying oven.

There is no reliable date for the construction of the building, but pottery from the destruction levels suggests that it was abandoned during the fourteenth century.

The malting complex (SP85)

Another area was devoted entirely to malting. It comprised a square drying oven, a paved surface, a stone foundation and a stone-lined tank (Fig 5.39). There was no clear evidence to suggest that the complex was ever enclosed by one or more stone buildings, but the survival of only the sunken lining of the malting oven does indicate that the ground laid outer walls of the oven, and perhaps other walls, had been completely lost.

The malting or drying oven, to the west, was set within a rectangular, flat-bottomed pit, 2.1m long by 1.45m wide

5. The Archaeological Evidence

foundation, measuring 2.3m by 1.7m, of closely packed, pitched limestone surrounding a central post-setting edged with stone. The foundation may have had an upper surface also of pitched stone, of which little remained.

A short gully ran between the stone foundation and a stone-lined tank. The tank measured 2.0m by 1.6m, and survived to a depth of 200mm. It bottomed on natural limestone bedrock, and the sides were lined with up to four courses of limestone, which may have been mortared. No evidence for a waterproof lining of clay was recovered, and the fills comprised only destruction debris that, in common with the rest of the range, contained fourteenth century pottery.

The northern yards (SP86)

To the north of the manor house, in the area between the north-west and north-east ranges, there were fragmentary remains of thin limestone surfaces that probably represent the vestiges of former metalled yards (Fig 5.35).

Demolition of the western manor (AD 1350/1400)

There were numerous and extensive demolition layers overlying the levelled structural remains of the manor house and its ancillary buildings, along with the shallow trenches left after the robbing of the walls (SP82 and SP83). Clear traces of a fire, perhaps associated with the process of demolition, were found in the service rooms of the north wing. A concentration of metal door fittings found close to the doorway between the western service room and the hall may have dropped directly from burning doors.

While it is evident that the walls of the manor house were very thoroughly robbed, an architectural fragment, part of a lancet window, found close to the manor indicates the quality of the building. A line of rubble lying adjacent to the end of the south wing may have been the remains of a pile of stone awaiting removal to the site of the new eastern manor, but never recovered.

These demolition deposits contained quantities of residual early–middle Saxon and late Saxon/Saxo-Norman pottery, but medieval wares dominated the assemblage. A small quantity of late medieval reduced ware suggests that the demolition occurred during the later fourteenth century, and had certainly taken place by AD 1400.

Finds that were probably contemporary with the occupation of the western manor included a silver gilt annular brooch, a stirrup-shaped finger ring, a pair of wide and narrow plain buckles, a pewter crowned head finger ring; a copper alloy key, fragments of glass including part of a glass linen smoother, and an unofficial English jetton of early fourteenth century date.

It would appear that structural metalwork, especially lead, was scavenged and recycled. Three small hearths lay within the destruction levels of the west wing, and one contained ash with a high lead content, as well as dribbles of lead and lead-rich ash slag. This, and the other hearths, also produced quantities of burnt oak, hazel or alder, and

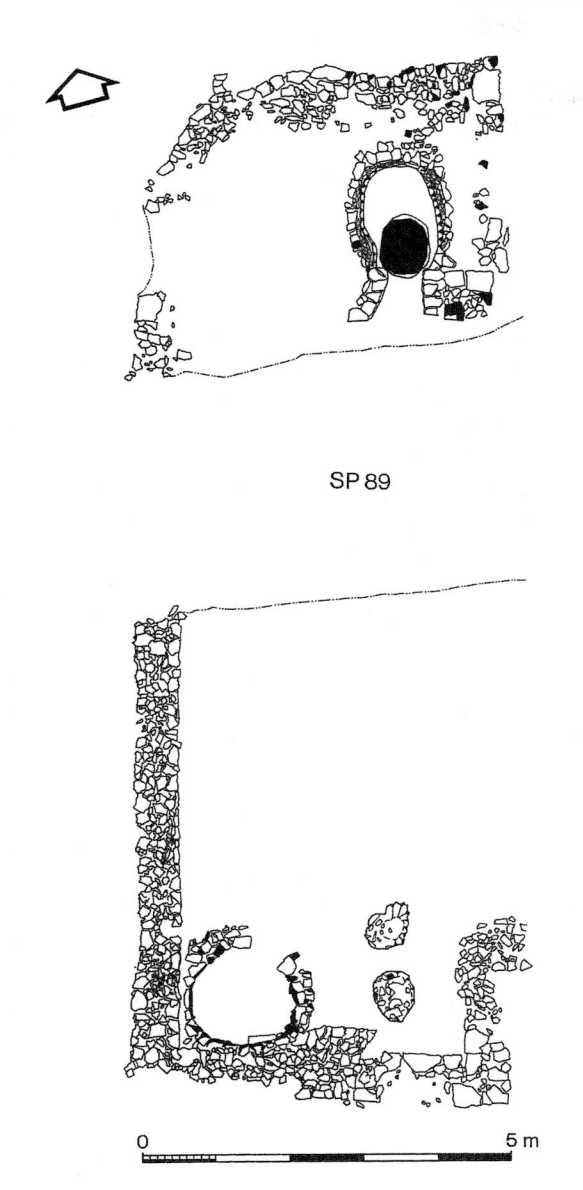

Fig 5.38: Furnells, the north-west range (SP89), with baking oven (south) and malting/drying oven (north)

and 0.45m deep. The oven chamber was 1.6m long by 1.4m wide, and was lined with up to nine courses of rough hewn limestone, surviving up to nine courses high, with a battered face. The flue opening was 0.6m wide, and the chamber floor comprised several large limestone flags. Burning was restricted to a small area close to the stokehole, and the oven chamber contained demolition debris including pottery dated to the early fourteenth century. The outer walls that would have retained the superstructure of the oven, which typically have walls at least 1.0m thick formed of soil and rubble to reduce heat loss during use, had been lost, as had any enclosing building to the south.

Running eastward from the oven, there was a setting of large limestone slabs, 4.0m long by 1.0m wide, of unknown function. To the east of this there was a rectangular

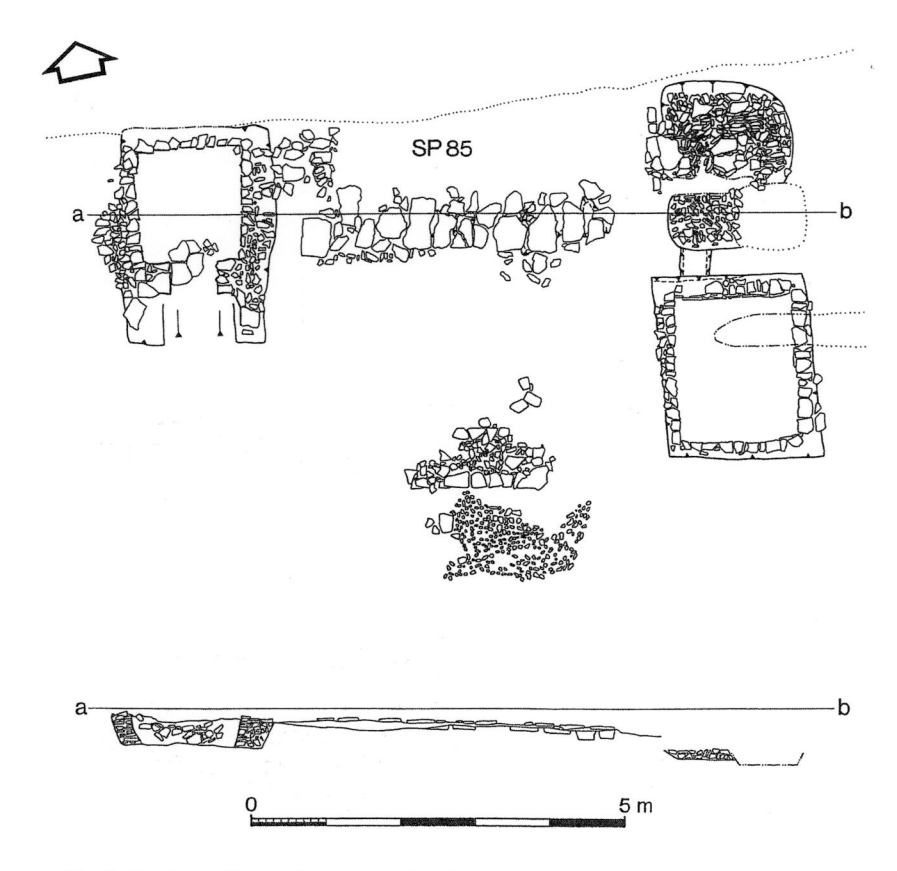

Fig 5.39: Furnells, malting complex (SP85), with oven (west) and tank (east)

some burnt grain and large legumes, suggesting the disposal of various kinds of demolition debris.

Furnells manor: The eastern manor (AD 1350/1400–1450)

A radical transformation of the whole manorial site occurred towards the end of the fourteenth century. The western manor was abandoned and the building was razed to the ground. The medieval church, which may have been redundant for some time, was similarly levelled. At the same time the minor boundary ditch systems were abandoned (Fig 5.40).

In this more open manorial enclosure, a new manor house, the eastern manor, was built on the former churchyard, over the levelled foundations of the medieval church, with a circular dovecote standing next to the service wing at the western end of the range (see Fig 3.17). A free-standing range, used for baking and brewing, stood 30m to the north, so that the two main ranges flanked an extensive central yard. The access to this yard and to the manor house itself was still from the east, as previously.

Only remnants had survived of former walled boundaries to this central area. A short length of wall ran northwestward from the dovecote, forming a western boundary, and remnants of wall ran eastward from the bakehouse range, forming a northern boundary, while the manor house itself formed the southern boundary. The door to the dovecote stood to the west, and was therefore only accessible from the west. Immediately west of the dovecote there were also remnants of walls and a spread of rubble forming a partial rectilinear plan. This area was not excavated at this level, but the evidence suggests the presence of a further stone building set within the western half of the rearranged manorial plot (Fig 5.44, visible in background west of dovecote). This would probably have served an agricultural purpose, perhaps as a barn and/or byre. The new arrangement therefore comprised the domestic facilities to the east with the ancillary agricultural buildings to the west, bordering the open field. This major rearrangement probably followed on from the loss of the seigneurial role of the manor at the acquisition of Furnells by the Greene family.

The western boundary between the manorial enclosure and the open fields was still defined at the time of excavation by a broad but shallow earthwork ditch with a low bank along its eastern edge. The margins of the lower lying ground to the south of the manor house were marked by a scarp above a ditch, which followed the former southern churchyard boundary. To the west a bank, with a marked drop on its eastern side, ran north–south roughly along the former ditched boundary between the manor house

5. The Archaeological Evidence   101

North Range

Eastern Manor

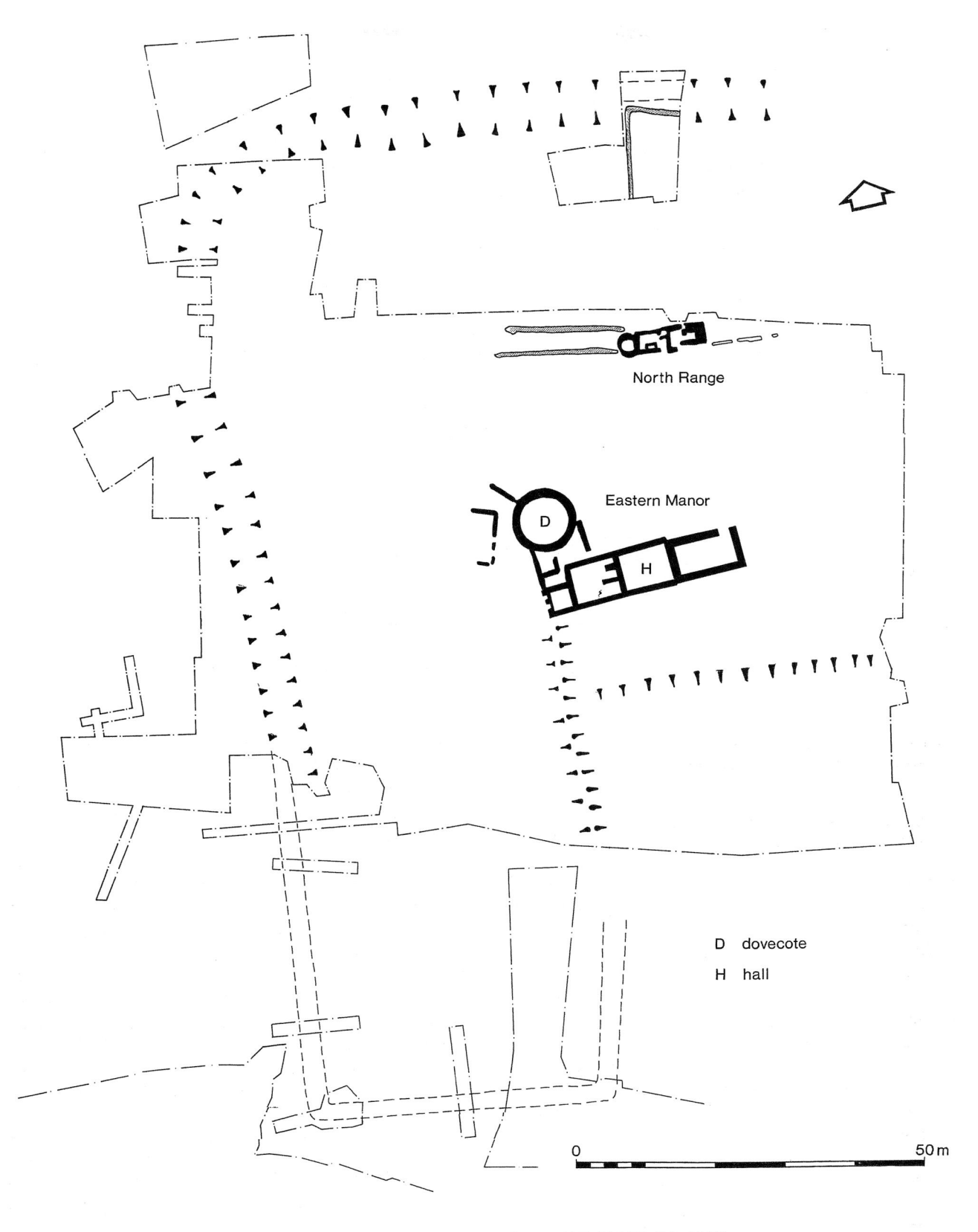

D dovecote
H hall

0   50 m

Fig 5.40: Furnells, the new manor house (AD 1350/1400–1500)

and church plots. These were also features that survived as earthworks up to the commencement of the excavations (see Fig 3.18).

After a relatively short life, the eastern manor was itself abandoned. It appears to have been left as a derelict shell for some years and during this time the hall was utilised as a makeshift smithy. Certainly by AD 1500, the remains had been levelled and manorial enclosure was turned into a simple pasture close, and remained so until the late twentieth century.

The manor house (SP7)

Following the levelling of the second church, a new manor house was built. In its final form, this building was 30m long, comprising the standard division into a central open hall, with a parlour/solar to the east and a service wing to the west, including an adjacent dovecote (Fig 5.41).

This was a completely new construction, although the fragmentary surviving lengths of the northern and southern walls of the hall appear to have been laid onto the levelled foundations of the nave of the former church. The partition wall between the hall and the parlour/solar to the east was also founded directly on the levelled inserted cross wall of the final church phase, but nothing survived of the new build. The eastern end of the parlour lay just beyond the former chancel.

Elsewhere the walls were effectively ground laid. They were built in good courses of rough hewn limestone, probably bonded with clay. In places they survived to a height of 0.90m. At the lowest courses they were 0.75m thick and the outer face was battered, the wall narrowing to 0.55m.

The hall

The central hall, room 3, was 7.8m long by 5.7m wide. The earliest floor comprised crushed limestone. This was succeeded by a clay floor, and eventually by gravel and sand. The base for a hearth, lying just east of centre, measured 1.4m by 1.5m. It comprised pitched limestone and pottery sherds, with by a burnt clay surface, surrounded by a low kerb of dressed limestone blocks (Fig 5.42). The presence of doorways towards the western end of the hall was indicated by external areas of stone surfacing. The surfaces were 1.5m wide, but were not quite directly opposed, as the southern doorway lay 1.0m east of the end wall while the northern doorway was directly in the corner of the room.

The parlour/solar

This eastern room, measuring 8.00m by 4.6m, contained few internal features. No floor surfaces were identified, and presumably it had a floor of beaten earth. A single course of stone abutting the eastern wall may have been the base for a stone bench, 0.70m wide, running the full width of the room. There may have been another bench against the southern wall. This was 0.35m wide, and ran the full length of the room apart from a central break 1.5m wide, perhaps the location of a doorway just west of centre. A break in the shallow robber trench may suggest the presence of another doorway in the north-eastern corner of the room.

The service rooms

The main part of the service wing was a room slightly shorter than the hall, at 6.5m long by 5.7m wide (Fig 5.41, room 5 and Fig 5.43).

It may originally have functioned as a single room. It contained a stone-lined trough, 2.0m long by 0.9m wide and 0.4m deep, which ran west–east down the centre of the room (not illustrated). The base and the steep northern edge were lined with large slabs of limestone. The southern side was also stone-lined, but stepping down more gradually and flanked to the south by a surface of large limestone slabs with worn surfaces. The stones lining the trough were stained grey, which at the time of excavation was taken to be burning. However, a number of identical features were excavated at the nearby deserted hamlet of West Cotton (Chapman in press). Here, the grey discolouration was evidently a result of chemical action on the limestone, often leaving crusted deposits on the edges of the stones.

While the exact process carried out in these troughs has not been established, they may have been used for the hand fulling of cloth, with the strong solution used for the scouring (cleaning), which probably contained urine, causing the grey staining and encrustation, while the worn limestone resulted from the trampling of the cloth to consolidate the fibres.

The trough was later infilled with limestone rubble and a floor, containing large flagstones up to 0.4m across, was laid above this (Fig 5.41, room 5). A finely incised nine men's morris board (see Fig 7.9) had been set face down within this surface.

Narrow partition walls, 0.35–0.45m thick, formed a small square chamber, room 4, in the south-east corner of the larger room, probably added once the processing trough had been infilled. There was a doorway, 0.9m wide, in one corner and the room had a floor of light blue clay.

To the north of this room, and abutting the wall of the hall, there was a rectangular stone pier, 1.5m long by 0.9–1.15m wide, which still stood up to seven courses high, c0.7m. It was probably the base for a flight of timber stairs leading to an upper floor.

It seems most likely that access between the hall and the service wing was via a single central doorway, between room 4 and the stair base, and part of a flagstone surface survived in this narrow passageway.

A square chamber, room 6, 2.9m long, was attached to the western end of the building (Figs 5.41 and 5.43). A gravel floor had been replaced by limestone, and was finally re-laid with large flagstone slabs up to 900mm across. In the western wall there were two external recesses, each

Fig 5.41: Furnells, the eastern manor house (SP7)

Hearth

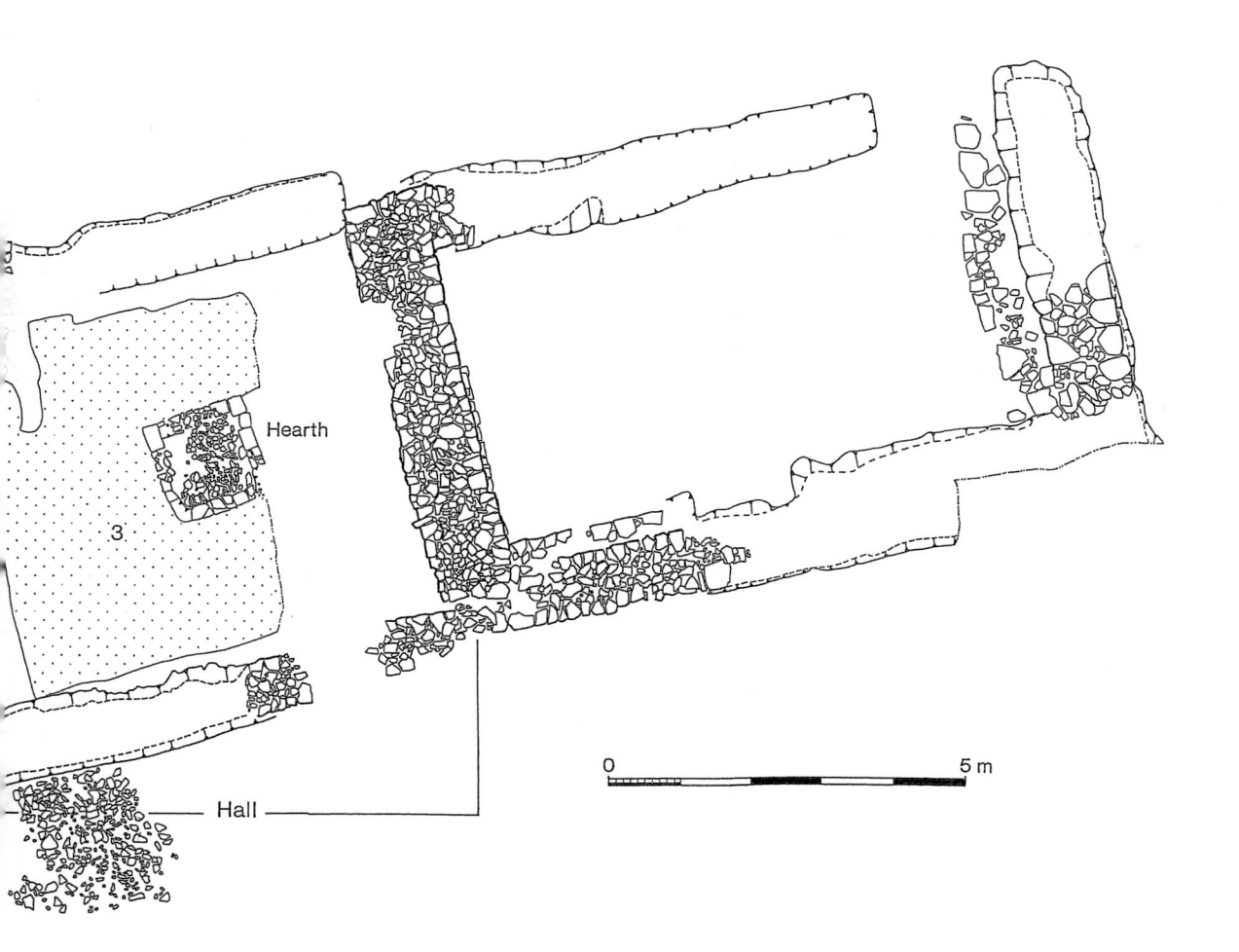

3

Hall

0　　　　　5 m

Fig 5.42: Furnells, the eastern manor house hall (left) and service room (right), looking south-west

Fig 5.43: Furnells, the manor house service rooms, with partially flagged floors, looking east

0.55m square, above small, shallow pits extending 100mm below the level of the wall foundation These served as garderobes. Each was filled with soft clay, and the southern pit contained fragments of eggshell and some pottery as well as mineralised plant and insect remains characteristic of badly drained deposits with a high faecal/urine content (Chapter 9, Table 9.2, samples 82 and 83). A row of three postholes within the room may have supported a small platform for seats and inclined chutes feeding material to the external pits.

The dovecote

A circular dovecote (SP8), 9m in diameter, was erected to the north-west of the manor house (Figs 5.41 and 5.44). The wall foundation was 1.1m thick, and was battered above this, reducing the thickness to 0.8m at a height of 0.6m, tapering by 200mm on the outside and 100mm on the inside. The exterior had been built using neatly laid limestone blocks. In contrast, the inside was more roughly constructed, with stones protruding up to 130mm, which may have offered convenient perches for birds. The surfaces of the stones were pockmarked, possibly due to acidity from bird droppings. There was a narrow, splayed doorway, 0.6m wide, on the western side.

During excavation of the walls, seventeen nesting boxes were identified in the lowest and only tier surviving. They appear to have been built at regular intervals of 700mm. The individual boxes were of a rounded L-shape, with narrow entrances that widened out and extended an average of 430mm into the wall. Each box was about 200mm high. Several contained pigeon bones.

No floor surface survived within the dovecote, possibly because of the repeated clearing of droppings for use as fertilizer. Similarly, there were no internal settings, apart from a slight central hollow which may have been the base for a central rotating ladder, or potence. Subsequently, the lowest tiers of nesting boxes had been blocked, possibly to deter predators.

The walled yard

The open space between the dovecote and the manor house was walled in to create a small yard and two small chambers (Fig 5.41, north-west wing, SP9). The western wall connecting the dovecote to the manor house was continuous, but there was a gateway at the southern end of the eastern wall. It was 1.2m wide, with a recess for a jamb, indicating the provision of a gate. The yard was paved with small limestone fragments.

Between the western wall and the dovecote, an L-shaped length of wall formed a small chamber, up to 3.5m long by 1.8m wide. The well preserved door jamb was recessed to take posts 180mm across, and the doorway was 1.3m

Fig 5.44: Furnells, the manor house dovecote, with remnants of a western range behind, looking west

wide. It was probably roofed, and had a floor of large worn flagstones, measuring 0.5–1.5m, which were set 200mm below the base of the wall, to form a slightly sunken chamber.

To the south of this, a small rectangular area lying between the surrounding rooms may have been utilised as a further storage area, accessed through a narrow gap, 0.7m wide, at the north-east. The ground level in this area had been lowered by 200mm, possibly through robbing of a sunken flagged floor. It may have had a lean-to roof set against the walls of the surrounding rooms.

Boundary walls

A limestone wall, 0.6m wide, which abutted the dovecote to the north-west, had probably formed a boundary between the domestic yard to the east and the agricultural area to the west. A length of 5.0m survived, and it probably once continued beyond this.

A western range

Remnants of two walls and a spread of stone rubble lying to the west of the dovecote clearly denote the presence of a further stone building (Fig 5.40). These remains were uncovered as part of the initial area of excavation taking in the eastern manor house (Fig 5.44). At this time, work was concentrated on the excavation of the manor house so that the primary objective of excavating the underlying church and cemetery sequence could be fulfilled. These marginal building remains were not fully excavated, and were not considered further in post-excavation analysis. Little can therefore be said about the nature of this building, but from the remnants of surviving walls it may have measured some 9m north-south by perhaps 6m east-west.

The location of this building to the west of the dovecote and facing its door, would suggest that this too served an agricultural function, perhaps as a barn or byre.

The northern range (SP21, SP22 and SP23)

A detached kitchen range lay 30m to the north of the manor house. The western room was a kitchen/bakehouse and the eastern room was a malting/drying room (Figs 5.45 and 5.46). A circular chamber abutting the western end of the building may have served as a vat stand.

The building was 10.5m long, not including the circular chamber. A central partition wall formed two rooms, which were entered by doorways in the southern wall to either side of the partition. The long walls and the partition wall were 0.6–0.65m wide, while both end walls and the circular chamber had thicker walls, 0.7–0.8m wide.

The eastern room contained the malting oven (G2005), which had a near square chamber measuring 1.30m by 1.15m, with walls 0.55–0.75m thick, largely of soil and rubble, which abutted the standing walls of the building. The chamber lining was battered, and survived to a height of 0.60m. The limestone bedrock that formed the base of the slightly sunken chamber had been burnt during use. The burnt debris within the chamber contained large amounts of carbonised grain, chiefly wheat, perhaps suggesting general use as both a drying and malting oven (see Chapter 9, Table 9.2, sample 76).

The western room had a floor of limestone fragments in a matrix of clay and sand. A circular baking oven, with a chamber 1.2m in diameter, was built into the walls in the north-east corner. A rectangular open hearth (G 621), measuring 1.4m by 1.0m, stood against the southern wall. It had a base of pitched limestone surrounded by a kerb of vertically set limestone, but had been partly removed. The occurrence of burnt daub in this area may denote the former existence of a smoke hood. There was a particular concentration of ash and charcoal in the south-western corner of the room, where the wall face had been disturbed. This may have resulted from the removal of stonework forming a small corner hearth or oven. The ash deposits from the floor of the room contained large quantities of

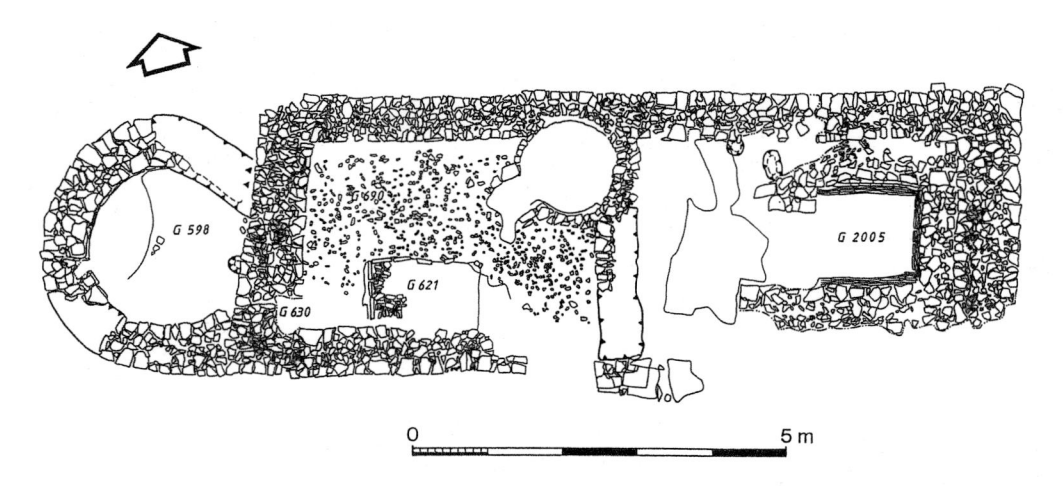

Fig 5.45: Furnells, the north range, kitchen with corner oven and hearth (west), brewhouse, with rectangular drying oven (east) and circular vat stand (west)

Fig 5.46: Furnells, the north range, looking east, with drying oven (top), bakehouse (centre) and circular vat stand (foreground)

herbage, wheat, rye, and barley chaff (see Chapter 9).

The circular chamber abutting the western wall had an internal diameter of 2.0m and an earthen floor. While there was no specific indication of use, a malt house at West Cotton, Raunds also had an attached circular chamber at the opposite end from the oven (Chapman in press). They may have held a large wooden barrel as a vat for the steeping of the barley, to prompt sprouting, prior to drying in the oven to create the malt for brewing.

Very little cultural material was associated with this range, so it is only possible to assume that it was broadly contemporary with the usage of the eastern manor house.

Demolition of the eastern manor (AD 1450–1500)

The eastern manor and its detached kitchen range were abandoned in the second half of the fifteenth century. The decay of the house seems to have been prolonged, in contrast to the sudden episode of demolition that had previously befallen the western manor. The roof was probably removed, and intermittent scavenging, linked with a varying intensity of stone robbing and the lighting of occasional fires in the former rooms, suggests that, for a time at least, the shell of the house stood derelict.

The smithy (SP12)

Later still the hall appears to have utilised as a makeshift smithy. It was suggested by the excavator that this had followed the levelling of the northern and southern walls, with these being partially, but untidily, rebuilt. In the centre of the room, narrow lengths of stub wall abutting both the northern and southern walls flanked the western side of two hearths. The northern wall and hearth was poorly preserved, although a deposit of iron slag was heaped against the adjacent wall. The southern hearth was well preserved, with a 1.4m length of wall flanking a square hearth base of flat laid flagstones. Above this there was a layer of scorched black silt and light blue clay.

In a final episode of use, the hearths were sealed beneath a floor of pitched limestone, which may suggest that the room had a more agricultural use, perhaps as an open-sided byre to house livestock.

The earthworks

The final state of the buildings and the associated manorial boundary system was indicated by the survival of various features as earthworks that were still visible prior to excavation in 1977. They had been recorded in 1970 by David Hall and were partly resurveyed in 1980 (Fig 3.18).

The western ditch, with a low bank on its eastern side, formerly separating the manorial plot from the open fields, was still a prominent earthwork feature. During heavy rain it still functioned as an effective water course, collecting the run-off from the higher ground to the west. To the north there were two shallower and less obvious east-west ditches, one running along the northern edge of the excavation, where it may have formed a northern boundary to the medieval manorial enclosure. An east–west ditch further to the north appears to have been the northernmost limit of the Furnells manorial plots. In this northern area, both on the line of the boundary ditch and within the enclosed space, there were a number of former quarry pits of unknown date. These may have supplied stone for various episodes of building through the lifetime of Furnells manor, but are also likely to have been in use into the post-medieval period to supply building stone for new houses on the Rotton Row frontage.

The area of the long range, the aisled hall and the western manor, for so long the focus of the domestic occupation of the site, had been so effectively levelled that it could not be detected on the surface. In contrast, the partial levelling of the walls of the eastern manor had left clearly visible rectangular earthworks (see Fig 3.18). The area of the former hall, the last part in use, still stood as a square platform, but more prominent still was the circular hump formed by the partial levelling of the dovecote.

A low bank ran southward from the manor house, lying at the top of the break of slope running down into the low lying area at the south-east corner of the excavated site. South of the manor house, there was also a broad shallow hollow along the line of the ditch systems that had bounded the southern side of the churchyard, and had stood at the upper edge of the slope running down to the south-east.

Langham Road

Following the completion of the excavations at Furnells in 1982, the adjacent fields to the west and south were also under threat from new housing development. A programme of trial trench evaluation in 1983 and 1984 identified an area of particular archaeological interest lying to the south of Furnells. Later in 1984, open area excavation began; the first phase of the Langham Road excavation. There were a number of subsequent extensions and additions, which were opened as land became available from the developers, and work continued through 1985 and into 1986. The excavated areas had to respect the physical constraints imposed by the layout and the site logistics of the new development, so the site had a convoluted outline. The area examined extended 140m east–west by 130m north–south and took in a total area of approximately 0.60ha, the equivalent of a single area about 78m square (Fig 5.47).

Archaeologically, the excavation falls into two distinct zones. The southern and central areas contained successive building groups and associated pits that appeared to relate to discrete areas of settlement. From the late Saxon period, these were constrained by the boundary of the open field system to the west and show the formation of a row of elongated tenement plots fronting onto Rotton Row. By the medieval period the excavated area was devoid of buildings, which are presumed to have migrated eastward onto the frontage; the forerunners of the present street frontage.

The northern part of the site contained ditch systems and buildings that appear to form the southernmost extent of the settlement at Furnells. The boundary between the manorial plots of Furnells and the tenements at Langham Road comprised a linear zone, 20m wide, which contained some small buildings. In the post-medieval period, and perhaps earlier, this zone appears to have been a track or lane running westward from Rotton Row onto the fields on the higher ground to the west.

Langham Road: Early Saxon settlement (AD 450–650)

While the site produced a substantial assemblage of early–middle Saxon pottery, the only features that can be ascribed to the early Saxon period lay at the northern end of the site. They are presumed to have formed the southern part of the extensive early Saxon focus at Furnells. To the south there were numerous undated pits and postholes, and others that produced early–middle Saxon pottery. As the only evident focus of occupation was the middle Saxon farm, the undated features are considered more likely to relate to this phase of settlement (Fig 5.47).

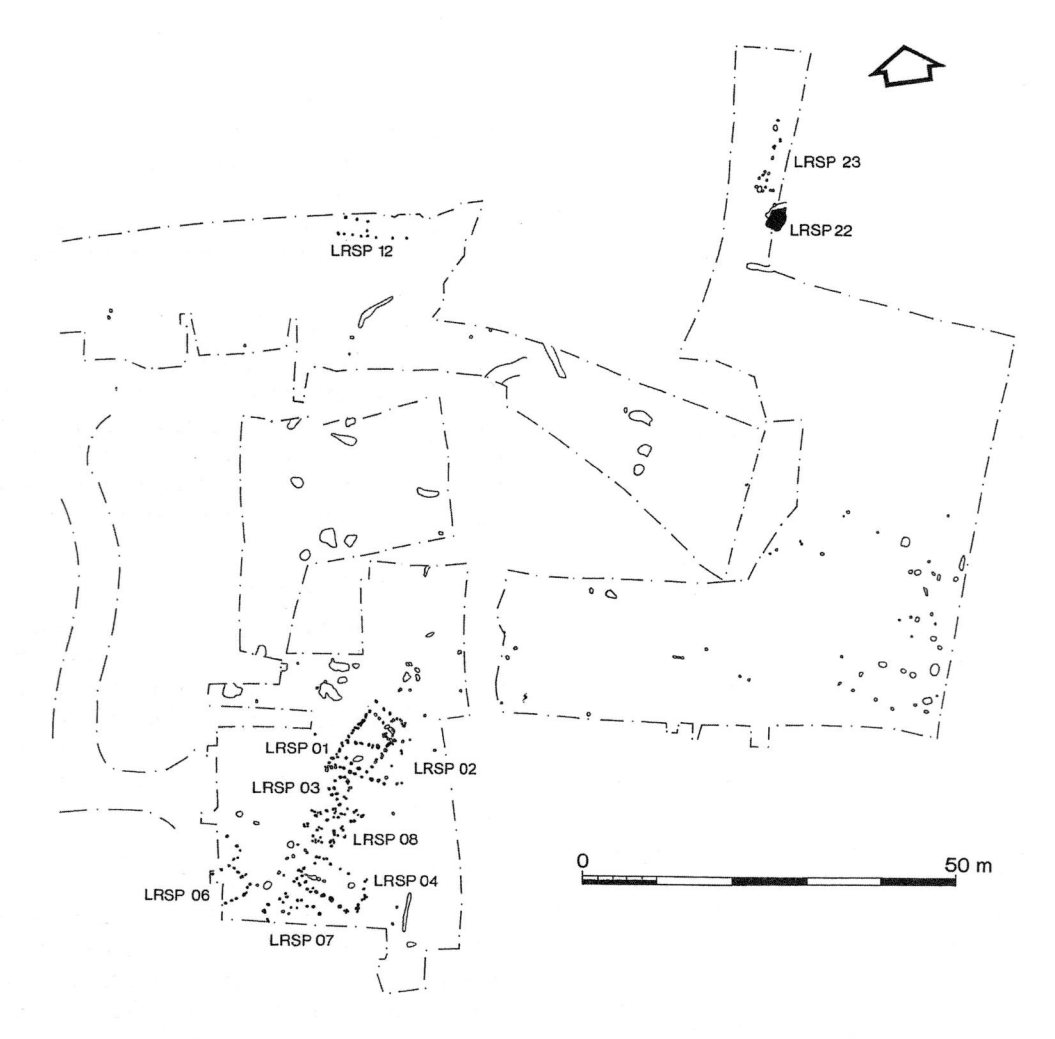

Fig 5.47: Langham Road, early–middle Saxon settlement (AD 450–850)

Sunken-featured building (LRSP22) and posthole group (LRSP23)

The sunken-featured building was located in the north-eastern part of the site at the southernmost edge of the Blisworth limestone outcrop (Figs 5.47 and 5.48). It comprised a shallow, sub-rectangular pit, 4.0m long by 2.5m wide and 0.4m deep, with a single posthole on the western side. The fill relates to its abandonment and contained a small assemblage of early–middle Saxon pottery along with a bronze girdle hanger, which has been dated to the sixth century (Fig. 7.11, 9).

To the immediate north of the sunken-featured building, there was a rough line of postholes on a south–north alignment (LRSP23). These may either have been an associated fence line or the western wall of a contemporary, post-built timber hall, c10–12m long.

Posthole group (LRSP12)

Also at the northern end of the site, and 50m to the west of the sunken-featured building, there was a rectilinear group of postholes cut into limestone (Fig 5.47). They may have defined a small post-built structure, at least 5m long by 2.4m wide, possibly with a fence line running eastward. The posthole fills produced a small assemblage of early–middle Saxon pottery.

Langham Road: The middle Saxon farm (AD 650–850)

The group of post-built timber structures at the southern end of the site (Fig 5.47) produced a large quantity of early–middle Saxon pottery that also includes smaller quantities of imported middle Saxon Ipswich ware and Maxey-type ware.

Pottery from a few of the building postholes included a local version of Maxey-type ware. This has been dated at Northampton to AD 800–1100. This, and the absence of St Neots ware from these contexts, suggests that the abandonment of these buildings may have occurred towards the close of the middle Saxon period (cAD 800–850).

The area of the middle Saxon farm had a slightly bet-

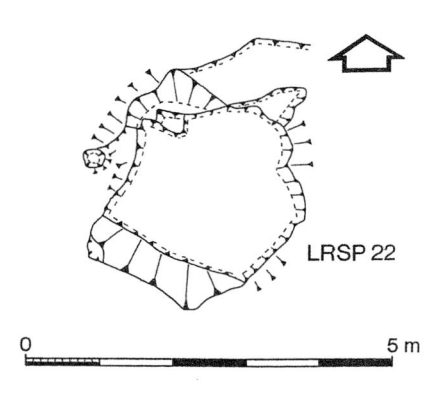

Fig 5.48: Langham Road, sunken-featured building (LRSP22)

ter quality of feature survival than elsewhere as it had lain beneath a medieval headland, and features were easy to identify in the underlying deposit of red sandy loam. A separate scatter of postholes further to the east, in the south-eastern corner of the excavation, lacked any clear pattern.

The building complex comprised two substantial halls (LRSP01 and LRSP04) aligned at right angles (Figs 5.49 and 5.50). The general pottery scatter extended eastward from these buildings, suggesting that they had faced onto a yard set in the angle between them. Between the two halls were two possible circular structures (LRSP03 and LRSP08), which have been interpreted as agricultural buildings, perhaps a stock pen and granary, as depicted in the reconstruction drawing (see Fig 3.3). A further hall, or halls, may have lain to the south (LRSP06 and LRSP07). There were no surviving traces of a ditched or fenced boundary enclosing the whole settlement.

Timber hall (LRSP01)

A rectangular post-built structure, 8.5m long by 4.5m wide (Fig 5.50 and 5.51). An internal line of small postholes and a shallow gully at the north may have screened a small end chamber, c1m wide. There was no clear entrance, unless a length of slot towards the northern end of the north wall denotes a threshold setting, with an internal line of small posts forming a screen adjacent to the door. A pit containing burnt refuse, which lay to the north-west of the building may have been associated.

A large assemblage of early–middle Saxon pottery was present in the postholes, including a single small sherd of Maxey-type ware. Chunks of a Rhineland lava quern had been used as packing in one of the postholes of the north wall, and a copper alloy pin was found in a posthole.

Timber hall (LRSP02)

This building appeared to be later than building (LRSP01) and was on a different alignment (Figs 5.47 and 5.52). It may originally have measured up to 8.0m by 4.0m. Two opposed pairs of larger and, deeper postholes in the north and south walls may define opposed doorways set east of centre. A small oval of scorched natural soil in the interior may be the setting of a hearth, lying west of centre.

Early–middle Saxon pottery came from nearly every posthole, and included a single sherd of shelly ware that appears to be a local version of Maxey-type ware. A single iron heckle tooth may indicate textile yarn production.

Timber hall (LRSP04)

A large rectangular structure, 9.5m long by 5.0m wide. A sparser scatter of postholes further to the west may have been part of an extension, perhaps a lean-to (Fig 5.53). A group of postholes and slots may have formed an internal partition at the western end of the building. A small assemblage of early–middle Saxon pottery was recovered.

Timber hall (LRSP06)

Part of a post-built structure, 4.0m wide and in excess of 4.5m long, lay in the south-western corner of the excavated area (Fig 5.54). Postholes beyond the north wall may have been an associated fence line. Although no dating evidence was present, the building is assigned to the middle Saxon complex on the analogy between its ground plan and the nearby structures.

Circular structure (LRSP03)

A few metres to the south of the northern timber hall (LRSP01) a group of postholes appeared to form a circular structure, up to 3.0m in diameter (Figs 5.49 and 5.55). A separate line of postholes could denote a fence running eastward. Pottery of early–middle Saxon date was recovered from the posthole fills.

Circular structure (LRSP08)

A cluster of postholes, including many which had been replaced (Figs 5.49 and 5.56), lay between the two timber halls (LRSP01 and LRSP04) and south of the smaller circular structure (LRSP03). They may represent another circular structure, c5.0m in diameter, which had been rebuilt on more than one occasion. Early–middle Saxon pottery was found in many of the postholes.

Timber hall (LRSP07)

Part of a possible further post-built timber hall at the southern end of the excavated area, was 5.0m wide and at least 7.0m long (Fig 5.49).

Other early–middle Saxon features

Fifty-seven small pits were scattered across the excavated area (Fig 5.47). A small group to the immediate north of the timber buildings may have been directly associated with the middle Saxon farm. Others lay more widely scattered further to the north and towards the eastern

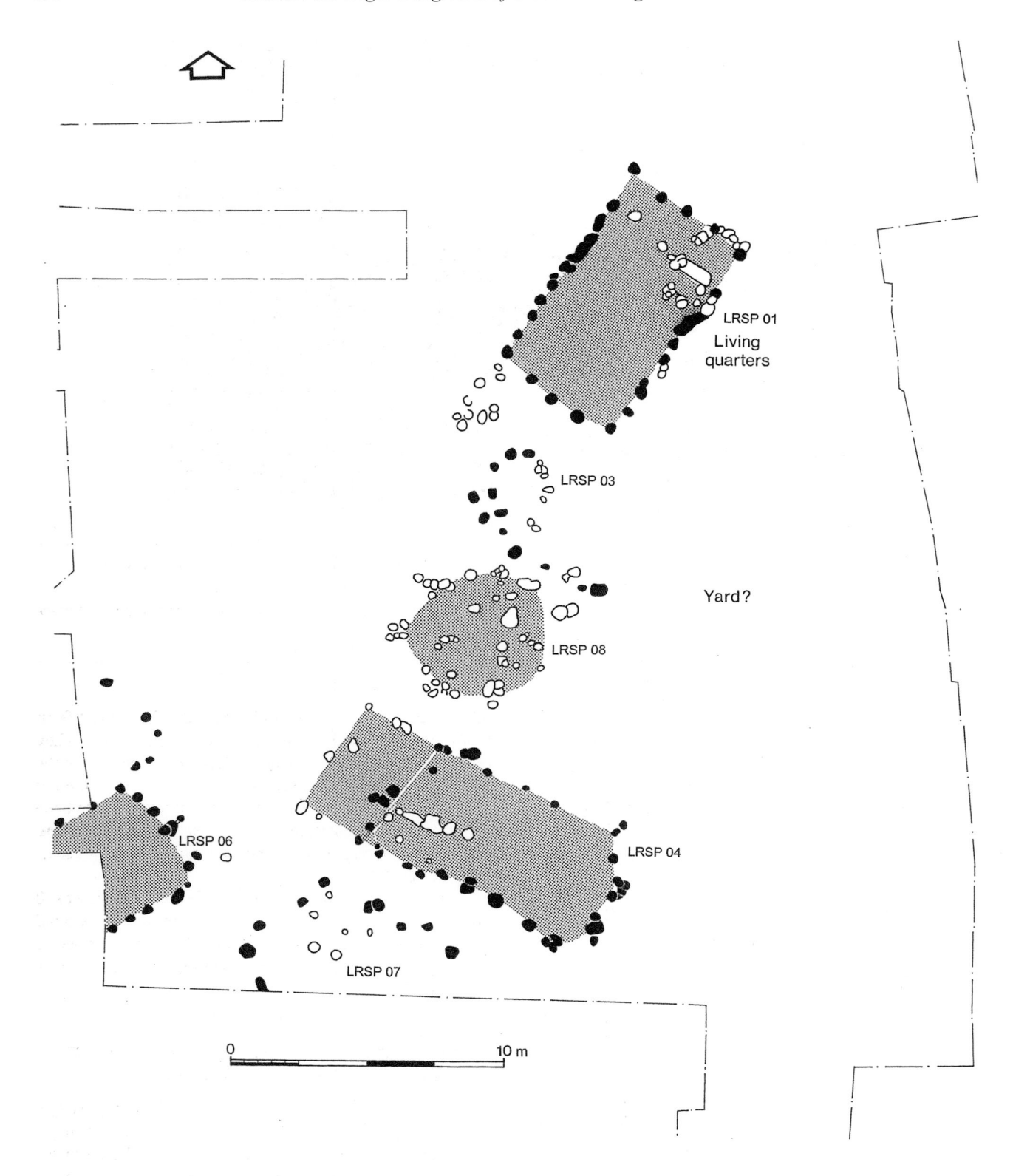

Fig 5.49: Langham Road, the middle Saxon farm (AD 650–850)

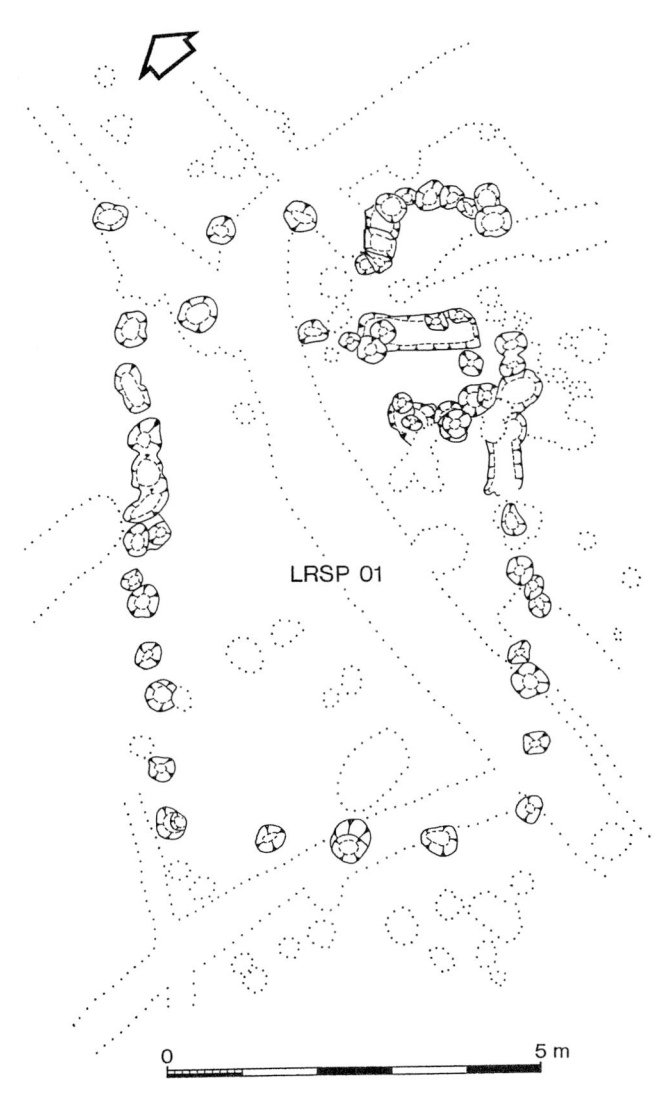

Fig 5.50 (above): Langham Road, the middle Saxon farm, building LRSP01 in foreground, looking south-west

Fig 5.51 (left): Langham Road, middle Saxon farm, timber hall (LRSP01)

limit of excavation. Their individual depths ranged from 0.3m–0.5m and their diameters from 0.5m–1.0m. They are all attributed to the early–middle Saxon period on the basis that only early–middle Saxon pottery was recovered from their fills, although some may obviously have been of later dates but containing only residual pottery. There were also eight separate segments of shallow gullies scattered across the site.

In addition, there was a background scatter of at least 158 postholes, which attest to the intensity of activity around the main structures. As with the pits, they are ascribed to an early–middle Saxon date on the basis of the pottery from their fills.

Langham Road: the late Saxon boundaries and farm (AD 900/950–1200)

The late Saxon period saw the creation of a complex system of ditched land boundaries, which included a major north–south boundary marking the division between the domestic plots to the east and the open fields to the west (Fig 5.57). A new building complex (LRSP14-16), largely of post-in-trench construction, may have been an eastward relocation of the middle Saxon farm at the creation of the new plot system. It may have been set within a one-acre plot fronting onto Rotton Row.

A separate area of activity at the northern end of the

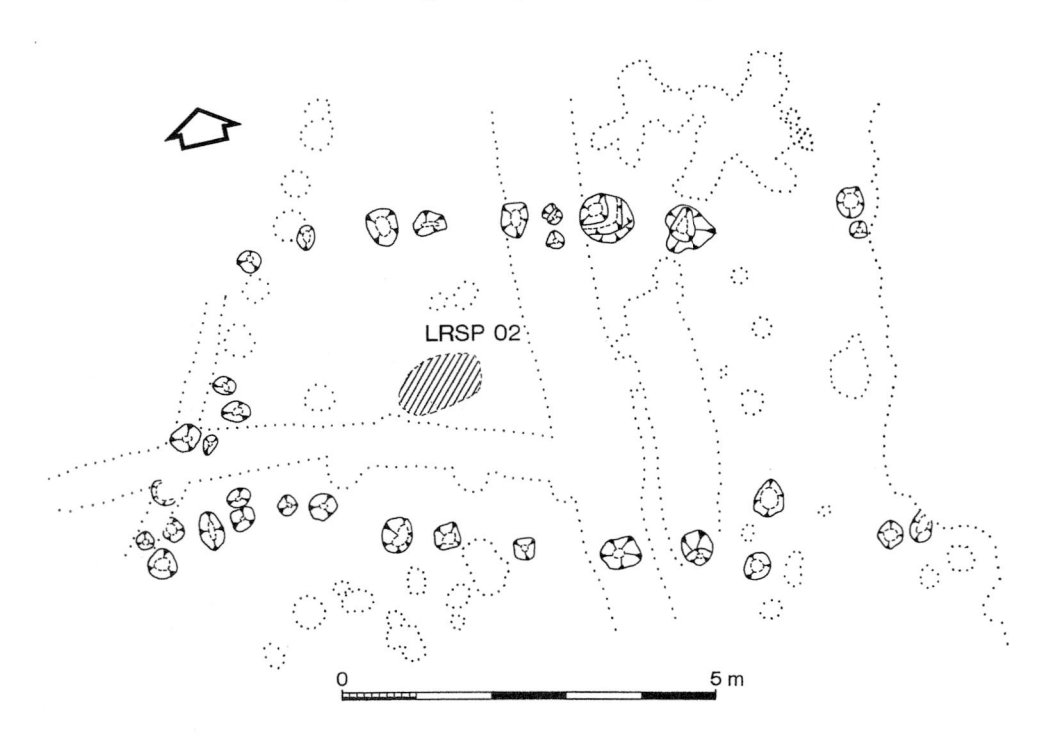

Fig 5.52: Langham Road, middle Saxon farm, timber hall (LRSP02)

site included the southern limit of the plots pertaining to the newly created late Saxon manor at Furnells. A strip of land along the southern margin of the Furnells plots, up to 20m wide, contained two minor buildings (Fig 5.57, LRSP13 and LRSP09). One of these (LRSP09) lay further west than any other excavated structure. It is suggested that this zone, where there was a trackway in the post-medieval period, was perhaps always a trackway providing access to the open fields. The occasional small buildings that appeared here in the late Saxon and medieval periods may have been squatter houses, built beside the trackway on the only land available to them, in a similar fashion to documented post-medieval squatter homes or the use of highway verges down to the present day.

A date for the creation of the plot system was not established at Langham Road, although it clearly post-dated the abandonment of the middle Saxon farm, which had occurred by the end of the ninth century. The fills of the boundary ditches, which were evidently recut and maintained for well over two hundred years, contained mixed assemblages of residual early–middle Saxon pottery, late Saxon pottery and medieval pottery through to around AD 1200. It seems most likely that the system was closely contemporary in origin with the plot system at Furnells, which was in existence by the mid-tenth century.

The late Saxon field boundaries

The basis for the arrangement of the boundary system was a linear ditch running south–north (LRSP26), which formed the boundary between the field system and the domestic plots (Fig 5.57). This ditch was traced for a distance of 75m, flanking the plot containing the late Saxon farm and adjoining plots to the south and north. In places, there was evidence that it had been recut. Further to the north, the line of this ditch lay largely beyond the excavated areas, but an equivalent south–north ditch on the northernmost part of the site, adjacent to Furnells manor, was offset some 4m to the east. This dislocation strengthens the argument that the Langham Road and Furnells plots systems were related but separate creations. To the south, the field boundary system was broken or cut across by a major west–east ditch system (LRSP25) which ran at least 85m further to the west (LRSP24); it was 1.0m wide and up to 0.15m deep. This west–east ditch appears to have been a major subdivision of the field system, and its partial continuation to the east of the field boundary may also suggest that it formed a southern boundary to the plot containing the late Saxon farm (see below).

Minor ditch systems branching from the western side of the field system boundary (LRSP86 and LRSP28), may have formed small abutting enclosures or pens. As at Furnells, the presence of these features suggests that in the late Saxon period this marginal area of the field system probably served several ancillary agricultural functions, with the cultivated land only beginning higher on the slopes to the west.

To the north of the field division ditch, a secondary ditch (LRSP28) formed a small rectangular enclosure or pen, 16m long by 4.5m wide. Adjacent to the field boundary ditch there was a group of nine intercutting pits (LRSP46), which cut or were cut by different phases of the boundary ditch.

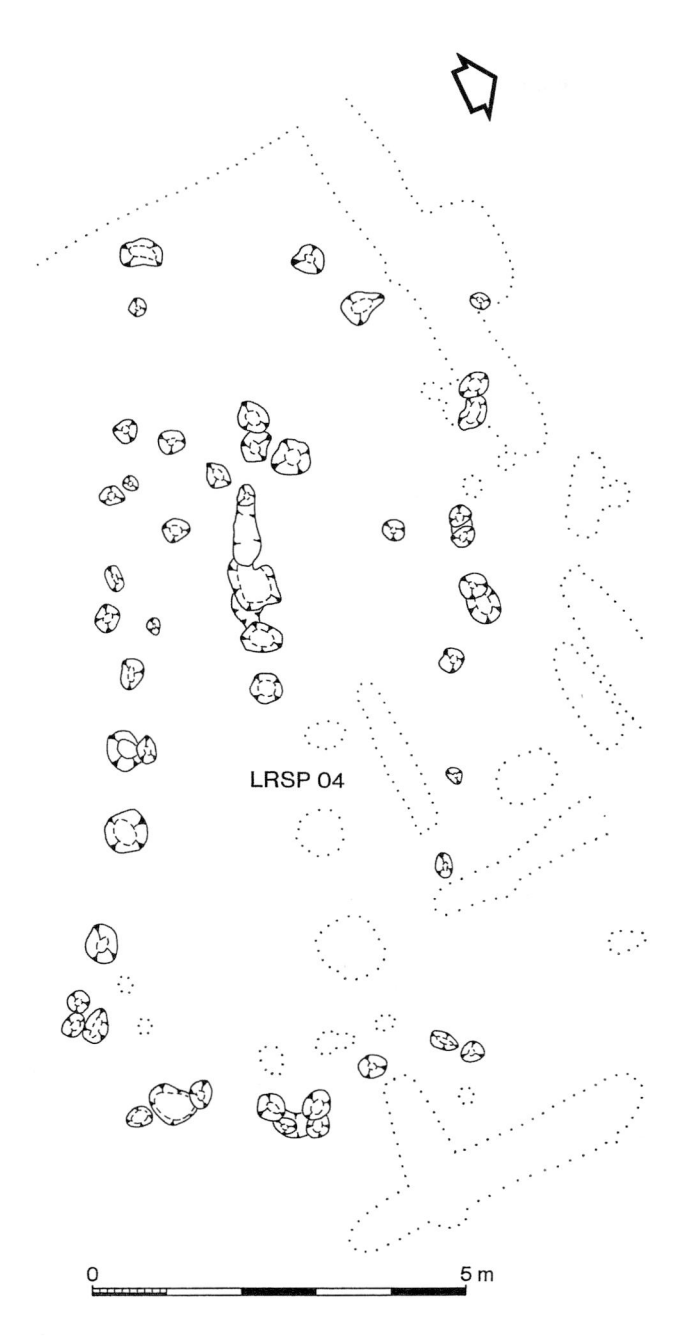

Fig 5.53: Langham Road, middle Saxon farm, timber hall (LRSP04)

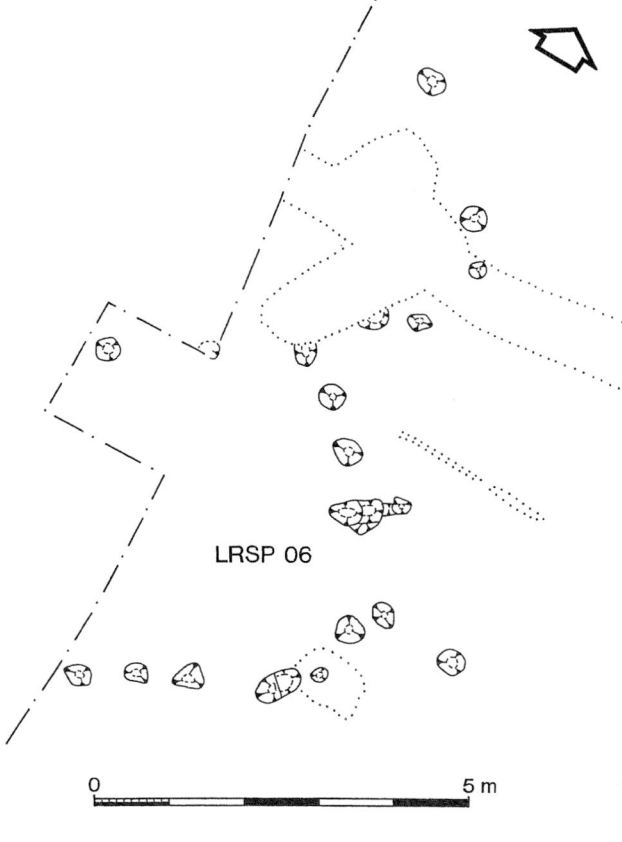

Fig 5.54: Langham Road, middle Saxon farm, timber building (LRSP06)

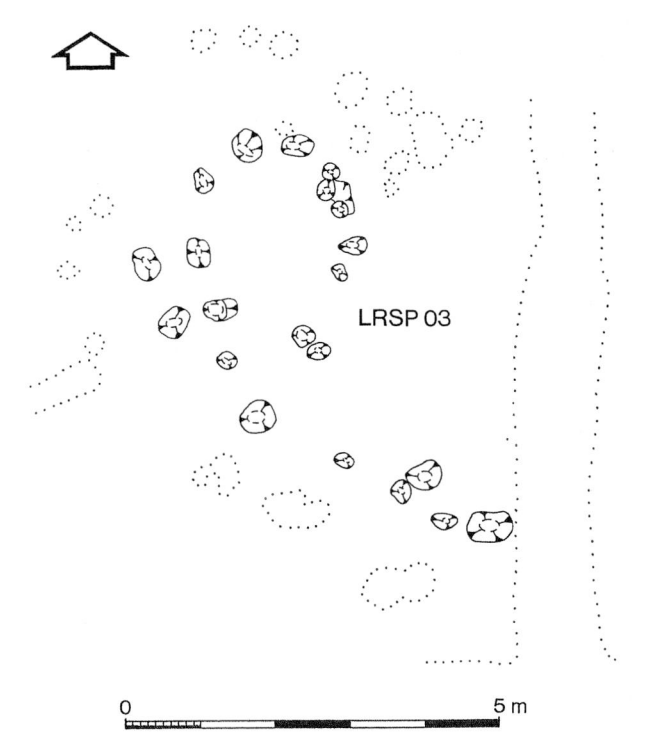

Fig 5.55: Langham Road, middle Saxon farm, posthole structure (LRSP03)

To the south curving ditches (LRSP86) formed pens on either side of the field boundary system, and both terminated about 2m short of the field-division boundary. This arrangement is perhaps most suggestive of the provision of restricted access at the corner of the fields to provide a stock control system.

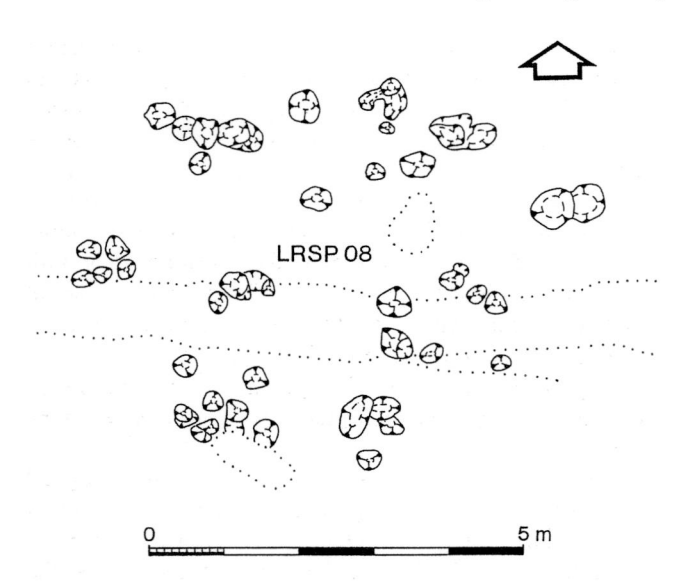

Fig 5.56: Langham Road, middle Saxon farm, posthole structure (LRSP08)

The late Saxon farm

To the east of the building complex there were two short lengths of ditch running west–east that may have formed plot divisions (Fig 5.57). The northernmost ditch (LRSP45) was a primary plot division, which was retained through the medieval period, when its location was respected by an extensive medieval quarry. A linear ditch 16m to the south, may have been a subdivision within the plot containing the late Saxon farm, as the buildings evidently continued to the south of this line.

The southern part of the plot was not available for excavation at the time, but it may be suggested that the southern boundary coincided with the east–west field division ditch (LRSP25). Confirmation of this was obtained in 2002 when a limited excavation on a house plot uncovered a system of boundary ditches that continued this line eastward (Fig 5.57, 2002 excavation: Morris 2002). Successive ditch systems were dated to the late Saxon and medieval periods, with a slight northward drift. The ditch system appears to have survived into the sixteenth century, when it was replaced by a limestone wall, located

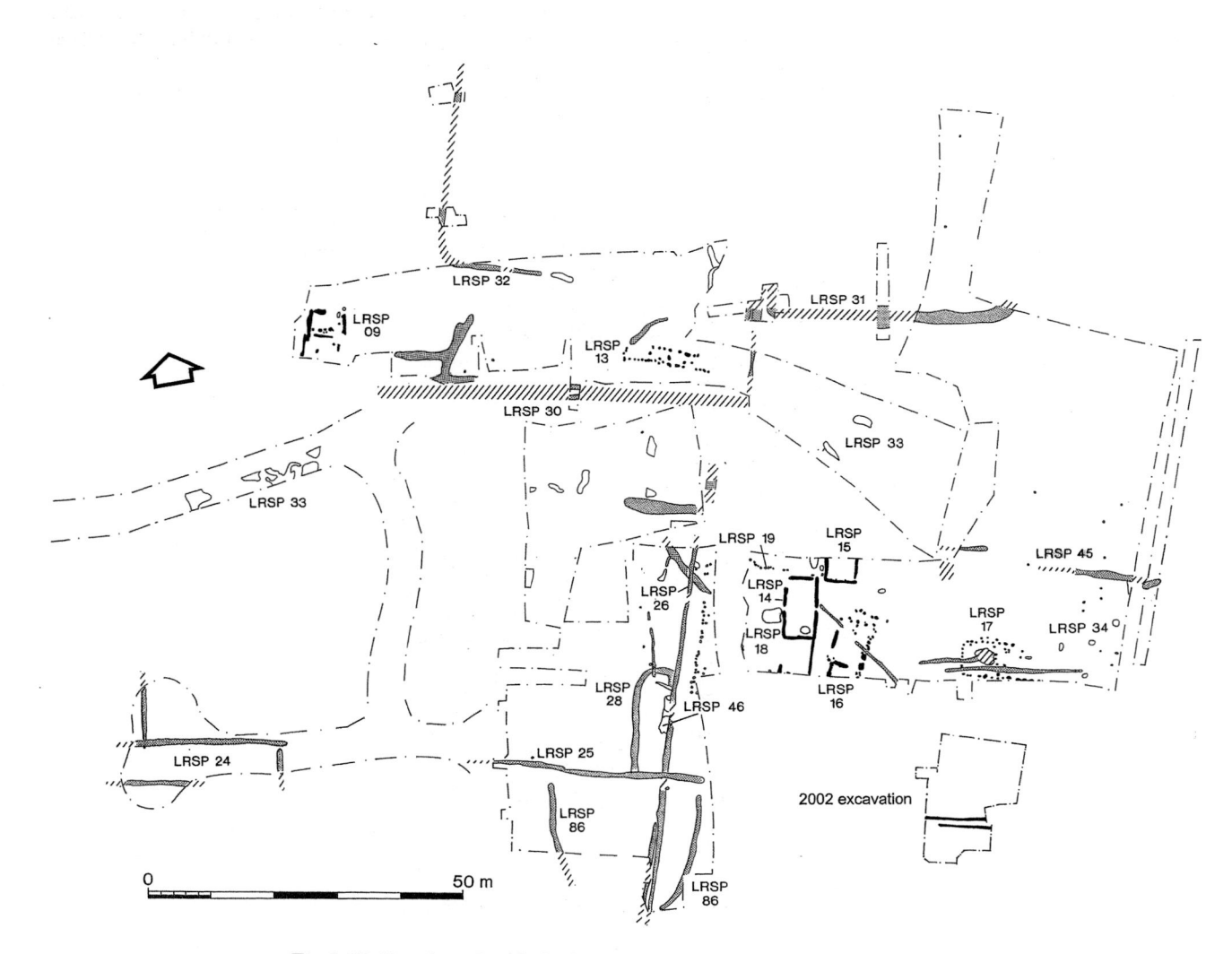

Fig 5.57: Langham Road, the late Saxon settlement (AD 900/950–1200)

slightly to the north of the ditches. The wall had stood until the late twentieth century, showing the durability of both the north–south field boundary system and the primary east–west divisions related to it.

The northern and southern boundaries of the plot containing the late Saxon farm lay 40m apart, indicating that the primary plot width was 8 rods, based on a rod of 16.5feet (5.03m) (Zupko 1968). In addition, it may be noted that the distance from the field boundary ditch to Rotton Row is approximately 110m. A plot measuring about 40m by 100m would be a one-acre plot, 8 rods wide by 20 rods long, the same as the one acre tenement plots identified at West Cotton (Chapman in press). It would therefore appear that the primary setting out along Rotton Row comprised a series of one-acre plots, of which the northernmost was excavated at Langham Road.

The farm itself comprised a group of at least three timber halls, two of which had their walls founded in continuous slots (Fig 5.58).

Timber hall (LRSP14)

A rectangular building of post-in-slot construction; most probably stave-built, measured 9.5m long by 4.5m wide, internally (Figs 5.58, 5.59 and 3.11, forground). The wall trenches ranged between 250–500mm wide and up to 400mm deep, with the shallowest trenches confined to the western part of the building. Central breaks in the eastern and western trenches formed opposed doorways, each 0.6m wide. Deeper post or plank settings on the southern side indicating the provision of more substantial timbers for the door surrounds. The break at the northern end of the western wall may suggest the provision of a further doorway. The northern wall slot terminated short of the long walls, suggesting that the roof was carried by the long walls, with the end walls probably of lighter build, although a central posthole setting on the southern wall might suggest the provision of an upright to hold a ridge beam.

A pit (Fig 5.58, LRSP18) adjacent to the western wall of the building, contained pieces of a single-sided bone comb.

The line of the east wall of the hall was continued southward by a further length of slot that may have formed part of a substantial boundary fence, perhaps of similar build to the hall itself. There is further evidence that the hall stood on the eastern side of a timber-walled enclosure. To the west, a line of postholes ran parallel with the field boundary ditch, and 2.5m to the east of the ditch (Fig 5.57). This line extended 23m north–south, and returned eastward to run past the northern end of the timber hall (Fig 5.58). This palisade enclosure would have been 23m long by 17m wide.

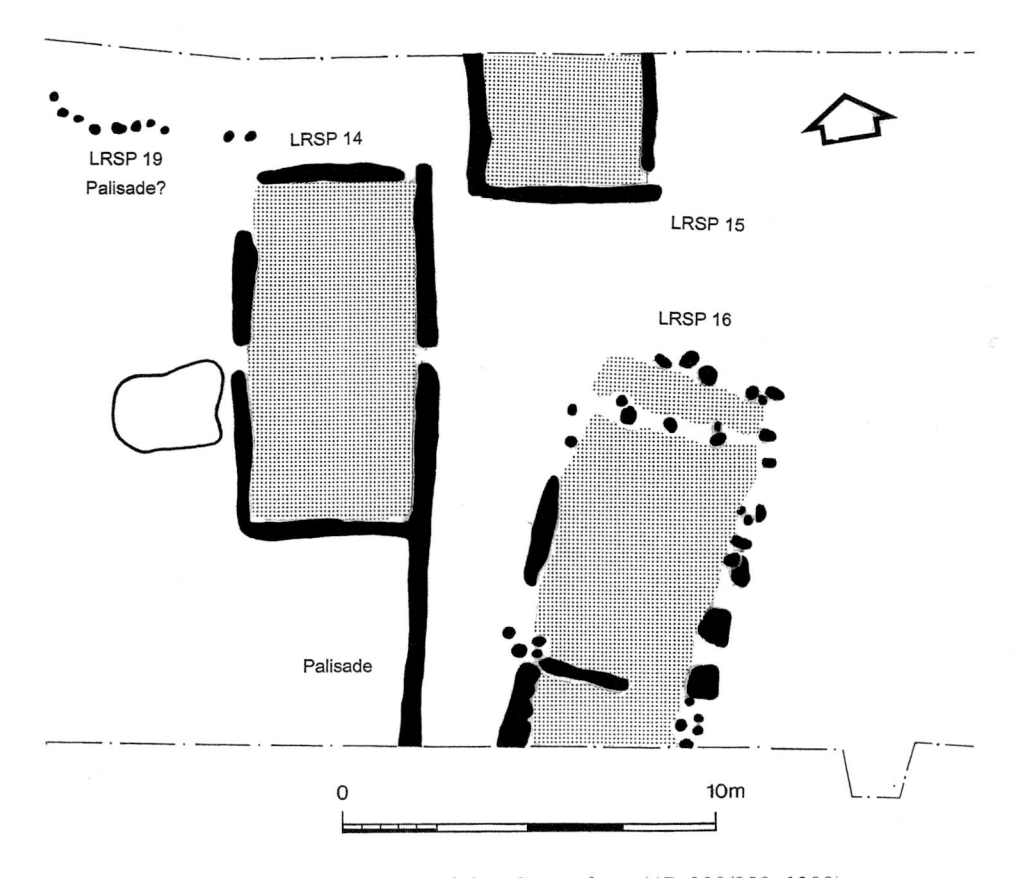

Fig 5.58: Langham Road, late Saxon farm (AD 900/950–1200)

Timber hall (LRSP15)

The southern end of a second hall of post-in-slot construction was 4.3m wide, internally, with wall trenches, 430–500mm wide and 200–300mm deep (Fig 5.60). Again, the southern wall trench was a separate from the long walls, and there was a deeper post setting at the end of the eastern wall trench.

Timber hall (LRSP16)

A third timber hall lay on a slightly different alignment (Fig 5.61). It appears to have been post-built, but while the eastern and northern walls contained discrete post-pits the western wall comprised postholes and two lengths of discontinuous slot, slightly offset, although the southern length did include several adjacent post-settings. The building appears to have comprised at least two rooms of separate structural build but with a common partition wall. The northern room was 6.7m long by 4.5m wide, although there may have been a further narrow chamber to the north. The room to the south was only 4.0m wide.

The pottery from individual postholes is largely of late Saxon date although some features contained later material.

Timber hall (LRSP17)

Another post-built hall (Fig 5.62), aligned east–west, lay some 15m to the east of the main group of buildings. It was 5.5m wide but the eastern end was poorly defined, although the southern wall appeared to be up to 11m long.

An area of scorched soil surrounding a setting of burnt stones may relate to a former central hearth. A separate, smaller setting of burnt stones and soil to the east may have been a further hearth either within the building or as dumped hearth debris outside a building 9.0m long.

Pit group (LRSP34)

A group of 11 pits were recorded on the limestone outcrop in the south-east corner of the excavated area, to the east of the timber halls (Fig 5.57). They contained late Saxon and medieval pottery

The central pit group (LRSP33)

A group of 22 broad but shallow pits, were cut into the clay in the central area of the site. They ranged in size from 0.62–1.40m and from 110–400mm deep (Fig 5.57). Their location was confined to a narrow corridor about 20m wide and at least 100m long which was bounded at the north by the southern end of the Furnells plots (LRSP30) and to the south by the plot boundary (LRSP45) of the late Saxon farm. The purpose of the pits is not clear but they may have been dug as clay extraction pits. They seem to show no respect for the north–south field boundary ditch, which may have been absent on at least part of this area, as some pits lay to the west on the field system. One possibility is that they occurred on an uncultivated margin on the heavier clay soils alongside the boundary between the Furnells and Langham Road plots. Associated pottery places them in the late Saxon/medieval period (up to AD 1200).

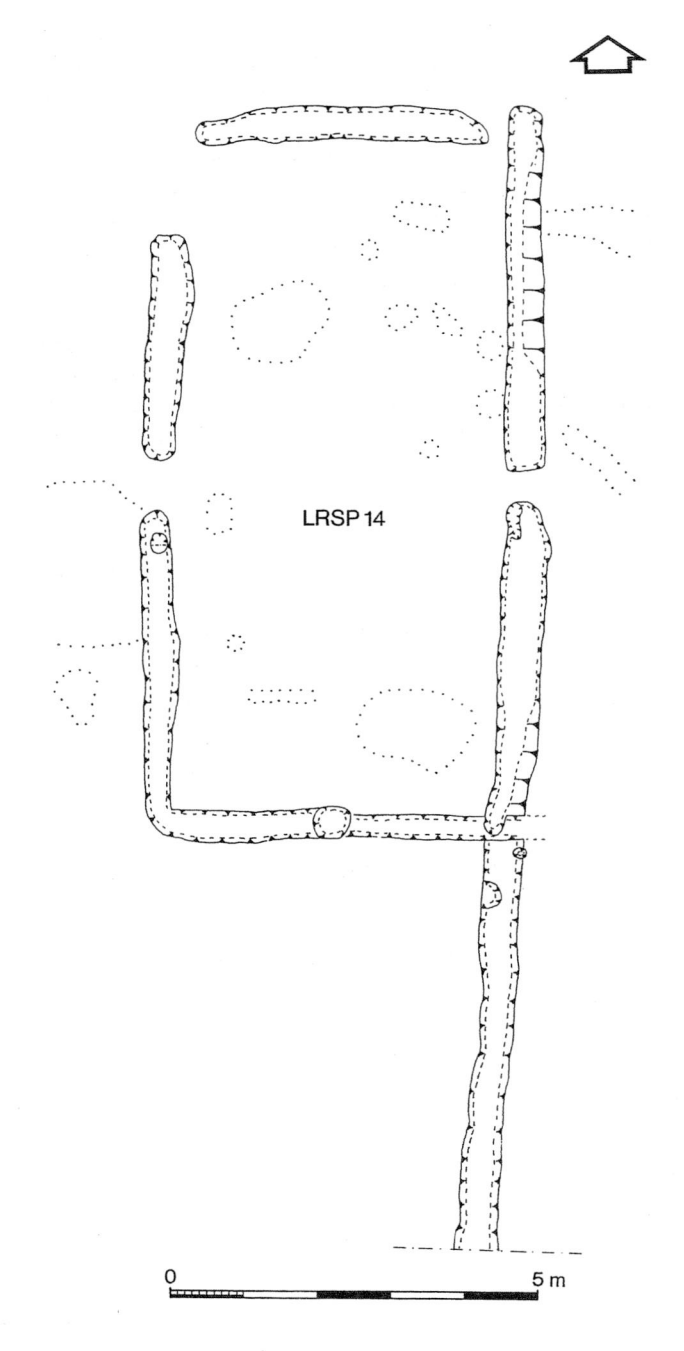

Fig 5.59: Langham Road, late Saxon farm, timber hall (LRSP14)

The northern boundaries and buildings

Two ditches probably formed the southern end of the Furnells plot system (Fig 5.57). The eastern ditch (LRSP31) would have been the end of the domestic plots, while the western ditch (LRSP32) was part of the agricultural enclosure abutting the western side of the settlement.

A further ditch to the south of these (LRSP30) was another primary and long-lived boundary system. To the west a hedge lay along the same alignment, and to east there was a late medieval/post-medieval wall, showing that the boundary was retained into the modern landscape. It is suggested that this ditch marked the northern end of the Langham Road plot system, with the narrow zone between this ditch and the end of the Furnells manor enclosure to the north serving as a trackway, as it apparently did in the post-medieval period.

In the late Saxon period two timber buildings stood here (LRSP13 and LRSP09). They were minor structures, one only 2.0m wide and the other comprising a single room with perhaps a lean-to to the rear. They have been

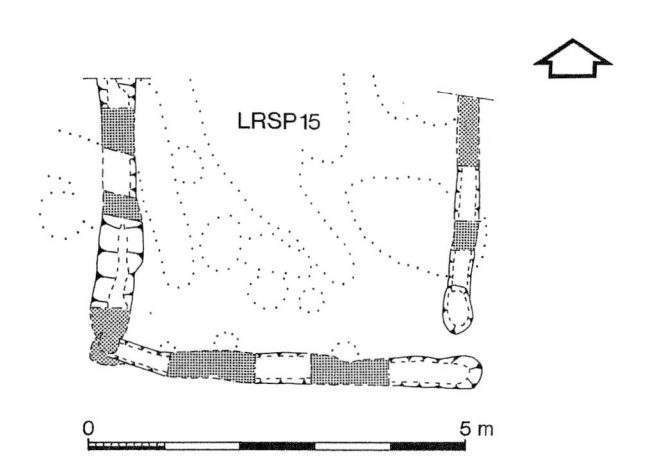

Fig 5.60: Langham Road, late Saxon farm, timber hall (LRSP15)

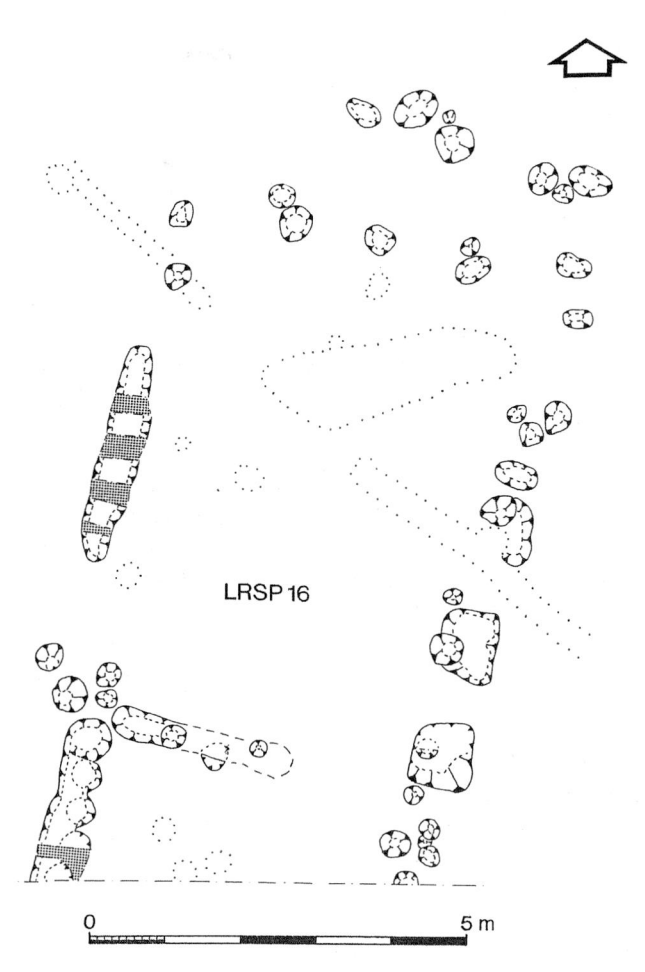

Fig 5.61: Langham Road, late Saxon farm, timber hall (LRSP16)

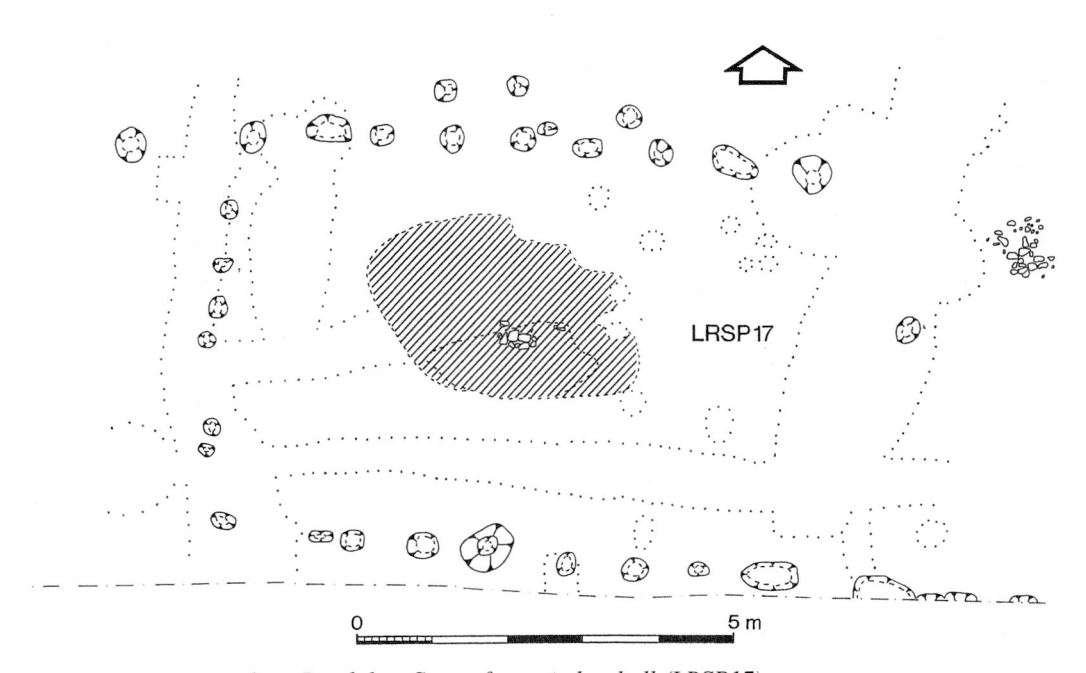

Fig 5.62: Langham Road, late Saxon farm, timber hall (LRSP17)

interpreted as potential peasant houses near the bottom level of society, and the term hovel may be appropriately used. They were located on a possible trackway, which may denote their status as the squatter homes of landless peasants built on a roadside verge. However, it must also be accepted that they could be interpreted as agricultural buildings, although the provision of animal housing did not generally occur at this date.

Timber building (LRSP13)

The main walls were formed by two parallel lines of postholes, set about 2.5m apart, and ranging from 240–580mm in diameter and 220–300mm deep (Fig 5.63). The southern wall was 13.5m long, but the building was only 2.0m wide, with single postholes forming partitions providing rooms 3.7m, 3.0m and perhaps 5.5m long.

Timber building (LRSP09)

An arrangement of four slots may have defined a small timber building 5.0m long by 3.2m wide (Fig 5.64). Only half of the northern wall was spanned by a wall slot, perhaps suggesting the provision of a broad doorway, at least 1.6m wide. The wall trenches were 300–800mm wide and up to 250mm deep. Narrower slots, slightly offset, indicate the provision of a second chamber to the south, perhaps open-ended.

Langham Road: The medieval tenement plots and field boundaries (AD 1200–1350/1400)

By the thirteenth century the late Saxon farm had been abandoned and thereafter there were no further domestic buildings on the excavated parts of the Langham Road plots. It is therefore assumed that from AD 1200 the domestic buildings had been relocated eastward nearer to, if not directly fronting onto, Rotton Row. The medieval activity on the excavated areas comprised redefinition of the boundary ditches and, on the tenement plots to the east, the eventual replacement of some ditches with boundary walls, together with quarrying and pit digging.

The field boundaries

The north–south boundary ditch between the tenements plots and the field system was maintained into the medieval period (Fig 5.65, LRSP55). The major west–east field division was also maintained (LRSP42), but it was also relocated slightly northward, perhaps with the double ditches flanking a hedge. The small enclosures or pens abutting the western side of the field boundary ditch had gone, and the minor ditches to the north and south of the doubled-ditched field boundary may have run along the line of the furrows of the medieval field system, which then ran right down to the boundary ditch. In fact during the medieval period the ditch was eventually lost beneath a low bank of soils that accumulated along the edge of the field system as a plough headland. The headland sealed two pits which contained pottery of thirteenth to fourteenth-century date.

The field boundary ditch terminated to the north at the edge of the area of underlying clays and, as in the previous period, it may have remained uncultivated. There was a series of shallow pits, perhaps dug as clay pits (LRSP37), scattered across this area.

The medieval tenement plot

The field boundary ditch, and later the headland, still defined the western limit of the tenement plot, and the northern boundary was defined by a new ditch (LRSP27). The excavations of 2002 (Morris 2002) also recorded a medieval ditch that probably formed the retained southern boundary (see Fig 5.57), suggesting that the basic

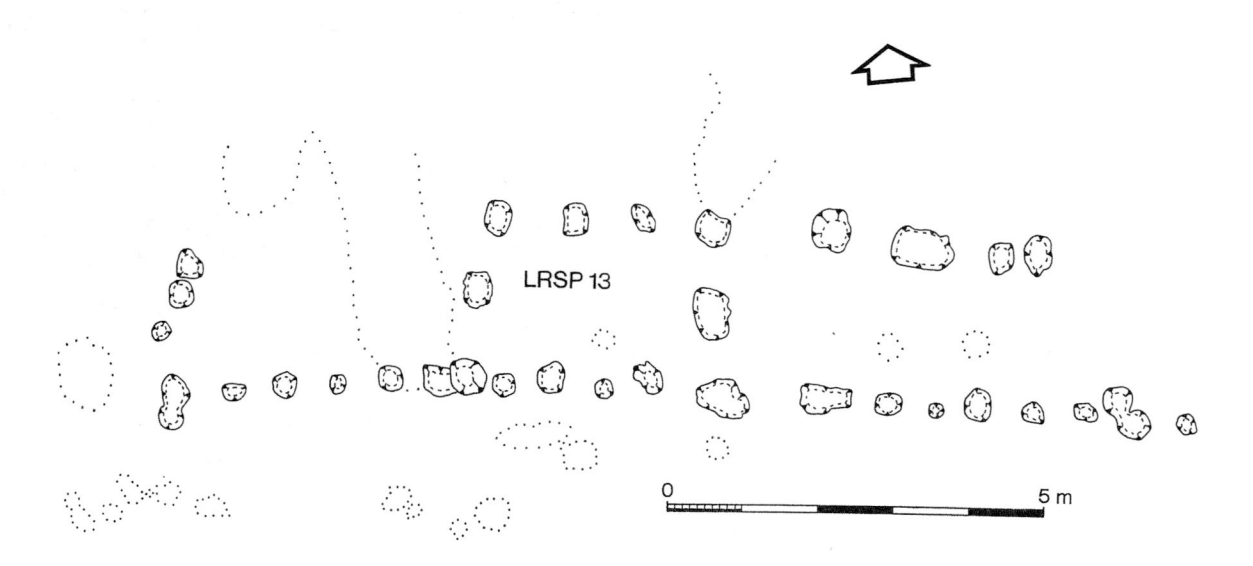

Fig 5.63: Langham Road, late Saxon farm, timber building (LRSP13)

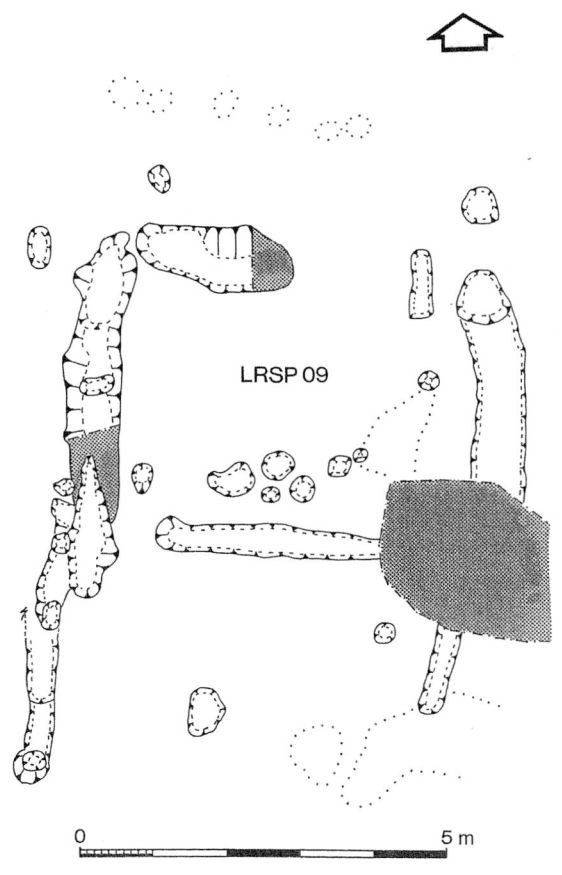

arrangement of the one acre tenement plot or toft remained unchanged.

Towards the east a new north–south ditch (Fig 5.65, LRSP29) may mark the introduction of a formal subdivision between a new domestic plot to the east and the open plot at the rear of the tenement. This ditch lay about half-way between Rotton Row and the field boundary, and therefore split the tenement into two half-acre plots. A probable continuation of this ditch system to the south was also seen in the excavations of 2002 (Morris 2002), where there was pair of parallel ditches, surviving to no more than 0.35m deep. The latest pottery from the fills here was dated to the fifteenth century.

The north-eastern corner of the rear plot was occupied by an extensive limestone quarry pit (LRSP20). This was partially excavated, confirming that it comprised several intercutting pits within an area of 25m by 17m, covering c225sq.m. The pits had been dug to various depths, in places up to 2.1m, to extract the underlying Blisworth limestone bedrock, but also to exploit the overlying shallow beds of broken limestone rubble. The individual pits

Fig 5.64 (left): Langham Road, late Saxon farm, timber building (LRSP09)

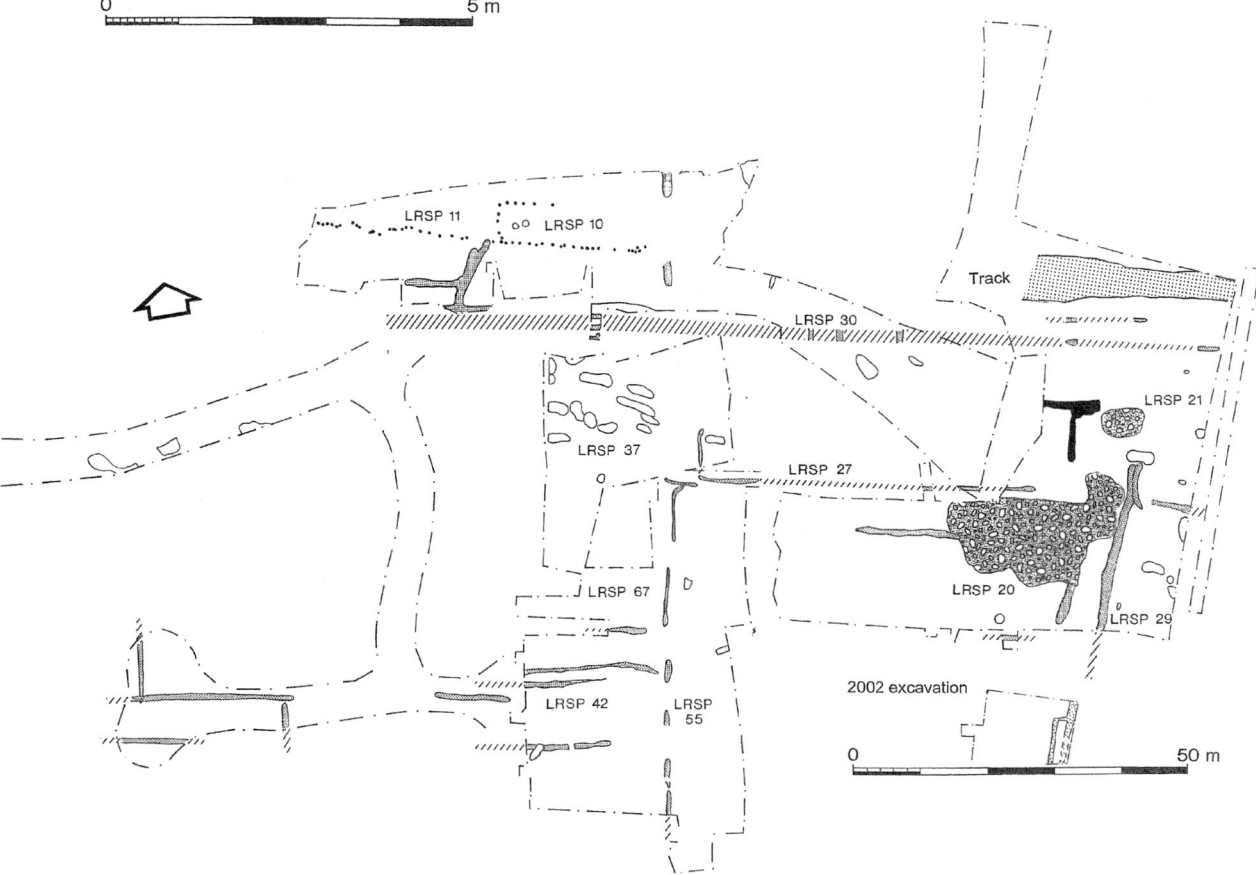

Fig 5.65: Langham Road, the medieval tenement plots (AD 1200–1350/1400)

had been backfilled with quarry-waste comprising small limestone rubble interspersed with thin layers of soil. None had any incorporated domestic refuse. A small quantity of medieval wares from the lowest fills of one pit provides a *terminus post quem* of AD 1200.

The quarry pit largely respected the northern tenement boundary, although one pit to the east crossed the boundary, and a further isolated quarry pit lay further to the north (LRSP21).

The stone from these quarries was presumably used in the building of stone domestic buildings on the eastern half of the tenement plots at around the beginning of the thirteenth century.

The northern plots and timber building (LRSP30)

The ditches of the Furnells plots had fallen out of use and only the main east–west division between Furnells and Langham was retained (LRSP30) (Fig 5.65). To the west this was still defined by a ditch but, at some point in the medieval period, to the east the boundary was defined by a limestone wall.

As in the previous period, the only buildings on the western part of the site lay on the narrow zone at the southern end of the Furnells plots. A line of postholes (LRSP 11) forming a fence line was traced for 50m, and an adjacent arrangement of postholes formed a timber structure, measuring 8m by 6m (Figs 5.65 and 5.66, LRSP10). The presence of two areas of scorched natural suggests that this was a roofed domestic building. However, lacking this detail the slight and widely-spaced postholes might have been interpreted as deriving from an open pen or, at best, a lightly roofed shelter. The dating is uncertain but it certainly existed after AD1200.

Langham Road: post-medieval activity

The overall pattern of agricultural and domestic usage established at Langham Road in the medieval period, with the long tenement plots fronting onto Rotton Row with the open fields behind, continued until at least the enclosure of 1798.

As established in the excavations of 2002 (Morris 2002), the southern boundary ditch of the late Saxon and medieval tenement plot appeared to have been replaced by a limestone wall in the sixteenth century, and this stood until well into the twentieth century, showing a retention of at least some of the earlier primary boundaries.

While the first medieval building of stone houses had utilised stone from quarry pits within the tenement, the absence of any later quarrying indicates that for subsequent rebuilding stone must have been imported from elsewhere. An indication of the uses of the rear halves of the tenement plots is provided by the pre-enclosure survey of 1739 (Hall *et al*, 69–71 and table 1), where the properties along Rotton Row are typically described as comprising a house and yard or yards, which would have occupied the eastern half of the plot, while spinneys, closes or orchards, would have occupied the western ends, thus explaining the rarity of any cut features of late medieval and post-medieval date in these areas. It is also evident from the enclosure plan of 1798 that the tenements along Rotton Row had undergone a process of sub-division (Figs 1.3 and 1.4, and Hall *et al*, fig 7). The identified medieval one-acre plot had certainly been split along its length into two plots and, along Rotton Row in general, there were both further sub-divisions and also amalgamations of plots, leaving the primary boundaries hidden beneath the complexity of later use.

Even immediately following enclosure in 1798, there was no change to the physical boundaries of the settlement pattern. However, with the abandonment of the open field system the previous ridge and furrow cultivation to the immediate west of the tenement plots was eventually turned to rough pasture, and sub-divided by new hedgerows. While the tenurial divisions were still there, the physical distinction between the former field system and the rear plots of the tenements, which were used as closes, spinneys and orchards, must have become progressively of less importance given the similarity of the functions and the declining economic importance of such usage.

It was in the late nineteenth century, in response to the rising population of the town as the shoe industry developed, that the final major re-division of the land was carried out. This led to the whole of Rotton Row being infilled with housing and other properties and, as part of this process new property divisions were set out. These were given new rear boundaries, the walls that still form the boundaries today. These typically lie some 40m west of Rotton Row, and therefore mark a major contraction in the length of the properties, reflecting the lack of a need for attached closes in a village rapidly taking on the appearance of a small industrial town. The new 40m plot length does, however, show another use of the 8-rod measurement that had been utilised nearly a thousand years earlier in the creation of the original system.

With the creation of the modern frontage, the former closes and orchards to the rear were largely abandoned as part of the general uncultivated systems of paddocks, which still existed in the late 1970s when the excavations at Furnells began. However, in one or two cases people subsequently arbitrarily re-enclosed parts of these rear areas in the 1960s, reflecting a modern interest in large gardens, and thereby continuing the constant cycle of adaptation to current needs and fashions.

The northern plots

To the north, the major boundary between the abandoned Furnells manorial plots and the Langham Road tenements was also retained. The enclosure map clearly shows the closes of the former Furnells manor, taking in both the area of the domestic plots and also a block of the former open fields to the north and west of this (Figs 1.3 and 1.4, and Hall *et al*, fig 7).

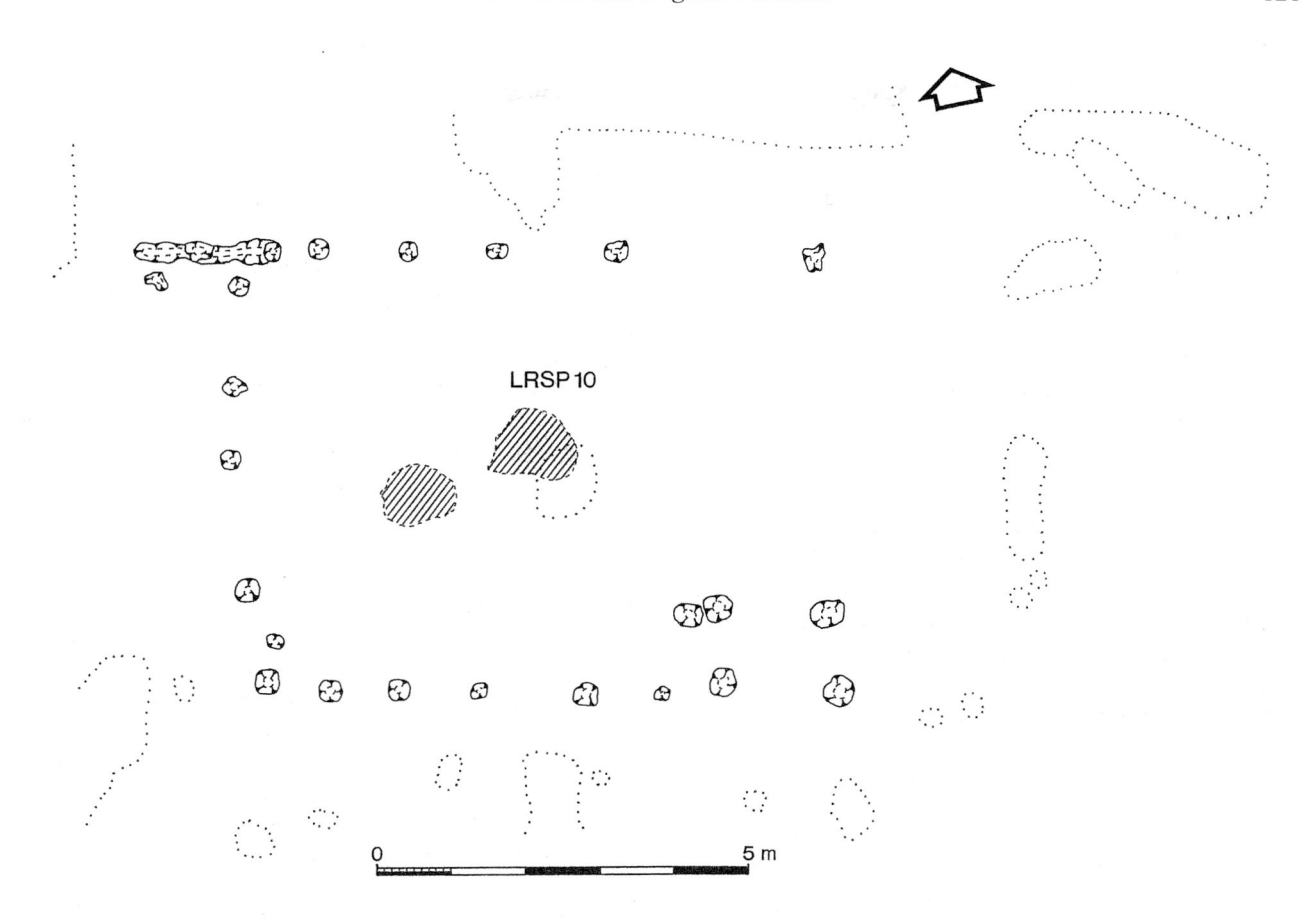

Fig 5.66: Langham Road, medieval timber building (LRSP10)

Archaeologically, this area saw the only principal new feature of the period: the construction of a crudely metalled trackway, c4m wide and heavily rutted (LRSP41). This ran along the eastern part of the narrow boundary zone between Furnells and Langham Road (Fig 5.65). On the enclosure map of 1798 (Fig 1.4), this area forms a narrow plot along the southern margin of the Furnells Closes. This was perhaps the 'blind lane' mentioned by historical documents as leading to Furnells Close (Hall et al 1988), and this may have been the first metalling of what might have been a green land running up onto the fields for several hundred years. The area to its immediate south is also distinguished on the enclosure map as a long plot that runs onto the former field system, perhaps reflecting the archaeological evidence for the late Saxon and medieval usage of this area as a marginal zone on a band of clay primarily utilised for clay extraction through the digging of small pits, and perhaps never actually under cultivation.

Burystead

At Burystead a large area of former paddocks and waste ground was available for excavation between 1985 and 1987 prior to and during the early stages of new housing development. It measured 106m north–south by 110m east–west, and a total area of 0.75ha was excavated. The southern boundary lay directly adjacent to the churchyard of St Peter's church.

The site was excavated in stages. The northern half was excavated in 1985–86. The southern half, which had been presumed to include the Burystead manor house, was excavated in 1987. The northern part of this second area, containing a dovecote, malting oven and other ancillary farm buildings was excavated in the early part of the year, while the southern half was opened for excavation later in the year. It was therefore only at the final stage of excavation that it became apparent that the manor house, which had been a primary objective of the work at Burystead, to provide a second manor house complex to compare and contrast with Furnells manor, did not lie to the north of the church, as presumed from an analysis of the documentary evidence. The location of the Burystead manor house is still unknown, but it may be tentatively suggested that it lay to the east of the church, in a similar arrangement to Furnells manor. This area was lost to housing long ago.

A separate area to the north, lying on the Midland Road frontage, is described separately (see section 5.6). A link between the two excavation areas was provided by a series of trial trenches excavated prior to the main excavations (Fig 1.5). These located either sparse archaeological features or areas of later disturbance, which is why no further excavation was carried out.

Burystead: Early–middle Saxon settlement (AD 450–850)

The presence of early–middle Saxon settlement on the eastern bank of the Raunds Brook is indicated by a large assemblage of pottery that included some imported Ipswich ware and Maxey-type wares. However, the bulk of the assemblage was unstratified or occurred as residual material in later contexts. This is indicative of the high level of disturbance from later activity, which made it difficult to isolate surviving features of probable early–middle Saxon origin.

The majority of the identified features, which include lengths of gully and a scatter of postholes and pits, lay within an area measuring 50m by 25m (Fig 5.67). All of these features contained pottery of the general period and some included middle Saxon wares. In addition, the oak plank lining of a probable waterhole on the southern margin of the area (BSP01), which also contained middle Saxon pottery, has given a radiocarbon date centred on the mid-seventh to late eighth centuries (660–770 cal AD, 95% confidence, 1308±36BP, UB-3420), confirming a middle Saxon date for the settlement. Whether the settlement began in the early Saxon period and continued through is less clear, although the presence of a small quantity of early Saxon stamped pottery suggests that there was at least some activity here in the early Saxon period.

No timber buildings can be positively assigned to this phase of occupation. However, a number of post-built structures that contained early–middle Saxon pottery but also small amounts of late Saxon pottery may have been of middle Saxon origin and were either abandoned at the beginning of the late Saxon period or there were small amounts of unrecognised contamination of the fills. These buildings comprised small post-built halls to the north (Fig 5.67, BSP08) and west (BSP09), and another building to the east (BSP11), largely lost to later quarrying. The most compelling argument for contamination being a factor may be provided by a sunken-featured building to the south (BSP51). This building form is typically associated with early Saxon settlement and appears to have fallen out of use within the middle Saxon period. The example at Burystead produced some late Saxon pottery but it certainly pre-dated part of the late Saxon boundary ditch system, suggesting that it belongs with the earlier settlement but the fills had been contaminated by later disturbance from the boundary ditch.

Early–middle Saxon features

Two lengths of shallow gully, 20m and 25m long, and several shorter lengths within the same general area may have served as boundaries and/or drains (Fig 5.67, BSP04). An L-shaped gully to the north (BSP05), with arms measuring 3m and 6m, might represent the remains of a small wooden structure.

A total of 28 shallow pits of varying shapes are dated to the early–middle Saxon period from the pottery in the fills and, in some instances, by their stratigraphic relationships. A number of postholes, including some forming loose groupings, contained early–middle Saxon pottery.

On the southern edge of the main concentration of early middle-Saxon features, a well or waterhole (BSP01) lay within a cluster of pits and short lengths of gully. The pit was 1.9–2.2m in diameter at the surface and 1.1m deep. The upper two-thirds were of sub-circular plan, while the lower third was rectangular, measuring 1.1m by 0.55m and 0.4m deep, and was lined with oak planks. A ledge or step towards the top of the eastern side could have facilitated access. Large sherds of Maxey-type ware, alongside smaller fragments of local early–middle Saxon pottery were present in the fills.

A cremation cemetery at Park Road (TL 0005 7298)

In 1989 evaluation trenches were excavated ahead of development at Park Road by the Raunds Survey team. The site lay 150m to the south of Burystead, and also to the south of St Peter's church. A number of pits and gullies contained early–middle and late Saxon pottery and a group of small pits, contained cremated human bone and early–middle Saxon pottery and other grave goods dated to the sixth century. This appeared to be part of an early Saxon cemetery, which is described in the Raunds Survey volume (Parry 2006, 225–228). While a sixth-century date may pre-date the main episode of early settlement at the Burystead site, it does confirm the impression given by a few sherds of stamped early Saxon pottery at Burystead that occupation on the eastern stream bank most probably began in the early Saxon period, as it did on the western stream bank at Furnells.

The Saxon timber buildings

As already noted, the Saxon timber buildings at Burystead are of uncertain date. A number of post-built structures (BSP08, BSP09 and BSP11) and a sunken-featured building (BSP51) may have been contemporary with the early–middle Saxon occupation, despite the presence of small quantities of apparently associated late Saxon pottery (Fig 5.67).

Timber hall (BSP08)

A rectangular structure, 9.6m long by 6.0m wide (Figs 5.68 and 5.69). The long walls are marked by irregular lines of postholes of mixed sizes, with 14 postholes along the northern wall, and no obvious doorway opening. The end walls are defined by smaller postholes, and the east wall appears to have lain at a slightly oblique angle creating a

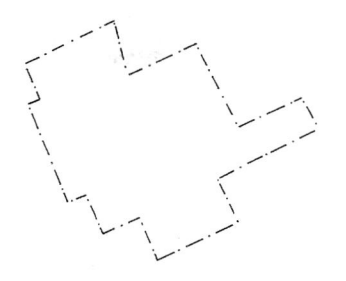

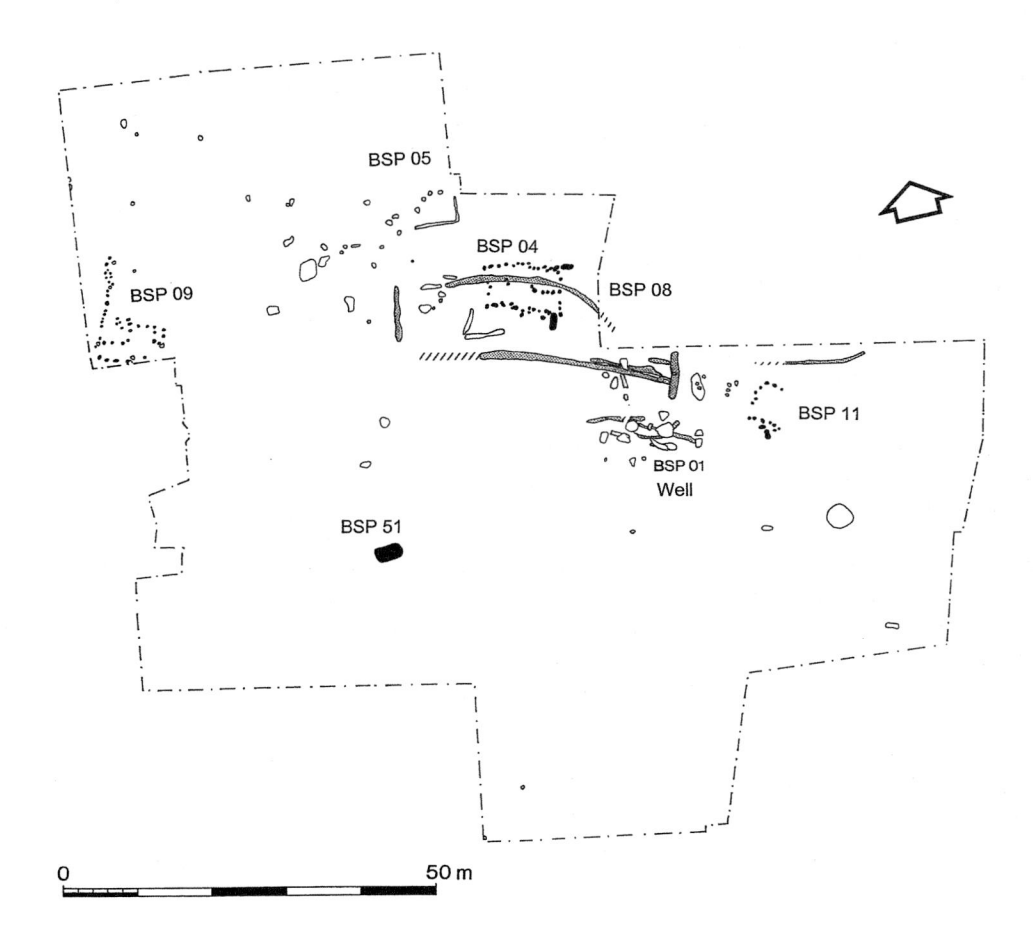

Fig 5.67: Burystead, the early–middle Saxon settlement (AD 450–850)

trapezoidal plan. The eastern half of the interior may have been divided into two chambers by a longitudinal partition based on a line of six postholes.

Some of the postholes contained a mixed assemblage of early–middle Saxon pottery and late Saxon St Neots-type ware. However, a boundary ditch that can be broadly attributed to the late Saxon/Saxo-Norman period cut across the structure, and an early–middle Saxon date is favoured.

Timber hall (BSP09)

A rectangular building, 7.0m long by 5.0m wide (Figs 5.70 and 5.71). Pairs of elongated postholes, perhaps double post-settings, in both the north and south walls may denote doorways, 0.9m wide. The western half of the interior may have been divided into two chambers by a longitudinal partition, 3.0m long. A 9m long line of postholes may represent a fence running northward. Pottery from some

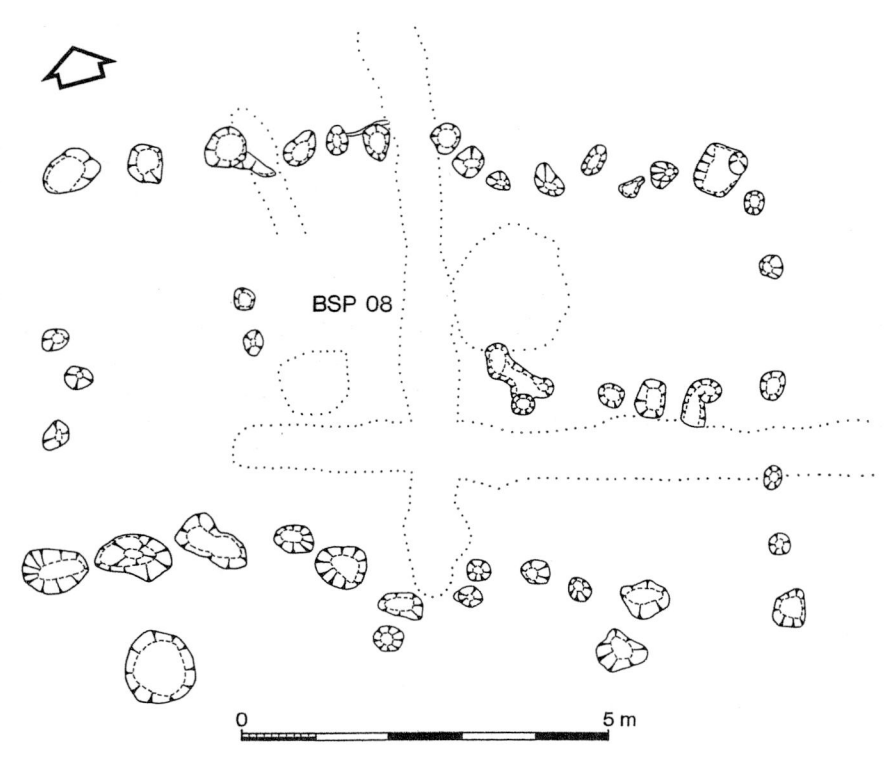

Fig 5.68: Burystead, early–middle Saxon timber building (BSP08)

Fig 5.69: Burystead, early–middle Saxon timber building (BSP08), looking south

of the postholes ranges from early–middle Saxon to the late Saxon.

Timber building (BSP11)

The western end of a rectangular post-built structure was 5.0m wide (Fig 5.72). The eastern end had been lost to quarrying.

Sunken-feature building (BSP51)

A rectangular, flat-bottomed pit, 3.4m long and up to 2.2m wide (but truncated by a later ditch) and 130mm deep (Fig 5.73). There were pairs of postholes at either end, and at the western end the outer posthole was much smaller. Three stake-holes, 1.3m and 1.5m apart, lay along the southern edge, while two postholes to the north, party investigated, were of uncertain association. The average dimensions of the postholes were 300mm in diameter and 240mm deep.

Burystead: Plot boundaries and late Saxon/ Saxo-Norman settlement (AD 900/950–1200)

At Burystead, as at Furnells and Langham Road, the late Saxon period was marked by the appearance of a boundary ditch system defining a set of rectangular plots (Figs 5.74 and 5.75). Contemporary activity included some minor timber buildings and a scatter pits, but the western parts of the site were dominated by extensive stone quarry pits, with smaller pits to the north which probably served as clay digging pits. The best date that can be provided

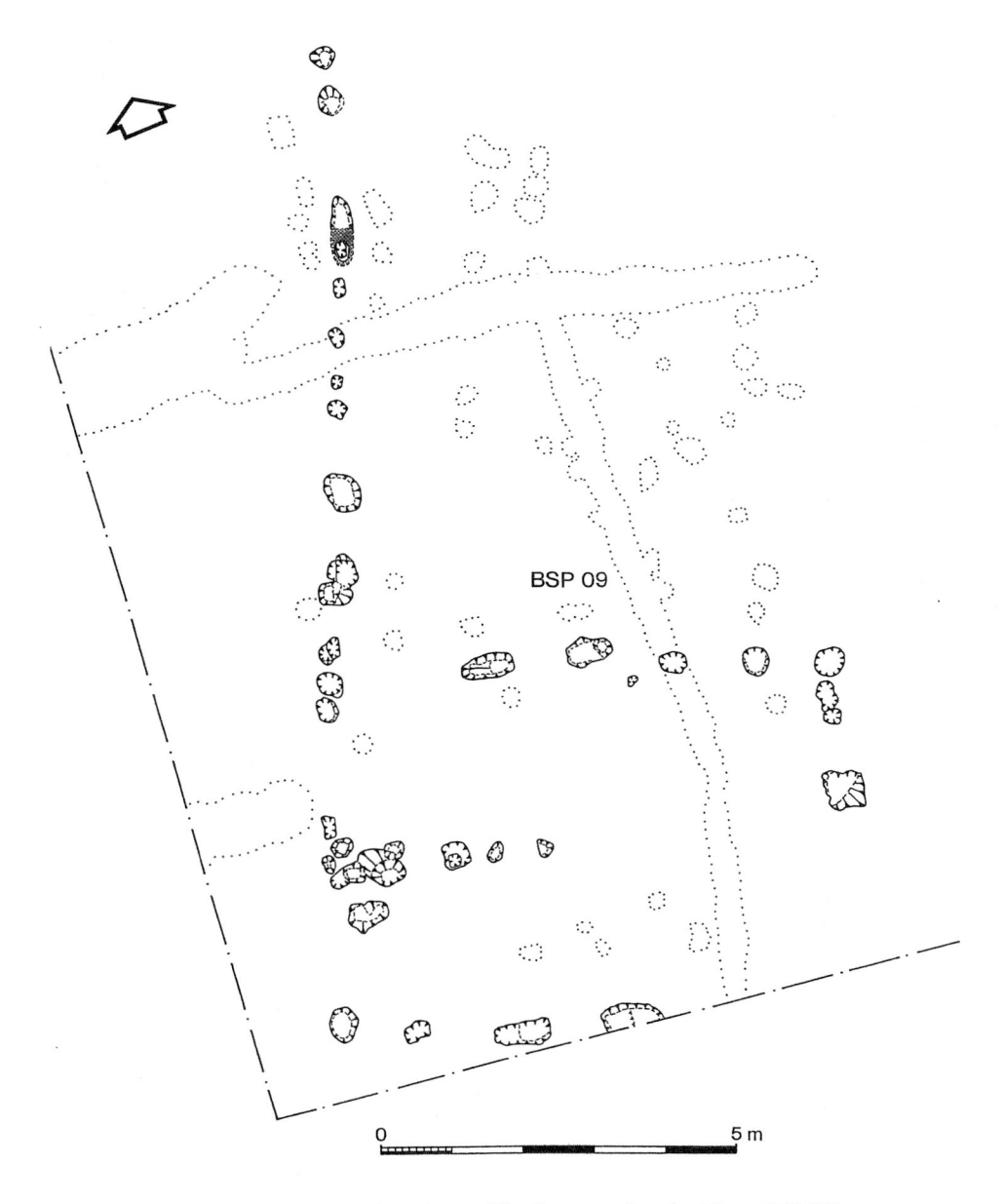

Fig 5.70: Burystead, early–middle Saxon timber building (BSP09)

Fig 5.71: Burystead, early–middle Saxon timber building (BSP09), looking south-west

for the commencement of this activity places it within the first half of the tenth century (AD 900–950, Ceramic Phase LS3).

Boundary ditch systems

While the lack of intersections and other stratigraphic relationships between the various ditch systems precludes any attempt to trace their development in detail, the simplicity of the overall plan form, essentially comprising east–west boundaries to the south and north–south boundaries to the north, lends support to the suggestion that they formed a single coherent system (Fig 5.75). It is the presence of St Neots-type ware, in addition to an apparently residual component of early–middle Saxon pottery, which suggests that the boundaries were established in the late Saxon period, AD 900–950. However, many also produced quantities of post-conquest pottery, indicating that the system remained largely intact until the end of the twelfth century.

The basic change in alignment and the longevity of a common boundary indicates that the area comprised two distinct zones. The southern block of land was bounded to the north by a linear ditch system (BSP17 and BSP99). This east–west boundary was still present in the modern property boundaries up to the time of the excavation, when it was defined by a hedge, and was only lost with the modern housing development. Twenty metres, or 4 rods, to the south there was a parallel boundary ditch (BSP15/16), which did not survive into the modern landscape, while the modern churchyard boundary lay slightly over a further 40m to the south of this. A further east–west system (BSP 18) appears to have been a partial sub-division of the southern plot, and there were further ditch systems immediately north of the churchyard. A north–south ditch system near the eastern limit of excavation, adjacent to a modern property boundary, may mark an eastern end to these plots. This eastern ditch lay 110–115m to the east of the lane that runs along the western margin of the site, Church Street. It may be suggested that the two southern plots at Burystead comprised a one acre plot to the south, and a half acre plot to the north.

It may also be noted that the junction of Church Street and Midland Road (Fig 1.5) lay around 100m to the north of the main east–west boundary (BSP17), although this distance increases steadily further to the east given the oblique alignment of Midland Road with respect to the plot boundaries at Burystead. On the northern half of Burystead there were two north–south boundaries (BSP06, to the west and BSP13 to the east). These were also 40m apart, so this central plot would have been one-acre in extent, while the narrower plot to its west would have been a half-acre. Most of the eastern plot lay beyond the excavated area, but plot boundary (BSP13) lay some 65m west of the

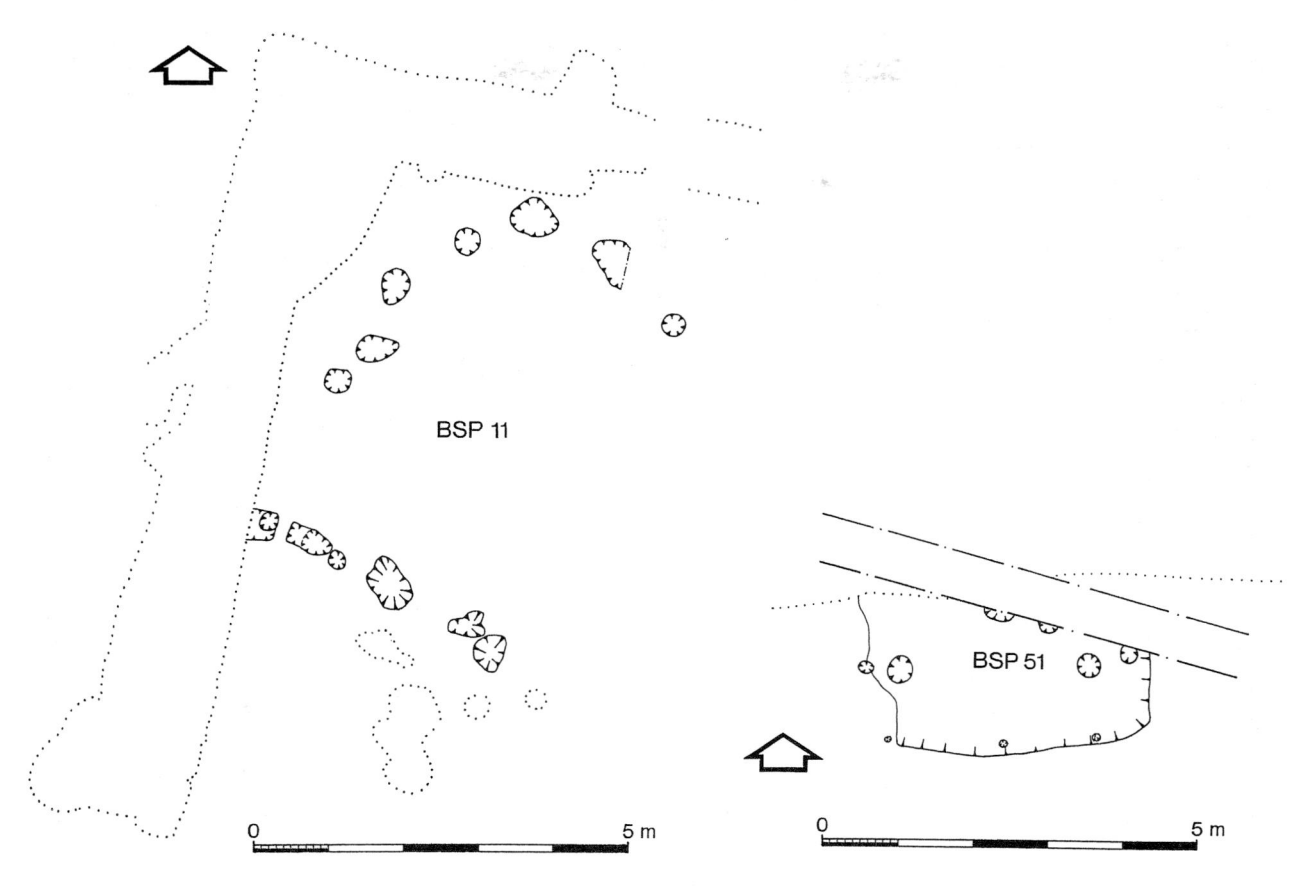

Fig 5.72: Burystead, early–middle Saxon timber building (BSP11)

Fig 5.73: Burystead, early–middle Saxon sunken-featured building (BSP51)

boundary to the two southern plots, suggesting that this eastern plot may have been of 1.5acres. It is recognised that, of course, none of these acreages are exact, but the frequent recurrence of measurements of the order of 40m and 100m suggests that the provision of one-acre plots, and fractions or multiples thereof, lay at the basis of the laying out of the plot boundaries, as has also been seen at Furnells, Langham Road and, most clearly, at West Cotton (Chapman in press).

Activity within the southern plots

In the eastern half of the southern plot there was a small timber structure, apparently with an open northern side, that may have been an agricultural building rather than a domestic hall (Fig 5.74, BSP19). No other buildings were noted by the excavators, although a rectilinear arrangement of postholes to the west of the recorded building may have been a less substantial structure or pen some 10m long by 4m wide.

Across the narrower northern plot there were a large number of scattered postholes that may have been of late Saxon or Saxo-Norman date on the basis of the small quantities of pottery recovered from them, but no rectilinear arrangements could be identified.

The western end of this northern plot was dominated by large, deep stone-pits (Fig 5.74, BSP12 and BSP107), which were only partially investigated. Within the backfill of these quarries were small quantities of domestic refuse which included ash and animal bone in addition to tenth to twelfth century pottery. These were all cut into limestone bedrock and, while the destination of the stone remains unknown, some may have been used in the construction of the predecessor of the present parish church, on the plot to the south, and perhaps also in the construction of the Burystead manor house.

Activity within the northern plots

A number of minor ditch systems and scattered pits lay within the northern plots. To the west there may have been a small ditched enclosure (Fig 5.74, BSP21), at least 10m wide, abutting the southern plot boundary. The northern end of this small plot was dominated by some 19 irregular pits cut into a surface deposit of clays that overlay the limestone in this area (BSP26).

Within the central plot a complex ditch system (BSP 25) may have partially enclosed a rectangular yard, 18m long by at least 10m wide, which lay to the west and south of the southern half of a substantial timber hall (BSP 20), that

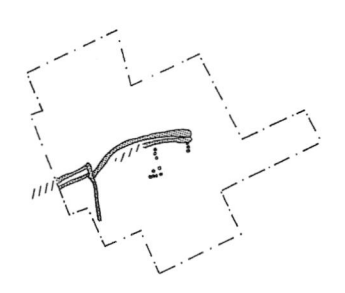

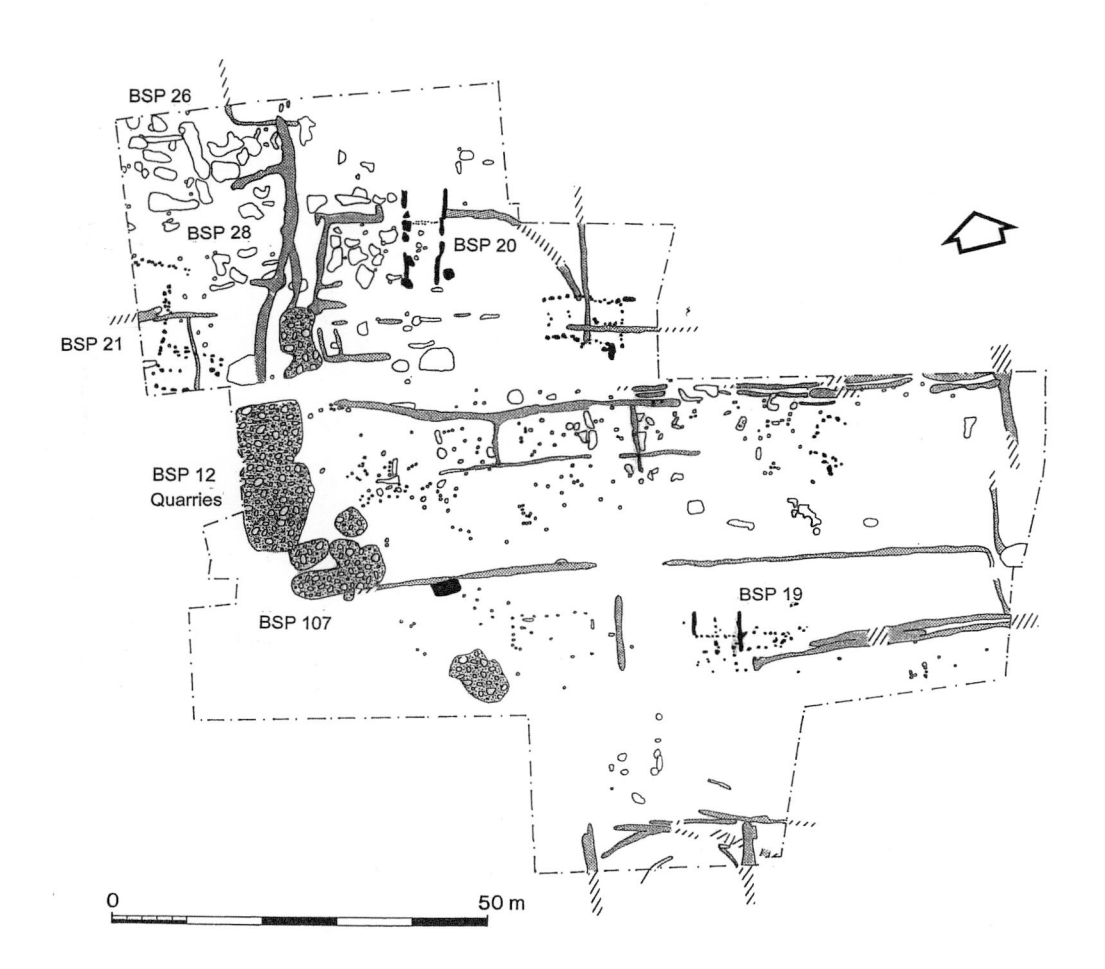

Fig 5.74: Burystead, the late Saxon to Saxo-Norman settlement (AD 900/950–1200)

appeared to have broad, barn-like doorways in its original usage. A dense cluster of smaller clay pits (BSP27) occupied the end of this enclosure to the west of the building, with further pits more scattered outside the enclosure to the west and north.

Timber buildings

Timber building (BSP19)

The end walls were post-in-slot construction, while the southern wall was post-built (Fig 5.76). The building was 6.0m long by 3.5m wide and was apparently open on the northern side. The eastern wall slot continued southward

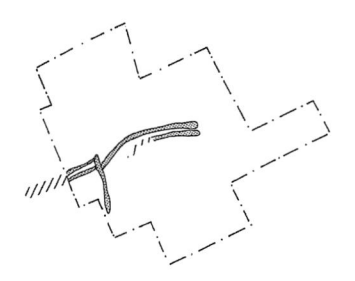

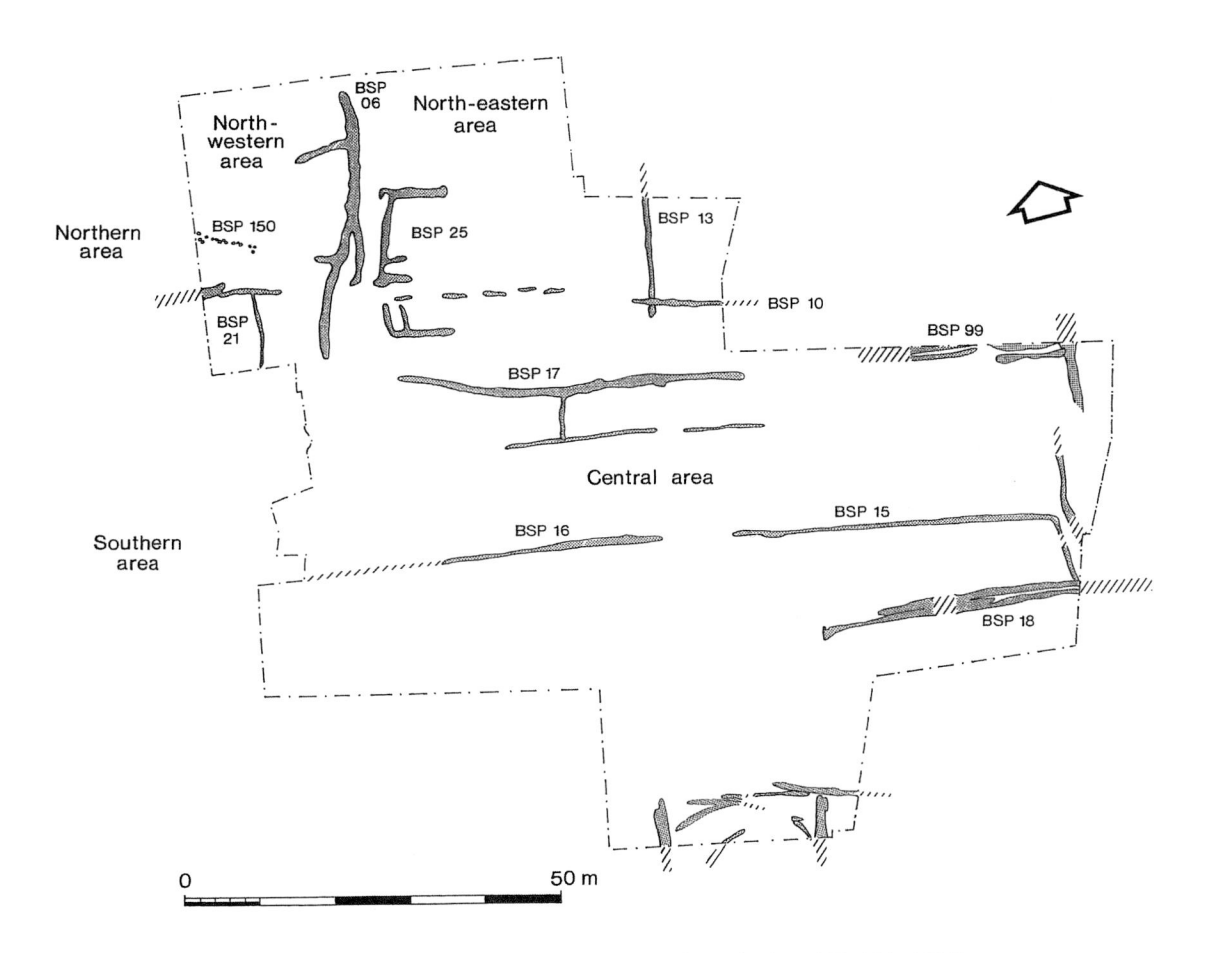

Fig 5.75: Burystead, the late Saxon boundary ditches (AD 950–1200)

for a further 2.0m and there was also an associated line of postholes. The open side suggests that this may have been an agricultural rather than a domestic building. If so, then it would suggest that the southern plots at Burystead they were always serving agricultural functions, and were never a focus of domestic activity.

Timber hall (BSP20)

The walls of this hall, which lay in the northern plots, were largely of foundation trench construction (Fig 5.77). The northern end had been lost to quarrying, and the main building survived to a length of 9.0m, with an internal width of 5.0m. To the south, slightly narrower wall trenches appear to form a separate, abutting room, with the internal width tapering from 4.0m in the north to 3.5m in south. The wall trenches were 0.5–0.7m wide and averaged 250mm deep, while those forming the southern chamber were 0.4–0.5m wide. While the main wall trenches were generally flat-bottomed, those flanking the southern chamber contained distinct timber settings suggesting that they had contained planks set along the wall line, indicating the use of the stave-building technique. While evidence of a probable internal partition wall survived, the end walls to the south had left no traces.

In the eastern wall there was a 2.5m wide break in the wall trench, which was partially blocked by a length of slot set along the line of the inner face of the wall, which reduced the width of the opening to 0.9m. This might suggest that an original broad doorway opening had been reduced to a standard doorway opening. The presence of an opposed doorway in the western wall, together with a further doorway to the immediate north, might account for the even broader opening in the western wall, with the post-pits perhaps marking the provision of the door surrounds, which were also set along the line of the inner face of the wall. The postulated second door in the western wall would have provided access into a separate room, as marked by the survival of a double row of stake-holes forming an internal partition. The room to the north was in excess of 4.5m long while the southern room, with its opposed broad doorways, was 4.0m long.

A small quantity of pottery in some of the postholes and foundation trenches provides a late Saxon date. This building was clearly the surviving part of a substantial timber hall set within a tenement plot running down to the Midland Road frontage. The probable presence of broad opposed doorways would suggest that it had served an agricultural function, perhaps as a barn, while the partial blocking of at least the eastern door might indicate a later conversion to a domestic hall.

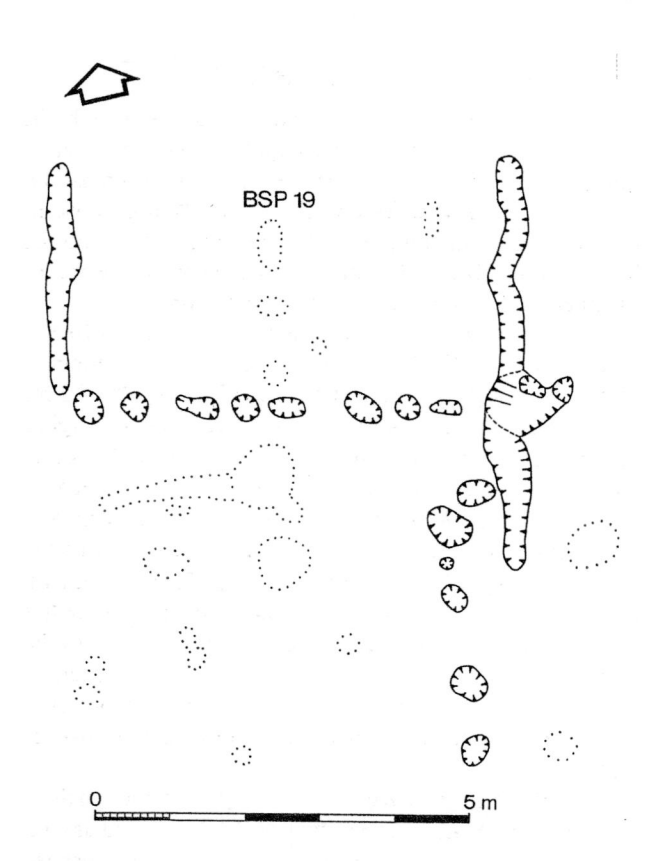

Fig 5.76: Burystead, late Saxon to Saxo-Norman timber building (BSP19)

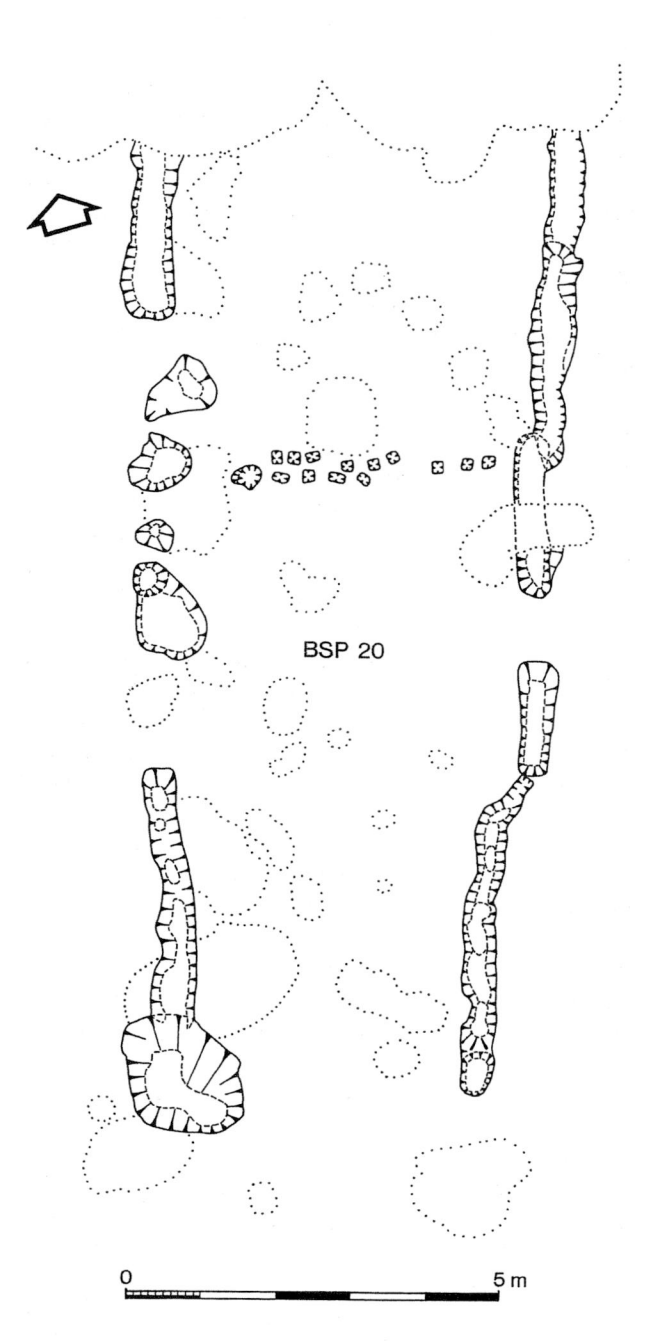

Fig 5.77: Burystead, late Saxon to Saxo-Norman timber building (BSP20)

5. The Archaeological Evidence

Peripheral evaluation

Subsequent to the main series of archaeological excavations at Burystead, a series of trial trenches were excavated at Gell's garage, which lies to the south-west of the Burystead site and immediately west of the churchyard (SP 999 731; Parry 1987) (Fig 1.5). At this site there were further ditches of probably late Saxon origin following north–south or east–west alignments, as well as postholes and pits that denote related occupation. Environmental evidence from this site is reported in this volume (Chapter 9, Table 9.11).

Burystead: A manorial farm and tenement plots (AD 1200–1350/1400)

From AD 1200 onward the basic arrangement of the plot system established in the late Saxon period was retained, although the boundary ditches were replaced by stone walls (Fig 5.78). The main absence was the presumed manor house, but the agricultural nature of the new stone buildings leaves no doubt that the southern plot contained the buildings of the Burystead manorial farm. The northern plots contained no buildings and served as the backage to tenements whose buildings had been relocated onto or at least nearer to, the Midland Road frontage.

The manorial farm

The east–west boundary between the two plot systems was retained, but now comprised a stone wall (Fig 5.78, BSP29), set slightly to the north of the earlier ditched boundary. All of the major features of medieval activity either directly abutted or lay closely adjacent to this wall, placing them within the northernmost of the two southern plots. While there was no surviving walled boundary between the two southern plots at this date it is assumed that either the ditch was retained or perhaps had been replaced by a hedge or some other barrier that had left no archaeological evidence. The southern plot appears to have been devoid of cut features in the medieval period.

Progressing from west to east, the buildings comprised a square, walled-enclosure (BSP32) with a drying or malting oven in its eastern arm (BSP33), a circular dovecote (BSP34) and a square building, perhaps a stable or byre (BSP36). The building remains were all fragmentary, with only partial survival of the walls and no associated floors or occupational deposits. As a result, dating evidence was sparse, but pottery from the fabric of the walls, and therefore comprising residual material, provides a *terminus post quem* of AD 1200. However, their actual dates of construction and use are difficult to determine. These areas produced only small quantities of medieval pottery and other finds, perhaps implying that the manorial farm buildings only appeared in the late medieval period. However, the low levels of medieval domestic artefacts might merely derive from the fact that such materials were less likely to be in use and discarded around farm buildings than around domestic buildings.

The walled enclosure (BSP32) and the village pound

At the western margin of the site there was a near square walled-enclosure abutting the southern side of the plot boundary. The walls were narrower than those of the plot boundary and the enclosure measured 17m by 14m. The western wall lay at the very edge of the excavation. The function of this enclosure is unknown, but one possibility is that it served as the medieval pinfold, or pound, for keeping the straying stock of tenants until a fine was paid. This is recorded in fourteenth-century documents as a walled and gated enclosure.

The basis for this interpretation is the adjacent presence of a site traditionally known as the village pound. Immediately west of the excavated walled enclosure the edge of excavation steeped back eastwards to avoid a sunken square enclosure fronting directly onto Church Street to the west. This appears to have been cut back into the limestone, perhaps utilising an earlier stone quarry, and it therefore lay at a lower level then the archaeology to the east.

This feature, although known locally as the village pound, was not examined or recorded in any detail, and has since been lost to redevelopment, but its location can be seen to have been directly related to the buildings that comprised the medieval manorial farm, and perhaps more specifically as a replacement for its medieval predecessor.

The drying or malting oven (BSP33)

To the immediate west of the oven chamber, and cut by it, there was a 2.0m length of narrow gully, 100–140mm wide, lined with small slabs of limestone set on edge against the sides. This drain-like feature has no apparent purpose in respect to the functioning of the oven, and such features have not been observed in other similar ovens. It is therefore assumed to be a remnant of an earlier drain.

The oven abutted the plot boundary wall (Figs 5.79 and 5.80), and the wall of the small enclosure ran up to the rear of the chamber. The structure was 5.0m long by 4.30m wide, with inner and outer facings in courses of roughly squared limestone surrounding an earth and rubble core, so that the walls were 1.5–2.0m thick. The chamber was built within a shallow construction pit, 300mm deep, and was 1.4m long by 1.0–1.2m wide, narrowing towards the rear. The splayed flue to the east was 0.6–1.0m wide, with the floor sloping down into the chamber. Traces of fire were observed within the oven chamber and close to the flue opening there was a flat hearth-stone, 400mm square and 40mm thick, which was still surrounded by the ashes and other residues of burning. The surrounding pit-base was also scorched.

The grain from this oven was mainly wheat, though there was also some barley. There was also a large weed assemblage that included *Brassica* species (cabbage or mustard) and many arable weeds as well as small legumes.

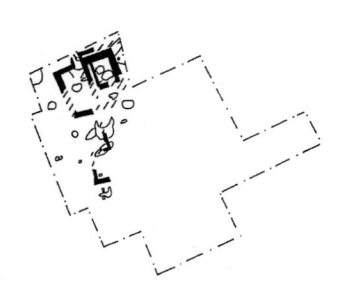

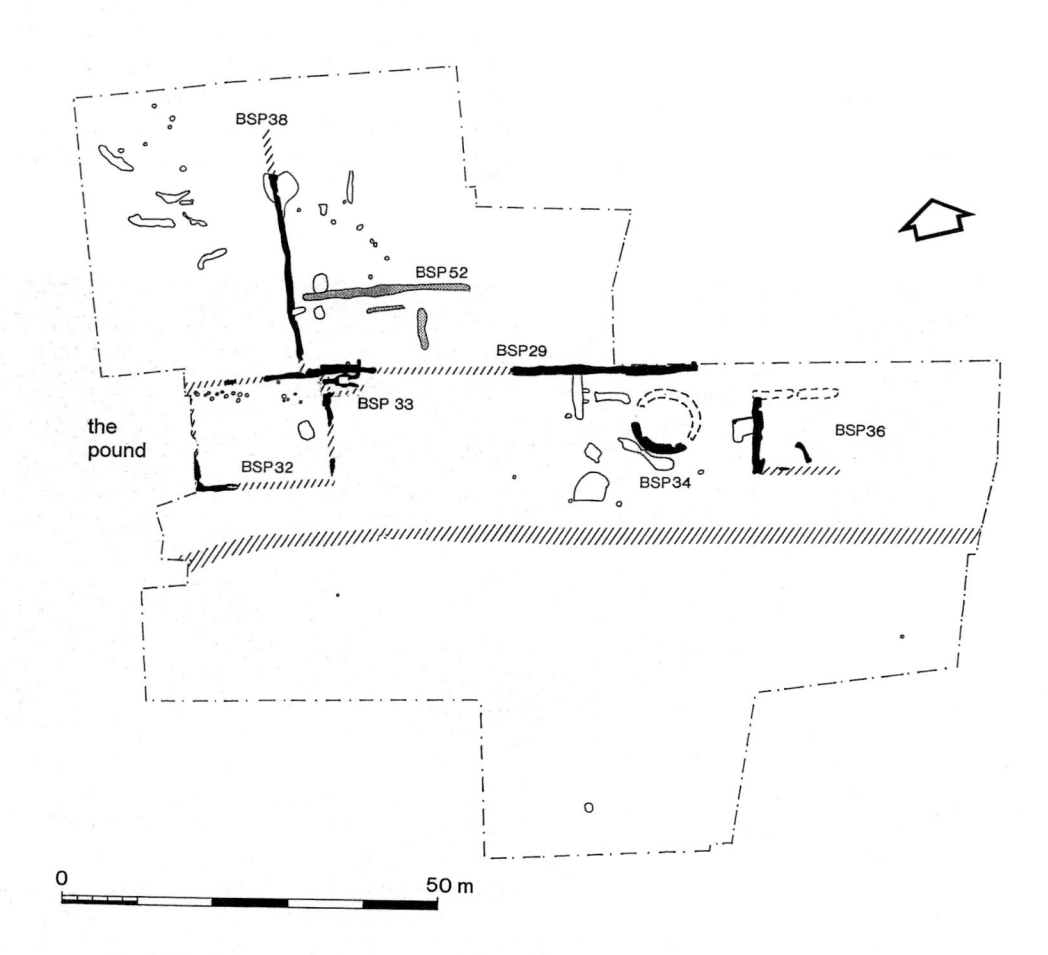

Fig 5.78: Burystead, the manorial farm and tenement plots (AD 1200–1350/1400)

While the oven structure had survived, there was no trace of any associated malting house, although evidence may have been lost in the later digging of a large stone-lined pit to the immediate east. Given the presence of the adjacent boundary wall, the malting house may have comprised a simple lean-to structure set against this wall.

The oven chamber was backfilled with limestone rubble and clay, presumably from the demolition of its superstructure. Pottery from the middle fills of the chamber indicates that it was demolished in the fifteenth century or later. Documents of the sixteenth century refer to a kiln house, which may have been a grander replacement located elsewhere within the Burystead plots.

The dovecote (BSP34)

Much of the southern half of the lower walls of a circular

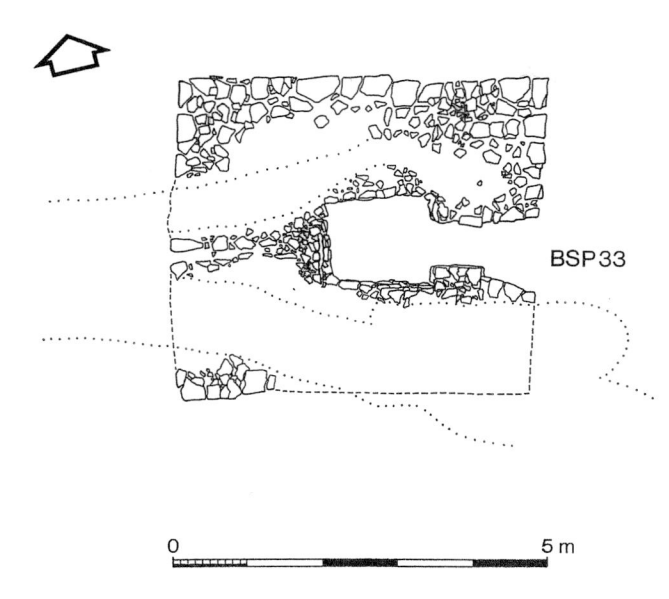

Fig 5.79: Burystead, medieval malt oven (BSP33)

dovecote survived, with the remainder defined by a shallow robber trench (Fig 5.81 and 5.82). It had an internal diameter of 7.0m, and the walls were 1.0m thick. It survived to no more than two courses high, 0.2m, and no nesting boxes survived at this level. A pit in the centre of the building might have held the central post supporting the rotating ladder, the potence, providing access to the nesting boxes. There is no secure date for this building, but a dovecote is first mentioned in the documentary evidence in 1298.

Building (BSP36)

To the east of the dovecote the western wall of a building survived, along with the robber trench of the northern wall (Fig 5.83). Both walls were 10m long, indicating that this was a building of some substance but no further details of its structure or internal arrangements survived. The wall footings were 1.25–1.40m wide and were constructed of rough courses of small limestone slabs in a foundation trench 500mm deep. Approximately half way along the

Fig 5.80: Burystead, the sunken, stone-lined chamber of the malt oven, looking west

western wall there was a 1.0m length comprising limestone fragments set on edge, which may represent the bedding for the threshold of a doorway, and there was an external area of limestone rubble surfacing.

The northern plots

The northern area was subdivided by a stone wall running north–south (Fig 5.78, BSP38). This lay just to the east of the more sinuous late Saxon ditch, but was a reinstatement of the same boundary. It coincides with a boundary shown on the Enclosure Map of 1798 (Fig 1.6). Other eighteenth-century boundaries to the east of this had no medieval predecessors, indicating that further sub-division took place in the post-medieval period.

The western plot only contained a few irregular, elongated pits. In the eastern plot, a pair of ditches (BSP52) formed a small enclosure or pen, 15m long by 10m wide, set in the angle of the southern and western boundary walls.

Burystead: Late medieval and post-medieval buildings (AD 1350/1400 onward)

The division of the Burystead site into northern plots, associated with activity along Midland Road, and southern plots pertaining to the Burystead manor continued into the late medieval and post-medieval periods (Fig 5.84).

The manorial farm

The boundary wall between the two plot systems was retained and, indeed, was extensively rebuilt in the post-medieval period (BSP30/31). At some later date it was levelled although the boundary survived up to the time of excavation, when it was marked by a hedge line.

Stone-lined pit (BSP 44)

To the west, a stone-lined pit, 3.1m long by 1.0m wide and 1.4m deep, abutted the boundary wall.

The dovecotes (BSP35)

The medieval dovecote was levelled and then totally rebuilt on the same site but to a slightly smaller internal diameter of 5.8m (Fig 5.85 and 5.86). The walls were 0.9m wide, slightly narrower than previously. Again, no nesting boxes survived, but there were guano stains left on some of the facing stones. A stone-lined drain cut through the western wall. The interior of the building was in-filled with collapsed stone or rubble containing much eighteenth-century pottery and roof tiles, although much of this may have come from the demolition of the adjacent square dovecote.

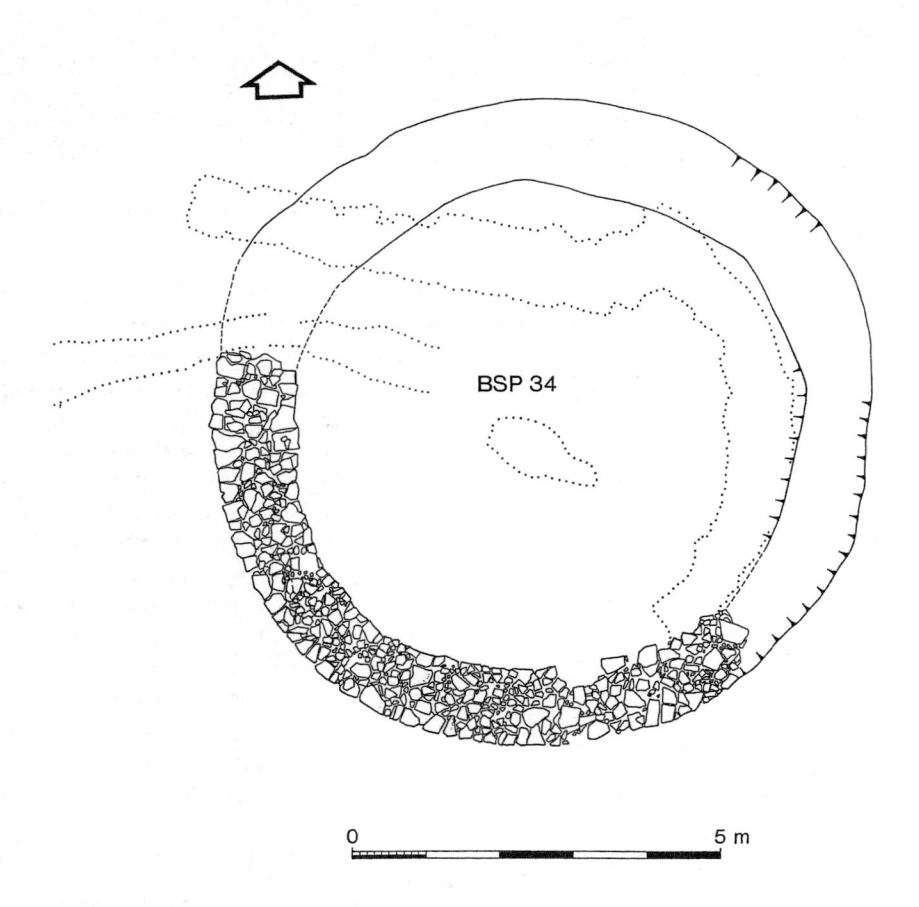

Fig 5.81: Burystead, medieval dovecote (BSP34)

Fig 5.82: Burystead, the circular dovecote (BSP34), looking north

The second dovecote was replaced by a building 4.0m square internally, with 0.8–1.0m thick walls, which seems most likely to have been a further dovecote. The north wall partly overlay the original plot boundary wall, and probably directly abutted the rebuilt boundary wall.

The transition from the circular to the square dovecote cannot be dated with any precision, but probably occurred no earlier than the late fourteenth century. Exactly the same sequence, with a square dovecote replacing a circular dovecote in the late medieval or early post-medieval period, was excavated at Bradwell Bury, a moated medieval house at Milton Keynes (Mynard 1994, fig 12, 23–26).

Building (BSP48)

To the immediate east of the dovecotes, very fragmentary remains of walling and robber trench suggest that a long rectangular structure, 12m long by 4m wide, had been built against the plot boundary wall (Fig 5.84).

Other structures (BSP42)

In the post-medieval period there was considerably more use of the southern plot, but the remains were fragmentary (Fig 5.84). Across an area measuring 30m east–west there were vestiges of stone-surfaced floors or yards, together with the fragmentary remains of stone walls and associated robber trenches. These betoken the ruthless destruction of a building or buildings which may have incorporated ovens and a threshing floor. The low levels of related domestic items, including pottery, suggest that these had been further agricultural buildings, and not the remnants of a substantial domestic range, but with the loss of so much detail it is impossible to ascribe individual forms or functions.

In addition, there was a series of broad but shallow quarry pits scattered between and around the two building groups (BSP42 and BSP171).

The northern plots

In the northern area the wall separating the two plots was retained (Fig 5.84, BSP36). On the western plot a

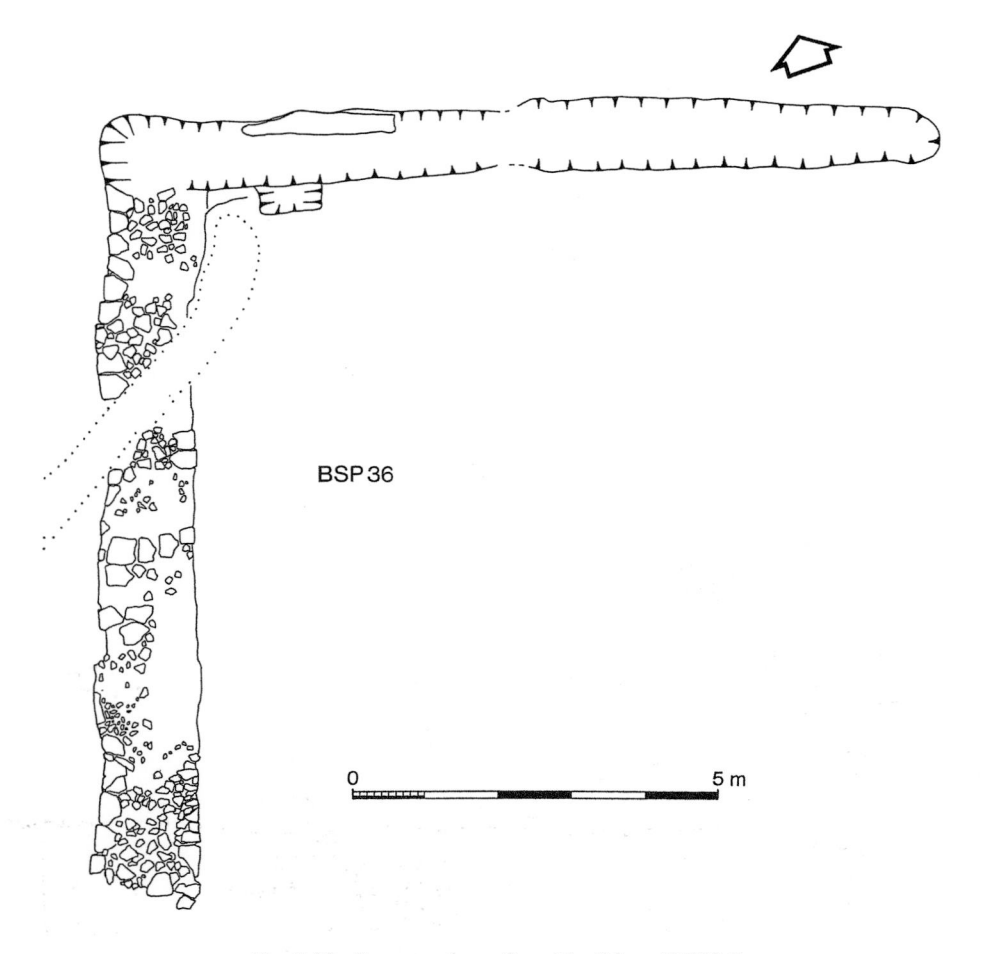

Fig 5.83: Burystead, medieval building (BSP36)

remnant of a stone wall may have been a subdivision of the plot, and to the south of this there were scattered irregular pits, and a few similar pits lay immediately north of this boundary.

There was also a scatter of small pits on the southern end of the eastern plot. The major feature on this plot was a large quarry pit, excavated into the limestone bedrock and probably providing building stone for new buildings along the Midland Road frontage (BSP180). It was 16m wide and in excess of 15m long. A second quarry pit lay adjacent to it in the north-eastern corner of the excavation. The narrow linear berm between the two quarries lay 20m east of the boundary wall, suggesting that there may have been separate quarries either side of a plot boundary or sub-division there had left no other sub-surface traces. The 1.0–1.5m wide berm may have been enough to hold a hedge line.

The tithe barn

The documentary evidence for Burystead refers to the spending of nearly £44 in 1444–5 on the building of a great barn (see Courtney above, Chapter 2). This building is probably to be equated with the great buttressed tithe barn, which stood on the southern side and towards the eastern end of the churchyard. The building is depicted in drawings of 1849 and was demolished in 1850 (Hall *et al* 1998, 118). The barn was of seven bays with a plain central doorway on the southern side and a porch to the north.

The fact that this building lay to the south of the churchyard, rather than with the buildings of the medieval and post-medieval farm to the north, adds to the suggestion that by the middle of the fifteenth century the plots to the north were becoming of lesser importance, and were thus beginning to fall into decline, as indicated by the archaeological evidence. While the dating of the construction and demolition of the buildings at Burystead is poor, the mid-fifteenth century date is closely consistent with the date for the abandonment of the eastern manor house at Furnells.

This change may well reflect the beginnings of the process of looking towards the growing new village centre to the south, a process that led to the decline and eventual abandonment of both manors at the northern end of the village, with their buildings levelled and their plots becoming neglected paddocks. At Burystead, it may only have been the new square dovecote that survived into the eighteenth century, as a sole survivor of the former medieval manorial farm.

5. The Archaeological Evidence 137

Fig 5.84: Burystead, late medieval and post-medieval buildings (1350/1400 onward)

Midland Road

The site on the Midland Road frontage that was chosen for area excavation was the only location where trial trenching had established that a substantial area of earlier buildings survived sufficiently intact to warrant excavation (Fig 1.4). Even so, over half the area available was occupied by quarry pits or modern disturbance (Fig 5.87). The site was excavated in 1986.

Late Saxon and medieval occupation

An L-shaped gully and a series of shallow curving ditches (Fig 5.74) produced late Saxon pottery. They indicate that while late Saxon occupation extended all the way down to the Midland Road frontage, there were no buildings here at this early date. Post-conquest activity was limited to a number of pits.

The late medieval and post-medieval buildings (AD 1300–1600)

The first appearance of stone-founded buildings at the Midland Road frontage occurred in the fourteenth century. There were fragmentary remains of three superimposed buildings, together with associated pits and drains (Fig. 5.87). A *terminus post quem* of AD 1300 for construction is provided by pottery from a large pit, B8505, sealed by the earliest building. This pit also contained the disarticulated skeletal remains of several horses.

Building (SP06)

Only the western wall and parts of the northern and southern walls survived. The building would have stood side-on to Midland Road, and was only 2.6m wide (Fig 5.88). The walls were 0.5m thick and up to seven courses of stonework survived to a height of 350mm.

Building (SP07/SP08)

The second building was a little more substantial (Fig 5.89). The northern end of the building survived, indicating that it stood end-on to the road. The floor was only 2.8m wide and, if a spread of rubble to the south denoted the location of the southern wall, it would have been only 3.7m long. Two small stone-lined drains ran diagonally across the interior.

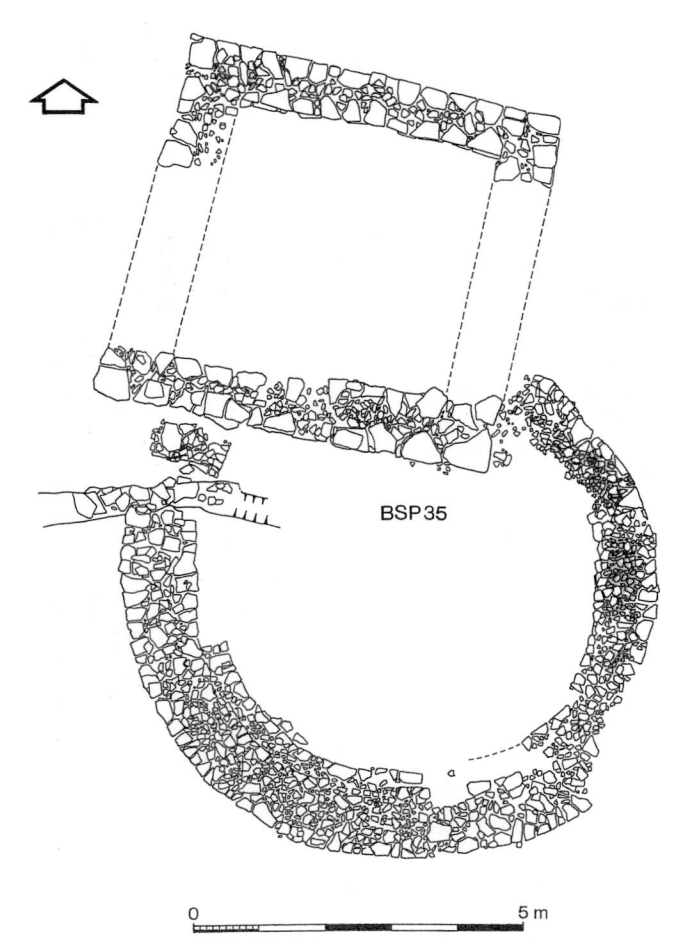

Fig 5.85: Burystead, late medieval circular and square dovecotes (BSP35)

Fig 5.86 (below): Burystead, the late medieval circular and square dovecotes, looking west

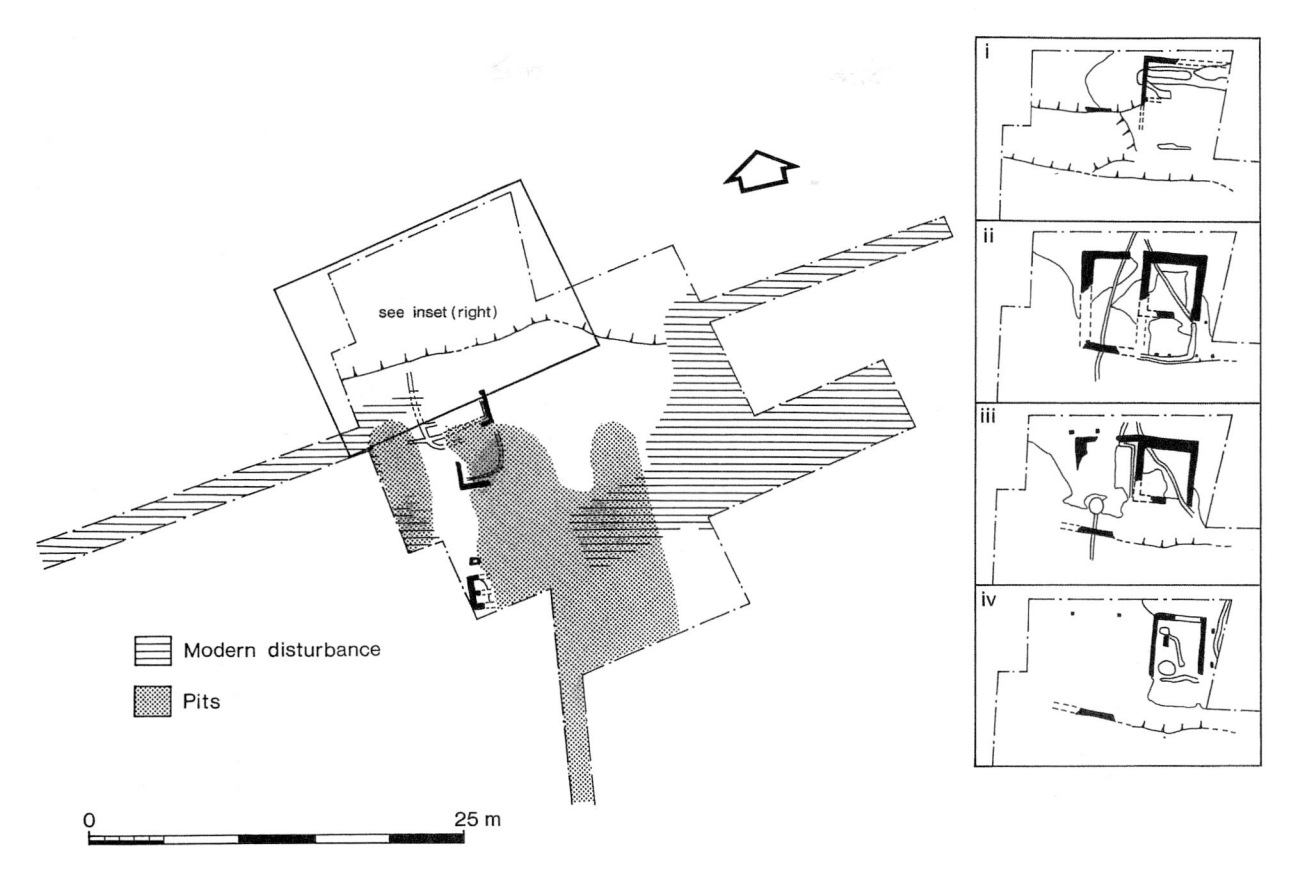

Fig 5.87: Midland Road, late medieval buildings (AD 1300–1600)

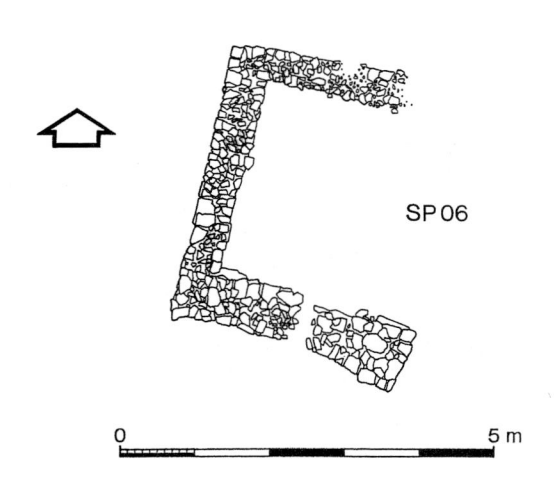

Fig 5.88: Midland Road, late medieval building (SP06)

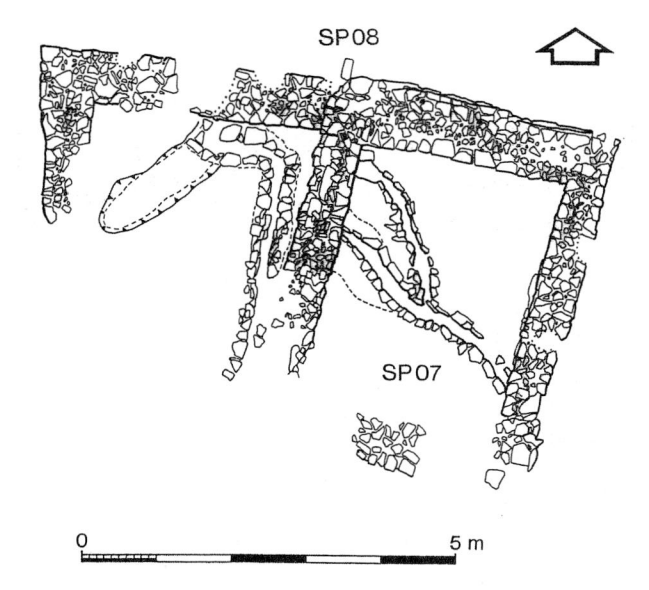

Fig 5.89: Midland Road, late medieval building (SP08)

Subsequently, a room was added to the west. This was slightly larger, at 3.0m wide. This room also contained a stone-lined drain, running alongside the eastern wall, along with remnants of stone floor surfaces and soil layers that contained a large amount of medieval pottery.

The small size of these rooms and the presence of the drains suggest that they were not domestic rooms, and it may be that initially only ancillary buildings were constructed on the road frontage. However, the quantity of domestic pottery recovered does suggest the nearby presence of a domestic range.

The smithy (SP09)

The third building was used as a smithy, although perhaps not for its entire lifetime (Figs 5.90 and 5.91). The new rectangular building stood end-on to the road, and had a floor area only 3.2m wide (Fig 5.90). There was a wide doorway in the northern wall, and fragments of mortar or plaster adhered in places to the face of the surviving stonework.

A stone-lined drain ran diagonal across the room, and adjacent to the drain there was a hearth base, 0.8m in diameter, comprising two scorched stone slabs abutted by a surface of small pitched stones. It was the large amount of hammerscale recovered from around the hearth which indicated that the building had served as a smithy. A small pit had later been cut through the drain to the north of the hearth.

To the south, a stone-lined circular well, 0.9m in diameter may have been contemporary, although it would seem unusual to have a well within a building.

The use as a smithy suggests that this period of frontage development, possibly dated as late as the sixteenth century, may have comprised only workshops, with the need to supply passing customers. This may have been a precursor to direct domestic occupation on the frontage.

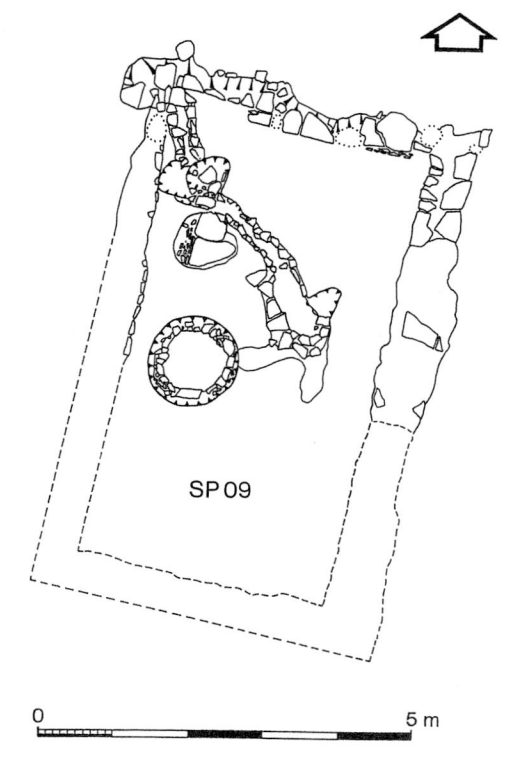

Fig 5.90: Midland Road, late medieval smithy (SP09)

Fig 5.91: Midland Road, the smithy, showing the stone-lined drain (centre to top right) and the well (centre left), looking west

Post-medieval tenements (1600 onward)

It was only into the seventeenth century that the appearance of larger new buildings along the Midland Road frontage marks the development of a frontage comprising domestic residences (Fig 5.92)

Building (SP10)

This building stood side-on to the road, and was 8.0m long by 6.0m wide, with a doorway in the northern wall, just west of centre (Fig 5.93). The eastern wall was apparently retained from the sixteenth century smithy, indicating that the narrow-walled construction method had not changed.

Building (SP11)

The latest building on the site had much broader stone foundations (Figs 5.92 and 5.94). Only the eastern end survived, but the building appears to have been 8.0m wide, standing side-on to the road. The western wall of building (BSP10) had been removed, but the remainder was retained as an abutting extension. It appears to have been built in the nineteenth century and remained standing into the twentieth century.

The rear yard (SP12)

Fragments of wall and soils layers of post-medieval date to the rear of the buildings presumably relate to backyard features (Fig 5.92).

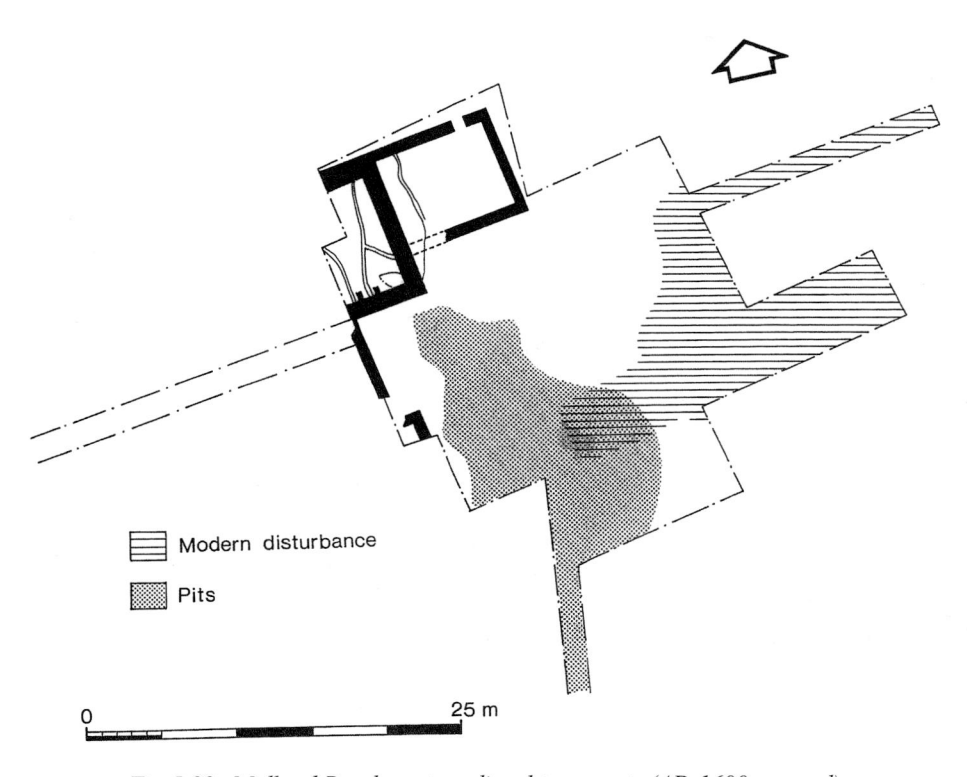

Fig 5.92: Midland Road, post-medieval tenements (AD 1600 onward)

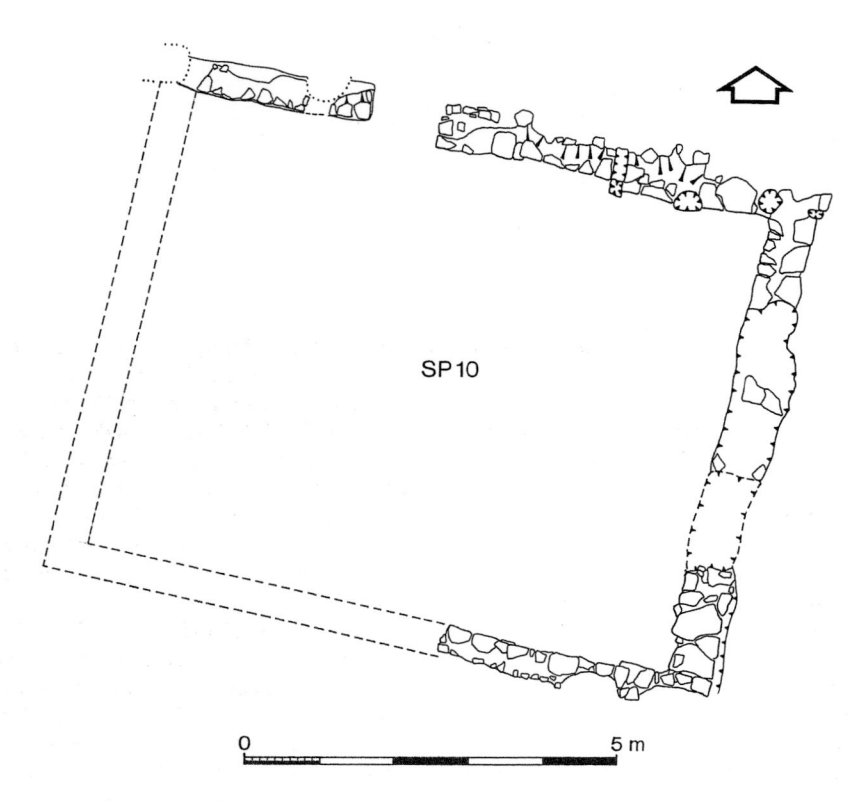

Fig 5.93: Midland Road, post-medieval building (SP10)

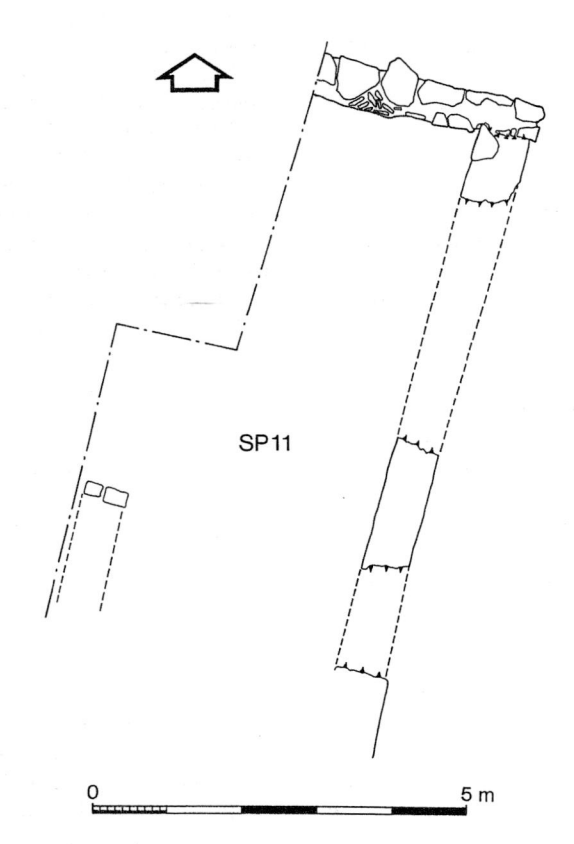

Fig 5.94: Midland Road, post-medieval building (SP11)

Bibliography: Parts 1 & 2

Abels, R P, 1988 *Lordship and Military Obligation in Anglo-Saxon England*, Berkeley

Allen Brown, R, (ed) 1984 *Anglo-Norman Studies*, **7**

Altshul, M, 1966 *A Baronial Family in Medieval England: Clares 1217–1314 (Study in History and Political Science S)*

Aston, T H, 1958 The Origins of the Manor in England, *Trans Roy Hist Soc*, **5** series **8**, 59–83

Barlow, F, 1963 *The English Church, 1000–1066*, London

Beresford, G, 1987 *Goltho: the development of an early medieval manor c.850–1150*, English Heritage Archaeol Rep, **4**

Blair, J, (ed) 1988 *Ministers and parish churches: the local church in transition 900–1200*

Blair, J, 1988 Introduction, in J Blair (ed) 1988, 1–19

Boddington, A, 1978 *The excavation record: part 1: Stratification*, Northamptonshire Archaeol Unit Occ Pap, **1**

Boddington, A, 1987 Raunds, Northants, analysis of a country churchyard, *World Archaeol*, **18**, 411–25

Boddington, A, 1996 *Raunds, Furnells, The Anglo-Saxon church and churchyard, Raunds Area project*, English Heritage Archaeol Rep, **7**

Bridges, J, 1791 *The History and Antiquities of Northamptonshire*, P Whalley (ed)

Brown, E A, 1974 The tyranny of a construct: feudalism and historians of medieval Europe, *American History Review*, **79**.4, 1063–88

Cadman, G E, 1982 Raunds: excavations 1981/82, an interim note, *Northamptonshire Archaeol*, **17**, 93–7

Cadman, G E, 1983 Raunds 1977–1983; an excavation summary, *Medieval Archaeol*, **27**, 107–22

Cadman, G E, and Audouy, M, 1990 Recent excavations on Saxon and medieval quarries in Raunds, Northamptonshire, in D Parsons (ed) 1990, 187–206

Cadman, G E, and Foard, G, 1984 Raunds: manorial and village origins, in M L Faull (ed) 1984, 81–100

Cadman, G E, Pearson, T, and Boddington, A, 1983 *Raunds Furnell's, a revised chronology*, Northamptonshire Archaeol Unit report

Campbell, G, in press The charred plant remains, in A Chapman in press

CAS undated *Raunds Area Project. Iron Age and Romano-British Project: the assessments*, Central Archaeology Service, English Heritage

Chapman, A, 2004 Prehistoric palaeochannels and a ring ditch at Stanwick Quarry, *Northamptonshire Archaeol*, **32**, 1–22

Chapman, A, in press *West Cotton, Raunds: a study of medieval settlement dynamics*, Oxbow Books

Chibnall, M, 1986 *Anglo-Norman England 1066–1166*, Oxford

Courtney, P, 2006a Raunds and its region, in S Parry 2006, 99–107

Courtney, P, 2006b Raunds Burystead: a manorial economy in decline, in S Parry 2006, 108–115

Crosby, V, and Neal, D, forthcoming *Raunds Area Project: The Iron Age and Romano-British landscapes of Stanwick, Northamptonshire*, English Heritage monog

Dix, B, (ed) 1986–7 The Raunds Area Project: second interim report, *Northamptonshire Archaeol*, **21**, 3–29

Dyer, C, 1968 A redistribution of incomes in fifteenth-century England, *Past Present*, **39**, 11–33

Fairbrother, J R, 1990 *Faccombe Netherton, Excavations of a Saxon and Medieval Manorial Complex*, British Mus Occ Pap, **74**

Fasham, P J, and Keevill, G, 1995 *Brighton Hill South (Hatch Warren): an Iron Age Farmstead and Deserted Medieval Village in Hampshire*, Wessex Archaeology Report, **7**

Faull, M L, (ed) 1984 *Studies in late Anglo-Saxon settlement*, Oxford Univ Dept External Studies

Foard, G R, 1979 *Archaeological priorities: proposals for Northamptonshire*, Northamptonshire Archaeol Unit Occ Pap **4**

Foard, G R, 1985 The administrative organisation of Northamptonshire in the Saxon period, *Anglo-Saxon Studies in Archaeol & Hist*, **4**, 185–222

Foard, G, and Pearson, T, 1985 The Raunds Area Project: first interim report, *Northamptonshire Archaeol*, **20**, 3–21

Franklin, M J, 1982 *Ministers and Parishes: Northamptonshire Studies*, unpubl PhD thesis, Univ Cambridge

Franklin, M J, 1984 The identification of Minsters in the Midlands, in R Allen Brown (ed) 1984, 69–88

Frere, S, 1975 *Principles of publication in rescue archaeology*, Department of the Environment

Gover, J E B, Mawer, A, and Stenton, F M, 1975 *The place-names of Northamptonshire*, The English Place-Name Society

Hall, D N, 2006 The open fields of Raunds and its township, in S Parry 2006, 116–122

Hall, D, Harding, R, and Putt, C, 1988 *Raunds: Picturing the Past*

Harding, J, and Healy, F, 2007 *The Raunds Area Project: A Neolithic and Bronze Age Landscape in Northamptonshire*, English Heritage

Hardy, A, Charles, B M, Williams, R J, 2007 *Death and Taxes: the archaeology of a Middle Saxon estate centre at Higham Ferrers, Northamptonshire*, Oxford Archaeology monog

Harper-Bill, C, Houldsworth, C J, and Nelson, J L, (eds) 1989 *Studies in Medieval History presented to R. Allen Brown*

Harvey, P D A, 1976 *Manorial Records of Cuxham, Oxfordshire, circa 1200–1359*

Holdsworth, W, 1922 *A History of English Law: i* (3rd edition)

Holmes, G A, 1957 *The Estates of the Higher Nobility in Fourteenth-century England*

Holt, J C, (ed) 1987 *Domesday studies: papers read at the novodentenary conference of the Royal Historical Society and the Institute of British Geographers: Winchester, 1986*, Woodbridge

Keevill, G, 1991 Evaluations and excavations in Northamptonshire by the Oxford Archaeology Unit 1989–1990, *Northamptonshire Archaeol,* **23**, 99–104

Kerr, W J B, 1925 *Higham Ferrers and its Ducal and Royal Castle and Park*

Lewis, C, Mitchell-Fox, P, and Dyer, C, 1997 *Village, hamlet and field,* Manchester UP

Lieberman, F, 1903 *Die Gesetze de Angelsachsen:* **i**

MacGregor, A, 1987 Objects of bone and antler, in G Beresford 1987, 188–93

Maddicott, J R, 1970 *Thomas of Lancaster 1307–132*

Maitland, F W, 1897 *Domesday Book and Beyond: three essays in the early history of England*

Miller, E, 1966 La Societe rurale en Angleterre X–XII siecles, in *Aoricoltura e Mondo Rurale in Occidentenell Alto Medioevo,* 111–34

Morris, S, 2002 *Excavation at 14 Rotton Row, Raunds, Northamptonshire,* Northamptonshire Archaeology report

Mynard, D C, 1994 *Excavations on medieval sites in Milton Keynes,* Buckinghamshire Archaeol Soc Monog, **6**

Palmer, J J N, 1987 The Domesday manor, in J C Holt (ed) 1987, 139–53

Parry, S, 2006 *Raunds Area Survey: An archaeological study of the landscape of Raunds, Northamptonshire 1985–94,* Oxbow Books

Parsons, D, (ed) 1990 *Stone: quarrying and building in England AD43–1525*

Reaney, P H, 1967 *The Origin of English Surnames,* Routledge

Reaney, P H, 1976 *A Dictionary of British Surnames,* London

Roffe, D R, 1981 The Lincolnshire Hundred, *Landscape History,* **3**, 17–36

Roffe, D R, 1990 Domesday Book and Northern Society: a reassessment, *English Hist Review,* **105**, 310–36

Rosser, G, 1988 The Anglo-Saxon Guilds, in J Blair (ed), 31–4

Round, J H, 1900 The Domesday Manor, *English History Review,* **15**, 293–302

Sawyer, P H, 1978 *From Roman Britain to Norman England,* London

Somerville, R, 1953 *History of the Duchy of Lancaster; 1: 1265–1603,* Duchy of Lancaster

Stenton, F M, 1910 *Types of Manorial Structure in the Northern Danelaw,*

Stenton, F M, 1971 *Anglo-Saxon England* (3 edition), Oxford

Walmersley, J F R, 1968 The "Censarii" of Burton Abbey and the Domesday Population, *North Staffordshire J Field Studies,* **8**, 73–80

Waterman, D M, 1959 Late Saxon, Viking and Early Medieval Finds from York, *Archaeologia,* **97**, 59–105

Williams, A, 1989 The King's Nephew: the Family and Career of Ralph, earl of Hereford, in C Harper-Bill *et al* (eds) 1989, 327–43

Zupko, E R, 1968 *A Dictionary of English Weights and Measures; From Anglo-Saxon Times to the Nineteenth Century,* Wisconsin Univ Press

Index: Parts 1 & 2

abbot of Thornton 17
advowsons 15, 17, 18
Anglo-Scandinavian farm 27, 29, 30, 31–32, 34, 52, 53, 60, 66, 67, 73, 74, 79
animal bones 58, 59, 88, 127

bailiff's accounts 16, 17
bakehouse 42, 47, 96, 98, 100, 105
Ballinderry 32
barns 9, 16, 17, 47, 100, 105, 136
Barton 15
Bedfordshire 15
berewick 14, 40
birds 50, 58
Bishop of Coutances, *see* de Mowbray
Black Death (1348–9) 45, 46, 57
bookland 14, 18
bookright 55, 56
boundary ditches/enclosures 30, 58, 84, 87, 88, 96
    Burystead 57, 122, 123, 125–127
    Furnells 32, 37, 41, 53, 63, 66, 74, 75, 78, 79, 100, 107
    Langham Road 47, 53, 57, 112, 114, 115, 118, 120
    see also ditches
Bradwell Bury, Milton Keynes 135
brewhouse 98
brewing 106
    see also malt; ovens
Brighton Hill South, Hampshire 54
Bromswold 1, 12
Bronze Age 6, 22, 62
brooch, annular 42, 99
Brown(e)
    Catherine 15
    Humphrey 15
Browne, Sir Wistan 15
buckles 99
Bungay, Suffolk 56
Burgred (thegn) 14, 39, 55
    Burgred's manor 14, 56
burials xv, 1, 27, 34, 41, 57, 59, 60, 62, 65, 84, 88, 93, 94, 96
Burystead 6, 9, 12, 22, 24, 27, 28, 31, 36, 37–38, 44–45, 48, 49, 50, 51, 52, 53, 57, 58, 59, 60, 66, 75, 94, 121–136
    manor/manorial farm 14, 16–17, 18, 37, 38, 41, 44–45, 47, 51, 57, 121, 131–134

Carlton, Notts. 56
Catlyn family 15
cereals/crop cultivation 28, 38–39, 47–48, 131
Chamberlyn family 12
Champernowne family/estate 15

charcoal 27, 59, 60, 65, 66, 71, 88
Chelveston 15
Church Street 126, 131
cistern 27
Clare family/fee 14, 15, 18, 39–40, 56
cloth 49, 102
Clowne family 15
coffins 34, 41, 57, 62, 88, 94
coins 59
    medieval 43, 78
    Roman 22, 62, 64
    Scandinavian 32
Cotes manor 15
Cotton Brook 1
Cotton Lane 12
court rolls 15, 16
Coutances, bishop of, *see* de Mowbray
Cranford 15
cremation cemetery (Burystead) 27
Crowhill (Iron Age hillfort) 9
Cuxham 17

D'Audley family 14
Danelaw xv, 51, 52, 54
Danish control/presence 29, 30, 32, 51, 52, 54, 66
de Coldale, Richard 16
de Ferrers, *see* Ferrers family
de Furneus family 14, 15, 42, 57
    Geoffrey 14
    Henry 14–15
    Roger 14, 15
de Hamptom, William 16
de Huggerford, Margery 15
de Mowbray, Geoffrey 14, 39
de Raunds family 15, 16
    Henry 15
    Herlewin 15
    Thomas 16
de St Lo, Hugh 15
de Trailly family 15
    Eleanor 15
    John 15, 16
    Reginald 15
    Reynold 15
    Walter 15
demesne 14, 16, 40, 51, 55, 56, 57
Denford 14, 40, 56
ditches/ditch systems 24, 36, 52, 55, 58,
    Burystead 127, 131
    Furnells 32, 34, 36, 41, 53, 63, 74, 78, 79, 84, 120

ditches/ditch systems (cont.)
   Langham Road 37, 44, 47, 107
   see also boundary ditches; enclosures
dogs 50
Dolben, Dr 16
Domesday Book 1, 14, 16, 39, 40, 55–57
dovecote/house
   Burystead 17, 44, 47, 57, 121, 132–133, 134–135, 136
   Furnells 46, 50, 100, 102, 104, 105, 107
   Gages manor 16
Drayton 15
duchy of Lancaster 14, 15, 16, 40

Earl of Aumale, William 18
earl of Lancaster, Thomas 16
earl of Peterborough 15
East Raunds 12
Eaton, Notts. 56
economy 1, 38–39, 57
   see also markets; trade
Ekins family 16
   John 15
   Thomas 15, 16
enclosures 24, 27, 29, 34
   see also ditches
estate map, *see* Map of Enclosure

Faccombe Netherton, Hampshire 54, 80
farmsteads 9, 22, 27–28
Ferrers family 15, 40
   Robert 18
   William (earl of Ferrers) 17, 18
field systems 9, 12, 28, 30, 31, 39, 41, 44, 118, 121
fish 50
fitz Marmaduke, Sir Richard 16
flax 48
founder's plot 88
Fourneux 14
Furnells Close 15, 31, 121
Furnells manor xv, 9, 14, 18, 22, 37, 41–42, 44, 46–47, 53, 57, 60, 62–107, 112, 125
   ancillary buildings xv, 31, 34, 37, 57, 63, 66, 74, 100
   domestic/kitchen range xv, 31, 32, 34, 41, 42, 47, 79, 82, 93, 100, 105, 106
   domestic enclosure xv, 34, 36, 41, 66, 68, 74, 79, 117
   halls xv, 27, 31, 40–41, 64, 66, 67, 68, 71, 73, 79, 80–81, 89, 91–93, 96–97, 102
   manorial chapel 12, 41, 42, 57, 94
   see also Anglo-Scandinavian farm; St Peter's church
Furneus/Furnellis family, *see* de Furneus

Gage family, 16
Gages manor 12, 14, 15–16
gaming pieces 32, 66
gardens 120
gatehouse 32, 34, 74, 79
geld 56
girdle hanger 26, 108
glass
   linen smoother 43, 99
   vessel 42
Gloucester fee 14, 40, 56

Goltho, Lincs. 32, 54, 80
granary 17, 27, 109
graves, *see* burials
Great Famine (1315–17) 46
Great Ouse 1, 25
Greene family 15, 47, 57, 100
   Henry 15, 16
Gytha (wife of Earl of Hereford) 14, 40

halls 54
   Burystead 17, 122, 123, 129–130
   Furnells 26–27, 28, 29, 31–32, 59, 66, 67, 68, 71, 73, 80–81, 89–93, 96–97, 102
   Higham 9
   Langham Road 57, 109, 115, 116
   West Cotton 53
   see also Furnells manor
Hampden, Edmund 16
Hargrave 3, 9, 14, 15, 18, 39, 40
hay-house 17
Headon, Notts. 56
hearth bottoms 27, 64, 65
Higham 9, 17, 18, 42, 49, 57
   castle 9
   estate 14, 16, 56
   soke 14
Higham Ferrers 9, 12, 14, 16, 20, 39, 40
horse gear/fittings 32, 66, 88
horses 50, 138

industries (local) 1, 27, 50
   see also economy; malt; shoe industry; weaving
Irchester 17
Iron Age 6, 22, 60
   see also Crowhill
iron peg 32
iron
   slag 27, 59, 64, 65, 88
   smithing 27, 28, 59, 64, 65
Irthlingborough 9, 62

jetton 43, 99
   see also coins

Kettleby, Lincs. 16
key (copper alloy) 99
kiln-house 17
Kings Meadow Lane 9
knight's fee 14, 15, 56

Langham Road 6, 9, 22, 24, 26, 27, 28, 30, 31, 36–37, 43–44, 47, 49, 52, 53, 57, 58, 59, 62, 64, 66, 75, 76, 78, 88, 107–121, 125
   farm 27–28, 31, 37, 108–109, 111–115
lead slag 99
leather-working 50
Lenton 18
linen 48
livestock 22, 28, 45, 107
   see also stock enclosures
London 9, 17, 32

loomweights 59
   see also spindle-whorls; weaving
Lyveden 43

Mallows Cotton 12, 22, 26, 28, 39, 40, 45, 56, 57
malt/malting 9, 17, 47, 57, 96, 98, 106
   see also ovens
malt-house 16, 42, 57, 96, 106, 132
malt mill 16
manerium 56
manorial centres/house xv, 12, 24
   see also Burystead; Furnells
manorial courts 56
manuring 22, 39, 46
Map of Enclosure (1798) 1, 9, 44, 45, 120, 121, 134
markets 9, 14, 42, 49, 57
Marriot, William 16
Mercia 14, 56
Middle Cotton 16
Middlecotes 15
Midland Road 31, 36, 47, 59, 126, 134, 137–141
Midland Road frontage 6, 9, 22, 37, 38, 44, 45, 48, 50, 57, 59, 121, 130, 131, 136, 137, 138, 141
Mill Cotton 12, 22, 26, 28, 39, 40, 45, 56, 57
moieties 15
Mordaunt, John 15
musical instrument 42

Nene
   river 1, 3, 9, 15, 22, 25, 26, 28
   valley 12, 22, 26, 62
Neolithic 6, 22, 62
Newark Hospital, Leics. 18
Newton Bromswold 15
Norman Conquest 24, 34, 41, 52, 57, 94
North End 9, 12, 39, 46, 51
Northampton 1, 108
Northamptonshire County Council Archaeology Unit 1, 3, 6, 13
Northamptonshire Field Group 1
Norway 32

Offa (Mercian centre) 9
Olaf Kyrre of Norway 32
orchards 120
ovens 60, 66
   baking 42, 47, 105
   drying/malting 27, 39, 42, 47, 64, 98–99, 105, 121, 131

Park Road 27
pasture/pasture closes xv, 1, 22, 47, 50, 62, 102, 120
Peterborough 1
Peverel family/fee 17, 18
   William 14, 16, 18, 40
pig-fibula pin 26, 64, 68
plots/plot system xv,
   Burystead 127, 131, 134, 75
   Furnells 29, 31, 34, 41, 44, 62, 63, 74, 75, 76, 78
   Langham Road 37, 43, 47, 57, 75, 111, 112, 116, 117
   West Cotton 24, 30, 53, 75–76
population size/growth 22, 39, 40, 46, 87, 120

post-medieval 6, 44, 50, 59, 120, 134, 138, 141
pottery 22, 24, 25, 26, 28–29, 32, 43, 44, 60, 62, 64, 68, 89, 94
   Cotswold Oolitic types 84
   early Saxon stamped pottery 122
   early Saxon wares 24, 65, 66, 68, 71, 73, 74, 78, 79, 82, 84, 88, 93, 96, 99, 107, 108, 109, 111, 122, 126
   Ipswich wares 24, 25, 27, 52, 108, 122
   late Saxon wares 68, 71, 78, 79, 84, 96, 99, 112, 122, 123, 126, 137
   Maxey-type wares 24, 25, 27, 52, 60, 108, 109, 122
   middle Saxon (imported) wares 27, 28, 60, 66, 68, 71, 73, 74, 78, 79, 82, 84, 88, 93, 96, 99, 107, 108, 109, 111, 122, 126
   oxidised wares 46
   reduced wares 46, 99
   St Neots-type wares 28, 29, 31, 65, 66, 68, 71, 73, 74, 78, 82, 84, 88, 108, 123, 126
   Samian wares 62
   Saxo-Norman wares 78, 84, 96, 99, 123
   shelly wares 109
   Stamford wares 88, 93
   Stanion wares 98
pre-enclosure survey (1739) 120
prior of Lenton 17

Ralph, Earl of Hereford
Raunds, parish of 3, 9, 14, 15, 17, 40
Raunds Area Project 1, 3, 6, 12, 22, 51, 57, 62
Raunds Area Survey 3, 9, 12, 22, 31, 51, 52, 62, 122
Raunds Brook 9, 31, 34, 79, 122
receiver's accounts 17
reconquest 29, 30, 31, 32, 51, 52
Redlands Farm 22
Resurrection Guild 18
rings 99
Ringstead 3, 12, 14, 15, 16, 18, 22, 39, 40, 55, 56
Roman 6, 26, 60
   coins 22, 62, 64
   pottery 22, 62
   road 12
   settlement 12, 22, 24
   see also Stanwick
Roper, William 15
Rothwell 20
Rotton Row 31, 37, 44, 47, 62, 76, 79, 107, 111, 115, 118, 119, 120
Rushden 16, 17

St Katherine's church, Irchester 17
St Mary's parish church, *see* St Peter's church
St Peter's church xv, 1, 9, 17–20, 24–25, 34, 41, 46, 50, 55, 57, 60, 62, 63, 74, 76, 79, 84, 85, 87, 93–94, 100
   churchyard xv, 18, 24, 34, 36, 41, 46, 55, 57, 62, 63, 74, 76, 79, 84, 87, 94, 96, 100, 121
   see also burials
Sepulchre Guild 18
sheep 49
shoe industry 1, 50, 120
smithy 47, 48, 50, 57, 107, 140
soke/sokeland 14, 55, 56

sokemen 18, 55, 56
spindle-whorls 26, 59, 64
   see also loomweights; weaving
stables 16, 131
Stafford 39
Stafford family 14, 15, 39
Stanion 43
Stanwick 3, 6, 9, 12, 15, 16, 22, 39, 40, 62
steward's chamber 17
stock enclosures 17, 32, 37, 47, 71, 109
sub-infeudation 14, 15, 39
sub-tenancy 15

Tawyer, John 16
tenements 1, 6, 12, 24, 31, 37, 44, 50, 52, 107, 115, 118, 131, 141
textiles 109
   see also cloth; weaving
thegn xv, 18, 34, 56, 74
Thornton Abbey 18
Thorpe End 1, 9, 12, 39, 46
trackway 31, 37, 44, 76, 79, 112, 117, 118, 121
trade 9, 17, 28
   see also economy; markets

tribute centre 9
Tyrwhite, Sir Robert 16

Viking 32
vill 56
villa regalis 14
Vivian, Christopher 15

Waldesshef, Joanna 16
Wash, The 1
watermills 12, 52, 55
Watling Street 52
weaving tools 26, 43, 59
   see also cloth; loomweights; spindle-whorls
Welland 1
West Cotton 3, 9, 12, 22, 24, 25, 26, 28, 29, 30, 34, 38, 39, 40, 41, 42, 45, 46, 51, 53, 55, 56, 57, 58, 62, 66, 75, 80, 81, 82, 102, 106, 115
Winchester 32
wolves 50
Woodford 15

Yelden, Beds. 16
York 32

I.D. No. b13553264
UNIVERSITY OF BRADFORD
LIBRARY

1 2 JAN 2010

ACCESSION No 0400603795.
CLASS No
LOCATION